Transnational Film Culture in New Zealand

Transnational Film Culture in New Zealand

Simon Sigley

intellect Bristol, UK / Chicago, USA

First published in the UK in 2013 by
Intellect, The Mill, Parnall Road, Fishponds, Bristol, BS16 3JG, UK

First published in the USA in 2013 by
Intellect, The University of Chicago Press, 1427 E. 60th Street,
Chicago, IL 60637, USA

A catalogue record for this book is available from the
British Library.

Cover designer: Holly Rose
Copy-editor: MPS Technologies
Production manager: Jelena Stanovnik
Typesetting: Planman Technologies

ISBN 978-1-84150-660-9

Printed and bound by Hobbs, UK

Table of Contents

Foreword

The idea that film is art, and not merely a source of entertainment or social information or moral example, has become an organising principle for film festivals and academic courses. But it is more than that – it is a revelation, a Eureka moment that has excited many film-goers and motivated them to devote a large part of their lives to unpaid work lecturing or writing on the subject or organising film societies and festivals, through the desire to share their discovery that the medium of film has its own aesthetics and is vastly more diverse than the latest crop of Anglo-American titles being screened in local cinemas. In New Zealand, these activities have been almost entirely an amateur enterprise, a labour of love, because of the shortage of public funding.

The lively personal recollections in the first chapter make it clear that writing the first detailed history of these campaigns has been much more than an academic exercise for the author because the idea of film as art is something he cares deeply about. Simon Sigley is a cinephile and filmmaker as well as a historian. He vividly documents the many ways in which New Zealand resisted the new approach to film, either through anti-intellectualism or through scorn for the medium because it was a vehicle for 'popular culture'. There were also moral panics, an Anglophile suspicion of 'foreign' films, the competitive attitude of the older arts towards a new rival, hostility to modernism, the dominance of commercial values, and so on. Of course these forms of opposition were not unique to New Zealand but Sigley's account leaves us in no doubt that this country has been a particularly 'unfriendly environment for the emergence of specialised forms of aesthetic taste'.

A distinctive feature of our history is the fact that there was no regular production of feature films in New Zealand until the end of the 1970s. The influence of film societies and festivals was an important factor in inspiring young adults to take up cameras as the first stage in the creation of our long-delayed industry. Strictly speaking, the creation of a film industry is a separate subject from the development of a film culture, yet in a small country like ours the two areas of culture were inevitably linked. Key people in the new industry such as Bruce Morrison, Leon Narbey, Robin Scholes, Geoff Steven, and Tony Williams were energised by the films they had seen in festivals and art-house cinemas. As Sigley notes, John O'Shea, the father figure of the new industry was prominent in the Wellington Film Society. And Lindsay Shelton helped to modernise the Film Society movement and was instrumental in establishing a Wellington Film Festival before becoming the Marketing Director of the newly created New Zealand Film Commission.

The other day I heard a young filmmaker become exasperated as he listened to a group of older directors discussing the hard life of one of their colleagues who had recently died. He exclaimed: 'Please, no more war stories!' His impatience was understandable since in his lifetime he had been able to take the existence of a local film industry for granted, with at least half-a-dozen features produced each year with the actors and crew members being paid for their work. In contrast, during the first quarter-century of my own life there were only four 35mm New Zealand feature films, each made on a minuscule budget.

Young filmmakers have also grown up with the opportunity to attend our major International Film Festival (which in recent years has been selling 90,000 to 100,000 tickets annually). Yet, as Sigley documents, the first year of the Festival in 1969 felt to its organisers like a scary leap into the dark. Auckland University now has a large Film, Television, and Media Studies department offering film history, theory, and production courses at all levels, but during the 1970s and 1980s all attempts to introduce the first undergraduate course were energetically opposed on the grounds that film was not a real subject.[1] There are plenty of war stories of this kind, and such campaigns deserve to be documented. Ultimately they are success stories, offering valuable lessons in the development of ideas and the growth of culture. Sigley's book is the first to record and analyse this history and he has done so with a great wealth of research and a shrewd eye for detail.

Admittedly no New Zealander has contributed anything highly innovative to world film culture, with the partial exception of Len Lye (1901–80), who earned a place in film history as the pioneer of 'direct film', the process of making films without a camera by painting and scratching images directly onto the celluloid. He was also a highly original film and television theorist, for example in his essays and interviews for magazines such as *Life and Letters Today, World Film News, Sight and Sound,* and *Film Culture.*[2] But Lye's theories lie outside the scope of the present book because he did most of his work in the United States of America or in Britain.

Peter Jackson and Weta Workshop have done original work in the field of computer generated imagery (CGI), but that is a matter of film production rather than film theory. New Zealand has one other claim to innovation, as Sigley explains in Chapter 8. Frank Stark, Director of the Film Archive, 'holds the view that at a fundamental level (and in the eyes of the world) the unique component of New Zealand screen culture is Māori-based.' Certainly the determined efforts of the Archive to involve the indigenous community of New Zealand in the management or guardianship (*kaitiakitanga*) of its collection, backed by the theoretical writing of filmmaker Barry Barclay, has attracted international interest as a new model for film archives, though it has also (as Sigley explains) produced some local controversy.[3]

For the most part, this book offers discoveries of a different kind. It tracks the history of ideas, not their genesis but their subsequent nomadic existence – how they have been encountered, imported, challenged, inflected, absorbed, and put to work in original forms of organisation. Radically new ideas are rare, such as the cluster associated with film culture (the notion of film as art, auteur theory, the editing ideas of Griffith and Eisenstein, and so on). New Zealand offers an especially clear situation for studying the process of dissemination because it is such a small country – just under 1 ½ million inhabitants in 1929, and just under 4 ½ million today. Also, this 'island' nation is relatively self-contained (unlike the countries of Europe, say). Even Australia is approximately 1400 miles or 2250 kilometres away and its culture is distinctly different.

Isolated as it is, it is still New Zealand's fate to be swamped by imports. Starting life as a British colony, the country was encouraged to export agricultural produce and to import most of its culture. Those involved with cultural matters saw Britain as the natural source of new ideas and quality products, though imports were limited and there was an intellectual time lag. In contrast, New Zealand's popular culture came to be dominated by the United States of America. The nation's culture at large has frequently been shaped by the struggle between British and American influences, and this can be seen particularly clearly in debates about the film medium. Meanwhile, it is fascinating to track the ways in which British and American ideas are subtly changed as they enter New Zealand cultural space. The process by which the DNA of an idea undergoes mutation in that space reveals the particular local forces at work, and also the culture-specific aspects of the original idea.

An unusually detailed knowledge of both the New Zealand and the French film cultures enables Sigley to make many interesting comparisons. As he remarks in his introduction:

> Over the course of my lifetime, I have seen [New Zealand film culture] progress along a comparable path [to French film culture], gradually to make the same kinds of discoveries, and to develop similar social and intellectual formations (with its cineastes, film societies, festivals, art cinemas, film archive or *cinémathèque*, and intellectual tendencies from 'auteur theory' to post-structuralism). There seemed an internal logic to the development of a national film culture, involving similar historical stages.

The 'logic' that provides the main driving force is intellectual in character, but, as Sigley shows, it is constantly pushed and pulled by the social, economic, political, and technological forces active at a given time in each territory. His account is particularly revealing because he takes care to avoid single-factor explanations. Cultural Studies has been bedeviled by vague definitions of 'culture', but in describing the specific field of New Zealand 'film culture', Sigley keeps a clear grasp of its many different elements and the ways in which they interact.

To take one example, his 'thick description' highlights the importance of distribution. For a long time, academic reception theory tended to focus on three elements – the text, its production, and its reception. Yet everyone in the media business – from filmmakers to book publishers, from music managers to festival directors – knew that those elements were all influenced by distribution. Sigley shows clearly how changes in the distribution of the so-called 'foreign' films in New Zealand, and in exhibition contexts, had a huge effect on how the art of film was understood and talked about. His case study is a reminder that we must not be tricked by today's abundance into overlooking the importance of scarcity in cultural history. When I was teaching in the 1960s and early 1970s, for example, I sought to champion "close reading" as a necessary first step towards the study of film aesthetics, yet I lacked the tools for doing so. Many of the films I wanted to screen were only available – if at all – in the form of a 35mm rental print, with a single copy shared by New Zealand and Australia. (My budget did not allow me to purchase prints.) If I was lucky, I could rent the film for a few days each year, but I was extremely nervous about trying to freeze frames for closer study because there was a risk of damaging the only copy available in our part of the world. Close viewing was revolutionised by the arrival of videotapes at the end of the 1970s.

Sigley's study casts light not only on film culture but on many aspects of New Zealand life. For example, overseas film people are astonished that our major film festivals have to rely mostly upon ticket sales because of the shortage of public and corporate funding; and they see the success of our film festivals as a remarkable achievement. Also important is the high value placed upon realism or verisimilitude in all areas of the arts. Gordon Mirams speculated in 1950 that 'The documentary is the only branch of film production in which this country has any chance of making a contribution of real value', and while the feature film directors of the last 35 years have overthrown this prediction, our country has certainly enjoyed an outstanding tradition of documentary filmmaking.

Many of the artists and intellectuals who crop up in the pages of this book saw film culture as one aspect of a general struggle to bring intellectual modernity to New Zealand, which was then an old-fashioned country with a derivative (colonial) culture. Many were better known for their work in literature and other areas of the arts – for example, James Bertram, A.R.D. Fairburn, Clifton Firth, M.K. Joseph, Bruce Mason, R.A.K. Mason, H. Winston Rhodes, and Hubert Witherford. Why did creative figures such as these not emigrate, following the precedent set by Lye or Katherine Mansfield? One reason was a sense of social involvement or community crusade – so much needed to be done. The situation encouraged eclecticism in the arts as there were not enough people to fill the required cultural roles, and this often resulted in a tendency to talk about film in literary rather than cinematic ways. Even those with knowledge of technical film terms were cautious about using them because of the strongly anti-intellectual attitude of the public. Cinéastes were accused of being elitist in their taste, pretentious in their talk, radical in their politics, and dubious in their morals. New Zealanders have always been passionate film-goers, yet reviewing and other forms of public discourse about films have tended to remain thin and populist. Nevertheless, while New Zealand has not developed a film culture as rich as the French, its activists have contributed in their own way to the same intellectual tradition, and following its 'internal logic' they have succeeded in building local versions of its institutions.

All over the world, film culture is now suffering a huge upheaval. Will it survive the digital age? It is encouraging to see so many young people making their own moving images with the new tools at their disposal; but those who watch films on their iPhones or computers seem unconcerned about the loss of quality. Digital experts lump 'texts' of all kinds together as 'content' and are not interested in the specificity of each source – the sense of 'the medium as message' that was so important to modernism and to the idea of film culture. Archives face a huge challenge in the need to migrate celluloid to high-definition digital formats. Film specialists in universities are being replaced by media specialists. Today's best-known New Zealand director, Peter Jackson, seems more interested in digital effects and computer games than in filmic qualities. The long-term future of cinemas and festivals is uncertain, and other media such as newspapers, magazines, printed books, and television are already in disarray.

While the tradition documented in Sigley's book may seem to be receding into history, it continues to offer a crucial education for our eyes and ears. Film culture with its understanding of the importance of details, the beauty of slowness as well as speed, and the countless other forms of artistry that have shaped great films, can still provide us with a firm basis for image-making and prevent us being swept away by the torrent of vapid digital images. Sigley's thoughtful study of the evolution of film culture in New Zealand is a fascinating contribution to intellectual history, reminding us of key issues that future digital generations cannot afford to forget.

By Roger Horrocks Emeritus Professor
University of Auckland

Notes

1   For other details of film education in New Zealand in recent decades, see my booklet *Media Teaching in New Zealand: Sketching out a History* (Department of Film, Television, and Media Studies, University of Auckland, 2007), and www.name.org.nz, the website of the National Association of Media Educators.
2   For sample essays, see *Figures of Motion: Len Lye Selected Writings,* ed. Wystan Curnow and Roger Horrocks, Auckland, Auckland University Press/Oxford University Press, 1984.
3   The most important text by Barry Barclay (who died in 2008) was *Mana Tuturu: Maori Treasures and Intellectual Property Rights* (Auckland University Press, 2005).

Introduction

This book is an investigation into the transnational nature of 'film culture', taking the film culture of one country – New Zealand – as a case study to investigate the dynamics of such a culture. 'Film culture' is used here to refer to the network of discursive and non-discursive activities associated with the idea of film as art. The term 'culture' is used in the cultural studies sense – that is, seen from a combination of perspectives including anthropology, intellectual history, and textual studies.

As an emerging research field, a lot remains to be written about the history of such networks, which are both individual and institutional, and which shaped in fundamental ways what was said and done amongst particular individuals, groups, and institutions as they created a (trans)national film culture. Filmmaking *per se* in New Zealand is a small – though sometimes important – part of this history. My principal aim is to describe and explain the rising cultural authority of the cinema – as it came to be taken seriously as an art. This involves looking at the interaction of various elements.

The diagram on the following page illustrates the main elements of film culture.[1] There are intricate links and 'multiplier' effects between different pieces in the web of film culture. Not all are exclusively parts of film culture – rather, some are allies or occasional contributors (for example, art galleries and museums which screen some films as part of a varied programme). The interaction and synergy between these elements weaves them together as a 'culture', a web of common interests and shared values.

The various components that constitute a more complete film culture have developed at different times, and often separately, in New Zealand, so they have not combined as productively as they might in order to produce a series of deeper and more varied discursive practices. For example, New Zealand still has no conceptually rich film magazine (with the partial exception of *Illusions*). The reasons for such gaps can be associated with several aspects of the country's history and geography, such as the country's small size, relatively short history, and isolation.

These aspects have an obvious 'downside', such as the one I have just mentioned, but they also have an 'upside' that puts a more positive gloss on them. Rather than seeing them as a disadvantage, which previous generations of literary and cultural critics have done, we may see them as providing a hot house atmosphere, which, as a prominent scholar has noted, 'is a historian's paradise' because the 'grand themes of world history are often played out more rapidly, more separately, and therefore more discernibly, than elsewhere' (Belich 1996: 7). The growth of film culture in New Zealand, which hardly qualifies as one of the 'grand themes' of world history, yet provides many micro examples to support this enthusiastic observation.

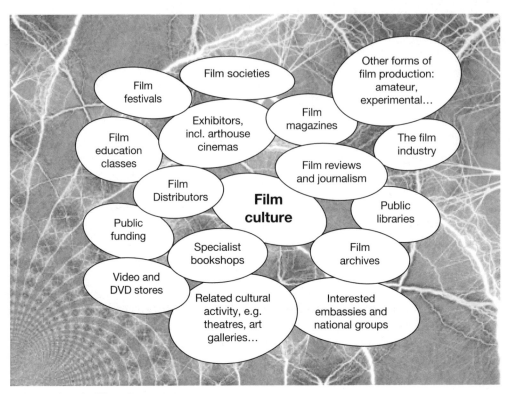

Figure 1: The web of film culture.

To introduce some key concepts, I will begin with a brief history of my own viewing – not to make claims for myself as a cinephile, but because my experience of growing up in New Zealand and then moving to France seems useful as a contrast between two kinds of film culture which represent extreme stages of development. Describing this contrast, as I experienced it on a daily basis, should serve to introduce some key concepts and contradictions.

The history of my viewing divides into three main eras: the conventional or mainstream viewing of my childhood; the discovery of 'art cinema' (but in the isolated, occasional, and under-theorised form that was available in New Zealand in the 1970s); and then immersion in the sophisticated, highly articulate film culture of Paris (where art cinema was a regular part of everyday life for those interested, and fully integrated with broader intellectual activities). These three stages represent three types of film viewing (in individual terms) and three forms of 'film culture' (in general terms). Obviously there were also many smaller stages within each era – such as the many discoveries I made during my nine years in France, including the new insights that accompanied my first experiences of filmmaking.

Returning to New Zealand forced me to become conscious of differences and to attempt to understand them in terms of cultural history and politics; and this served as the stimulus or provocation for writing this book. As a 'film enthusiast', making a living as a film editor, this was a topic I cared deeply about. France represented an advanced form of 'film culture', while New Zealand illustrated film culture at a much less developed stage; yet over the course of my lifetime, I have seen it progress along a comparable path, gradually to make the same kinds of discoveries, and to develop similar social and intellectual formations (with its cinéastes, film societies, festivals, art cinemas, film archive or *cinémathèque*, and intellectual tendencies from 'auteur theory' to post-structuralism). There seemed an internal logic to the development of a national film culture, involving similar historical stages. Yet it was difficult to generalise about these phenomena because no one had documented them in any detail.

Examining New Zealand as a case study in the formation of such a culture, this book provides both an intellectual history and a social (or sub-cultural) study, and it also observes the interaction between these two elements. New intellectual concepts created new social and industrial possibilities, and at the same time were dependent upon an infrastructure of importers and exhibitors, societies and cinemas, magazines and educational institutions.

I would first like to expand a little more on my own history as a viewer if only to stress the fact that the issues at stake have deep roots in lived experience. For anyone who cares about film, they are matters not only of intellectual curiosity but also of everyday modes of experience and of passionate cultural allegiances.

The First Stage

As I was of the first New Zealand generation to experience televised home entertainment, film going was an infrequent distraction for me growing up in various towns and cities throughout the 1960s and 1970s. In comparison to other western countries, New Zealand acquired this technology relatively late in 1960. There were only 4600 television licences in 1961, although by 1966 these had exploded to 500,000 (*New Zealand Official Yearbook* [hereafter *NZOYB*] 1990: 340). At the end of the decade, television was available in 77 per cent of New Zealand homes (Belich 2001: 427). This might help explain why my parents seldom took us to the cinema – and when they did, our big screen experience was casual, and never discussed. As a child, I remember seeing several musicals, such as *The Sound of Music* (USA, 1965), *Chitty Chitty Bang Bang* (UK, 1968), *Oliver!* (UK, 1968), and *Fiddler on the Roof* (USA, 1971), but those are almost the only films that have stayed in my memory.

When I think of the immediately preceding generation of school children and their parents, it is clear that film was a more central part of New Zealand life. Film-going hit 40,632,000 cinema tickets sold in 1960, with 545 cinemas, in a population of approximately 2.4 million (*NZOYB* 2000: 287 and 91), so the average New Zealander went to the cinema approximately 17 times a year, or almost as often as once a fortnight. The arrival of television then began relentlessly to erode this figure, so that by 1966 the number of admissions was down to 19,606,000 and the number of cinemas to 312 (Dennis and Bieringa 1996: 224–25). But despite the inroads of television, film-going continued to be a major activity for New Zealanders. What the pioneering film critic Gordon Mirams said of New Zealanders in 1945 was still largely true in 1966, that 'Only tea-drinking is a more popular form of diversion with us than picture-going' (1945: 5).

In my teenage years, films offered weird, magical, and sometimes traumatic, experiences. The cinemas were semi-public social spaces that allowed me glimpses into illicit sights. At the local 'flea pit' (the grandly named Crystal Palace) in Mt Eden, an Auckland inner city suburb, I can recall seeing a bizarre Scandinavian 'documentary' that was ostensibly about human sexual reproduction, but I remember it chiefly for the naked bodies on display and the close ups of male and female genitalia. One really curious shot even purported to show the frantic liquid struggle of spermatozoa as they raced towards an egg and assailed it in comic desperation. Unsupervised viewing could occasionally produce genuinely scary experiences. Seeing one of the Hammer studio's horror films in which a psychopath jammed a bunch of hat pins into a woman's eye kept me away from that genre for years. Although I'm sure that censorship restrictions at that time prevented the filmmaker from showing this literally – with the pins actually entering the eye – 'constructive editing' and my imagination supplied the missing detail. In my mind's eye today I can still see the woman turning her head towards the camera in close up so that the audience could see the effect of the completed action.

Even though my film-going was infrequent, experiences of the sort just described serve to underline the power and importance of the medium for me. It was a source of weird entertainment and shock, family values, and gross sentimentality. One thing it never seemed to be was art. Film thus formed part of the mainstream of New Zealand life during my early years, and a popular 'film culture' certainly existed, but in my own personal experience, it was a culture without clear definition that simply blurred into the general run of entertainment activities, experienced now and then in the company of family.

The Second Stage

My delayed discovery of 'the cinema', with its multifarious lessons and pleasures, was connected with films positioned at the seriously artistic end of the celluloid continuum. The term 'the cinema', referring to the art of the film was one that I did not encounter until many years later. Everyone spoke of 'going to the pictures' in the literal terms of the local theatre, and there was no talk in my vicinity about 'cinema' as something generic, as a medium or as an art. My discovery that such extraordinary films existed began with film society activity. The Auckland Film Society had been the prime mover in the founding of the Auckland International Film Festival in 1969, a showcase for provocative world cinema. (Auckland is New Zealand's largest city. At that time it had a population of just over half a million.)

The annual film festivals were like celluloid rivers in which I would swim, session after session; sometimes sucked down into deep dark holes, I was also made to rise as another current swirled around me. Directors of the various national cinemas associated with successive 'waves' of innovative, modernist-inspired filmmaking (French, Czech, Russian, Japanese, West German, and South American) were screened during the festivals, along with arresting examples of documentary, animation, and underground films. I learned that movement, light, and sound could be combined as a form of art that made my pulse quicken, stimulated my curiosity, and aroused my desire to understand. Films could incorporate the expressive possibilities of so many other artistic forms – poetry, literature, theatre, music, dance, photography, and architecture. Although the range of films seen at the festivals did not extend to films that could be described as 'abstract' or 'experimental', the feature films I did see were as stimulating as modernist literature, as engaging as political theatre, and (importantly) more sensual than either.[2]

I supplemented participation at the annual film festival with attendance at Auckland's iconic cinemas, the Academy and the Lido. These were 'art-house cinemas', though that was another term I did not hear until later. These were my cinematic equivalents of an art gallery or museum, more regular sources of supply than the annual festivals, and less intimidating. But like them, they functioned as places of learning for me, where shocking, enthralling, and perplexing sights and sounds might be sampled at a modest price. One of the most confounding films I saw at the Academy was Hans-Jurgen Syberberg's *Hitler: A Film from Germany* (1977). Although it had been cut from its original seven-hour length when shown in New Zealand, it still seemed extraordinarily long, and to have been put together using a strange alchemy comprising collage, montage, and bizarre theatricality. Strangeness was an attraction, the weirder the better, *pourvu qu'on ait l'ivresse*. Was Syberberg exorcising modern Germany's fascist past? I don't think I understood much about the film although it was certainly arresting enough to hold me throughout its length, and I knew that I was watching something unique.

Enrolling as an undergraduate at the University of Auckland in 1978, I continued my cinematic experimentation. In a large lecture theatre (B28) in the basement of the University Library, I went to weekly screenings. The organiser of these sessions was a reticent cinephile who let the films speak for themselves. There were no introductions to any film, its director, genre, period, or style. The audience was not directed towards readings of the film but left to commune with it, grapple with it, alone. If the festivals were like celluloid rivers, the sessions in B28 were like a pool you jumped into. There was always the anticipation of discovering something new, possibly weird, and usually thoughtful.

Art cinema offered many insights into the human in all its confusion, yet suggested that narratives with which to structure that welter could somehow be fashioned. The idea of film as an art became a given for me but I still lacked both the social dimension of an art film *culture*, and the ability to articulate my instinctive judgements. Clearly there *was* a culture – or a loose community – around the Film Society, the Film Festival, and the art-house cinemas, represented by familiar faces and styles of clothing. National groups (coming to the films more to hear a native language than in search of filmic innovation) rubbed shoulders with students and hippies. But my own film-going was still not especially social. I wasn't there to see or be seen by others. Reading books is obviously a solitary practice, and so too, for me, was going to the cinema; I shared the same physical space with others but when the lights went down, I was on my own with the film.

Not that watching art cinema was a voyeuristic affair, partly because such films gave the impression that they were watching me, too. We interacted – the film and I – in an unrehearsed *pas de deux*. This was not an unpleasant experience; it was like reading the pages of a precious book whose words found a resonance inside my experience of the world up to that point. Such words and images allowed me to slice through another of the Gordian knots that life presented. Alongside this existential thrill, popular pleasures were dubious – not the real thing, not art. This did not mean, however, that I was immune to the attractions of Bruce Lee's kung fu revenge fantasies when they screened in Auckland, or the sardonic shocks of *Lenny* (USA, 1975), where Dustin Hoffman's poet rebel railed against 'the American way of life'. The latter was seen (experienced would be a better physical description of its effect on me) at the cinema in the Waiouru Military Camp where the remains of the Army Education and Welfare Service's cultural programme could still be found. *Lenny* challenged sweeping generalisations about Hollywood, proof that some American films could offer stimulations and provocations different from those of the mainstream.

If I had seen a film with other people, I had no wish to have instant opinions once we left the cinema, since such opinions tended to seem pretentious or be divisive, and if the film had left its mark in me, then I wanted to be left alone to reflect on it. In any case, from my untutored taste and sensibility I could not have proffered much more than impressionistic comments. I had no way to formally analyse a film's 'internal' structure or to relate it confidently to its social or aesthetic contexts. The sense that cinematic art was more than just entertainment was something I felt very strongly but could not yet articulate. I was certainly filling in gaps in my knowledge of world cinema, but there were still many lacunae in my knowledge of film history. Some concepts were gradually taking shape in my mind – that directors were important, that 'serious' films often departed from straightforward narrative patterns, that they offered a new vision of the world or some part of it, and that all this meant that spectatorship had to be more *active* – but I was still a long way from being able to put together the various pieces of the jigsaw into coherent theories.

I did know that something strangely important was going on, and I wanted to understand it. I did not assume, as some seemed to do, that avant-garde perplexity necessarily meant profundity. But all the head-scratching occasioned by narrative dislocation at least had the advantage of making me think. And even when a director's preoccupations were more classically configured, art cinema's moral and thematic searching made it impressive and challenging. I became convinced that Robert Bresson's films were self-evidently of the first order while George Lucas's were of the seventh, though not many of my peers seemed to agree (*Star Wars* was a huge hit in 1977) and it was years before I could argue my case other than intuitively.

My experience of art films up to this point had been as beacons. They rose above the sea of popular cinema, projected a bright light, and signalled the existence of an exciting, albeit more solemn, art form, whose presence in this country was still somewhat tenuous. They existed, at least for me, in a discursive vacuum. They came, were seen, and went away, leaving little trace in their wake. I have subsequently learned that there were individuals thinking and talking about the cinema, even making their own films, in New Zealand at this time, but what my personal experience suggests is that such activities were marginalised. Certainly, I never learned of their existence from mainstream magazines, newspapers, television, or radio stations. Film reviewing had existed here since the mid-1930s but it was basically limited to what we now call the 'consumer guide' variety. The brief blurbs for films in film society magazines and film festival booklets were the closest thing I encountered to historically and theoretically informed film talk.

I had not even acquired a clear idea of 'authorship', the concept that for many overseas enthusiasts represented the point of entry into film theory. The English film magazine, *Sight and Sound*, published by the British Film Institute from the early 1930s, had been available in New Zealand for decades on subscription or in the main public libraries, yet I knew no one who read it. Similarly, there were no undergraduate film classes on offer at my university, although one of the lecturers in the English Department was active in the Film Festival and had been teaching an MA course in film studies since 1975 that attracted graduate students from many departments. There were also other initiatives around New Zealand – enthusiastic individuals teaching filmmaking in art schools in Auckland and Christchurch, an annual Winter Film School in Wellington and a filmmaking co-op movement picking up steam – but I remained a solitary viewer, unaware of their existence.

The Third Stage

In April 1985, undergraduate degree in my suitcase and with money saved from being a part-time taxi driver, I went to France with the aim of studying for a post-grad degree in political science at the Sorbonne. One cultural difference that caused early surprise was seeing Bernardo Bertolucci's *Last Tango in Paris* (France/Italy, 1972) on one of the State-run television channels. Obviously France had a liberal approach to screening intellectually and emotionally contentious material.

Another signal difference was demonstrated by French public television's commitment to providing specialist programmes having particular films or the cinema as their subject. *Cinéma cinémas* was a 50-minute monthly television programme that never failed to be informative and visually arresting. It was produced and often directed by André S. Labarthe, a former critic with *Cahiers du cinéma* in the 1950s and 1960s. He was also responsible for the valuable *Cinéastes de notre temps* series, produced with Janine Bazin from the early 1960s on. The learned Claude-Jean Philippe, an erudite and passionate cinephile, writer and journalist, hosted his weekly *Cinéclub* on Friday nights on Antenne 2. He introduced each film with a short infectious talk that contributed to my understanding of it, the director, or the genre. The *Cinéma de minuit* was another regular television rendez-vous on France 3 introduced by the more discreet but equally erudite Patrick Brion, whose face we never saw, but whose distinctive voice provided, in its curiously syncopated way, a wealth of detail about the personnel involved in the film and the period in which it was made.

Arte, a Franco-German television station with high culture ambitions, broadcast thematic *soirées* on a wide variety of subjects that often included film – sensuality in Chinese cinema was one memorable example. *Radio Nova* had a weekly round table discussion intelligently reviewing the films of the week. *Les Inrockutibles* was a monthly magazine devoted to contemporary culture, basically music, literature, and a strong section on the cinema written by Serge Kaganski. Their accent was on the marginal, the independent, and the personal in each of the three arts.

What the various people in these different media shared was a common stock of knowledge about film culture – one that had been developed over many generations by critics committed to the idea that film was the art form of the twentieth century, a protean cultural phenomenon, and one that deserved intelligently argued and reasoned critical comment. This *common culture* was, of course, added to, disputed, and individually interpreted. However, many people were deeply versed in it and used a set of common concepts.

The best theory is in constant dialogue with practice, represented by the impressive number of films on show in Paris, with respect for the old as well as the new. There were not just two art-house cinemas but a multitude, which together formed a dense network in the *quartier latin*. Instead of waiting for Auckland's annual Film Festival, which transformed film-going into a bulimic-type sickness to which one fell victim for two weeks each year, there was a permanent 365-day festival. Watching films was now *à la carte*. I became a cinephile, watching several films a week for many years. I can no longer recall which films sparked things off for me – too many were fusing in my mind; but the most important effect was to fill in gaps, providing me with sequences and clusters that encouraged the generation of labels, ideas, historical and aesthetic generalisations. Viewing films from different periods and countries allowed me to better understand the cinema's aesthetic evolution. Specialist cinemas allowed me to explore styles and periods – early silent films (shown to be not as 'primitive' as I had assumed); restored films from the 1920s screened with orchestral accompaniment in the Pyramid of the Louvre; Hollywood's classic era (screened exclusively by the small Action Gitanes cinema group); retrospectives of little known *auteurs* (Japan's Mikio Naruse, Mexico's Arturo Ripstein, India's Ritwik Ghatak); discoveries of the latest crop (Hal Hartley, Abbas Kiaorastami, and Jane Campion in the early 1990s); genre celebrations (for example, Anthony Mann's westerns with Jimmy Stewart); national cinemas past and present (at the Centre Georges Pompidou); and North African cinema at the Arab World Institute, Egyptian most notably.

Moreover, the art of cinema *mattered* in a way it had never mattered in New Zealand. There was *public* debate and critically stimulating discussion in a variety of media. If Auckland's two art-house cinemas had been my local art gallery and museum, then the film culture of Paris was the equivalent of the Tate Gallery, the Louvre and the Museum of Modern Art combined – both quantitatively and qualitatively more powerful and more challenging.

Their impact was not confined to the films themselves, although they were vital, but also to the cultural field in which they were embedded and debated. The importance accorded the cinema, the variety of discourses, the number of magazines, radio and television programmes devoted to analysing the cinema in social, political, industrial, and aesthetic terms – these were impressive. The air seemed full of such messages. I felt connected. And notwithstanding the considerable cultural shock that awaits provincial yokels who go to the 'big smoke' for the first time, I felt at home. Living in France validated cultural and intellectual aspirations.

There were personal exchanges, both heated and relaxed, between friends and strangers over the thematic and *cinematic* merits and meanings of particular films. Did Stephen Spielberg 'have the right' to represent what was deemed unrepresentable (Nazi Germany's Final Solution) in his film *Schindler's List* (USA, 1993)? Was there anything more to be said on that subject after Claude Lanzmann's monumental *Shoah* (France, 1985)? Was the Jewish holocaust *representable* in fictive form? Could a *politique des acteurs* inflect the time-honoured *politique des auteurs*? In France, debate over, under, and around the cinema was well informed, aesthetically complex, and politically alert, not to mention personally stimulating and liberating. Films were no longer merely private experiences – I had friends with some of the same interests as myself. The range and number of voices speaking and thinking the cinema allowed me to find mine.

La politique des auteurs was the powerful conceptual weapon that I first got to know well. I moved through a series of expanding concentric circles, as auteurism was inflected and complicated by more general considerations of the cinema. A psychoanalytical discourse (then very active) worked on the relationship between the screen, the unconscious, and the process of identification. The Althusserian approach that posited the cinema as a hegemonic ideological apparatus of the State was declining in influence. Narratology explored concordance and discordance in written and filmic stories. A Neo-Hegelian method sought new ways to link national cinemas with the social and political realities of those countries. Metzian semiotics looked at the cinema as a complex language or signifying system. There was sometimes a confusing richness and intoxication in this ferment of ideas.

Even as I grappled with the ideas of Jacques Derrida and Michel Foucault, I was still catching up with the film theories of the 1950s. And though the theoretical legacy of André Bazin – as a version of realism – now had to contend with everything from post-structuralism to the rise of special effects technologies that blurred the boundaries of the real, his work was still well known and widely discussed. The idea of authorship and the influence (or mythology) of the *nouvelle vague* retained their power. Authorship was more than a concept in Paris as it was embodied by so many famous directors appearing in person. One night I cycled across Paris to be one of the many that filled the Max Linder Cinema to see Martin Scorsese present his early student films.

The history of film criticism also sprang to life – for example, in a series of public lectures organised by the *Cinémathèque française* in a small theatre connected to the Palais de Chaillot.

There, for instance, I heard Jean Douchet, one of the young critics in the 1950s writing for *Cahiers du cinéma* whose collective effort gave a robust form to the idea of the director as the intelligence outside the film shaping its visible events. At the *Cinémathèque* he talked about a Japanese filmmaker of the 1960s, obscure for me but highly significant for him. Of particular interest was the way Douchet was able not only to point out the innovative stylistic features of this film but also to relate them to the social context in which it was made. At the time this was a new insight for me – that films were not merely rarefied aesthetic objects but points of entry into a society or culture at a particular moment in history.

Two matters of importance – the work of the individual filmmaker and the conditions of the society – were both revealed through *mise en scène*. Films were a confluence of individuals and wider social forces. Such ideas had a powerful influence on me since they encouraged both closer forms of reading and a more serious consideration of contexts and implications. This was a broad conception of film criticism that took authorship as its starting point. Although constantly under attack in the wake of structural anthropology and 'the death of the subject', authorship still informed some of the most lively film discussion in Paris. The high status of film within French culture owed much to this idea that had first made it possible to align filmmaking with arts such as literature and painting. Alexander Astruc's 'camera-pen' was still writing, though critics now paid more attention to its contexts.

Return to New Zealand

I returned to New Zealand in 1994 with three short films I had made, and began researching subjects that might interest *Thalassa* and '*Faut pas rever*', two long-running French television programmes. For the French, New Zealand is always rediscoverable. For me, it had become a problematic place. In the wake of two neo-liberal ('free market') governments, television was more commercially minded than ever, with films interrupted by an ad break every ten minutes or so.[3] Filmmaking had moved further away from the 'art' end of the spectrum towards the 'industry' end. Media coverage of film focused on celebrity stars or the colourful prejudices of journalists with no knowledge of film history or aesthetics. (Almost all specialist reviewers had been fired, either as a cost-saving measure or because they were out of step with the general shift towards a chatty, populist approach.)

There was no shortage of 'film culture' in New Zealand if one concentrated on the public's interest in mainstream Hollywood films and stars, expressed in a discourse of entertainment rather than art. Film-going had reached an all-time low in 1991 with an average of only 1.79 cinema admissions per year per person, but a wave of re-investment had enabled the building of new, more comfortable multiplex cinemas, and this brought the average number of admissions back by 1997 to 4.71.[4] By now, however, the kind of 'film culture' that most interested me centred round the idea of film as art. In New Zealand, the Film Society and the Film Festival still soldiered on, and undergraduate Film Study courses had emerged at some universities; but this kind of film culture seemed extremely thin compared with that of France.

The shock of returning was one of the reasons I decided to write the history of film culture in this country. I wanted to understand the local situation and the reason for the enormous differences in relation to France and other European countries. As I researched film history in New Zealand, I became more intrigued by the dynamics of culture and questions such as these:

- Was there a set of stages through which film culture normally developed; and if so, was New Zealand gradually progressing along the same path that would lead to a sophisticated film culture like that of France – or were the necessary cultural foundations simply not present?
- How did the history of overseas film cultures compare with New Zealand's?
- How to account for the presence or absence in New Zealand of ideas circulating in film culture overseas?
- Was my gaze so coloured by my French experience that I was failing to recognise a unique film culture developing along different lines in New Zealand? (To what extent was film culture locally specific?)

These and a number of other questions began to occupy my curiosity. It was clear that the first stage of answering them would involve a history of the development of film culture in my own country, and no one had researched and written such an account. A preliminary search convinced me that this was a fascinating area of cultural history that had not been explored. I discovered some interesting writings on film in the pages of *Tomorrow* (1934–40), a local radical fortnightly newspaper; and unearthed evidence of a forgotten Auckland Film Society in 1929, which published a column in the *Auckland Star*.

Research on the formation of the Wellington Film Society, and the reasons for its prosecution by the Government in 1933, encouraged me to learn more about the cultural climate that could produce such events. In schools in the 1950s, the application and discussion of film was diverted from the idea of it as a medium in its own right, towards its purely functional use as a moral and educational 'tool' that permitted a closer engagement with literature and theatre – films of Shakespearean plays, for example. Obviously the growth of a national film culture was intricately linked with the political, moral, and artistic developments that made up New Zealand history; and I found that my research on film was giving me a new perspective on the general evolution of this society. It was also yielding insights into the nature and functioning of 'culture' itself.

The book then took shape as an investigation of the growth of film culture in New Zealand. More specifically, I investigated the arrival of the idea of 'film as art', and the individuals and organisations responsible for the diffusion of this idea, the films most closely associated with it, and the concrete cultural practices that supported this discourse. In other words, this book documents and analyses the history of a particular subculture, albeit from an aesthetic as well as a sociological perspective. In detail, I seek to illuminate questions such as these:

- In a young and thinly populated country, with its 'high culture' still under construction, how did a national film culture become established?
- How did a subculture develop around this idea? (For example, what was the process of audience formation for 'art cinema', and how did this relate to other social identities, practices, and institutions?)
- How have the various aspects of film culture worked together – intellectual discussion, film distribution, film exhibition, school and university education, publishing, and local film production?
- In the course of history, what social and political forces have impacted on and shaped the film culture (or subculture) in question?
- By analysing the adaptation of overseas ideas and institutions to the local situation (such as 'the film society', 'the film festival' or 'the art-house cinema'), what do we learn about the dynamics of local cultural development?
- How has cultural growth been funded in New Zealand (for example, by the State, wealthy private patrons, business interests, or some other means)? How do these sources interact?
- What are the main drivers of cultural development – individual enthusiasts, say, or small 'ginger' groups, or large social and economic trends? How important are immigrants or overseas influences?
- What role have new technologies (such as the 16mm projector and the Internet) played in the growth of film culture?

The overall aim is to document and analyse the development of a national film culture. I hope that my study may also make a distinctive contribution to the history of a post-colonial intellectual and artistic culture; the study of the dynamics of such a culture (how does it develop); and the transnational history of 'film culture' and 'art cinema'.

Majority and Minority Film Culture

As a simple starting point, New Zealand film-going can be divided broadly into majority and minority forms. During the period covered by this study, majority film culture was centred on the American films distributed by the major exhibition chains (Fullers-Hayward, Amalgamated, and Kerridge-Odeon). The screening of American films was supported by reviews, stories, gossip, and advertising that appeared in the press and on the commercial ZB radio network. This vibrant 'majority film culture' was well established by the 1920s.

Support for 'art films' as a form of minority film culture was centred on 'foreign films' – that is, 'foreign (or non-English) language' films from countries other than England or the United States, whose exhibition was facilitated by independent distributors, embassies, and members of the fledgling film society movement. This so-called 'serious' film culture (the closest thing to 'film as art' culture, but somewhat diluted and with particular New Zealand inflections) had its reviews, stories, and gossip, too, but these appeared in the 'quality' press: *Tomorrow, NZ Listener, Landfall, Here and Now,* or on the 'highbrow' YA radio network programmes: *Leaves from the Diary of a Film Fan, Footnotes to Film,* and *Cinema.* 'Serious' weekly film reviews first appeared in a daily newspaper on a regular basis at the end of 1954, written by a prominent local academic, John Reid. His reviewing appeared on page two of the *Auckland Star,* separated from the section that displayed majority film culture taste many pages later. Film study and analysis, a second aspect of minority film culture, was fostered by members of the film society movement (including educators, filmmakers, and other enthusiasts). This study tracks both of these aspects, but pays particular attention to the second as the most active and innovative local site for thinking about film. I do not wish to imply that majority film culture should be seen as of lesser importance, and I hope my study encourages other researchers to write histories of this other (and larger) tradition in New Zealand. There are also, of course, a myriad of minority film cultures (such as those associated with the terms 'cult', 'gay and lesbian', 'ethnic groups', 'porn', 'political', etc.). Such films have their own circuits and contexts, although there is a certain amount of overlap with 'art film' venues.

The present study on the construction of a (trans)national film culture is organised chronologically, based on a firm belief in the importance of history, and the importance of cause and effect sequences in understanding ideas and the way they work in society. Today, the electronic transfer of information is so rapid that it is difficult to appreciate the relative isolation of New Zealand in earlier decades, and the time lag involved in the dissemination of overseas ideas. It was, for example, customary for ideas emerging on the 'continent' to become acclimatised in London before 'trickling down' to New Zealand.

This study is an archaeological project that seeks to excavate the past, to identify the various stages in the construction of film culture, and to resurrect the texts and contexts that played a part in that development. They were thoroughly buried – most areas of the history have never been previously touched by any researcher.

References

For French titles (of books and films) I use the French system, which is to capitalise the first letter of the first word (and any proper nouns) with all other words in lower case.

Belich, J. (1996), *Making Peoples: A History of the New Zealanders from Polynesian Settlement to the End of the Nineteenth Century,* London: Allen Lane; Auckland: Penguin Press.

——— (2001), *Paradise Reforged: A History of the New Zealanders from the 1880s to the Year 2000,* Auckland: Allen Lane and Penguin Press.

Dennis, J. and Bieringa, J. eds. (1996), *Film in Aotearoa New Zealand*, Wellington: Victoria University Press.

Mein-Smith, P. (2005), *A Concise History of New Zealand*, Melbourne: Cambridge University Press.

Mirams, G. (1945), *Speaking Candidly*, Hamilton: Paul's Books.

New Zealand Official Yearbook (1990), Wellington: Government Printer.

NZOYB (2000), Wellington: Government Printer.

Notes

1   I thank Emeritus Professor Roger Horrocks for allowing me to reproduce the diagram.

2   I later learned that some films of that kind were being screened at the university in a free 16mm season held each year in the week before the Festival.

3   'Rogernomics' is the popular designation of this period: a portmanteau of 'Roger' and 'economics', the term describes the radical monetarist policies followed by the Finance Minister Roger Douglas following his appointment in 1984. Briefly, the reforms dismantled the Australasian model of state development that had existed for the previous 90 years, and replaced it with the Anglo-American neo-liberal orthodoxy based on the monetarist policies of Milton Friedman and the Chicago School. See Mein-Smith 2005: 201–16.

4   2011. *A trip to the flicks: watching cinema admission prices in the CPI.* n.d. [Online.] Wellington: Statistics New Zealand. Available at: http://www.stats.govt.nz/browse_for_stats/economic_indicators/prices_indexes/watching-cinema-admission-prices-in-the-cpi.aspx. Accessed: 20 May 2012.

Chapter 1

In Defence of Films as Art

This chapter explores the work of New Zealand's first film society at the end of the 1920s. This will serve as a touchstone to the emergence of various conceptions of film as art. Key issues include the relative value of types and sources of film (such as 'Hollywood' versus Europe), debates about morality, and attempts to identify those aspects of filmmaking in which artistry can most clearly be identified. These discussions also represent an attempt to establish an adequate lexicon and discourse for film aesthetics.

At the moment in history at which these debates reach some kind of critical mass, New Zealand was a country of less than one and a half million people. It was still in many respects a British colony, lacking any depth of high culture, and what there was tended to be mostly an importation. The creation of a film society was no exception, for – as we shall see – the idea was derived from the London Film Society, founded in 1925. (This society subsequently liked to describe itself as the first film society in the world.) Alongside the popular consumption of film, the 1920s also saw the development of specialised minority film cultures in the major European film-producing countries as well as in Britain.[1] As Tom Ryall has noted, this was 'a decade of self-conscious artistic experiment in the cinema in which the key artistic revolutions of the twentieth century – Expressionism, Cubism, Futurism, Dadaism and so on – found an outlet in the cinematic experiments of filmmakers in Germany, France, and the Soviet Union' (1986: 7). The 1920s therefore saw the emergence of cinemas that bore the imprint of 'art' and 'high culture', attracting the attention of the educated classes who had previously scorned the medium. This was not yet the case in New Zealand, but the arrival of a film society was one of the first signs.

In the work of the Auckland Film Society (AFS) it is also possible to see the lineaments of broader cultural patterns: in opposition to a narrow, strict, and relatively sterile colonial vision more preoccupied with respectability than stimulation, the AFS participated in the formation of informal networks conducive to local expressions of cultural modernity during the interwar period – a time of major change and upheaval in which 'the cumulative effects of the social, economic, technological and demographic developments of the late nineteenth and early twentieth century became increasingly obvious and began to have a significant impact on New Zealand society' (Sprecher 1999: 142; see also Hilliard 2006: 120, for more on the 'informal networks' that structured cultural life in the 1920s and 1930s).

Film had become a hugely popular medium in New Zealand, with exhibition and distribution following the same pattern as other countries – starting with film as a novelty attraction associated with fairgrounds and vaudeville, then progressing to store-front cinemas (existing buildings hired for film screenings), then to purpose-built cinemas, and by the end of the 1920s to elaborate 'picture palaces'. The growth of public interest was fuelled during the Great War (1914–18) by the demand for newsreels. Improved projection technology and more skilful cinematic storytelling techniques also fed the public's appetite for narrative. 'By 1917, 550,000 New Zealanders went to the pictures every week' (Hayward and Hayward 1979: 11–12). The 1920s also saw a huge increase in Auckland suburban theatres with over 25 new theatres opening. In 1929, Auckland's Civic Theatre was completed as a giant picture palace with exotic architecture and seating for 3500. Three other large cinemas had already been built in Auckland: the Majestic (1925) with seating for 2000 people; the Regent (1926) held 1700, and the St James (1929) a similar number. By the late 1920s, one-sixth of Auckland's population (about 230,000) went to the movies every Saturday night (Hayward and Hayward 1979).

Sound technology arrived in 1928–29, which made it possible to produce and screen 'sound films' (that is, films with synchronised soundtracks physically combined on celluloid with the images). This development caused a huge upheaval in the film business, in both economic and technological terms. It also involved an upheaval in the art of film, and debate within the new film society would reflect this shake-up.

New Zealand, like other countries, drew its films from particular national sources. Its white settler culture was extensively and intensively connected to Britain, and most other forms of art were dominated by British products and ideas. Officially, New Zealand had been an independent dominion since 1907, but this was a nominal change; unofficially, it was still a colony. But from the beginning its citizens could not resist the temptation of Hollywood films. This tension would generate many fierce debates over the decades between the enthusiasts of American films and their critics (moralists disturbed by the risqué tendencies of 1920s American films, in an uneasy alliance with intellectuals who saw the influence of American popular culture as politically and educationally dangerous).

Inevitably, these historical factors influenced the particular form taken by emerging ideas of what constituted a 'good film', 'a serious film' or 'an artistic film'. (It is important to recognise that these were separate ideas, although there was considerable overlap between them.) As we shall see, the AFS was initially distinguished by its strong strain of aestheticism – its emphasis on 'artistic' films and the pure (medium-specific) art of film. Yet the surrounding context of moralism was so strong that its aestheticism was sometimes diluted.

Among local moralists, not only American films but the popularity of the cinema in general was suspect, particularly in the influence of the medium on children. In Freudian terms, that influence was seen as weakening the social institutions designed to keep libidinal energy in harness and individuals hard at work. A letter written to the editor of the *Otago Daily Times* in April 1921 expressed the sense of outrage produced by *Dr Jekyll and Mr Hyde* (USA, 1920):

Sir, On more than one occasion I have written to you condemning immoral, debasing kinema shows in our town. Two or three months ago I went to the American dramatisation of *Dr Jekyll and Mr Hyde*, and came away with the intention of writing to you again, but could not find decent English words to express my feelings. Such an abominable travesty of the story by our beloved Stevenson, introducing long drawn out sensuous music-hall scenes that have no part in the original at all.[2]

In contrast, the writer expressed pleasure in the British film *Darby and Joan* (1919). The title itself has come to mean a happily married couple leading a placid, uneventful life – a condition the irate letter writer clearly prefers.

Such a response linked several forms of disapproval: a puritanical dislike of any public display of sexuality (or 'sensuousness'); a concern with declining standards of English (taking BBC-style Received Pronunciation as the ideal); a fear that entertainment was crowding out education; an hostility to films that vulgarised great literature or other forms of art (instead of doing what they should do, which was to attract people to high culture in a serious way); a suspicion of the United States as the principal source of commercial, mass-produced culture and vulgar populism; and an unwavering allegiance to Britain and its cultural products ('our beloved Stevenson'). But protest as he might, the writer was on a sticky wicket since the game to capture audiences was not going England's way. In 1927, 350 out of 400 films shown on New Zealand screens were American (Belich 2001: 251).

The cinema of the 1920s and 1930s was but one of a number of new technologies that provided a distinctive electric hum to life. Whilst many wealthy New Zealanders were 'early adopters' of these new technologies, there were conservative voices who espied in them the harbingers of modern times and modern morals, neither of which was viewed favourably. Fears concerning the growing cultural invasion of Hollywood were vividly expressed in the popular New Zealand women's magazine *The Mirror*.[3] An editorial declared that 'Instead of ennobling and inspiring influence, the majority of present day pictures are calculated to arouse the primitive emotions which we are forever endeavouring to check, control and guide by a complex system of customs and conventions that are supported by the strongest sanctions of law and religion' (*Mirror* 1929b: 8). An article by Dr Mildred Staley, 'The Child and the Cinema', demanded to know 'what steps we have taken here in New Zealand to ensure – as the report advises – that our children shall see only good films and be "protected from all demoralising influences"' (*Mirror* 1929a: 35).[4] Another expression of alarm was heard in a September editorial, 'Crime and Sex in Films', which spelt out the dangers likely to develop if the country's moral vigilance weakened and allowed 'the lowest phase of American life' to enter New Zealand. It added: 'If we were to believe the [film] producers, the United States would be a sink of iniquity, with people living a jazz life, depraved in morals, with minds and souls warped by sex instinct, corrupted by crime and depraved by drink' (*Mirror* 1929b).

Strong reactions of this sort need to be balanced with other moral crusades of the period, some of whose achievements are not to be sneered at – such as votes for women and better care for babies.[5] Nevertheless, the perceived threats to moral harmony could create excessive

Figure 2: The American hegemon was economic and cultural.

responses – Balzac and Zola joined the *Illustrated Marriage Guide* as 'offensive publications', and cinemas, veritable dens of iniquity, were linked to the spread of venereal disease and female smoking (Belich 2001: 157–58).

For many of the *Mirror*'s writers, any sense of art in films was seriously compromised by their American links with the vulgar clichés of mass-produced popular culture. Isobel M. Cluett's neo-Luddite article, 'The Menace of Mechanical Art', took issue with both gramophones and the cinema – diabolical markers of modernity. She associated the latter with 'crude, nasal American voices, the hideous argot of the Bowery slums freely flashed on the screen, the travesty of passionate emotion in long drawn-out embraces and provocative behaviour', and added: 'For these and other reasons ... if we must have the pictures, the intelligent and artistic section of the public should make every effort to encourage the production of British films in British countries' (*Mirror* 1930: 33).[6] The marked preference among educated New Zealanders for BBC English, and the sometimes vehement contempt of American dialects appear to reflect a fear of the new and the different. So long as films were silent, the 'otherness' of America was not so evident.

It is hard now for us to appreciate the value accorded 'correct' pronunciation by British audiences in the early 1930s. Vicky Lowe has drawn attention to its importance for film reception in marking out symbolic boundaries: 'Voices acted out representations, setting out a constituency from which the audience could be excluded or incorporated.' She goes on to argue that 'the sound of actors' voices on films was crucial in both reinforcing and challenging national, regional and gendered identities' (2004: 182). The negative local reaction to the influence and sound of Hollywood mirrored similar concerns in Britain and in other European countries. From today's perspective, however, the most striking aspect of the public debate in New Zealand was the absence of any reference to a distinctive local or national cultural identity. Educated New Zealanders were still happy to regard themselves as 'Better Britons' and to refer to Britain as 'Home'. They saw Hollywood not as a threat to New Zealand's national (or nationalist) culture – such as the potential growth of local filmmaking – but rather as a threat to British values, seen as synonymous with civilised values generally. The prevalent anti-Hollywood attitude would mean that the recognition of artistic achievement in the best American films (as promoted later by the French 'politique des auteurs') would be a slow and controversial development.

The Overseas Context

Although the attitudes and activities described so far in this chapter have been mainly of a middlebrow character, similar attitudes permeated the discourse of intellectuals. And this was not only a New Zealand phenomenon. In England, intellectual film culture had a strongly anti-Hollywood slant. As Duncan Petrie has observed, much of Paul Rotha's influential 1930 book, *The Film Till Now*, 'displays little more than contempt and scorn for what he regards as "the lowest form of public entertainment", the product of a factory system governed by the profit motive' (1999: 55). In 1927, Harry Potamkin, a left-wing American film critic and theorist, had sought to place such attitudes in context:

> Europe has America on the brain. America is either the last bulwark, proof, or justification of European civilisation or America is degraded and degrading – hope or despair. ... The result is a resentment against America intensified by the intrusion of Americans into the industrial life of every other country. And in no enterprise has the presence of America been so treacherously felt as in the movie – of England, Sweden, Germany, France, Italy and even Russia.
>
> (Potamkin 1927: 4)

As an example, Potamkin cited a diatribe on 'American Film Propaganda' written by 'a pathetic little journal', *The Patriot:*

> We hope, but do not expect, that the agitation over British films will arouse English people to the danger in their midst of American propaganda through the agency of American films. England is being suffocated by American films; they lead in East and West, and, thanks to our apathy, a promising British industry is being strangled before our eyes.
>
> (Potamkin 1927)

The process of strangulation was slowed by the introduction of tariffs and quotas for the screening of British films in the United Kingdom. The 1927 Cinematograph Films Act was designed to protect the British film industry from further decline. To offset American economic and cultural dominance, British cinemas were required to screen a certain number of locally-made films; the quota was set at 7.5 per cent for distributors, raising to 20 per cent in 1935 (Chibnall 2007: 2). An unintended consequence of this was the production of 'quota quickie' films, many of them financed by American distribution companies and made in the United Kingdom to satisfy British regulations.[7] A few films from the colonies gained access to the British market thanks to the quota, but were often savagely re-cut or treated with condescension. The one New Zealand example would be Rudall Hayward's 1939 version of *Rewi's Last Stand* – a film that dramatised an episode in the New Zealand Wars of the 1860s (Martin and Edwards 1997: 50).

One of the most important sites for the development of ideas of film-as-art was the magazine *Close Up* (1927–33), which was based in Britain and Switzerland but had a strongly international perspective. Writers for this magazine (which included Potamkin) had their own intellectual reasons for resisting the appeal of Hollywood. Instead, they championed the aesthetics of German and Soviet feature films, and avant-garde filmmaking in other countries, including England.

By way of contrast, French film critics and artists had, from the mid-1910s, reacted to the films of Mack Sennett, Charlie Chaplin and Harold Lloyd with great pleasure. Some of this difference may be attributed to a wider respect in France for the fact that the medium was a popular democratic art, but there was also an aesthetic in American cinema to which they reacted favourably. For the iconoclastic poet Pierre Reverdy, the chief value of the best American films 'was in the pleasure of surprise they contained':

> For the first time, simply and directly, someone had applied to film a key aesthetic principle that had developed out of the innovations in avant-garde painting and poetry: Perhaps the value of a work is in direct proportion to the quantity and especially to the *duration* of surprise that it can elicit. I have felt before some films an emotion *more intense* and at least as pure as that before the art works I love most dearly.
>
> (Abel 1975: 29)

To such French artists and intellectuals, cinema could be an art even in its most popular manifestations. It also seemed to them peculiarly in tune with modern life. There was thus an emerging alliance between high culture (in its avant-garde forms) and popular culture, united in opposition to the stuffy morality of middlebrow taste.

Although French film culture was developing on a broader base, British film culture certainly became more sophisticated during the 1920s. I have already noted the publication of the influential magazine *Close Up*. Even more important was the establishment of the London Film Society in 1925, which set to work expanding the range of films, promoting the discussion of film aesthetics, and encouraging innovative filmmaking (for example, by its 1929 filmmaking workshop with Sergei Eisenstein and Hans Richter, and its funding support for a film, *Tusalava*, by New Zealand-born filmmaker Len Lye). There were obviously close links between educated New Zealanders and British culture – lecturers in New Zealand universities were often imported from Britain, and New Zealand intellectuals headed to London for their 'OE'.[8] It is therefore not surprising that news of the London Film Society and copies of *Close Up* would soon reach New Zealand.

Film Availability in New Zealand

Before focusing on these innovations, we should complete our survey of the period by turning from film criticism to the business of film distribution and exhibition, an aspect little understood and seldom included in academic analysis. In the days before video, the DVD or the Internet, the only way to see films was by the projection of prints, and many films never reached New Zealand. Even those that did were often represented by a single, well-worn print that circulated through Australia and New Zealand.

Debates about the negative influence of popular films had an impact on the cinema business in New Zealand. One exhibitor was particularly active in exploring alternatives. Henry Hayward started Auckland Cinemas in 1930, following the demise of his larger national distribution and exhibition chain, a casualty of the Depression in 1929. His venture was initially shaped by moral concerns and by loyalty to Britain. In 1930, he and Lady Alice Fergusson (wife of the then-Governor General) set out 'to establish Educational Matinees throughout the Dominion – especially for children – not a "goody goody" show, but programmes of healthy adventure, comedy, combined with travel and scientific subjects' (*Tomorrow* 1938). This initiative covered cinemas in both town and country and was supported by some film distributors who placed their libraries at the disposition of the committee headed by Lady Fergusson.[9]

Hayward also established a theatre devoted exclusively to the screening of British films when he inaugurated his British-only policy at the London Theatre in Lower Queen Street in June 1930: 'The All-British Talkie Theatre. The only one of its kind in the Empire' (*Sun* 1930b). The first film was Maurice Elvey's *High Treason* (1928), an anti-war film 'predicting the regimentation of women in a hypothetical war of the future' (Davis 1994: 12).[10] This venture was praised by *The Sun* as a 'commendable scheme that should meet with the approval of the Auckland public' (*Sun* 1930a). An astute businessman, Hayward had realised that there was going to be a significant increase in the number of British-made films available for exhibition throughout the Empire as a consequence of the 1927 Act, and was hopeful that a sizeable local audience existed. However, despite the *Sun*'s optimistic forecast, the exclusive screening of British films at the London Theatre failed to win public approval and closed after only three months. Australian reception of 'British Voices for British People' may have been more enthusiastic. The Lyceum cinema in Sydney began screening exclusively British pictures in 1931; Melbourne had three such dedicated cinemas by 1934, and 112 British feature films went to Australia in 1933, which was much more than the whole of Europe and America combined (Chibnall 2007: 176).

That a broader taste in films was developing in Auckland as the 1920s ended, however, may also be inferred from another of Hayward's initiatives. This was the Tudor in Remuera (Auckland's most affluent suburb), billed as 'the repertory theatre for the intelligentsia'. Hayward not only had a definite flair for detecting cultural change but also an ability to act on his intuitions. As a first step towards what would later be known as the 'art (or art house) cinema', the Tudor screened the best of popular (or, as he put it, 'box office') films together with what he called repertory films: 'Those few subjects that appeal to the "Intelligentsia" by their purposeful drama, their special art or technique, the outstanding histrionic performances of individual players, or pictures we can get of Radical outlook, as well as those which we can occasionally present of Russian or French origin' (Hayward 1944: 130). Hayward's broad interests extended from British to continental films, particularly those linked with 'high culture' or with left-wing politics. Examples of the films he designated as Tudor material included *The Wandering Jew* (UK, 1933), *Hungarian Rhapsody* (Germany, 1928), *Turk-Sib* (USSR, 1929), *Sous les toits de Paris* (France, 1930), *Payment Deferred* (USA, 1932), *The Congress Dances* (Germany, 1932) and *Crime and Punishment* (USA, 1935) (Hayward 1944).

Through Hayward and a few other interested exhibitors, some European films did reach New Zealand, with exhibitors doing their best to exploit their associations of 'quality', 'culture' and educational value. Mainstream cinema-going continued to consist almost entirely of Anglo-American fare, which inevitably shaped and limited any discussions of the art of film. Among the European (or 'Continental') films that did reach major New Zealand cities, many were distributed and exhibited by a company called, pointedly, Cinema Art Films. Such titles were also known as 'foreign films', as though British and American material was already native to the national culture.

The changeover to sound at the end of the 1920s meant that audiences for silent films had shrunk dramatically, a consequence of which was that films produced at the end of the silent era could be purchased cheaply and screened to audiences who had heard of their cinematic qualities but had not had the opportunity to see them. Cinema Art Films, for example, obtained the New Zealand rights to the entire output of the German Ufa studios, which the owner promoted with great energy in *The Sun* (an Auckland newspaper with a strong interest in the arts), often taking out half page advertisements that emphasised their 'quality' and links with traditional high culture. For example, on Saturday 12 November 1927, F.W. Murnau's silent film *Faust* (Germany, 1926) was presented by Cinema Art Films at the Regent Theatre in Auckland, giving it local credibility by reporting that royalty and high-class English society had attended its 'triumphant opening in London'.[11]

It would be interesting to know how it fared at the box office against Clarence Brown's *Flesh and the Devil* (USA, 1926) with Greta Garbo and John Gilbert, screened on the same day by one of Davis's rivals, the Fuller-Hayward distribution and exhibition circuit. (Film critics today would see that Hollywood film, whose director was influenced by German Expressionism, as no less significant in cinematic terms.) Cinema Art Films screened Fritz Lang's *Metropolis* (Germany, 1927) on 28 June 1928, while in September Fuller and Hayward offered *Sunrise* (USA, 1927), directed by Murnau. The fact that Murnau was now resident in the United States, and *Sunrise* had won several Oscars, illustrated the complex overlaps that sometimes occurred between the categories of 'American' and 'European' films.

One result of the interest in 'serious' films was an initiative that saw the New Zealand Rationalist Association (1927) organise public lectures followed by the screening of a film. The choice of lecture and film could sometimes be felicitous as, for example, the programme on Saturday 12 October 1929, which combined a lecture on 'Science and the Future – A Challenging Forecast' with the film *Metropolis*; another paired a lecture on 'Free Thought and Social Progress' with Frank Borzage's 1927 Academy-Award-winning *Seventh Heaven* (USA); F.W. Murnau's *Sunrise* (1927) accompanied 'A Pagan's Thoughts on Easter'. Sometimes the link between lecture and film was less evident; on Sunday 3 November 1929, for example, the subject of the lecture was 'The Fight against Cancer', followed by a screening of *Faust* (although perhaps there was an ingenious Rationalist interpretation of the link?). These regular Sunday lectures took place at the Majestic Theatre, which was part of the Fuller-Hayward chain of cinemas and had the support of Henry Hayward himself. Hayward understood the value of aligning the cinema with cultural events as a way of building the audience for unusual films.

Films deserved thoughtful attention not for their art but for their serious subject matter. At the same time, however, this may have been a commercial opportunity as screenings were not then permitted on Sundays in New Zealand for religious reasons.[12]

Such European cinema clearly varied the range of films available to a public whose curiosity was increasingly stimulated by news from distant metropoles – the controversies around the screenings of Soviet films in the United Kingdom received particular attention. On Saturday 10 May 1930, *The Sun* ran an article on *Storm over Asia*: 'Moscow's most notorious anti-British propaganda film', directed by Vsevolod Pudovkin, after its screening by the London Film Society (which had struggled to obtain a special dispensation from the London Country Council to screen these controversial films privately) (Samson 1986: 310). The article also noted that Soviet films *The End of St. Petersberg*, *Battleship Potemkin*, *Mother* and *Bed and Sofa* had also been shown, and that Pudovkin had been allowed into Britain by the Home Office to meet members of the London Film Society. A week earlier, the *Auckland Star* had reported that a British left-wing organisation, The Masses Stage and Film Guild, was attempting to secure the screening of *Mother, Armoured Cruiser Potemkin* [sic],

Figure 3: Advertising for *Faust* in the *Sun* in 1927.

Storm over Asia, Modern Babylon, Ten Days that Shook the World and *The General Line*.[13] The political controversy around these films gave them a great publicity boost. Overseas, the Russian cinema and Eisenstein's championing of montage were becoming central to debates about the art of film.

The Auckland Film Society (1929)

The background to the emergence of New Zealand's first film society included the moral and aesthetic debates described above, the upheaval created by the arrival of sound films, and the gradually widening – though still limited and uneven – range of films available in local cinemas. On Saturday 14 September 1929, readers of *The Sun* encountered the first column of film comment by an organisation calling itself the 'Council of the Film Society, acting on behalf of the Film Society'. Its first film recommendation was John Ford's first talking feature, *The Black Watch* (1929), described by Ford scholar Tag Gallagher as 'a neo-Wagnerian music-drama, exploiting aural-visual storybook pageantry in order to intensify milieu – the social structures (ethnic customs, values, rituals, myths) by which an individual is formed and of which he becomes a perpetuating instrument' (1988: 61).

It is perhaps not by chance that the AFS announced its existence with this film. Reviewing it rather than one of the many others being screened at the same time implicitly foregrounds one of the Society's *raison d'être*: an incipient post-colonial mission to reconcile the transparently competitive British and American cultural presences in order to arrive at a hybrid form of film culture cognisant of both, enthralled by neither, and charting its own course on the path to an indigenous understanding.

Of particular interest, given the cultural circumstances of the Society's establishment, John Ford's film speaks about identity formation; more especially, it illustrates the social mechanisms that construct the conditions for being one type of person rather than another. In this and other films by Ford, the degree of freedom available to the subject of these mechanisms resides in the force with which the individual either succumbs to or resists the instruments of social control, some of which, 'by their insularity, breed intolerance, greatest of all evils' (Gallagher 1988: 61). Clearly, the AFS was resisting widespread insular intolerance, and can therefore be seen as engaging in a process of proto-nationalist identity formation through their work on film reception.

Though brief by today's standards, the analysis was one of the first independent and reasonably detailed film reviews to appear in print in New Zealand. Previous writing about films in newspapers had been almost entirely of the kind described as 'puff-pars', the self-serving promotional hype provided by film distributors and exhibitors and published by the papers as a favour to their advertisers.

The existence of a film society in Auckland at this time is surprising. Previous accounts of the emergence of film societies in New Zealand locate the first appearance in Wellington in 1933 (Dennis and Bieringa 1996). The AFS arrived four years earlier,

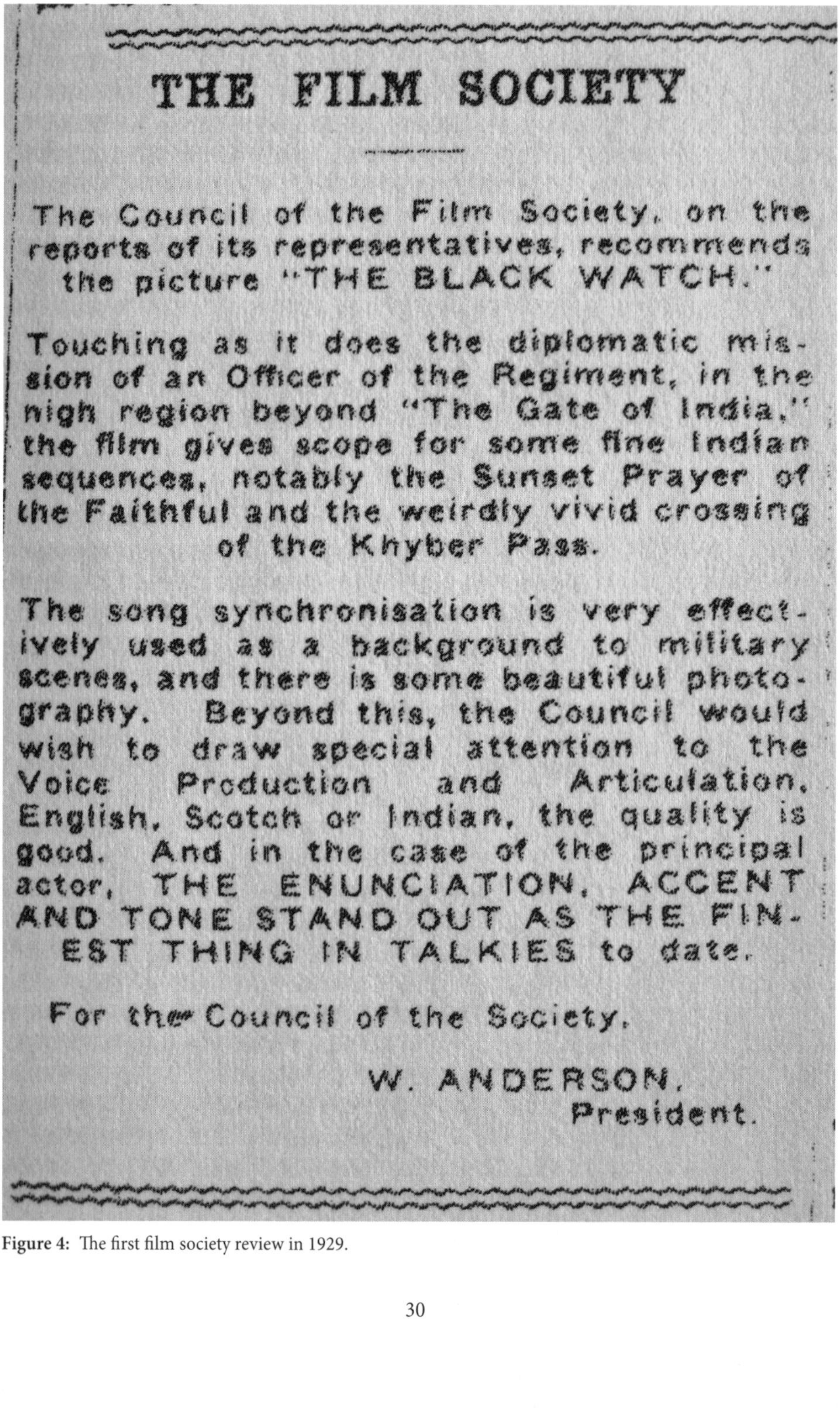

THE FILM SOCIETY

The Council of the Film Society, on the reports of its representatives, recommends the picture "THE BLACK WATCH."

Touching as it does the diplomatic mission of an Officer of the Regiment, in the high region beyond "The Gate of India," the film gives scope for some fine Indian sequences, notably the Sunset Prayer of the Faithful and the weirdly vivid crossing of the Khyber Pass.

The song synchronisation is very effectively used as a background to military scenes, and there is some beautiful photography. Beyond this, the Council would wish to draw special attention to the Voice Production and Articulation. English, Scotch or Indian, the quality is good. And in the case of the principal actor, THE ENUNCIATION, ACCENT AND TONE STAND OUT AS THE FINEST THING IN TALKIES to date.

For the Council of the Society.

W. ANDERSON,
President.

Figure 4: The first film society review in 1929.

though it appears not to have become involved in film exhibition. In that respect, the later Wellington Film Society would operate more closely on the London Film Society model. The AFS concentrated on film criticism and theory, on intellectual and aesthetic defences of the cinema. Three aspects of the review just cited would prove to be characteristic of the Society. First, the review shared some of the familiar preoccupations of the period – such as the emphasis not only on the novelty of the soundtrack but on the 'quality' of the English accents.

The second aspect was unusual. Despite its concern over accents, the Society promoted a generally open-minded appreciation of American as well as European cinema. The AFS was established out of an enthusiasm for 'pictures of quality' and a desire to make more people aware of such pictures. Refreshingly, it proceeded on the assumption that 'the finest films' were to be found among American as well as British or European productions. The Society was on a crusade to rescue the cinema from the censorious attitude then widespread, aimed particularly at American cinema. At the same time, the AFS was no less supportive of Hayward's exclusively British cinema (*Auckland Star* 1930: 5).

Third, the AFS made a genuine attempt to consider any film in artistic terms. For example, the review of *The Black Watch* mentioned the story and the subject matter but did not (in the usual way) devote most of the review to them; it also considered the photography and the soundtrack, and attempted to identify the best 'sequences'. While evaluative words and phrases remained vague ('fine', 'good', 'beautiful', 'very effectively used'), there was the striking phrase 'weirdly vivid', and the principal focus was aesthetic – notably different from most of the other 'serious' film discussions of this period which ignored the texture, style or form of films and focused on their perceived moral or political subject matter.[14]

There is no information about how many members the AFS may have had. All we have are the newspaper columns written by the mostly anonymous members of the Society. These texts do, however, enable us to understand the type of films that the Society promoted and their conception of the art of cinema. I will examine a few examples closely because they illustrate the range of current issues and attitudes, and confirm that the AFS received *Close Up*, the British magazine 'devoted to the art of films' that was a rich source of information about European film culture.

The *Auckland Star* Film Reviews

Of the 23 articles written by ten people between January 1930 and August 1931, only one writer's identity has been established clearly: W. (William) Anderson, who wrote the review cited earlier, was a professor of philosophy at Auckland University College (for more information on Anderson, see Sinclair 1983: 132). This was the first instance of a later trend where 'university men' occupied prominent positions on the committees of film societies after 1933. This was the case in Wellington where Professor Thomas Hunter of Victoria

University College was president; a similar occurrence took place in Christchurch with Professor James Shelley[15]; while Dunedin went even further in the quest for social legitimisation when the Mayor, the Reverend E.T. Cox, was elected president (*Otago Daily Times* 1934).

Other AFS writers used either their initials (such as JCT or MN) or sobriquets (Marcus Finola, Peter Vivandier, Kotuku, Reginald Ramontier, John Storm and, my personal favourite, Écran, later changed to E. Cran D'Argent). Écran was the most prolific of the group, responsible for six of the 23 columns. When the AFS first appeared in *The Auckland Star*, Écran wrote the first three articles over successive weeks. Under the subtitle 'The Art of the Picture', these offered a résumé of the past year and proceeded to forecast film's future in the sound era.

'A Confession of Faith of One of Us', the title of the first article, purported to be 'an expression of purely personal and unofficial opinions and desires from a critic who is not quite a "movie-fan" and not quite a "highbrow"' (Écran 1930a: 5) – a promising description for someone who aimed to explore the art of the film. What did Écran see as the salient features of this new medium of artistic expression? In the first column, he pointed out thoughtfully that film was an 'inherently artificial medium … since it has to represent solid bodies, moving in three dimensional space, by lights and shadows projected in monochrome on a flat screen' (Écran 1930a: 5). This fact set it apart from the stage and gave it both 'powers and limitations'. The more purely visual quality of silent films made them rely on 'facial expression, gesture, pantomime, attitude and "significant form"' (a term rich in associations that will be explored further), which had yet to find 'their proper balance and emphasis'. Écran attributed these 'vital limitations' to a then widely shared and enduring belief that 'the film became an industry before it had time to develop as an art' (Écran 1930a: 5). Against these defects the cinema possessed a quality that the stage could never emulate, 'It can show us at one moment every minute detail of a face or a hand, at the next a city, a forest valley, a battle' (Écran 1930a: 5). This, for Écran, made it especially suited to spectacle and pure fantasy: 'No stage could show the galley and the sea-fight of *Ben Hur*, the dream architecture of *Secrets of the East* or the nightmare city of *Metropolis*.' Films suited epic subjects and narrative methods. Stories were the necessary framework. Because film was primarily a visual experience, Écran asked of it that it 'please the eye' in its depiction of 'beauty'.

Écran's approach displayed a great deal of visual sensitivity. He was obviously interested not only in literary or theatrical qualities but also in matters of space and what the French would call *mise en scène*. He was not, however, sympathetic to avant-garde or other extreme styles. The more esoteric, poetic pursuits of the cinema – its efforts to show internal states of the mind through effects obtained in the camera such as soft focus, double exposure or unusual camera angles – were given short shrift by Écran who deemed them to be tricks to amuse the mind if their use did not develop the 'mood and "atmosphere"' of the picture'. He somewhat grudgingly conceded the value of close-ups, but he described the effect of panning the camera from one object to another as like trying to follow a tennis ball; clearly unacceptable behaviour in a camera. One can only wonder what he would have made of

Dreyer's *The Passion of Joan of Arc* (1928), composed almost exclusively of close-ups and hailed in Europe as one of the first films to prove that the cinema was an art and that the silent film could speak eloquently. Dreyer's work drew upon several avant-garde traditions of film from France, Germany and the USSR – but such modernist experimentation remained almost entirely unknown in New Zealand at this time.

Écran did, however, recognise some of the innovations of European experimentation indirectly, through their influence on Alfred Hitchcock's narrative feature films. He enthused that 'most of the London scenes of *Blackmail* were highly effective in their contribution to the actuality of the story' (Écran 1930b: 5). Écran was aware of décor and its important role at the time in the development of film as art; setting could be character, with its own psychology, or used to comment upon, illustrate or refract the mindscape of a protagonist. Hitchcock had worked in the German Ufa studios in 1925–26, and been exposed to the work of Paul Leni and Fritz Lang, and was thus familiar with the expressionistic use of décor, costume and lighting. *The Lodger* (1926) and, especially, *Blackmail* (1929) were films in which Hitchcock was able to refine his style in reference to what he had encountered in Germany. What held Écran back from a fuller appreciation of the possibilities of *mise en scène* was his basic assumption that films must stick closely to verisimilitude. He took a common-sense view of historical films: 'When the producer shows me an Englishman's letter, it must not be in the American idiom and script; he must not introduce a fox terrier into the streets of ancient Jerusalem, nor clothe soldiers of old Byzantium in modern football shorts' (Écran 1930b: 5). This principle appeared to contradict the critic's enthusiasm for the medium's ability to explore 'fantasy', but he would reconcile them by a broad conception of realism.

Not surprisingly, a key theme of the period was sound. In the second part of his article, Écran examined this development, noting that 'for some sensitive critics, the speaking film may continue to be a sheer calamity' (Écran 1930b: 5). While many exponents of a 'pure cinema' feared the contamination and dilution of the silent era's visually rich 'language', Écran felt, anticipating André Bazin, that sound was another means by which the talkies might 'progress towards realism and beauty'. Écran's discussion of speech in early sound cinema reflected a thoughtful awareness of restricted and open narrative strategies – the way information could be communicated to the spectator but withheld from a character in the film, thereby generating various narrative strategies to increase audience participation in the film, either confirming the public in their superior knowledge or confounding them with unexpected twists and turns. His example focused on language as the vehicle for conveying information denied to a protagonist: 'Deftly used in this way, speech would serve to throw into relief the vital scenes of crisis and climax' (Écran 1930b: 5).

Sound has often received less attention than image in the development of film theory, but during the first years of sound films, this dimension of the cinema received a great deal of thoughtful (and anxious) discussion. The AFS writings included many interesting examples. Écran's third column illustrated a concern shared by many film enthusiasts around the world that the introduction of sound would compromise the cinema's visual strengths by encouraging films to tell rather than show their stories. The cinema would thus come to resemble canned theatre and lose its already established singularity.

> The great danger of the speaking film is that the movies may put an 'enemy in their mouths to steal away their brains'; in plainer language, may sacrifice their freedom, and their peculiar effectiveness and strength, to the 'picturisation' or imitation of stage-plays.
>
> (Écran 1930b: 5)

He added: 'The film, in its own idiom, can show us a life, and not merely the crisis of a life, can follow the making of a character or a situation which the stage-play must grasp when the fuse is already lighted' (Écran 1930b: 5). Écran was developing an interesting line of argument here but he seemed unable to come to terms with editing, which constructs a properly cinematic spatial and temporal coherence (or incoherence). Écran seemed better attuned to the unity and dramatic intensity that typified the stage than to the possibilities of montage or continuity editing. It is not surprising that many critics of the period turned to the stage, with its long tradition of aesthetics, as the most useful way of understanding sound films.

A welcome alternative view was advanced by 'Kotuku' (the Māori word for heron) who argued that the essence of cinema was movement. Where the stage was static, 'the film knows no confines. As unfettered as thought itself' (Kotuku 1930: 5). This writer was concerned about the advent of sound, as it initially required cameras that were big noisy machines needing to be encased in even bigger soundproof boxes. This severely limited their ability to be moved around the set and 'as soon as the camera becomes anchored the lantern at once begins to lose its magic' (Kotuku 1930: 5).

Another key issue was realism. This concept was frequently invoked by those looking for signs of seriousness in films – usually from an uncritical 'common sense' standpoint, but sometimes from a left-wing political standpoint (which would become increasingly common as the Depression deepened). It came to be widely assumed that reality defined in terms of politics, economics and class had to figure prominently in any serious film. At the same time, some saw films as a welcome escape from realism. Écran saw reality as 'the muddle of sordid cares and trivial satisfactions, which we "really" live' (Écran 1930c: 5), and this had no place on the screen, whose primary purpose was to provide a distraction from life's travails.

An interesting aspect of Kotuku's thinking emerged in his attempt to flesh out *significant form* – a concept linked to the influential British critic and philosopher of art Clive Bell (1881–1964), who claimed in his book, *Art* (1914), that a uniquely aesthetic response, akin to the ecstasy of religious contemplation, could be experienced in certain works that had the requisite 'significant form' – a distinctive combination of lines and colours. For Kotuku, 'Mere realism is not art and does not awaken any aesthetic sensibility in us. Good art does not remind us of our common existence, our everyday world, but transforms everything and takes us into another world' (Kotuku 1930: 5). The perception altering abilities of art made it most valuable. This aestheticism, shared by some of the other AFS writers, was a striking alternative perspective. It was not simply a call for Hollywood entertainment but expressed an expectation that film could provide mind-altering and mind-opening experiences of a mystical sort. Kotuku's writing had a particularly clear link with the *fin-de-siecle* tradition of Symbolism and 'art for art's sake', expressing the hope that cinema might serve a transcendent purpose:

> In the hands of real artists, the sound picture may hold in store for us a veritable cup of delight; colour ... will serve further to enhance our ecstasy; appropriate music motifs will complete our emotional thrill. Indeed, if these several media should be wielded by genius into an artistic whole ... then we may experience a rapture that not even Scriabin envisaged in his most advanced excursions into the mystic realms of sound and colour.
>
> (Kotuku 1930: 5)

Kotuku's choice of composer was significant. Alexander Scriabin was an avant-garde Russian composer who experimented with 'colour music' and other forms of mixed media, and glorified art as religion. Works such as his *Poem of Ecstasy* (1905–08) and his later piano sonatas displayed a strong strain of mysticism (Scriabin n.d.). The introduction of sound to film could be seen as a further development in the direction of the Wagnerian *gesamtkunstwerk* (total work of art).

In addition to the debate between realism and aestheticism, there was a constant battle between uncompromising champions of high culture (recognisable through unmistakable signs of artistry, serious moral purpose, and intellectual content) and those who insisted that a different kind of artistry was to be found in creating an entertaining and emotionally rich film. The latter view was more open to the best work from Hollywood, but it also had more difficulty in finding adequate forms of expression. These positions were illustrated by an AFS debate between Walter Kron (on behalf of high culture) and 'Marcus Finola' (in defence of entertainment). Finola no doubt saw Kron as an intellectual snob, and Kron would probably have seen Finola as a poorly educated provincial. The sympathies of most New Zealand readers today would go to Finola – particularly if they have a liking for American films – yet such an exchange does serve to remind us of New Zealand's peripheral, and hence provincial, position in relation to European and American metropolitan centres where, before the arrival of the talkies, 'there did exist, however marginally, a dynamic and fractious sphere of production and exhibition in which the ontology of cinema could be investigated and expanded' (Donald, Friedberg, and Marcus 1998: 30).

The AFS had mainly a second-hand knowledge, through newspapers and magazines, of much of the cinema that was being made in Europe (especially in the Soviet Union and Germany where most of the cutting-edge developments had taken place). Their basic ambitions were therefore more modest – to rescue films (including some popular American ones) from snobbish and puritanical attack. Members of the AFS genuinely liked this new medium and their discussion of film aesthetics was, in one sense, a way to justify guilty pleasures, and, in another, a means to develop a more discursively sophisticated appreciation of cinematic variety.

On 15 November 1930, a new voice was heard praising *King of Jazz* (USA, 1930). The review by JCT illustrated how hard the AFS struggled to come to terms with Hollywood, again held back by the limits of current critical discourse. While JCT was dismayed by the success of 'the uninspired and raucous *Gold Diggers of Broadway*' (USA, 1929) and its ill-begotten progeny – 'shows made hideous with noisy voices, unconvincing nocturnal orgies, meaningless ballets, and other direful things' (JCT 1930: 5) – this critic hailed *King of Jazz* as representing a quantum leap forward. It was the ideal AFS film in the sense that it could satisfy 'Low, medium, high and, in fact, the veriest outside in brows'. Certainly *King of Jazz* has come to be regarded by historians as an outstanding musical, with lavish colour production numbers (it won an Academy Award for Best Art Direction), excellent cinematography by Hal Mohr, and music by Paul Whiteman – the self-proclaimed 'King of Jazz'.

How did JCT explain its success as a film? A 'rollicking pace' was established from the outset by a 'brilliantly clever and riotous cartoon de luxe (in colour)' and maintained throughout the film. The effects were so 'kaleidoscopic that one's brain is besieged with thrilling sensations' (JCT 1930: 5). The arrival of colour presented reviewers with as great a challenge as the arrival of sound. In this case, JCT turned to painting as his frame of reference.

> Take, for instance, the beauty of the bridal veil scene with its exquisite effects of gold and van dyke brown suggestive of a background by the late Claude Shepperson; or a portion of the Spanish scene with its rhythmic figure or two, a grotesquely exotic tree, rich colouring, enhanced by patches of black and a general sense of design; or again, a group of ballet girls suggesting the influence of Dégas – these impressions were alone worth going to see.
>
> (JCT 1930: 5)

The carnivalesque appeal of this film was not neglected either: 'To some, however, the barbaric vigour of the drum-dancer, the lavish ensembles of the Melting Pot, and the Rhapsodies in Blue, will appeal more deeply' (JCT 1930: 5). The real significance of the film, however, marking 'an immense step forward', lay in its emancipation from the stage, which revealed 'the artistic possibilities of the new medium'. Design, colour and rhythm (musical, visual) were all to feature more prominently, 'thus providing for our delight interludes of superlative beauty and distinction'. This was a brave attempt to describe the art of a popular film, but it required film-specific discourses (the discourse of filmmaking or that of film genre studies) to do the job properly.

One AFS commentary – by 'Marcus Finola' (8 March 1930) – is important evidence that *Close Up* was known in Auckland. Finola attempted to defend Hollywood from a savage attack in *Close Up*'s June 1929 issue. Walter Kron's article, 'The Coming Heritage of the Films', had been a Nietzsche-inspired polemic that savaged Hollywood for being 'a seething factory, making miles of transparent rubber and phonograph discs. For the amusement of English speaking peoples, this hive is controlled by a group of gamblers as gaudy and as tasteless as any side-show barker' (Kron 1929). Kron called for a revolution in taste that would bring about a 'nobler', more spiritually exciting world, ruled by intellectuals and creative artists (like Murnau and Lubitsch in their pre-Hollywood period). He added: 'The real ill in the world to-day is the absence of cosmopolitan ideals of aristocracy; not the inferior blooded aristocracy of the Bourbons but the aristocratic, universal ideals of the intellect (Kron 1929). Finola, however, argued that Hollywood had already opened its doors to European genius and that continental directors had made a difference to films made there, and that the very films Kron had scorned – *The Broadway Melody* (USA, 1929) and *Sunrise* (USA, 1927) – 'delighted many people of serious views concerning the cinema on account of the forward step that they themselves marked!'

Kron's sweeping rejection of Hollywood overlooks a number of films that we would today regard as classics; but its context needs to be acknowledged. The last years of the silent era had been rich in reflection about the nature of the cinema, and innovative forms of film attained a strong position through such directors as Jean Epstein, Louis Delluc, Germaine Dulac, Hans Richter, G.W. Pabst, and Sergei Eisenstein. The coming of the 'talkies' had undermined this position, both by increasing the cost of filmmaking and rendering many of the visual techniques of the silent era no longer appropriate. Hollywood also controlled many of the patents associated with sound technology, and several of its early talkies were based on a return to the Broadway stage (de Baecque 1991: 18). In contrast, *Close Up* had long supported the German cinema, especially the psychological realism of Pabst and of the Soviet filmmakers; it had translated and published Eisenstein's writings; and it had given sympathetic coverage to the avant-garde.

One other important concept is seen in the Society's published writings – the idea of national cinema. This would become a controversial concept in the 1930s in the context of extreme forms of politics such as National Socialism, but it survived as an important aspect of film criticism, and came to have a particularly deep resonance for film culture in New Zealand as the country emerged from colonialism.

The 'national' approach was given detailed presentation in the article 'A World Review' of film which appeared in the *Auckland Star* on 28 February 1931. This was not an AFS text and was probably reprinted from a British source. The AFS had announced in that newspaper in the previous month that it needed 'to pause for breath' (*Auckland Star* 1931a: 5) and its column was then replaced by articles on film from other sources. In its generalisations about national character and psychology, 'A World Review' was more confident and essentialist than today's criticism of this kind would dare to be, but it did contain some sophisticated insights and was obviously informed by a wide knowledge of films, including two from New Zealand.

The central idea of the review was a neo-Hegelian belief that each nation's 'true spirit' expressed itself in its art. Films revealed group psychology and shared values, or reflected historical experience. Using 'humble' westerns as an example, the writer saw that '[Although they were] conscientiously manufactured from a standardised thriller recipe, at the same time [they] glorified the American pioneers. ... [chronicling] three great stages ... of pioneering, of prospecting, and the final conquests of the vast spaces by science and industry' (*Auckland Star* 1931b: 5).

Drinking from the 'Orientalist' fountain, the article also made the interesting suggestion that the best films from the 'Empire' were those 'acted entirely by natives, who have succeeded in imparting to them the spirit of their peoples' (*Auckland Star* 1931b: 5). He cited two films from New Zealand in which he had detected this 'spirit': *Rewi's Last Stand* (1925) and *Under the Southern Cross* (1929), 'beautiful and vivid pictures of Māori New Zealand'.[16] Some Japanese films embodied a Samurai ideal 'of perfection of character'. French films 'reflected the democratic spirit' of France. Religious, moral, and social conditions were portrayed in the best Swedish films, which also revealed 'the William Tell spirit' (natural forces personified, physical strength, endurance, and love of adventure). German films were singled out as being excellent examples of national cinema. *Caligari's* Expressionist characterisation, setting, and costume 'revealing the dynamic movement of insanity', which was based on 'actual suffering, yet urged by a powerful desire to be free'. Later German films were believed to reflect the changing moods of the German people confronted with 'urgent and bitter political, economic or social experience'. Such comments strikingly anticipate Siegfried Kracauer's famous study, *From Caligari to Hitler: A Psychological History of the German Film* (1947).

It is tempting to speculate that the review sowed critical seeds that would soon inject an ethical and political imperative to local film criticism. When the AFS returned from its silence to the public sphere in early 1933, its concern for a more politically engaged film culture was sharp. Film criticism under this new dispensation was to shape a form of spectatorship that used film not to redeem existing reality but to question and challenge it, and to encourage viewers to see through reified aspects of the visual world created through film. Control of the AFS would pass from a predominantly older generation whose primary sources of reference were the theatre, literature, and traditional aesthetics, to a younger, more determinedly political group who drew inspiration from revolutionary Soviet cinema (see Chapter 2 for more details).

The AFS deserves credit for encouraging New Zealanders to feel more confident in talking thoughtfully about films without fear of being chided for taking popular culture too seriously. Among the issues that have emerged from this chapter of early history have been the need to overcome a general suspicion of Hollywood, and equally – in a country with an underdeveloped critical culture – the need to overcome a general suspicion of intellectualism. Above all, we see the need to develop adequate discourses for the discussion of film, with a relevant vocabulary and set of critical concepts.

References

Abel, R. (1975), 'The Contribution of the French Literary Avant-Garde to Film Theory and Criticism, 1907–1924', *Cinema Journal*, 14(3), p. 29.
Anderson, W. 'President' (1929), 'Council of the Film Society', *Sun* 14 September.
Anon. (1930a), 'Films and Lecturette', *Sun,* March 15.

—— (1930b), 'Rationalist Association', *Sun,* Saturday 7 June.

—— 'Crime and Sex in Films', *Mirror* (1929b), September, p. 8.

—— (1934), 'Dunedin Film Institute: Successful Inaugural Meeting', *Otago Daily Times,* 12 December, p. 13.

—— (1931b), 'Their Spirit Revealed', *Auckland Star,* 28 February, p. 5.

Belich, J. (2001), *Paradise Reforged: A History of the New Zealanders from the 1880s to the Year 2000,* Auckland: Allen Lane and Penguin Press.

Brookes, B. (2007), 'Gender, Work and Fears of a 'Hybrid Race' in 1920s New Zealand', *Gender and History,* 19(3), November, p. 507.

Chibnall, S. (2007), *Quota Quickies: The Birth of the British 'B' Film,* London: BFI.

Cluett, I. M 'The Menace of Mechanical Art', *Mirror* (1930), July, p. 33.

Davis, B. (1994), 'Beginning of the Film Society Movement in the U.S.', *Film and History,* 24(3–4), p. 12.

Dennis, J. and Bieringa, J. eds. (1996), 'Timeline'. In: *Film in Aotearoa New Zealand,* Wellington: Victoria University Press.

de Baecque, A. (1991), *Histoire d'une revue, tome 1: à l'assaut du cinéma, 1951–59,* Paris: Cahiers du cinéma.

Donald, J., Freidberg, A. and Marcus, L. eds. (1998), *Close Up, 1927–1933: Cinema and Modernism,* London: Cassell.

Écran (1930a), 'A Confession of Faith of One of Us', *Auckland Star,* 4 January, p. 5.

—— (1930b), 'The Art of the Picture', *Auckland Star,* 11 January, p. 5.

—— (1930c), 'This Year, Next Year: The Art of the Picture', *Auckland Star,* 18 January, p. 5.

F.S. 'Vice-President' (1930), 'British Talkies', *Auckland Star,* 24 May, p. 5.

Gallagher, T. (1988), *John Ford: The Man and His Films,* Berkeley: University of California Press.

Hagener, M. (2007), *Moving Forward, Looking Back: the European Avant-garde and the Invention of Film Culture, 1919–1939,* Amsterdam: Amsterdam University Press.

Hayward, B.W. and Hayward, S.P. (1979), *Cinemas of Auckland, 1896–1979,* Auckland: The Lodestar Press.

Hayward, H.J. (1938), 'The Cinema – Yesterday – Today – Tomorrow', *Tomorrow,* 16 March.

—— (1944), *Here's to Life,* Auckland: Oswald-Sealy.

Hilliard, C. (2006), *The Bookmen's Dominion: Cultural Life in New Zealand, 1920–1950,* Auckland: Auckland University Press, p. 120.

JCT, *Auckland Star* (1930), 'New Horizons', 15 November, p. 5.

Kotuku, *Auckland Star* (1930), 'Art and the Talkie', 22 March, p. 5.

Kron, W. (1929), 'The Coming Heritage of the Films', *Close Up,* IV(6).

Lowe, V. (2004), 'The Best Speaking Voices in the World: Robert Donat, Stardom and the Voice in British Cinema', *Journal of British Cinema and Television,* 1(2), pp. 181–96.

Martin, S. and Edwards, H. (1997), *New Zealand Film, 1912–1996,* Auckland: Oxford University Press.

Petrie, D. and Kruger, R. eds. (1999), *A Paul Rotha Reader,* Exeter: Exeter University Press.

Potamkin, H.A. (1927), 'The Plight of the European Movie', *National Board of Review Magazine,* 2(12), p. 4.

Robinson, R. and Wattie, N. eds. (1998), *The Oxford Companion to New Zealand Literature*, Auckland: Oxford University Press, p. 520.

Ramontier, R. (1931a), 'Film Society', *Auckland Star*, January, p. 5.

Ryall, T. (1986), *Alfred Hitchcock and the British Cinema*, Urbana: University of Illinois Press.

Samson, J. (1986), 'The Film Society, 1925–1939'. In: C. Barr, ed. *All Our Yesterdays: 90 Years of British Cinema*, London: BFI in assoc. with the Museum of Modern Art, p. 310.

Scriabin (n.d.), R.E.B., Scriabin's *Poem of Ecstasy*, Op. 54. n.d. [Online]. Available at: http://classicalcdreview.com/scriabin.htm. Accessed: 29 April 2009.

Sinclair, K. (1983), *A History of the University of Auckland, 1883–1983*, Auckland: Auckland University Press, p. 132.

Sprecher, D. (1999), 'Good Clothes are Good Business: Gender, Consumption and Appearance in the Office, 1918–1939'. In: C. Daley and D. Montgomerie, eds. *The Gendered Kiwi*, Auckland: Auckland University Press, p. 142.

Staley, M. 'The Child and the Cinema', *Mirror* (1929a), August, p. 35.

Notes

1 For detailed analysis of this development, see Hagener 2007, especially chapter three, 'The Film Societies and Ciné-Clubs of the 1920s and 30s', pp. 77–120.

2 The term 'cinema' – originally 'kinema' – was derived from the Greek word for motion.

3 Originally titled the *Ladies Mirror*, this magazine was published monthly in Auckland from 1922 to 1963.

4 A League of Nations Child Welfare Committee report prompted her concern. Dr Mildred Staley, an ardent Anglican medical missionary, had trained in Britain and worked for 19 years in India, the Federated Malay States and in Fiji. She was on the National Council of Women and was a woman of strong opinions who had sparked controversy by advocating in the *Sun* that Chinese people be kept out of New Zealand (see Brookes 2007).

5 New Zealand women won the right to vote in 1893, and in 1907 the Society for the Promotion of the Health of Women and Children was founded. Better known today as the Plunket Society, it was credited with giving the country the lowest infant mortality rate in the world after 30 years of existence.

6 Isobel M. Cluett (1881–1973) was a teacher, writer and radio broadcaster.

7 England was not the only European country to impose quotas in an effort to develop a national cinema and 'protect' its people from 'the American way of life' as represented in its cinema. American films also dominated the screens of France, Germany, the Soviet Union and the Scandinavian countries; Germany imposed quotas in the 1920s and a combination of both State and private money was used to establish the giant Ufa studios. Britain's response was the Cinematograph Films Act 1927.

8 A term in common parlance used to designate young New Zealanders overseas experience.

9 After some initial success, with theatres full due to the influence of the Governor's Lady and her committee, interest waned 'until the enterprise had to be abandoned for want of attendance'. The lack of a sufficient number of films made specifically for children was a factor.

10 Although not well known today, Elvey was a prolific director whose career began in 1912 with *Maria Marten* and ended in 1957 with *Second Fiddle*.

11 Arthur C. Davis, an Australian immigrant who established a film distribution company in Wellington in 1923 to import both American and European films, was the owner of Cinema Art Films.

12 Exemptions from the legislation that prevented 'trading' on Sundays were given if the spectacle (or performance) could be shown to have an educational purpose.

13 While *Ten Days that Shook the World* (1927) and assorted short documentaries were seen (probably in the mid- to late-1930s) by small audiences as part of the Friends of the Soviet Union cultural programme, the Wellington Film Society only obtained a 16mm print of *Battleship Potemkin* after Word War II, and gave its first New Zealand screening on 21 October 1946 at the Wellington Town Hall Concert Chamber. *Mother* was purchased by the National Film Library in the immediate post-World War II period. *The General Line* was first screened in Wellington in 1948.

14 There were no more film reviews in *The Sun* after it folded in 1930 but the AFS contributed a fairly regular series of articles, from 4 January 1930 to 1 August 1931, to *The Auckland Star* which had purchased 'the copyright, goodwill, property and plant' of its rival. See Robinson and Wattie 1998: 520, for more on *The Sun*.

15 Archives New Zealand, File IA 1 1933/15/19.

16 Rudall Hayward made a silent and sound version of *Rewi's Last Stand*.

Chapter 2

Second Thoughts About Art

In the struggle to establish independent film exhibition and develop an aesthetic and cultural awareness of film, the nascent film society movement in 1930s New Zealand encountered many obstacles: distance, dearth, and demonisation figuring prominently. The events and analysis that follow are components of a cultural history that seeks to incorporate 'high' culture within a broader understanding of what culture is and does: 'Rituals, symbolic systems, and the meanings and stories attached to everyday aspects of life are analysed in a rich array of topics that range from smells to carnivals, from promenades to reading, and everything in between' (Dalley and Labrum 1999: 2). Film screenings were monthly rituals charged with symbolic meaning and pregnant with expectation. That they were urban and tantalisingly urbane Pakeha rituals allows this chapter to contribute to the 'scholarly – as opposed to popular – examination of cultural history, especially Pakeha cultural history' (Dalley and Labrum: 3), and to explore the dynamics of constructing high culture in a settler society still largely rural and provincial in its self-understanding.

Specifically, the chapter examines the attempts to create an infrastructure for the distribution and exhibition of 'arthouse' cinema as well as a conceptual framework for understanding film, whose 'proper' appreciation distanced film society members from popular film consumption. This aesthetic distancing rethought the cinema and spectatorship in several ways: an emphasis on film art as a legitimate element of high culture; an instrumental perspective that valued the pedagogical uses of film in visual education; and a political optic that explored the ideological component of films and their suasive power. These aims were pursued in several ways: by introducing an innovative screening programme of contemporary and 'classic' (generally silent) films from Europe and the USSR that had either not been shown here, or so rarely that their deeper artistic, political, or (unmentionable) erotic merits had not been properly appreciated; by treating film society screenings as events similar in nature, for example, to an art exhibition or an evening of chamber music; and through political polemics published in fledgling intellectual journals.

As a result of these multiple initiatives, film culture continued to grow in New Zealand but not without a variety of problems. Film societies began to appear throughout the country in 1933, not only in the four major cities of Auckland, Wellington, Christchurch, and Dunedin but also in smaller centres such as Wanganui, Hamilton, Hastings, and Hawera. Pioneering practices, both material and discursive, were developed as more people became involved in film society activity: as a forerunner of independent film exhibition in New Zealand, the Wellington Film Society (WFS) established a screening programme; a national federation of film societies was set up to co-ordinate the fledgling movement and pool scarce resources as controversial films entered the country;[1] contacts were made with the British Film Institute (BFI) and assistance sought in procuring a wider range of films; libraries began to stock a slowly increasing number of specialist books that talked about film as art; local writings about 'intellectual film culture' by members of New Zealand's intelligentsia began to appear in small magazines, notably *Phoenix* in 1933 and *Tomorrow* in 1935; and Gordon Mirams began to make a name for himself as a film critic for *Radio Record*, the forerunner of its more influential successor, the *New Zealand Listener* (1939), for which Mirams would also write.

Another area of growth in film culture was the state's use of it. New Zealand's first Labour Government, elected into office in December 1935, was interested in the use of film for educational purposes (the development of 16mm sound technology facilitated this development) and in broadening the range of narrative films for local audiences (essentially, this meant more European and fewer Anglo-American ones). Increased government awareness and interest in film had its downside, however, in terms of bureaucratic and legal scrutiny. The film industry in New Zealand, especially its distribution and exhibition branches, had earlier discovered the onerous weight of state interest when the United Government introduced the Film Hire Tax in 1930, which coincided with a period of profound economic insecurity.

The Great Depression, the worst economic crisis of the twentieth century, made itself felt in 1929 when it 'settled on New Zealand like a "grey and ghastly visitor to the house"' (Mulgan 1947 cited in Sinclair 1991: 264). Despite numerous warnings, New Zealand was very badly placed to deal with this crisis. In three years, national income was estimated to have fallen from £150,000,000 to £90,000,000; the value of exports fell by 40 per cent over a similar period and by 1933 more than 20 per cent of the population was unemployed. It is believed that the community at large suffered a 20 per cent drop in their standard of living and farmers were as hard hit as the urban working class (Belich 2001: 255).

The effects of the Depression on film culture were many and varied. The Fuller-Hayward Theatre Corporation, which controlled 63 cinemas throughout New Zealand, collapsed. Thomas O'Brien, the man responsible for building New Zealand's largest 'picture palace', the Civic, in 1929, and who owned eight other cinemas in Auckland, went out of business in 1932 (Hayward and Hayward 1979: 28). The expense involved in converting silent cinemas to sound left their owners vulnerable to rapidly mounting debt as cinema attendance fell off markedly. One estimate puts the loss as high as 45 per cent (Hayward and Hayward: 28). Although figures of cinema attendance and takings were not gathered until 1938–39 (*NZOYB* 1960: 1160), the introduction of the Film Hire Tax in 1930 does allow us to measure some of the impact of the Depression on people's disposable income in terms of their purchase of cinema tickets. This tax was assessed on the net monthly receipts that the distributor obtained from hiring out 'sound-picture films'. British films only attracted a ten per cent tax, whereas all foreign films were taxed at 25 per cent. In a gesture of support for New Zealand filmmakers, locally made films were exempted (*NZOYB* 1937: 486). The tax earned the state £41,756 for nine months in 1930–31. This dropped off dramatically in 1932–33 to £30,102 before rising slightly the following year to £32,960 (*NZOYB* 1937: 486). In 1935, when the Depression is thought to have ended, the tax brought the state £60,657, and by the end of the decade, in 1939, it earned the Government £85,882 (*NZOYB* 1940: 591). Regrettably, the Film Tax was never ploughed back into local filmmaking or film culture.

Another way to measure the effects of the Depression on people's disposable income is to look at the Amusements Tax (1917), which taxed 'any exhibition, performance, amusement, game, or sport to which persons are admitted for payment'. Exemptions were made to a heteroclite range of activities, including 'shows promoted by agricultural, pastoral, horticultural, or poultry societies', and entertainments whose proceeds went to 'charitable, philanthropic, patriotic, or educational purposes'. This included 'any society or institution not established for profit', and benefited the film society movement (*NZOYB* 1940: 592). Between 1930 and 1940, the state collected the following:[2]

Table 2.1   Amusements Tax collections

Year	Amount in £	Year	Amount in £
1930	79,887	1935	49,526
1931[i]	105,936	1936	56,507
1932	74,763	1937	70,564
1933	53,564	1938	98,646
1934	48,715	1939	92,993

i.   Although the introduction of the Film Hire tax might have been expected to reduce the amount of Amusement taxation in 1930, the marked increase in 1931 is to be attributed to an increase in the tax itself that year.

We should note that the new Film Hire Tax was especially high on 'foreign films' (i.e. films not made in New Zealand or Britain). As dutiful scion of the British Empire, New Zealand appeared to be doing what it could to limit the allure of American cinema. Indeed, New Zealand was recorded as 'screening a higher percentage of British films than has been screened in England itself' (Belich 2001: 252). Unfortunately, combined with the introduction of sound, which made foreign language films less accessible, this punitive taxation hit European films hard as they struggled to find commercial distributors and exhibitors in New Zealand. French, German, and Russian films held a potential 'niche market' appeal that required 'boutique' distributors, and while the number of people interested in these films was growing in this decade as film society activity demonstrates, New Zealand did not attract a dedicated arthouse distributor until Natan Scheinwald reinvented himself as one in 1939.

Other effects of the Depression on local film culture included a significant drop in specifically New Zealand filmmaking. Between 1921 and 1929, 15 films had been produced, but in the following decade only eight were made, seven of which were shot after 1934 when the harshest effects of the Depression were subsiding (Martin and Edwards 1997: 28–50).[3] Meanwhile, local intellectual film culture began to look at the political issues associated with the development of the new 'mass' media. Most of the new office holders of the AFS, for example, which resurfaced from its hiatus in 1933, were on the extreme left of the political spectrum. While Russian films were lauded for both their rectitude and their cinematic innovation in intellectual journals, the aesthetic appreciation of films from Europe or Hollywood was out of favour in these turbulent times in which a sympathetic emphasis on the 'common' man and his problems found more favourable reception. This political turn reflected international developments in film culture. Opposition between two distinct avant-garde trends (the aesthetic versus the politically radical) came to a head at the second (and final) International Congress of Cinematography, held in Brussels in 1930. It was at this conference that the obituary of 'film as film' was written. Members recognised that 'the Avant-Garde as a purely aesthetic movement had passed its climax and was on the way to concentrating on the social and political film, mainly in documentary form'. Artists working in film increasingly decided to adopt a more practical commitment to social action: 'Our age demands documented fact' (Donald, Friedberg, and Marcus 1998: 33).

In some quarters, these trends intensified problems that already existed in New Zealand: puritanism, an egalitarian suspicion of aestheticism, and an antipathy to Russian films for those who were wary of communism. One of the original organisers of the WFS in 1933, Read Mason, recollected the public perception of film societies in an interview given 50 years later: 'When the Society was started, uninformed and unthinking people assumed that anything like the Film Society must exist for communist or pornographic purposes and had to be stamped out' (Cooke 1987: 16). Mason attributed this attitude to years of official and unofficial censorship, and it was true that social malcontents of various stripes – radicals, liberals, socialists, and communists – were very vocal at this time, both inside and outside film societies. A further factor that prejudiced 'Almighty Norm'[4] against the film society was the nationality of the films screened. The First World War may have ended in 1918 but many New Zealanders had lost their lives fighting in it and anti-German sentiment had not disappeared from popular memory. In its first year of operation, in 1933, the WFS screened 15 films: three were Russian and six were German; half the second season's films were German. The menace that such films, especially those from the Soviet Union, held for God-fearing New Zealanders found expression in theatres being picketed in Auckland because of their screening of continental films. Seventy-seven churches and religious organisations sent a petition to government in 1935, which asked that 'All films that had their origin in Russia should be banned from the screens in New Zealand' (Hayward 1936: 13).

Notwithstanding (or because of) this culturally intolerant attitude, the extreme homogeneity of 1930s New Zealand society led some individualists to want to see life from perspectives that were not exclusively British. Unfortunately, as we have just seen, local film societies had an 'image' problem. Large sections of the New Zealand public reckoned that such societies were seedbeds for perverts, radicals, and 'arty' types, or all three combined. If puritanism and censorship were major problems in New Zealand for minority film culture, so too was a national fear of difference. A politician could declare proudly (in 1943) that 'New Zealand's world leadership in social legislation was due largely to the quality of the people of the Dominion, where the proportion of British-born was higher than in any other part of the Empire. That position should not be jeopardised by the admission of aliens with different ideologies' (*Whim Wham* 1944: 7). This fear of difference was also frequently a fear of anything perceived as extreme, including any form of cultural activity that might be labelled as élitist. Allen Curnow in his persona of Whim Wham cleverly summed up the situation:

What did the Nation-builders build?/How was the World impressed?

Oh, Some went up and Some went down,/'Twas Life in the Looking-glass, Sir,/The same old Scenery back to front,/The Victorian Middle Class, Sir.

And What was the net Result, my Boy?/What became of the Plan?/What was the Fruit of the Enterprise/For the average Pig Island Man?

Oh, they crossed the Upper and Under Dogs/To produce this Island Race, Sir,/A Society neither Up nor Down

With a puzzled Look on its Face, Sir.

Is This a very good Thing, my Boy?/Or What do you think about it?/Is it Civilisation's finest Flower,/Or could we manage without it?

Oh, yes, it IS a very good Thing,/A very good Thing indeed, Sir –/Here's looking at Me, and looking at You,/Of that identical Breed, Sir.

(*The Best of Whim Wham* 1959: 11)

Clearly, New Zealand of the 1930s was a troubled nation in which many saw their traditional way of life threatened from many directions. Although the country did not experience a comparable level of strife and turmoil as occurred in France, Germany, and Italy, there were spontaneous outbursts of rioting and violence, which disposed a nervous centre-right coalition government to acts of political and cultural suppression.

The Wellington Film Society (1933)

The WFS was the brainchild of 'Two gentlemen who were very earnestly and very seriously interested in filmic art'.[5] They approached one or two 'of their intimate friends who they thought might hold similar views and suggested that something might be done in the way of creating a small private society in order to view some films'.[6] In his modest way, James Tucker was the catalyst and driving force behind the formation of the Society in March 1933. 'A sensitive, artistic person from Christchurch who worked in advertising for the Commercial Printing Company', Tucker had cooked up the project with a journalist colleague, Read Mason, during conversations about films they had seen or wished they had seen (Cooke: 1).

One of those films was a 'mountain' film co-directed by Dr. Arnold Fanck and G.W. Pabst, *The White Hell of Pitz Palu* (1929), which had had a brief public exhibition in the capital. Fanck, one of the earliest promoters of Germany's popular mountain films, was a professional geologist and a climber himself, and, following World War I, he began a series of fictional and documentary films about mountain climbing. In these films, the physical effort and technical prowess of climbing were not mere sporting exploits but means through which man could liberate himself from the mundane toiling and moiling of the world. The symbolism of this may not have been lost on the pioneers of the WFS, who formed the project of a film society towards the end of March 1933, setting out on their own adventure to carry film reception to heights not yet attained in New Zealand.

Anxious to avoid problems with the commercial theatres, the founders stated at their first meeting that the Society would only use films 'not screened commercially, or films which had failed on a commercial circuit'. They further believed that they could actually help the commercial film exhibitors by forming a public less ignorant of the cinema as an art. They even cherished the notion that, in time, 'they would enlighten many people on the potentialities of the film as a dramatic vehicle'.[7] The impetus behind the desire to form a film society was in large part an expression of the frustration they felt at the lack of films from countries other than the United States and England. The rise of the sound film resurrected national and linguistic boundaries, and the international reach silent film had enjoyed through the strongly visual nature of the medium had been reduced with its emergence. Film society members still wanted, however, to see as much of world cinema as was available, and experience the varied forms of narrative that innovative filmmakers were making of this emergent art, with its singularly powerful expressive abilities. In contrast to the *Mirror* writers, technology was welcomed by film societies as a means to reduce New Zealander's powerful sense of isolation. Some of the effects of the 'tyranny of distance' could be reduced by it. Read Mason felt that:

> The world was moving forward to better times … a time of artistic awakening in Europe. Although films provided by far the greatest source of entertainment in the early '30s, they were being prevented from participating in, and being stimulated by, one aspect of this movement in the older countries.[8]

Innovative film style, thematic seriousness, and occasional nudity, differentiated much European cinema from Anglo-American films. The revolutionary Soviet cinema, exalting proletarian culture and extolling the virtues of the Workers' State, also fired some film society members' imagination, not simply for the content but also for the form in which that content was shaped and expressed.

In its inaugural Sunday evening programme on 30 April 1933 at Short's Theatre, the WFS screened *Giant*, and *The Animal Kingdom* (USA, 1932, aka *The Woman in His House*). This initial offering – one Soviet and one Hollywood film, risqué fiction and no nonsense documentary, stars and ordinary people – made it clear that the WFS would take an eclectic approach. Membership in the WFS grew quickly, 'climbing to 166 within a fortnight of the first screening' (Cooke: 3). Membership had to be capped at 280 because of the seating restrictions of Short's Theatre but another reason for limiting membership was a concern that commercial exhibitors might bristle at the competition. Some 50 years after these events, Read Mason evoked the emotion he had felt at the screening of the silent films for which the Society had provided the gramophone music: 'The matching of music to evocative photography [in *Turksib*] created an emotional effect that I had never believed possible except in opera.'[9]

The Road to Ruin

The film culture practised by the New Zealand film societies was still in its emergent phase when the United-Reform Government took the WFS to court in 1933 for having shown an uncensored film. The Society's wings were severely clipped and the nascent film society movement brought to a limping halt when an already tenuous relationship with commercial film distributors collapsed in the aftermath of the 'scandal' as the trade distanced itself from the Society and its now discredited cultural agenda. Although it had a short life of one and half years, attracted hostility from the commercial film exchanges, encountered a lack of understanding in government, and struggled to overcome a chronic problem of film supply, the WFS stimulated the establishment of similar societies throughout the Dominion, initiated the cultural programme for film societies that found more lasting expression in the post–World War II period, and made submissions to the 1934 Parliamentary Committee of Inquiry into the Motion Picture Industry, which led to some relaxation of censorship requirements for film societies.

On Sunday 15 July, the WFS arranged for the screening of what it claimed to be the first Soviet picture shown in New Zealand. Presumably they meant the first *fiction* film as Soviet documentaries had been shown as part of the cultural activities of the Friends of the Soviet Union (FSU). Members were informed that *The Road to Life* (1931) carried subtitles, that it was well known in both Europe and America, and that it would 'afford members an opportunity of seeing Russian cinematic technique' – an exceptionally strong drawcard as the Soviet innovations in film langauge had inspired many Western artists and intellectuals to write strongly in support of Soviet film theory and film practice from the mid-1920s on (Samson 1986: 311).[10] *The Road to Life* explored the problems of rehabilitating delinquent and unemployed orphans thrown up during and after the civil war (1917–20). This still constituted a major social issue at the time the film was made. It met with immediate success both at home and abroad, and had a significant influence on later films based on the same theme.[11] The title, message of the film, and the figure of the teacher were based on the pedagogy and practices pioneered by the Soviet educationalist Anton Makarenko, and expressed in his trilogy *The Road to Life*. The significance of this outstanding educational pioneer was recognised at the time by Emeritus Professor John Dewey whose filmed talk preceded the screening (Dickinson and de la Roche 1948 cited in Leyda 1983: 285).[12]

It was fortunate that members of the WFS had the opportunity to see this film as events began to take a turn for the worse in the fortunes of the Society. On Saturday 14 July 1933, the day immediately preceding the scheduled screening of *The Road to Life*, the Police Commissioner sent a memorandum to the Wellington Superintendent of Police, informing him of the imminent projection of an uncensored film. The ostensible concern of the Commissioner was that as the film had not been submitted for censorship, it was likely to be in breach of Section 7 of the Cinematograph Films Act (1928). Section 7 provided for the prosecution of any person who charged an admission price for entry into any place where a film (or any part of it) was shown, which had not been approved by the censor. Soon after the projection, the Commissioner was directed to 'cause enquiry to be made and furnish details of (1) the control and objects of the club and (2) the titles and description of pictures that have been shown'.[13] Questions remain concerning the intent of the action brought against the WFS: was it politically motivated; or the conditioned reflex of an administration charged with overseeing public and private compliance with statute; or was there some other agenda?[14]

Within the WFS, radical elements, frustration, and opportunism (film availability) may have convinced the Society's committee to see just how far they could push against narrow state-fixed boundaries. Such an attitude would not have been foreign to many of the Society's office holders, starting with its president, Professor Thomas Hunter, at that time the first working Vice Chancellor of the University of New Zealand. Hunter had a passion for the social and liberalising effect of education that drew him towards activities outside the college. His encouragement of independent thought in students led the conservative and conventional to distrust the college because of its radical reputation (*Dictionary of New Zealand Biography* 1999: 243). Although less obviously radical than the Auckland group, the involvement of socialists, academics, and assorted liberals gave the Society a profile that pushed against customary behaviour and conservative statutes. These were heroic days for the arts in New Zealand, when an interest in 'modern' ideas had something of the feeling of a shared crusade or conspiracy. The 1930s saw the laying of foundations for a new culture, on which the post-war years would later build national institutions. Yet this was not a simple process – it was fraught with difficulties, especially in the early years.

Opposition to censorship has always provided a forum for dissent and for introducing elements of sophisticated metropolitan culture into parochial New Zealand. James Tucker's remarks at a committee meeting, held on 29 September 1933, that 'although we may screen films that do not pass the censor we do not screen them in order to pass judgement on [him], nor does the censor's ban necessarily make a film desirable for our purposes' (Cooke: 11), accords with a comment he later made during the WFS visit to the Minister of Internal Affairs to explain the *bona fides* of the Society at a time of impending crisis; he declared that insofar as the WFS was concerned, they were not interested in censorship as they had their own standard of values.[15] Such openly professed bohemianism or élitism was strategically inept, even if the WFS did see itself as David battling with Goliath.

In August 1933, the Solicitor-General reported to government that a prosecution of the WFS was likely to be successful, if pursued. His opinion depended upon a contentious point of legal argument. In the first instance he found that Short's Theatre could not be considered a place to which the public were admitted, as admission was limited to members of the Society and their friends. However, he did find that 'the substantial purpose of the subscription is to confer on them the right of admission to a place where entertainment by exhibition of films will be provided',[16] and this seemed to contravene Section 7 of the Films Act. The final decision to prosecute emerged from a ministerial cabinet meeting – the matter was therefore one that accrued political significance.[17] It may well be, as some contended at the time, that the political and cultural orientation of the film societies was antithetical to the United-Reform Coalition Cabinet of 1931–35, which 'consisted of nine farmers and a lawyer' (Belich 2001: 256). By way of contrast, the police report into the WFS revealed that it included 'the names of well known citizens – Solicitors, Doctors, businessmen and such like. For instance, Dr R.M. Campbell, the Acting Prime Minister's Secretary, is one of the members'.[18] This government of farmers was unlikely to appreciate the cultural pretensions of a film society who seemed to think they could thumb their noses at the common man by claiming to be exempt from censorship standards that applied to everyone else.[19]

More concretely, the dire circumstances of the Great Depression were encouraging the growth of protest organisations of the right, left, and middle. 'The New Zealand Legion, the Communist Party and Social Credit are examples in each category' (Belich 2001: 257). Mass rioting had broken out in an intense spasm in the four main centres in April and May of 1932, resulting in violent clashes with the thousands of 'special constables' recruited by the Government. The riots were profoundly shocking to both Cabinet and the public at large: 'Some thought they portended Red revolution', and Parliament passed draconian legislation, making arrest for 'sedition' easier (Bassett 1995: 179). 'Some 185 prosecutions resulted from the riots; 72 men were imprisoned' (Belich: 258). The prosecution of the WFS should be seen against this heated political background. 'With feelings running high, a lot of New Zealanders held that communists, who were influential in the Unemployed Workers' Movement, were threatening not just law and order but the very foundation of society' (Beaglehole 2006: 173).

There are other cultural traits that can also be factored in to help explain the relative ease with which a decision to treat the WFS harshly was made. It could be argued, for example, that New Zealand was particularly prone to the suppression of any emerging form of difference – something the parliamentarian satirised by *Whim Wham* has already given us a clear expression of. Another writer has noted of the period that 'Clots of difference, including the cream of society, were homogenised out; the bacilli of tight class, sin, racial "inferiors" and non-conformity were pasteurised out in practice, on paper, or both' (Belich: 121). New Zealand was a powerfully conformist and conservative society – the dark side of paradise (Pratt 2006). Even during the worst of the rioting, the state's authority was never seriously in doubt, and there was nothing comparable to the political extremism that racked other democracies. Several elements thus converged in the case against the WFS, which can be seen as a lightning rod for some of the concerns of the period, many of which had a powerful social resonance that echoed long after the court case, and culminated in the Government's action, which took the WFS to court on

21 October 1933 in what amounted to a test case to determine whether or not the activities of the Society circumvented the law. Such a maverick group (and the risk of contagion) could not be allowed to operate with impunity. Instead of welcoming the diversity that it offered, the state sought to impose its narrowly normative colonial code.

During the court case, the Crown Prosecutor argued that the work of the censor would be nullified if the Society were permitted to screen whatever it wanted, and that many similar societies would spring up with no state control over their activities and no way to stop them 'spreading subversive propaganda'. In a prescient remark, the lawyer for the defence (a film society committee member himself) noted that the decision of the court would have 'a very important bearing not only on the operations of such societies but also on the cultural development of film in New Zealand' (*Evening Post* 1933). The 'high art versus popular art' argument received further exposition when the defence compared the aims of the WFS with kindred cultural organisations which sought to introduce distinctions where none had been before. The development of repertory theatre was an example since it allowed for the expression of an 'aesthetic emotion' not found in most travelling players' presentations of plays that merely appealed to popular taste. In like manner, film societies wanted to promote a form of cinema unlikely to have sufficient popular appeal to warrant exhibition by local distributors. Film societies offered the only way to see films of 'technical merit' that developed the 'cinematographic art in Continental countries' (*Evening Post* 1933). In an appeal to the civilised values of the United Kingdom, the defence pointed out that the WFS was modelled on its metropolitan mentor, the London Film Society (1925).

However, the law was (apparently) the law. The WFS was convicted on 3 November 'for exhibiting cinematograph films that had not been approved by the censor in a place to which a charge was made in respect of persons admitted thereto.'[20] On the charge relating to the exhibition of *The Road to Life*, a token fine of £1/11s, the cost of the proceedings, was imposed. The public defeat, combined with the film trade's refusal to supply films, no doubt hurt more – and was in fact an eventually crippling tactic. The film supply obstacle proved insuperable. Making the Society subject to the usual forms of censorship meant that it incurred unaffordable financial costs, which handicapped the procurement of films from private sources.

The promising debut the Society had made was compromised. Undeterred, it invited the Minister of Internal Affairs to attend Fritz Lang's *Siegfried* (1924), pointing out that the film was regarded as 'a landmark in cinema history' that had yet to be screened in New Zealand; the Minister declined (*The Dominion* 1933: 21). Attendance figures at the films do not exist, so it is impossible to know what happened when the Society screened *Siegfried* two days after newspaper reports of the case appeared under headings like 'Film Society Convicted' and questioning the suitability of the films shown to members (Cooke: 12). Another consequence of the court case was the resignation of 21 members (*The Dominion* 1933: 11). The 'scandal' had repercussions the following year, too, when membership for the second season fell significantly with only 73 members renewing. There were 52 new members but total membership was well under half that of the first season.[21] If many of the Society's rank and file were lower middle class, then we might suppose that a need to be seen to be respectable was stronger than the allure of the cinematic 'sirens' the Society's programmers were scheduling. An appeal against the conviction was considered by the Society but discarded with the thought that: 'Even if we did win, the victory might be a short one, and that it would probably be followed by amended legislation. What we wanted was some way of regularising the Society's position for we considered it was obviously wrong to impose the restrictions required of public entertainment on a private society' (Cooke: 12). Stressing high culture credentials, the Society had ended its first season strongly with Lang's *Seigfried* and went into the summer recess with a resolve to improve matters in New Zealand with regards to both film supply and censorship.

A Parliamentary Inquiry

An opportunity to right a perceived wrong soon presented itself when a parliamentary committee of inquiry was established in March 1934 to investigate the film industry (Beaglehole n.d.). The WFS took full advantage of this to present its case to have legislation more favourable to film society objectives enacted into law. Preparation of their submission to the committee of enquiry involved careful international research: 'All available information was collected about the position of film societies overseas'. During this process it became apparent 'that what we were seeking was in line with enlightened opinion of the day' (Cooke: 12). One of the recommendations came from C. Palmer Brown, a solicitor and member of the Wanganui Film Society, who suggested that the Societies be allowed to screen free of New Zealand censorship, 'provided the films imported had passed the London County Council for film society or general exhibition' (Cooke: 12). It is interesting that loyalty to Britain in this case was associated not with cultural cringe (an internalised inferiority complex with regards to the value of indigenous culture) but with a plea for greater freedom.

Hunter and Tucker attended the enquiry and presented the submissions on behalf of all the film societies in the country. They thought that 'the existence of a strong film society movement, able to show a fair assortment of international films will prove a tremendously valuable link in keeping us abreast of world developments … in helping remove the curse of distance from us New Zealanders' (Cooke: 12). They informed the committee of the film society movement's cultural and educational aims and prudently recommended that the Minister be given the power to exempt film societies from the censorhip provisions of the Cinematograph Films Act (1928) so long as he was satisfied of the *bona fides* of a duly incorporated film society. This attempt to inflect the state's stringent control over what adults could watch in cinemas represented the first collective shot by the film society movement in New Zealand to establish a more liberal censorship regime.

At the end of the inquiry the committee were of the opinion that there was no 'reasonable objection to members of a film society, constituted as proposed, attending the exhibition of films which might not be suitable for general audiences as a public entertainment'.[22] All but one of the recommendations made by the representatives of the film societies were adopted in new legislation voted by Parliament in October into The Cinematograph Films Amendment Act (1934). The Minister of Internal Affairs rejected the submission to exempt societies from local censorship in favour of the ratings of the London County Council on the grounds that 'all parties that have pictures for exhibition [should be] treated alike'.[23] That was the egalitarian impulse opposing any signs of élitism, including those derived from Britain. The Minister's decision did not exempt the societies from censorship but it did accept that only a nominal fee for censorship should apply to a film society. Under the amended Act, the censor could 'approve a film to be exhibited only by, or on behalf of, an approved film society, or to adults only'.[24] This was a victory of sorts, but it depended upon the presence of a sympathetic Minister.

Notwithstanding this small concession, censorship of films that the societies wished to see was a persistent ill with which they had to cope. Murnau's 1926 film of Molière's play *Tartuffe*, which the Christchurch Film Society (CFS) had programmed for 6 May 1934, had to be cancelled when the censor acting under the older legislation prohibited it for exhibition, thus provoking the ire of Hypatia Johnson, occasional film critic for *Tomorrow*:

> The ways of Censorship in New Zealand, and in the rest of the world for that matter, vary from the mildly exasperating to the decidedly irritating and the absolutely imbecile. Australia, for instance, bans Aldous Huxley's *Brave New World* – a splendid satire on the increasing mechanisation of our age – and then … has the quaint audacity to ask Mr. Huxley to attend the Melbourne Centenary celebrations. Not even to our own Film Societies will our Censor allow the film version of Molière's *Tartuffe* to be shown, an incredible fact to anyone familiar with the play and surely grounds for a serious international dispute between France and England.
>
> (*Tomorrow* 1934: 14)

Tartuffe is also known as *The Hypocrite* and it is tempting to suggest that the censor may have rejected it because he saw too much of himself in it. It is hard to see what other aspect can have disturbed him, though Molière was admittedly controversial in his own day.

The reasons that led the censor to ban films are for the most part unknown because he was not required to explain. He did, however, leave some trace of his decisions in the 'Weekly Return and Report of Films Examined'.[25] A Soviet documentary film, *The Five Year Plan*, that he examined on 18 June 1932, for example, was rejected on the ground that it was propaganda for Soviet Russia. 'It will be sent out of the Dominion' was his peremptory decision.[26] René Clair's film *Sous les toits de Paris* was considered to be a 'Paris gangster story', with 'an unnecessary bedroom scene', that he had removed. *The Animal Kingdom* (USA, 1932) appears to have been rejected simply because it satirised married life. The Russian origin of *The Road to Life* was sufficient to warrant its immediate ban. Professor Shelley, president of the CFS, said 'The censor would not, I think, have censored our films because they were purely of an educational nature. The police decided to ban *The Road to Life* for quite another reason than censorship'.[27] This was a widely shared sentiment, echoed by

Figure 6: A view of the censor in *Phoenix*, 1933.

C. Palmer Brown of the Wanganui Film Society, when he criticised the censor for being 'more concerned about our politics than our morals and passes things we do not want, while refusing to pass the Russian and Italian films which naturally advertise the Soviet and Mussolini'.[28] A.R.D. Fairburn, in *Tomorrow*, said of *Sous les toits de Paris* (1930): 'There is not a bedroom scene in it from beginning to end. The most bitter prude could sit through it without a blush.

If indeed it was banned, I can only conclude that the word "Paris" was fatal' (Fairburn 1935: 7). Fairburn ended with the hope that 'an improvement under the new dispensation' might usher in a new era. The 'new dispensation' was a reference to the incoming first Labour Government, which had won power in December 1935. Fairburn, and others further to the left of the political spectrum, believed that many glittering prizes would now come their way.

Turning Left

Notwithstanding the case brought against the WFS, 1933 was also a year rich in events for the growth of minority film culture in New Zealand. Aucklanders with a serious interest in film included several influential communists such as R.A.K. (Ron) Mason and Clifton Firth (Gillam n.d.). Mason had taken over the editorship of Auckland University College's influential literary magazine, *Phoenix*, in 1933 and had already written many of the poems that would later make him a major figure in New Zealand literature. A 'fierce man exploring politics and a man of granite when he had made up his mind' (McEldowney 1991: 560), Mason, as if echoing the sentiments of the International Congress of Cinematography, which had heralded a turn towards documentary film, repudiated aestheticism and announced that the condition of society required an urgent attention to politics: 'This is no time to be studying the tonal values of the minor works of T.E. Brown. It is the greatest hour in history. ... This is no time for optimism, no time for pessimism: the hour for realism is here.' (Gillam n.d.)[29]

Like Mason, Clifton Firth was an enthusiast for Soviet cinema, seeing it as the only cinema that could be called an art form (1933 2(1): 17). Born in 1904 (a year before Mason), he was the eldest son of a wealthy family, had met the poets Mason and A.R.D. (Rex) Fairburn in 1925 and became good friends with both. The young men's shared political beliefs provided one area of early concord but their friendship was cemented through discussions of philosophy and art. Firth was also heavily involved in agit-prop activities associated with the FSU and Auckland's People's Theatre (founded 1936). The first of the FSU's objects was to make known the achievements of the USSR in the building of socialism, and a variety of films that flattered the Soviets and attacked fascism were made available throughout the 1930s, for example, *Ten Days that Shook the World* (aka *October*, USSR, 1928), *Modern Russia, A Day in a Soviet Kindergarten*, and *Defence of Madrid* (UK, 1936).

Another of Firth's cultural commitments was in resurrecting and radicalizing the AFS, which was officially incorporated as a society in December 1933. The objectives of the Society seemed innocuous: 'The showing of films of an artistic, cultural and educational nature and the general encouragement and advancement of same', but actually represented a significant development. Where the AFS of 1929–31 had sought only to draw the public's attention to a variety of 'good pictures' released commercially, thereby rescuing them from an opprobrium that sectarian interests had attached to the cinema, the revamped AFS now wanted to organise screenings of films that would otherwise not get seen – notably, but not exclusively, those of Russian origin. The political involvement of most of the 15 signatories to the application for incorporation of the Society suggests that it was wrested from the former group of enthusiasts so as to become an instrument for the advancement of left-wing cultural aspirations. This is not to suggest that the members were all communists or narrow ideologues – many were prominent in drama, the visual arts, or education.[30] What they shared was what would have then been described as a 'progressive' outlook in cultural matters. Of the 15, at least half are known to have had strong left-wing sympathies and several of these were on the extreme left.

The cinema, which Lenin had already declared to be the most powerful propaganda medium (and German National Socialists and Italian Fascists had concurred), was an obvious weapon to be aimed at the more reactionary areas of culture. However, in order for this weapon to work, spectatorship would have to be refashioned via a knowledge of Soviet films and of the formal stylistic invention and ideology that informed their production. Firth provided a useful synthesis of the ideological, political, and technical developments in revolutionary Soviet cinema in the two articles he wrote for *Phoenix*. Although the readership of this periodical was small, its influence rippled out far beyond a tight circle of intellectuals. The periodical's very existence was an inspiration to other frustrated individuals who sought to create a space in which innovative, 'modern' culture might exist in populist and provincial New Zealand.

If modernism was an international development, so too was communism. In 1933, no New Zealander had seen films by Eisenstein, Pudovkin, Vertov, or Dovzhenko, unless they had travelled overseas. Firth had not, but he and his friends knew that 'the vitality of the Russian Cinema [was] one of the seven wonders of the modern world' because they had read Anglo-American film critics, such as Christine Lejeune, whom Firth cited in the first of his two *Phoenix* articles. In them, he tried to understand and to explain, in the absence of the films themselves, why this was and should be so. Revolutionary principles underpin the faith that is apparent in his verbal raptures about Russian films. The idea of them was so satisfying because the films, from an ideologically inflamed distance, demonstrated that a political revolution could go hand-in-hand with an artistic revolution. Another influential source of ideas was the journal *Experimental Cinema* (1930). *Phoenix* included a review of its fourth issue, which was used to express dismay at New Zealand society's multiple conservatisms:

> By this time intelligent people the world over know that the Communists have made of the cinema a new art-form worthy to take its place with the noblest of old. It is unlikely that we New Zealanders, rotating dully in our little backwash of the world's waters, will ever so much as glimpse a fragment of this work. Even if our intelligentsia were sufficiently numerous and united to cause an effective demand, it is not to be thought of that our business-men lords and masters would allow their Parliament to allow their police to allow us to see their films.
>
> (Firth: 54)

Figure 7: Soviet filmmaking and film theory finds expression in this influential magazine.

Experimental Cinema had articles on American, Russian, and Continental filmmaking, 'including the most merciless analysis of Hollywood methods that [Firth had] ever seen', as well as an article by Eisenstein himself, 'The Principles of Film Form', which related 'cinematic practice [to] sociology and philosophy'. There was also a description of Eisenstein's Mexican film *Que Viva Mexico*, where the parsimony of its production, 'a 400-foot load French camera, two reflectors, and five actors, each earning one peso', contributed to its moral and material superiority over any Hollywood film. The writer concluded that Eisenstein had 'so completely covered Mexico that it will be difficult for another picture-director to enter the country without repeating' (Firth: 54).

In the first of his two articles, Firth's intention was to give the layman 'some inkling of the principles on which the Soviet Republics have been built', so as to 'grasp the reason for the extraordinary interest that is being taken in Russian films [and] understand the complicated principles on which [they] are constructed' (17). This required a crash course in Marxist fundamentals. Lesson number one involved an understanding of the concept of 'surplus value'. Lesson number two led Firth to define the nature and purpose of art, now disinfected of its religious roots. Art was defined as a 'condensation of experience and its symbolic expression' (17), involving sensory perception formulated intellectually – an aesthetic emotion, as the Argentinian writer Jorge Luis Borges would have said. In a perceptive analysis that reveals affinities with Gramsci's concept of cultural hegemony as spontaneous consent by the dominated to oppressive power structures under capitalism, Firth noted that while Hollywood films appealed to the subordinated in society their ideological structure served the interests of the powerful; one class had succeeded in persuading another to accept its own moral, political, and cultural values. He also noted how sporting events functioned as convenient distractions for audiences who devoted more time and energy to them than to politics and power – a notion that Noam Chomsky would later develop in his critique of the media and professional sport culture in the United States. Another of the veils producing a state of 'false consciousness' was the distortion of sex into 'love' with its attendant romance and idealistic falsification of reality, considered by Firth to be 'gravest charge that can be laid against Hollywood'. This last concept is one that the present-day French feminist and filmmaker, Catherine Breillat, has been exposing in the course of her study of masochistic heterosexual female desire, with *Romance* (1999) perhaps the clearest statement of the cost of conflating sexuality and a culturally oppressive romantic attachment to a man.

Firth was one of the first critics in this country to remark that a film's form was not *mere* form, but comprised an indispensable part of its meaning. Although Firth's treatment of Soviet 'cinematics' and montage passed through the ideological filter of dialectical materialism, he was certainly presenting a new way of talking about film for New Zealand readers. He went on to argue that capitalism's inability to employ 'cinematics' had led to an over reliance on such 'non-cinematic' aspects as story, sets, acting, and speech, all of which could be attributed to a theatrical legacy. This placed Firth firmly in the camp of those who saw editing as the primary language of film. It is not hard to imagine the contest that he and his comrades waged against the 'apolitical aesthetes' of the earlier AFS who had focused on *mise en scène*. (An Eisenstinian aesthetic gave greater emphasis to editing and the juxtaposition of images, to 'strife' rather than consonance.) According to Firth, while Hollywood had made no cinematic advance in 30 years, the Bolsheviks had made 'the discovery that the medium of the cinema is FILM' (17).

Firth was working hard to grasp the aesthetics of film on the basis of such information as he had and the least that can be said of his articles is that they provided the readers of *Phoenix* with a thought-provoking introduction to some of the technical-aesthetic aspects of revolutionary Soviet filmmaking, making them better prepared to appreciate silent Soviet narrative cinema when it did arrive in New Zealand. As we will discover in Chapter 3, *Tomorrow* (an influential fortnightly magazine) would later expand upon the ideas about Soviet cinema in a series of articles written by an expat Australian academic, H. Winston Rhodes, from 1935 on.

The Federation of Film Societies

The first WFS Management Committee meeting was held in May 1933 with James Tucker and Read Mason in charge of a sub-committee to encourage the development of film societies in other provincial centres. The aim was to establish a federation, share knowledge, pool resources, and increase the purchasing capability of the individual societies. Success was reasonably swift:

> The result is that Dunedin and Christchurch have been formed, Dunedin showing its opening programme on 27 August and Christchurch on 3 September. Auckland has yet to report progress. The greatest care was taken to ensure these societies would operate along the sound lines we have provided by experience in Wellington. I recommend that the Committee keep in view the affiliating of these various societies in one association with headquarters in Wellington. The formation of these societies will materially strengthen purchasing power and is yet another reason why the committee should immediately investigate the question of importing overseas productions.[31]

The pooling of scarce financial and administrative resources was always going to strengthen the nascent film society movement in New Zealand, but even the purchasing power of the combined societies was never going to rival that of the film exchanges and would always make film supply both problematic and haphazard. As Tucker conceded: 'After all, with, say, 1000 members in various Societies in New Zealand, it is only the equivalent in purchasing power of half a house at, say, the Regent Theatre or St James.'[32]

In the months preceding the inaugural Conference of New Zealand Film Societies in November 1934, members of the WFS had had the opportunity to see a range of films, including: *The White Devil* (Germany, 1931) – an adaptation of Leo Tolstoy's *Hajji Murad*; *The Last Company/Die Letzte Kompagnie* (Germany, 1929); re-releases of Fritz Lang's

Metropolis (Germany, 1927), E.W. Dupont's *Variety* (Germany, 1925), F.W. Murnau's *Faust* (Germany, 1926), and Dr. Arnold Fanck's *Peaks of Destiny/Der Heilige Berg* (Germany, 1927); the opulent Erich Pommer production of *Hungarian Rhapsody/Ungarische Rhapsodie* (Germany, 1929); and René Clair's *Le Million* (France, 1931). This was certainly an eclectic selection but not of the standard set by the London Film Society. Nor could it be. Films of high historical importance with regard to technical and aesthetic achievements mingle with films that are now largely forgotten.

At the inaugural screening on 24 September of the renaissant AFS, members saw *Turksib* (USSR, 1929), *The Mysteries of Life,* and *The Life of Beethoven* (Austria, 1927) at Henry Hayward's 'theatre for the intelligentsia', the Tudor, in Remuera (Auckland's wealthiest suburb). The police were still taking an interest in film societies. Under-Secretary of Internal Affairs Malcolm Fraser had received a memo from the Commissioner of Police on 5 October informing him of the formation of 'an organisation known as the Auckland Film Society', and the titles of the films screened.[33] With an eye to another prosecution, the ever-vigilant Fraser then memoed the censor to find out if all the films had been passed for exhibition – by this stage they had.

The geographical centrality of Wellington had made it the obvious business location for the film exchanges to establish their headquarters; films were stored and distributed from there throughout the country. A similar reasoning also made it the logical place to hold the first Conference of the New Zealand Film Societies, which occurred on Thursday 29 November 1934. Present at this event were Professor Hunter (in the Chair); John Robertson represented Wellington (Tucker had left the country for Sydney); Professor James Shelley and F.G. Dunn represented Christchurch; Dunedin sent its apologies; and its first President, Arnold Goodwin, represented Auckland. Three small towns (Hasting, Hamilton and Hawera – to name the 'Hs') had given notice of their intention to form societies 'as soon as a supply of programmes was assured'. Invercargill, too, was 'desirous'.[34]

Film supply remained a crucial issue, but involved making a place for the societies in a highly complex and competitive environment. In an effort to ensure a regular supply of films, the societies considered becoming licensed exhibitors in order to obtain films from the Film Renters Association. However, because other participants at the conference were not sure that it was either desirable or constitutional for the film societies 'by becoming licensed exhibitors to place themselves in the position of being regarded as Commercial Institutions', no decision was taken (Cooke: 21). The conference also resolved to form a New Zealand Federation, consisting of one member from each society 'and that a circuit for programmes be followed to minimise freight charges and that the previewing of programmes be dispensed with as much as possible to reduce costs' (Cooke: 21).

The drive to secure a steady supply of films was a matter very much on the minds of the Management Committee of the WFS as initial cooperation from the film exchanges evaporated. 'Very early in its career your Society quite unexpectedly met with the determined and planned opposition of the American Film Exchanges operating in New Zealand whose members banned supplies.'[35] At the same meeting the committee heard that the 'field of local supply was thus almost totally barred, but it was found possible to obtain a few subjects from "free" exchanges. From these and certain private sources it was possible to secure material for the 1933–34 Season' (Cooke: 5). Gordon Mirams later took the film exchanges' greed to task in his book *Speaking Candidly* when he wrote: 'If there is any money to be made out of showing films they want to make it' (1945: 212). The exchanges feared that the pool of filmgoers was fixed and that any incursions by film societies necessarily took part of that fixed pool from them. However, we have also seen that film societies, in fact, formed new audiences for 'non-commercial' films; nevertheless, the suspicious film exchanges withdrew their support.

Mirams was a key figure in the resurgence of local film society activity in the aftermath of World War II, and played a key role in developing a more independent role for film criticism before the war. In his book, he drew on his intimate knowledge of the difficulties encountered in obtaining films:

> [It] was the success of the German film *Maedchen in Uniform*, acquired by two astute Englishmen for a mere song and shown to big audiences, that gave the film trade a shock from which it has never quite recovered. Ever since, they have given the impression of being on guard against all such amateur enterprises (1945: 213).

The suspicion and lack of cooperation that characterised relations between film societies and most of the film exchanges continued, with no significant change until the early 1950s when smaller independent distribution companies, such as New Zealand Film Services, run by Ron Usmar and Russell Rankin, in Wellington, and Eddie Greenfield's Exclusive Pictures, in Auckland, began to source 'continental' films and specifically target film society audiences as likely publics for them. This did not resolve the tensions with larger exchanges but meant that there were smaller exchanges with similar interests. The 'art film' market was to become commercially stronger from this time on, as arthouse cinemas became more viable.

In an effort to circumvent the local film exchanges, the WFS had set out in June 1934 to establish contacts with American and European film companies and with the BFI. These initiatives were supplemented by individual efforts to obtain films by persons travelling to London (a precedent-setting endeavour that would be repeated many times by later members of film societies). During an overseas conference trip 'Home', R.M. Campbell, a committee member (and leading light of the local Fabian Society), had tried without success to procure films. There was a similarly unsuccessful attempt by Miss Foreman of the Wanganui Film Society, who 'attended to the interests of the film societies whilst in England' (Cooke: 6). She did, however, establish contact with Miss Cohen, Secretary of Film Societies Inc., and Miss Harvie, Secretary of the London Film Society. In an imperious manner, Cohen stated that films would not be sent to New Zealand 'until their run is absolutely finished in England and are no longer required by any British film society'. Possible titles included *Le Million* (France, 1931), and three German flms: *Maedchen in Uniform* (1931), *Kameradschaft* (1931) and *West Front 1918* (1930).[36] In more conciliatory mode, Misses Harvie and Cohen did promise, nevertheless, 'to go into the matter almost immediately and try to arrange for a number of suitable films to be sent out to New Zealand for the next winter season … for something under £100 each'.[37]

The entrepreneurial A.S. Fielding also travelled to England in September 1934 and offered to act on behalf of the societies 'until such time as a Federation of NZ Film Societies is formed, when I will be appointed as buying agent of such Federation' (Cooke: 6). A condition attached to his offer allowed him to exhibit the films commercially after film society use. True to his word, Fielding cabled an offer of five films in November at a cost of £50 each, a figure substantially less than that proposed by Miss Cohen. The films were *Kameradschaft, Atlantide* (France/Belgium, 1921)*, M* (Germany, 1931)*, West Front,* and *War Is Hell/Niemandsland* (Germany, 1931). At the conference of the film societies in November 1934, a committee was asked to report on his offer and on the 'advisability of his permanent appointment as Film Societies' representative' (Cooke: 7). In the event, none of Fielding's films were taken by the WFS, although the Christchurch Film Society (CFS) did eventually screen Jean Vigo's striking poetic realist feature *L'Atalante* (1934) and G.W. Pabst's mining drama *Kameradschaft*. These varied attempts to obtain films independently did not lead to a steady supply as Robertson ruefully remarked at the Extraordinary General Meeting in 1936, which had been called to officially disband the WFS:

> Suitable films could only be obtained at a cost beyond the capacity of the society. Purchasing power was at this stage weakened by Societies in other parts of New Zealand not being able to continue to function, a position brought about by their not being in the strategic position of your Society in obtaining supplies locally. The principal difficulty of the overseas market was the freight payable on transit, insurance and the length of time the film would be hired. Also, because of the ban of the Exchanges and in some cases, censorship, it would not be possible to recoup any part of the cost by subsequent commercial screenings.[38]

Although most of the films that the WFS arranged to screen in its inaugural season had come from Robertson's contacts with local distribution companies, contacts had been made with 'kindred Societies in London and Sydney to acquire the use of unusual films of merit'. The creation of the BFI in 1933 gave further hope to the WFS who had every intention of establishing contact with it 'for the purpose of acquiring its films for exhibition here'.[39]

From letters sent by the WFS to a variety of overseas companies in New York, London and the Continent in search of a more regular and independent supply of films, the first to reply was documentary maker and film critic Paul Rotha. Unsurprisingly, given his involvement, he urged the Society to consider the many 'first rate films' from the Empire Marketing Board and the GPO film unit run by John Grierson, and to contact the Federation of British Film Societies. The newly appointed general manager of the BFI, J.W. Brown, also replied in August, but the news was not good: 'We are not at present in a position to offer you very much practical assistance.' He did, however, send a copy of *Sight and Sound* and the *Monthly Film Bulletin* (Cooke: 6). J.M. Harvey, who headed Film Society Ltd. (1925–26), forerunner of the LFS,[40] noted that as there was no import duty on film in New Zealand 'your position becomes much more possible'. As his society was a licensed distributor of films, Harvey offered to talk to European film distribution companies if the WFS appointed an agent. Despite these varied attempts to procure suitable films from overseas distributors, success eluded them; 20 months after its last screening the WFS finally closed in June 1936.

The Film Institutes (1934–39)

The official demise of the WFS and its 'sister societies' in 1936 did not mean the complete absence of any forum where non-commercial interests could express their interest in film. An organisation calling itself the Wellington Film Institute (WFI), which certainly had an instrumental interest, had formed in 1934, not long after the WFS court case. It is probable that in an attempt to distance themselves from this 'scandal', and because their interest was not in the 'art' of film, the newly formed film institute's aims were oriented towards the pedagogical and moral use of films in schools and society. The officers elected to the Institute at its annual meeting in 1935 reflected this more 'conservative' ambition and character: school, church, educational, mother's and women's organisations all had their representatives. Tellingly, the WFS was not included in the roll call of officers invited to join the Institute (*The Dominion* 1935a). The idea for the formation of institutes had originated in Auckland, where the Headmasters' Association had 'formed itself into a body which had as its principal objective the censorship of pictures' (*Otago Daily Times* 1934). Social and moral control of the cinema was one of the objectives the institutes shared in their quest to 'discountenance unwholesome pictures and posters' (*Otago Daily Times* 1934).

Membership was never high: only 23 new members joined the WFI in 1935, and a year later total membership had increased only to 31. Reasons for this limping progress included a lack of advertising, no permanent home and 'a certain vagueness and lack of definition in our aims and objects' (*The Dominion* 1935b). The rather woeful cinematographic ignorance of the Institute's members was signalled with the admission that notwithstanding the poor membership, the executive council had 'usefully employed' the year 'in educating themselves on many matters connected with the cinema so that we now possess a much clearer idea of the lines along which we can usefully work' (*The Dominion* 1935b). Those 'lines' were spelt out as being made up of 'inquiry as to good releases and announcements to the public ahead of good releases so that these will be patronised rather than poor or unsuitable pictures'; the use of educational films in schools and elsewhere, and the introduction of lectures or 'addresses from experts' (*The Dominion* 1935b). The innocuous institute received praise from the film trade, which compared it favourably with film societies whose salient characteristics were their 'pathetic ignorance of an industry into which they were endeavouring to poke an antagonistic nose and their colossal vagueness about the whole reason for their existence' (*The Dominion* 1936). This last remark might have been more profitably directed against the Institute itself with its self-confessed lack of clear direction. However, the Institute had come into being not to criticise the film trade but to curry favour with it, and collaborate as closely as possible in promoting 'better films'.

Its dismal first year of existence did not prevent the Institute from wanting to expand into the other provincial centres. The annual report of 1935 made it clear that a comparable body had formed in Dunedin and that another was 'on the eve of formation in Auckland' (*The Dominion* 1935b). However, the Educational Council in Christchurch was considered adequate by that city to watch over the aims professed by the Wellington Institute, who nonetheless opined that 'before long Christchurch would do as other centres are doing' (*The Dominion* 1935b). Once this had been accomplished, the four would federate as one into a New Zealand Film Institute, 'which might be able to link up with the British Film Institute and perhaps with the International Institute of Educational Cinematography at Rome' (*The Dominion* 1935b). The Institute was still in operation in March 1939 when it organised a screening of health and educational films at the Dominion Museum in Wellington. The work of the League of Nations featured in a film called *Fight for Life*, which described the war on disease; *Children at School* showed some of the work being done in 'special schools and classes in London [which fostered] the creative and artistic spirit of the children' (*The Dominion* 1939).

The notion that film was a form of art received a serious setback with the demise of the WFS. Dunedin followed Wellington in reducing film activities to educational and moral (rather than aesthetic and political) aims when the Dunedin Film Institute (DFI) was established in December 1934. Dr. Sinclair, a committee member, made a study of the recently established BFI. Her report provides additional evidence of the influence of this organisation on the development of the New Zealand film institutes and societies, and deserves comment. Certainly some of its aims were emulated here, although New Zealand has never had a National Film Theatre, or a periodical of the stature of *Sight and Sound*.

Besides wanting to accentuate the positive and eliminate the negative in film production, the DFI sought a closer liaison between 'the trade and cultural and educational interests in the Empire, and also between the trade and public' (*The Dominion* 1939). It valued the BFI as a resource centre 'on all matters dealing with film', although one of the subjects the BFI applied itself to may have been of concern for New Zealand as it brought up the sensitive issue of race and the sometimes harmful consequences of empire. Sinclair noted:

The [BFI] hoped to be able to keep in touch with the various dominions and colonies and to advise certain films suitable for backward races, such as those requiring agricultural tuition and training in the prevention of disease. The institute also aimed at keeping a record of dying things, for the march of Western civilisation was so overwhelming that many customs, costumes and even landscapes were disappearing.'

(*The Dominion* 1939)

The BFI's activities were so extensive that both sophisticated, art-oriented groups and more conservative, moralistic groups could find areas of interest. Obviously the Britishness and cultural status of the BFI made it particularly influential in colonial New Zealand.

As the 1930s went on, the film activities of 'educational' and moralistic groups on the one hand, and left-wing political groups on the other, continued, but there were also small cultural groups with an artistic agenda that met informally. Perhaps the most notable example was a loose organisation that included the film critic Gordon Mirams, who later became Chief Film Censor (1949–59), Stanhope Andrews, editor of *National Education* and the first manager of the National Film Unit (NFU) (1941–50), Michael Forlong, who worked for the NFU, making many films, notably *Journey for Three* (1950), and Jim Harris, a filmmaker who also worked for the NFU. John O'Shea, a towering figure in terms of local film culture and film production, and a student at Victoria University College at that time, described them all as 'Labour Party-type people'.[41] Carrying on the film screening and appreciation begun by the WFS on a less formal basis, O'Shea considered this group to have been politically liberal and 'quite influential' in government circles whern Labour was in office.[42] Many of the screenings took place in homes where, O'Shea recalled, he saw both *Turksib* and *Metropolis*. He also believed they had a copy of Leni Reifenstahl's formidable *Triumph of the Will* (1936), a celebration of Nazi Germany's hosting of the last Olympic Games prior to World War II.

In the late 1930s, O'Shea acted as the liaison between this group and other students, arranging for some of its leading lights, such as Forlong, to come and address the students about the cinema and their left-wing vision for documentary film, which was expressed more widely when Stanhope Andrews became a film critic for *Tomorrow*. O'Shea rather improbably thought that John Grierson's visit to New Zealand in 1940 (actually at the behest of the very English-based Imperial Relations Trust) was the result of lobbying by this 'ginger group', but his interpretation of Grierson's agenda stands up well: 'Grierson was the greatest confidence trick pulled in the world. By talking about the creative interpretation of reality, what he was really talking about was the creative propagation of liberal, left-wing Labour views.'[43]

Grierson was something of a *cause célèbre* to 'progressive' minded people in this country (and the Commonwealth) because of his earlier work producing British documentary film. Before World War II, many of these films and others made by the Shell Film Unit were screened on Friday nights in the lecture hall of Wellington Public Library, and other cities, and continued to be shown during the war by enthusiasts and those left behind as unfit for active service. It is not known whether GPO films by expatriate Len Lye were also screened in New Zealand during the 1930s or 1940s, a period that mobilised left-wing political forces on all sides.

To conclude, the WFS had laid some important groundwork but it had not been able to overcome the existing financial and regulatory problems. It had suffered above all from a lack of public and government understanding of the very concept of a film society. Efforts to educate both the powers-that-be and the public through printed material and official deputations to government and Parliament came up against several insuperable political and cultural obstacles. Unfortunately, not enough progress could be made to sustain the WFS once its association with commercial exhibitors and distributors was sundered through the toxic fallout of the court case. Perennial challenges, such as New Zealand's small population and physical isolation, made it extremely difficult to import enough cinematic variety (experimental, foreign language, 'classics') to sustain a film society programme. Though they had gained some legislative recognition in the amendment to the Cinematograph Films Act, its 'founding fathers' moved on to other fields (Tucker to Sydney, and Robertson to Parliament for a six-year term as Labour MP for Masterton). The film society movement would only recover from the court case and its aftermath in the post–World War II period when like-minded energetic individuals with friends in high places would lay firmer institutional foundations for the development of film culture in New Zealand. However, before this could occur, there was more discursive work to be done in shaping perceptions and understandings of the place that film could play in the new social order that the Labour Government sought to engineer upon being elected into office in 1935, and it is to the radical magazine *Tomorrow*, an important forum of both political and cultural opinion, that this study now turns.

References

Anon. (1933), 'Sunday Shows: Society Charged', *Evening Post* (EP), 21 October.

———— (1933), 'Picture Screening: Film Society Convicted', *The Dominion,* 4 November.

———— (1934), 'Dunedin Film Institute: Successful Inaugural Meeting', *Otago Daily Times* 12 December.

———— (1935a), 'Better Films: Work of Institute', *The Dominion,* 30 April.

———— (1935b), 'For Better Films: Efforts of Wellington Film Institute', *The Dominion,* 27 April.

———— (1936), 'Film Institute's Work: Wellington Organisation Praised', *The Dominion,* 1 July.

———— (1939), 'Film Institute: Screening at Dominion Museum', *The Dominion,* 3 March.

Barrowman, R. (1991), *A Popular Vision: Arts and the Left in New Zealand, 1930–1950,* Wellington: Victoria University Press.

Bassett, M. (1995), *Coates of Kaipara*, Auckland: Auckland University Press.

———— (1997), *The Mother of All Departments: The History of the Department of Internal Affairs,* Auckland: Auckland University Press.

Beaglehole, T. (n.d.), 'Hunter, Thomas Alexander 1876–1953' [Online]. From the *Dictionary of New Zealand Biography*, Te Ara – the Encyclopedia of New Zealand. Available at: http://www. TeAra.govt.nz/en/biographies/3h47/1. Updated 31 July 2003. Accessed: 19 October 2010.

———— (2006), *A Life of J.C. Beaglehole: New Zealand Scholar*, Wellington: Victoria University Press.

Belich, J. (2001), *Paradise Reforged: A History of the New Zealanders from the 1880s to the Year 2000*, Auckland: Allen Lane and Penguin Press.

Cooke, P. (1987), 'Wellington Film Society 1933–4', Unpublished MS.

Dalley, B. and Labrum, B. eds. (1999), *Fragments: New Zealand Social and Cultural History,* Auckland: Auckland University Press.

Dickinson, T. and de la Roche, C. (1948), *Soviet Cinema*, London: The Falcon Press, cited in J. Leyda (1983), *Kino*, 3rd ed., Princeton: Princeton University Press p. 285.

Dictionary of New Zealand Biography (1999), Auckland: Auckland University Press with the Department of Internal Affairs, vol. 4.

Donald, J., Freidberg, A. and Marcus, L. eds. (1998), *Close Up, 1927–1933: Cinema and Modernism*, London: Cassell.

Fairburn, A. R. D. (1935), 'Notes by the Way', *Tomorrow*, 11 December, p. 7.

Firth, C. (1933), 'Russian Film', *Phoenix*, 2(1), March.

Gillam, J. (n.d.), 'Firth, Reginald Clifton 1904–1980' [Online]. From the *Dictionary of New Zealand Biography*, Te Ara – the Encyclopedia of New Zealand. Available at: http://www.TeAra.govt. nz/en/biographies/5f7/1. Updated 31 July 2003. Accessed: 19 October 2010.

Hayward, H. (1936), 'The Churches and the Cinema', *Tomorrow*, 22 July, p. 13.

Hayward, B.W. and Hayward, S.P. (1979), *Cinemas of Auckland, 1896–1979*, Auckland: The Lodestar Press.

Johnson, H. (1934), 'Those Films', *Tomorrow*, 15 August, p. 14.

Leyda, J. (1983), *Kino*, 3rd ed., London: George Allen & Unwin, p. 285.

Martin, S. and Edwards, H. (1997), *New Zealand Film, 1912–1996*, Auckland: Oxford University Press.

McEldowney, D. (1991), 'Publishing, Patronage, Literary Magazines'. In: T. Sturm, ed. *The Oxford History of New Zealand Literature*, Auckland: Oxford University Press.

Mirams, G. (1945), *Speaking Candidly*, Hamilton: Paul's Book Arcade.

New Zealand Herald (1970), Obituary Notice, 13 June.

New Zealand Official Year Book (*NZOYB*) (1960), p. 1160.

NZOYB (1937), p. 486.

Pratt, J. (2006), 'The Dark Side of Paradise: Explaining New Zealand's History of High Imprisonment', *British Journal of Criminology*, 46(4): 541–560.

Samson, J. (1986), 'The Film Society, 1925–1939'. In: C. Barr, ed. *All Our Yesterdays: 90 Years of British Cinema*, London: BFI in association with the Museum of Modern Art, New York.

Sigley, S. (2008), 'How *The Road to Life* (1931) Became the Road to Ruin: the case of the Wellington Film Society in 1933', *New Zealand Journal of History*, 42(2): 196–215.

Sinclair, K. (1991), *A History of New Zealand*, 4th rev. ed., Auckland: Penguin Books, p. 264.

The Best of Whim Wham (1959), 'Pioneer Stock', Hamilton: Paul's Book Arcade, p. 11.

Whim Wham 1943 (1944), Wellington: The Progressive Publishing Society, p. 7.

Notes

1 As a non-profit-making organisation, the individual film societies often had to rely on members' travels abroad to secure films when cooperation with the commercial film exchanges ceased; and relying on the good will of amateurs was an unsustainably haphazard affair.

2 Although the introduction of the Film Hire Tax might have been expected to reduce the amount of amusement taxation in 1930, the marked increase in 1931 is to be attributed to an increase in the tax itself that year.

3   *The Romance of Maoriland* (1930) was billed as New Zealand's first feature-length talking picture. The next New Zealand film was a travelogue shot using a new colour process, Trucolor: *Romantic New Zealand* (1934).

4   A local term that refers to the cultural influence of mainstream New Zealand.

5   Anon. 'Notes on a Deputation to the Hon. J.A. Young, Minister of Internal Affairs', from the Wellington Film Society, IA 1933/55/19. Archives New Zealand. Read Mason appears not to have been related to R.A.K. Mason.

6   Ibid.

7   Ibid.

8   Ibid, p. 1.

9   Read Mason in an interview with P. Cooke, 5 February 1984, in Cooke 1987.

10 The London Film Society (established in 1925 and model of the WFS) had even invited Soviet filmmakers – such as Pudovkin and Eisenstein – to speak to the Society in 1929.

11 *Nous les gosses/Portrait of Innocence* (France, 1941), *Valahol Európában/Somewhere in Europe* (Hungary, 1947), *Los Olvidados/The Young and the Damned* (Mexico, 1950), and two, more sensational, American derivatives, *Wild Boys of the Road* (1933), and *Blackboard Jungle* (1955).

12 Although this film did not demonstrate the more innovative 'cinematic techniques' associated with Soviet silent films, it did contain some vivid scenes. The eminent film critic Catherine de la Roche, who emigrated from England to New Zealand in 1958 and played an important role as film critic, radio broadcaster, and WEA lecturer in Wellington, was struck by 'the night scene on the railway where Mustafa was murdered: the metallic noise of wheels and Mustafa's carefree song, as he rides alone in a rail handcart; further along the line, the stillness of the night, broken only by croaking frogs and the light clinking of tools while the murderer loosens a rail; then Mustafa's distant song becoming louder and louder as he approaches danger'. (Dickenson and de la Roche 1948).

13 Anon. 'Notes on a Deputation to the Hon. J.A. Young, Minister of Internal Affairs', from the Wellington Film Society, IA 1933/55/19. Archives New Zealand.

14 For a detailed cultural history of the prosecution of the Wellington Film Society, see the article 'How *The Road to Life* (1931) Became the Road to Ruin: the case of the Wellington Film Society in 1933', in Sigley 2008: 196–215.

15 'Notes on a Deputation', IA 1933/55/19. Archives New Zealand.

16 The Wellington Film Society (Incorporated), Inwards Letters c.1933–c.1937, IA 1 1933/55/19. Archives New Zealand.

17 Memo for the Hon. Minister of Internal Affairs, 1 September 1933, IA 1 1933/55/19, Inwards Letters c.1933–c.1937. Archives New Zealand. Signed by the Cabinet Secretary, F.D. Thomson, this memo reveals that the WFS prosecution was considered and approved in Cabinet on 19 September.

18 Report of Detective Murray, 29 July 1933, IA 1 1933/55/19, Inwards Letters c.1933–c.1937. Archives New Zealand.

19 The Censor's Office had existed in New Zealand since 1916 when an official censor had been established by parliament in September following 'agitation by women's and church

organisations about the need to protect children from films of a "highly suggestive character"' (Bassett 1997: 88).

20 Young to Franklin, 4 November 1933, IA 1933/55/19, Inwards Letters c.1933–c.1937. Archives New Zealand.

21 Chairman's Report, cited in Cooke 1987: 12; an earlier draft reportedly spoke not of amended legislation but of 'harsh and repressive legislation'.

22 Anon. Report of the Committee of Inquiry into the Motion Picture Industry, April 1934. Appendices to the Journals of the House of Representatives (AJHR).

23 Parliamentary Debates, Vol. 240, 2 November 1934.

24 Ibid.

25 IA 1933/55/3. Archives New Zealand.

26 Ibid.

27 Ibid.

28 IA 1 1933/55/2. Archives New Zealand.

29 T.E. Brown was a nineteenth century British poet, scholar, teacher and theologian.

30 Among other members, Eric Blair, at that time president of the Workers Educational Association (WEA), was one of the first enthusiasts to introduce modern drama to Aucklanders, and was 'hailed by fellow producers as one of the best actors on the New Zealand stage' (*New Zealand Herald* 1970). A.J.G. Stuart was an art critic. The two Tornquist brothers, Fred and Herbert, who both enjoyed success as society photographers, were next on the list. Archie Fisher, the second Director of Elam School of Fine Arts, was a known socialist (Barrowman 1991: 6). Norman Richmond was the Director of Tutorial Classes at the WEA. John Harris was a journalist. Stephen Champ was an English artist employed to teach at Elam. A.F. Goodwin was another staff member at Elam; he was also one of the founders of the People's Theatre. R.A.K. Mason's brother Walter was also there. D.A. Monro had been on the editorial committee of *Phoenix*. In 1948 he was a lecturer in philosophy at Otago University. John Barr, City Librarian and Administrator of the Auckland City Art Gallery, seems to have been a pillar of the establishment.

31 Secretary's Report to the Management Committee, in Cooke 1987: 19.

32 Tucker, 29 September 1933, in Cooke 1987: 20.

33 Report of Detective Murray', 29 July 1933, IA 1 1933/55/19, Inwards Letters c.1933 – c.1937. Archives New Zealand.

34 'Minutes of the New Zealand Conference of Film Societies', 29 November 1933, Cooke 1987: 21.

35 John Robertson, Management Committee Report to an Extraordinary General Meeting, 22 June 1936, in Cooke 1987: 4.

36 *Mädchen in Uniform* (1931), a pre-Hitler sound film, had been a surprising success in London as recorded in a *New Zealand Herald* article (The Screen, its Plays and its Stars, 28 January 1933, p. 10). The film had gone from being screened at the 'art-house' Academy Cinema in June 1932 (German dialogue and the absence of stars marked this film as likely to have limited appeal) where it played for an astonishing six months to around 200,000 people, to a general London release (six months later) where it was shown simultaneously 'at five of the biggest cinemas outside the West End circle'. In one week, 300,000 people

had seen it. The film's 'scandalous' content seems to have been the principal driver in its enduring appeal: a frankly erotic depiction of heterosexual female friendship in an exclusive girls' boarding school, becoming a lesbian romance.

37 Letter, Foreman to Palmer Brown, 2 August 1934, in Cooke 1987: 6.
38 Robertson, 22 June 1936, in Cooke 1987: 9.
39 Franklin's Statement to Detective Murray, 29 July 1933, IA 1 1933/55/19. Archives New Zealand.
40 It became better known as the London Film Society later when others were established.
41 John O'Shea in an interview with P. Cooke, 8 October 1986, in Cooke 1987.
42 Ibid.
43 Ibid.

Chapter 3

Thesis and Antithesis - *Tomorrow* on Film

This chapter focuses on the magazine *Tomorrow*, not in terms of its role as the 'principal forum in New Zealand for the discussion of issues and international developments of left-wing culture in the 1930s' (Barrowman 1991: 27), but in terms of its attention to film. It is an exercise in intellectual history that seeks to relate the texts found in that journal to the contexts that shaped their writing. Obviously its discussions of the cinema often echoed the wider political and cultural debate around the struggle between communism and fascism. Such writings also touched upon many aspects of New Zealand's social environment. Indeed, attitudes to the cinema were in some respects a revealing touchstone to key issues of the period. The cinema was not a neutral territory, a pristine Switzerland. Conflicting ideologies disputed its purpose and practice. There were a number of writers for whom its potential links with realism suited it for immediate enlistment in a battle with capitalism.

Although the film society 'movement' fell on hard times as supply problems persisted during the 1930s, this did not mean that intellectual interest and commentary disappeared; quite the contrary. A new intellectual journal gave expression to an ongoing engagement with the medium. The shortage of films did make it difficult, however, for nascent film aesthetics to develop with any breadth or sophistication. This is an example of the extent to which one aspect of film culture is dependent upon another. What the period did encourage was a closer look at the political aspects of film and its possible educational uses.

The 1930s was a period that saw a great deal of polemical writing by intellectuals attacking commercialised forms of popular culture. However much their sympathies and convictions inclined such writers to an imaginary identification with 'the people', it was *their* definition of the said 'people', *their* judgement of what constituted 'true' and 'false' consciousness, *their* understanding of the differences between 'mass' and 'folk' culture, and *their* division of the world into left and right, high and low, bourgeoisie and proletariat that found expression in the pages of 'the only paper in New Zealand in which vital issues may be freely discussed' (Barrowman: 27). This involved an ongoing tension between sympathy for the 'masses' yet antipathy to many existing forms of popular culture.

If the readership of *Tomorrow* was any reflection of its writers' backgrounds, then it was in no way a working-class one, notwithstanding the attempt to induce such a public to buy it – for 'only the price of a beer' – at the mere cost of sixpence. A progressively-minded middle-class intelligentsia held sway in its columns, composed largely of 'public servants, professionals, educationalists and academics' (Barrowman: 31). The tone and content of the paper, too, conveyed clearly that it was written for an informed, educated public. Founded in 1934 and published initially in a weekly, later a fortnightly, edition, *Tomorrow* was the brainchild of Kennaway Henderson, ably assisted from the outset by two Canterbury University College academics, Professor Frederick Sinclaire and H. Winston Rhodes. This triumvirate became a five-member editorial group with the addition of Denis Glover, a poet and burgeoning printer of Caxton Press fame, and Bruce Souter, an official with the Public Trust Office who acted as the paper's business manager. The mixture of left-wing politics, literature, and academia represented by this group was typical of much 'progressive' cultural activity in the 1930s. Despite the fragility of its financial position, the paper continued publishing regularly until 1940 when the Government effectively suppressed it in May under wartime emergency regulations. The important and innovative role that *Tomorrow* played in New Zealand cultural history as a conduit through which, for example, elements of transnational film culture were filtered justifies a close look first at the main editors and then at the new forms of film criticism developed in its pages.

Henderson, an artist by profession, had arrived in the 'colony' in 1885 at the age of six with his father John and mother Alice. He later earned his living in the 1910s as a caricaturist, contributing drawings of prominent figures and local celebrities in Christchurch to the *Weekly Press* and the *New Zealand Illustrated* (Rhodes 1988: 11). Although he referred to himself as a radical rather than a socialist, he grew up at a time when socialist ideas were starting to attract attention in New Zealand.[1] The writings of Tolstoi, and more particularly his attitudes to war and militarism, remained an abiding influence in Henderson's life, according to his close friends, Leonard Booth and Blanche Baughan (a poet and social reformer), who both testified at his trial in 1918, where he was court-martialled as a conscientious objector and sentenced to two years and nine months of back-breaking hard labour at Paparoa Prison, where conditions for objectors were harsh; he was one of only some 100 or so objectors being held in prison and prison camps throughout the country (Anon. n.d.).

Upon completion of his sentence he left Christchurch, travelling to Auckland where he stayed with his friends Alan and Marguerita Mulgan (Alan was a journalist with the *Auckland Star* and became supervisor of talks with the Broadcasting Service in 1935). It was during his stay with them that he met people who would later come together to establish *Tomorrow* such as Frederick Sinclaire (Rhodes 1988: 27). In 1925, Henderson crossed the Tasman and found work as a caricaturist in Australia. In Melbourne, Sinclaire introduced him to the 'Y Club', with its stimulating dinner discussions about political and social issues. In 1931, Henderson returned to New Zealand carrying the hope of creating a radical but independent journal with its headquarters in Christchurch as a way to generate the type of intellectual nourishment that he still found wanting in his young and raw country.

Born in extremely straitened circumstances in Auckland in 1881, Sinclaire was the son of John Sinclaire and Mary Carson, Irish migrants who arrived in 1867. His family had hoped to prosper but endured, like many thousands of others, the hardships of an economic slump in New Zealand that lasted nearly two decades (Rhodes 1984: 3). At the age of 11, Sinclaire won the Rawlings Scholarship, which entitled the holder to free tuition at Auckland Grammar School. Six years later he won a University Scholarship. In 1903, he was awarded a First Class MA in both Latin and French. Influenced by the ideas of Rev. William Jellie, Sinclaire went to Oxford, where he studied for the Unitarian ministry and gained a First Class in the final examinations in 1907. He capped his Oxford years by winning the Dr. Williams Theological Scholarship, which was open to all nonconformist students. He had a reputation for being 'a man of uncommon ability and very strong character', as well as being aggressively left-wing in politics and a great admirer of Bernard Shaw (Rhodes: 20). He was then appointed Minister to the Eastern Hill Unitarian Church in Melbourne, 'where he served for three years before his outspoken political views finally exhausted the tolerance of his congregation' (Barrowman: 29). Sinclaire became the first minister to join the Victorian Socialist Party, accepted, too, the post of secretary of the recently formed Fabian Society, and was closely associated with *The Socialist*, the journal of the Victorian Socialist Party, which he co-edited (with Marie Pitt) from 1911 to 1913 (Rhodes: 29). Comments that Sinclaire made as a theatre critic for *The Trident* and *The Socialist*, under the pseudonym 'John Tanner' (a character from Shaw's play *Man and Superman*) anticipated his later condemnation of the cinema in his erudite 'Notes by the Way' column in *Tomorrow*. He took a serious stance in his criticism of Melbourne's theatres, which offered 'melodrama instead of tragedy, farce instead of comedy, and vaudeville instead of opera'. In his review of *The Country Girl*, which 'being neither comic nor musical is obviously a musical comedy', he observed that 'as a community, we have no standard by which to judge the worth of a thing except that of its price in the market' (Rhodes: 35–36). He joined with Bernard Shaw in repudiating 'the demon of Americanism', and in comments on the performance of *The Lion and the Mouse* concluded: 'If I were censor, I would incontinently damn all plays containing any allusion to that abomination of desolation known to geographers as America; and I would do this on ethical and aesthetic grounds' (Rhodes: 36–37). This anti-Americanism anticipated his left-wing attacks on Hollywood in *Tomorrow*, which began after he arrived in Christchurch to take up a position as Professor of English Literature in 1932.

It was in Melbourne, in the 1920s, that Harold Winston Rhodes formed a friendship with Sinclaire. This was followed in 1933 by his appointment as Sinclaire's assistant at Canterbury University College where Rhodes arrived with his wife, Sophie, to begin a long and eventful career in the English Department. Rhodes had been born in 1905 in Melbourne, the son of Winifred Mary Short and her husband, Thomas Rhodes, a doctor. (He thus belonged to a younger generation than Sinclaire or Henderson, and was a contemporary of *Phoenix* writers such as Rex Mason, A.R.D. Fairburn, et al.) Switching from medical studies, Rhodes graduated from the University of Melbourne with an MA Honours in English literature. It was at that university that he became interested in politics and was secretary of the Melbourne University Labour Club. He was also involved in the Melbourne Workers' Art Club and joined the local branch of the Friends of the Soviet Union after graduating (Barrowman n.d.).

Soon after his arrival in Christchurch, Rhodes was drawn into discussion with Sinclaire and Henderson about the new independent weekly that the latter was planning to establish. Sinclaire's involvement became increasingly problematic and his association with it diminished after two years as its increasingly left-wing position was articulated. More precisely, his older Fabian and Unitarian brands of socialism differed from the newer pro-Russian forms of Marxism. Rhodes, however, was at ease with the evolving editorial stance and wrote for the paper 'until its demise at the hands of a nervous Labour Government' (Barrowman n.d.). He contributed articles on a variety of subjects – 'the Victorians, the modern novel, Milton, Chesterton, Soviet cinema [and] the cultural climate in New Zealand' (Barrowman n.d.) – in the course of which he espoused a philosophy of humanist Marxism. Rhodes' involvement with *Tomorrow* and, more especially, his articles on the cinema make him an important figure in the writing of a transnational film culture.

The original overseas model for *Tomorrow* was the influential English weekly, *The New Age*. Both Henderson and Sinclaire had been subscribers, 'greatly impressed by its sturdy independence and the quality of its writing and stimulating articles' (Rhodes 1988: 42). A tribute to A.R. Orage (editor of *The New Age*), written by Hilaire Belloc and quoted by Sinclaire after *Tomorrow* had been in existence for more than half a year, could equally apply to Henderson: 'Orage directed what was for many years the only newspaper in England at once intelligent and incorrupt ... The date of this public venture was 1907; and for seven years – that is until the war came to eclipse all intelligent public discussion – he maintained the character of the journal without flagging in any single number' (Rhodes: 42). The parallel with *Tomorrow*'s achievement is striking. *Tomorrow* began in 1934 and for nearly seven years – that is until war came to eclipse all intelligent public discussion – Henderson maintained the character of the journal without flagging. It is salutary to observe how much of the labour involved in creating New Zealand culture in the early years was unpaid – with no Creative New Zealand or university subsidies available in those days. So strong was the desire to establish an intellectual life that contributors wrote on a voluntary basis and editorial boards consisted of unpaid enthusiasts.

Early Film Criticism

The first articles concerned themselves with developing three topics: the moral and political content of film; film censorship in New Zealand; and the absence of critical standards comparable to those at work in literary and theatrical criticism. Of the three, it was the last that provoked the most interesting reflections and suggestions for improvement, although the political content of films ran a close second in this essentially political paper. 'James Sunshine', the pseudonym of a school teacher who may have requested anonymity for fear of losing his job with the Education Department, wrote the first film review in the pages of *Tomorrow* when he roundly denounced the morality of *The Red Ensign* (UK, 1934), a film shown to hundreds of New Zealand school children as a companion picture to *Romantic New Zealand* (*Tomorrow* 1934: 10–11). Sunshine was not concerned with artistic issues since his primary purpose was to expose the bankrupt capitalist morality that informed the film's ideology and to bemoan the effect the film would have on school children. Speaking of the filmic representation of workers, he noted:

It is obvious that the hordes, dishevelled, gaunt and hungry, who flock to the yard gates would take on practically anything short of filling the bunkers of Hades for the sake of a square meal. It is also true that these workers are apt to fall for the kind of virile appeal made by the excellent actor who impersonates Mr Barr.

(*Tomorrow* 1934: 11)

Intellectuals in the 1930s had much to say about working people. But outside of Marxist discourse, it was difficult to find the right rhetoric. Although Sunshine's primary purpose was to attack the film, and his tone was ironic, nevertheless his use of terms like 'hordes' and workers being easily spellbound had an uneasy ring. This representation of the urban poor by middle-class observers such as Sunshine had a long history. In its extreme form, the tradition

represents the urban poor as a cultureless class, lost in the abyss of filth, depravity, criminality and sin. Comparisons were made throughout the nineteenth century between the urban masses living in *terra incognita*, and the 'savages' of Africa. Ungodly, habitually drunk, sexually active from a young age, and physically debilitated – some observers were led to the belief that the degeneration was so extreme that the poorest classes had reverted to an animal state.

(Dodd and Dodd 1996: 42)[2]

The problem was compounded by Sunshine's apparent inability to separate the explicit content of the film from its narrative and directorial strategies. Common to intellectuals at the time, the reviewer's paternalistic sympathy for the masses looked back to the nineteenth-century notion of a 'social conscience'. Such a stance involved, according to Raymond Williams, 'a persistent sense of a quite clear line between an upper and lower class. … It is a matter of social conscience to go on explaining and proposing at official levels, and at the same time to help in organising and educating the victims' (Dodd and Dodd: 42–43). This was a fundamentally different role to (say) Lenin's idea of the vanguard of the proletariat or Gramsci's 'organic intellectuals', though it sometimes leaned towards those Marxist conceptions. The point is not that such a paternalistic stance was wrong or insincere, but that it was a problematic stance for someone seeking to analyse popular culture. A writer needs a complex discourse and a nuanced understanding of how such texts work to avoid the uneasy rhetoric and simplistic moralism of reviews such as this.

It is unfortunate that not much is known of Hypatia Johnson (1908–92) and even more to be regretted that her pioneering film criticism and later teaching (in print, on the radio, and for the WEA) have largely disappeared from the historical record. For the moment, the only surviving example of her thinking is an article she wrote for *Tomorrow*, entitled 'Those Films', in which her defence of the cinema as a form of art was clarion clear, as was her frustration with the censor for prohibiting 'even to our Film Societies' the screening of Murnau's adaptation of Molière's play *Tartuffe*. 'Films and Film Criticism', a course she taught for the Otago branch of the WEA, began in 1937 with 15 people enrolled for 20 sessions. The same course was offered the following year and 'showed a decided increase in enrolments and attendance'.[3] The course was still being taught in 1939 and marks the gradual widening and penetration of intellectual film culture in the 1930s.

By this time Hypatia Johnson had become Mrs. F.R. Thompson. Under her married name she was invited by Alan Mulgan, supervisor of talks on the 'highbrow' YA network, to give a three-part series on 4YA, broadcast from Dunedin. These 'Winter Talks' were an innovation and formed part of the continuing programme for cultural improvement that was a feature of Professor James Shelley's energetic tenure as the inaugural Director of Broadcasting (1936–49) during the first Labour Government's time in office.[4] Her first talk, broadcast on 12 September 1939, took as its subject 'The Educational Aspects of Film', a topic that exerted a significant influence in the Labour Ministry and among educationalists generally. The topics of Thompson's two other talks, broadcast on 15 and 29 September, were in keeping with the article she had written for *Tomorrow* in 1934: 'The Film as an Art' and 'Drama vs. Film'. Although no records of these talks have been discovered, her spirited defence of the cinema against accusations of its close connections with Mammon was demonstrated by the article she had written for *Tomorrow*. Also evident in that article were her wit, intelligence, and learning, exercised with a light touch:

> The much-maligned cinema is a form of art and is to be criticised from that point of view. True it is that its inclusion in the family of the arts may be contested on the grounds that its mother was suspiciously familiar with Commerce, but Shakespeare was a shareholder in the Globe Theatre, and his age was proportionately less commercial than ours.
>
> (Thompson 1934: 14)

'If one were to listen to the addicts of cinema', wrote Frederick Sinclaire, 'one would be forced to believe that it rains masterpieces, and that to be a regular patron of the films is to bathe in a perpetual fountain of goodness, beauty and truth such as all the superlatives in the American language are inadequate to describe' (Sinclaire 1934a: 2). Other than being a ferocious denigrator of the cinema *per se*, Sinclaire also waged an aesthetic war on the inadequate standards of film criticism. However, in a delicious irony that he may have appreciated, given his declared wish to spark debate in this 'land of dreadful silence', his thundering sermons had unintended consequences: the gradual formation of a 'defence' of the cinema by some of his readers, and a plan for developing film criticism. Such a project was not without formidable obstacles given that the 'New Zealand mind [was] so morbidly sensitive to hostile criticism, so nervously respectable, so deferential to outside opinion, so lacking in independence – in a word, so provincial' (Sinclaire 1934a: 2).

One film that provoked Sinclaire's particular ire was Thorold Dickinson and Maurice Elvey's screen version of Richard Brinsley Sheridan's eighteenth-century comedy of manners, *A School for Scandal* (UK, 1930). The film was shown under the auspices of the Christchurch Film Society and Sinclaire had been persuaded to attend despite his 'own forebodings'. He confessed that his knowledge of the cinema was slight but that his prejudice against it was based on experience, as he had 'During the last decade ... paid no fewer than three visits to the cinema' (Sinclaire 1934a: 2). As one of these had been 'by mistake' and the other two 'under suasion from enthusiasts', it seemed he had never attended a film on his own initiative. But let us not accuse Sinclaire of superficiality just yet (a reader of his column will do that for us soon). He was an apocalyptic critic, according to the definition of this type given by Umberto Eco in his analysis of intellectual reactions to the rise of 'mass civilisation'. In his terms, Sinclaire was a representative of a misunderstood humanist tradition:

> What [such a critic] is displaying here is not an act of personal dishonesty, but a mental vice which has claims to nobility – and which is often justified on account of its desperate good faith. It will come as no surprise, then, when the apocalyptic critic derides the suggestion that the mass media (like machines) are instruments, and as such may be instrumentalized. For in reality, the apocalyptic critic refused from the outset to examine the instrument and to test its possibilities (1995: 47).

These comments highlight the kind of problems a morally earnest highbrow critic had in coming to terms with modern popular culture; and those problems were exacerbated by both the 1930s sense of political urgency, and the particular environment in New Zealand where all forms of high culture struggled to survive. In this situation, an intellectual like Sinclaire was not going to waste any energy attempting to understand or to draw fine distinctions within popular culture. Sinclaire supposed that in Sheridan's day 'the performance of his comedy must have occupied from three to four hours. At any rate it was nutriment for the whole evening. What I saw the other night lasted barely an hour, which ... seemed unconscionably long' (Sinclaire 1934a: 1). Sinclaire was determined not to return to the cinema 'this side of the grave'. The single saving grace of the evening for him had been that he now knew what was meant when a film was 'recommended for adults'. This provided him with another opportunity to lambaste the present: 'An adult, for the purpose of this recommendation, is a person who unites the mental capacity of a child with the prurience and vulgarity of a decivilised modern' (Sinclaire 1934a: 1). Sinclaire still retained something of the style of the preacher. We should remember, however, that this was a troubled age when many eminent intellectual figures – from the Frankfurt School to T.S. Eliot, D.H. Lawrence, W.B. Yeats, and Ortega y Gasset – delivered sweeping diagnoses of what was wrong with the modern world. Many of those diagnoses focused on the increasing influence of popular culture via the mass media. Sinclaire continued in this vein in his next film critique two months later when he nostalgically compared the cultural wasteland of today with the splendour of yore.

Yet while I was still a schoolboy I had seen Kryle Bellew's company in three or four Shakespearean plays, and in the *School for Scandal*, and I had been, with the school, to see Rignold in *Henry V*. I had also seen the Broughs in several of the best modern comedies then offering – the work of Wilde, Pinero, and Jones … In the three or four years following my schooldays, I saw, besides melodrama and musical comedy and farces, a least a dozen Shakespearean performances, including several different *Hamlets*. These performances, in what was then a third-rate provincial town, were, broadly speaking, on the same level of excellence as what we might have seen in the larger cities of the world.

(Sinclaire 1934b: 3)

Clearly, Auckland was not then the cultural desert it had become in 1934 when the conquering cinema swept the travelling players and their repertoire from the stage, setting up shop in their stead. Sinclaire saw his beloved high culture (writers he was passionate about, such as Milton) being submerged beneath the rising tide of a popular taste represented by the songs of American crooners on the ZB stations, and comic book characters from 'that abomination of desolation known to geographers as America'. Film played a key part in the rise of this new Babylon: 'The cinema is a school of vulgarity and imbecility, and its lessons are being absorbed everywhere. Only a fool or a knave could be cheerful about the effect of these lessons' (Sinclaire 1934b: 3).

'A fool or a knave' duly arrived in the person of Henry Hayward who shrewdly took issue with Sinclaire's denunciation of the cinema:

One week F.S. decapitates the hydra-heads of Capitalism: the next he slays the Australian Federal Government for its unfair usages of its Immigration Language Test. Last week he executed the cinema – and it is as dead as mutton, and without any "sure or certain hope of resurrection". Then he scattered its ashes to the winds.

(Hayward 1934: 19)

Hayward had an intimate knowledge of the commercial cinema in terms of distribution and exhibition, as he had been one of the first to establish it on a national scale in New Zealand, eventually owning or leasing 68 theatres employing 800 people (Hayward 1944: 104). With the onset of the Great Depression, his exhibition circuit had collapsed, but by the early 1930s he had re-established himself on a reduced scale in Auckland, and had initiated several projects to increase the range of films available to a variety of publics. He was, for instance, one of the patrons of the Auckland Film Society in 1933, which organised its infrequent screenings at his 'theatre for the intelligentsia' in Remuera. Hayward represented a more complex and ultimately more productive attitude to culture that rejected rigid distinctions between high and lowbrow, or uplift and entertainment. He was the New Zealand equivalent of sophisticated cinema-owners in Britain such as Sydney Bernstein who was both a patron of the London Film Society and the manager of popular cinemas.

In contrast to the 'apocalyptic intellectual', Eco posits another category, the optimistic response of the 'integrated intellectual'. Hayward can be seen as an example of this type:

'Not least because, if apocalyptics survive by packaging theories on decadence, the integrated intellectuals rarely theorise. They are more likely to be busy producing and transmitting their own messages in every sphere, on a daily basis. The apocalypse is a preoccupation of the dissenter, integration is the concrete reality of non-dissenters' (1995: 29).

While Eco's account points to some limitations in the 'integrated' approach, it was certainly a more productive perspective in relation to the development of film culture in New Zealand. It pointed towards a style of media analysis that implied a respect for local complexities and a practical commitment to local activism (growing the culture from within). Hayward wrote frequently on behalf of the cinema and worked energetically to introduce films into New Zealand that would appeal to a variety of publics. He saw the rise of popular culture as a process of wider democratisation. In his letter to the editor, he asked: 'But was the stage of 1904 the glowing temple of Art and Beauty [Sinclaire] would have us believe? In contradistinction to the "school of vulgarity and imbecility" that he says the cinema of 1934 is?' (Hayward 1934: 19). Hayward's query was far from being merely rhetorical.

His riposte drew on facts from *The Australian and New Zealand Stage Annual for 1904*. In that year, 28 theatrical companies had toured Australia and New Zealand, only one of which had played Shakespeare in only three towns of the 28 visited. For the most part, and excluding two musical shows, the 27 other touring companies performed melodrama and 'included such examples of the Theatrical Art and Beauty as *The Face at the Window, The Stranglers of Paris, The Worst Woman in London, The New Magdalene, The Painted Woman, The Man They Could Not Hang*, and others of the same type' (Hayward 1934: 19). Hayward pointed out that the 'once in a blue moon' performance of Shakespeare generally spelled ruin to the average theatre and that although some films might be 'vulgar and imbecilic', they could not 'plumb the depths which Melodrama reached in the golden days of F.S.' (Hayward 1934: 19).

Hayward, in the terminology of 'brows', was somewhere in the upper middle and was obliged to defend the cinema from many types of critics: 'The Churches with the ceaseless wail for censorship, and still more censorship; the highbrows, who with tip-tilted noses, profess contempt for most things common folk enjoy – and the journalistic freelances who tilt at any windmill they see' (Hayward 1934: 19). The cinema was, in his apt phrase, the 'Poor Man's Theatre', which brought 'to untold millions happiness, contentment and forgetfulness, and is their antidote to the cruel economic and social injustices that *Tomorrow* is so bravely fighting' (Hayward 1934: 19). His use of the words 'happiness, contentment and forgetfulness' would be used against him by left-wing critics engaged in waking 'the masses' from their cinema-induced narcotic slumber. It is interesting that pleasure was not a value advocated by many intellectual critics in the grim years of the Depression. Hayward was clear about its importance.

He was particularly incensed at the hypocrisy of the arguments used against the cinema when critics expected it to be of a standard comparable with the long evolution of the other arts, or that it should conform to a single standard when there was a variety of publics with a variety of expectations.

> The Cinema, like the Bookshop or the Music seller, has to cater to a wide gamut of taste ... Why should the cinema be expected to reform itself to the ideals of the few superior highbrows who seldom patronise (which is a good word) the picture houses, and who, when the occasional artistic film comes along – still stay away, and allow it to pass unnoticed like a "ship in the night"?
>
> (Hayward 1934: 19)

The last point has always been a matter of particular annoyance to those involved with film (or television) exhibition.

New Zealand's Labour Government, in the latter part of the 1930s, did consider ways of raising the standard and variety of films available to the public, which was a programme Hayward agreed with, and in later articles written for *Tomorrow* he explored the possibility of a system where the state might subsidise cinemas (as they do in France) and participate in the distribution and exhibition of films. The control of culture, both he and Sinclaire agreed, was too important to be left in the sole charge of capitalists. Such arguments reflected the sense of paternalism still strong in the 1930s and a confidence in the Government's cultural leadership, combined with awareness (at least in Hayward's case) that government intervention was necessary in a country with a small and fragile market.

While the moral and aesthetic values symbolised by Disney's Mickey Mouse threatened many intellectuals who saw a vulgar age of comics and cartoons replacing the literary tradition symbolised by Shakespeare,[5] what Hayward understood, but they did not, was the way cinema would help to keep that very tradition alive among the popular audience. Shakespeare's romantic tragedy *Romeo and Juliet*, for example, has been filmed many times, from Ernst Lubitsch (1920) to Baz Luhrmann (1996). Sinclaire and Hayward's controversy did not end there. Hayward observed wryly in another letter to the editor that it was incumbent upon a critic to have actually seen what he was criticising. Sinclaire had already admitted to having ever seen only three films prior to 'enduring' the screening of *School for Scandal*, and to make his point, Hayward quoted a passage from one of Sinclaire's favourite writers, G.K. Chesterton:

> I think a man may praise Pindar without knowing the top of a Greek letter from the bottom. But I think that if a man is going to abuse Pindar, if he is going to denounce, refute, and utterly expose Pindar, if he is going to show Pindar up as the utter ignoramus and outrageous impostor that he is, then I think it will be just as well perhaps –

I think at any rate it would do no harm – if he did know a little Greek, and had even read a little Pindar.

(Tomorrow 1935a)

Defending the Cinema

We cannot know what plans the editorial committee of *Tomorrow* had made concerning articles on the cinema prior to this debate. In order to protect the identities of many of the paper's writers, Henderson destroyed most of the documents he held when the Labour Government caused the paper to shut down. In practice, the attempt to develop serious film criticism proved to be a complex process. In particular, the contributors of *Tomorrow* had to find ways to critique popular culture without leaving themselves exposed to the very effective counter-attack that Hayward had mounted, in effect accusing Sinclaire of highbrow snobbery and out-of-touch assumptions.

In his 'Notes by the Way', Sinclaire had thrown down a critical gauntlet in talking of the inadequacy of aesthetic standards in film criticism in the press, which was literally true as nobody had ventured to set themselves up at this early stage as a public film critic – Gordon Mirams would not appear regularly in the pages of the *NZ Listener* until the end of the 1930s. Now *Tomorrow* began publishing attempts at serious film discussion, starting with an anonymous essay on Robert Flaherty. This began by reassuring readers that it was a mistake never to go the pictures: 'While a good deal of the adverse criticism that has appeared in *Tomorrow* is justified and more than justified, nevertheless entertainment and useful social knowledge are both obtainable in these places for approximately one shilling' (*Tomorrow* 1935a: 8). The film discussed – though primarily as a negative example – was Flaherty's ethnographic documentary *Man of Aran* (UK, 1934), a genre he had virtually invented with *Nanook of the North* (USA/France, 1922). Flaherty's work had raised extremes of enthusiasm and criticism. He had been reproached for his flights of exotic fancy, his predilection for distant lands and small human communities; his rejection of social forces, his political disengagement, his 'Rousseauism' and, graver still, his 'special effects', or confusion of facts and fiction in his use of re-enactment – in reality, Nanook hunted with a rifle and not a harpoon; sharks had not been hunted on Aran Island for 50 years; the missionaries had forbidden both dancing and tattooing in Samoa. Flaherty explained his approach judiciously: 'At a time when it was still possible, I wanted to create a document about these people that could be archived, so that we could see the human spark that distinguished them from all the others'[6] (*Dictionnaire du cinéma* 1995: 254). His films were made in long and intimate collaboration *with* the people he filmed, not in the fashion of an entomologist observing insects with a supposed dispassionate objectivity, so Flaherty did not have any qualms about recreating former conditions. He was concerned not merely with naturalism but with 'celebrating man's grandeur caught in this struggle and this multifarious dialogue with nature, from which civilisations are born' (1995: 254).

Tomorrow's reviewer, however, showed little interest in Flaherty's merits – he focused on his limitations. The film was used as an object lesson in how not to make a contemporary documentary. Damnation through dubious praise came early in the piece when it informed the reader that the US National Board of Review had declared *Man of Aran* the best film of the year, and that it had also received 'the highest commendation from Signor Mussolini' (*Tomorrow* 1935a: 8). Given the prevailing leftist tide of anti-American sentiment and outright opposition to fascism, this 'praise' came from ideological adversaries. Flaherty's trickery was evidenced in a malicious rumour: the islanders had forgotten how to hunt with a harpoon and the producer had lent them one for the film. However, the most heinous charge levelled against him was that economic forces had been overlooked in favour of natural ones:

> The conflict between the islanders and their savage environment was made the dominating motive force for their activities, whereas a little consideration would show that their main enemy is neither the sea nor sharks but those economic conditions in their islands and on the mainland which prevent them ... from making a decent living as fishermen.
>
> (*Tomorrow* 1935a: 8)

By implication, Flaherty was as guilty as any Hollywood producer in using the medium to promote false consciousness: *Man of Aran* was a romantic fantasy that masked unpleasant economic facts.

In his first defence of films, H. Winston Rhodes noted that the cinema was in need of protection both from its enemies and its friends, as the recent controversy between Sinclaire and Hayward demonstrated. Rhodes rehearsed some of the common complaints made against the cinema: that it was the illegitimate offspring of the legitimate stage with certain mechanical disadvantages; that it was an independent art form appropriated by commerce to coin money for the few; that it was in its infancy and lacked technical resources, qualified artists and qualified critics. Overseas film critics would have challenged all these arguments, but Rhodes had evidently had only a limited exposure to such debate.

New Zealand was handicapped by a shortage not only of world cinema but of sophisticated film criticism. Understanding the material and discursive constraints of the local context makes other statements by Rhodes more comprehensible. For example: 'Few have bothered to concern themselves with the way in which a film is made. Fewer still have kept pace with the latest artistic developments' (Rhodes 1935: 11). Yet Rhodes was not unaware of intellectual film culture and regretted rash judgements about the cinema *in toto*, such that moralists and ill-informed critics could either 'condemn the cinema lock, stock and barrel', or regard it 'as nothing more than a mechanical means of providing mass amusement' (Rhodes 1935: 12). In the idealising ferment of his age, he noted how fortunate it was that film societies and overseas cinema magazines were 'treating the cinema as it should be … and preparing … for the time when it will be an educational and artistic force in the community' (Rhodes 1935: 12).

Quoting Eisenstein's remark that the cinema was the art of the future, Rhodes, a Marxist, took issue with Hayward's 'Poor Man's Theatre' definition of the cinema because more needed to be done to make it 'an adequate theatre for the poor man' whose taste was standardised and debased. It was inappropriate to talk of the 'happiness, contentment and forgetfulness' it brought to untold millions without noticing that critical standards were required to categorise what sorts of happiness, contentment and forgetfulness were operative, because some of it 'was good, some bad [and] some indifferent' (Rhodes 1935: 11). The social implications of the cinema's influence needed to be made clear because it remained 'a potent influence for evil'.

In further response to Hayward's defence of film, Rhodes fumed that 'it was sheer humbug to pretend that all hostile criticisms of the cinema come from highbrows', which was not quite what Hayward had said. Displaying his familiarity with overseas film magazines, Rhodes quoted from David Schrire's article in the autumn issue of *The Film Quarterly* condemning *Man of Aran* as 'evasive documentary' because it focused on nature rather than on society (the correct alternative approach taken by the Russians and by John Grierson):

Man's struggle with nature to wrest from [it] his means of subsistence has lost importance to-day. It is his struggle for the right to divert what he has produced to the interests of humanity that is the vital question. And it is there that the documentary has the justification, in truthfully depicting modern economic relationships, in rendering audiences conscious of their interests, of their economic claims, aware of their remedy. That is the true sphere of the documentary if it is to serve the most urgent purpose beyond itself.

(Rhodes 1935: 11)

Extending the journal's cultural remit with regards to forming another type of spectatorship and taste, 'Observing Ernest' (O.E.) began a regular column of film reviews entitled 'Sound Films and Silly Ones' at the end of July 1935. It appeared regularly until 4 March 1936 when differences between O.E. and the editorial committee over the role and nature of the cinema became too great. The rise of fascism in Europe and the increasingly Marxist stance of the journal had by then made his style of reviewing seem inadequately political. During its period of operation, however, the column served as a touchstone to many of the ideas then 'in the air' around film, illustrating the struggle to develop aesthetic standards in film criticism within the left-wing environment of the 1930s.

The editorial committee made it clear that in making motion pictures the subject of a regular feature of the magazine, their aims ranged 'from increasing our readers' enjoyment of picture shows to counteracting the vicious social-political-economic propaganda content generally present in films' (*Tomorrow* 1935b: 2). Evidently the pleasure principle had to be balanced by a healthy dose of 'reality'. The paper also saw itself as called upon to attack 'the star racket', which put actors on pedestals for the crowd to worship leaving directors with insufficient attention and credit. This practice inhibited 'the development of the true technique of film making, for the film is more than a photographic record of plays' (*Tomorrow* 1935b: 2). The proper apportioning of credit would open viewers to the 'full realisation of what is potentially one of the greatest cultural instruments of all time' (*Tomorrow* 1935b: 2). This desire to attribute authorship to the director revealed two motivations: it countered the tendency to deprecate the cinema as being artless because its production was both collective and industrial; and it challenged the ability of Hollywood to manipulate audiences through their imaginary identification with stars. The reigning left-wing theory of audience response to the products of mass production attributed an unwholesome passivity to the consumers of film. Anything that roused a passive public from this state could create in them a critical awareness to counteract Hollywood's influence. The need for *auteur* theory was thus based on Marxist premises. There was, however, a potential contradiction in Marxists using the individual basis of *auteur* theory to challenge industrial production.

The Importance of Documentaries

By the mid-1930s as British documentary film grew in critical stature, more were made, with some addressing pressing socio-economic concerns. They attracted increasing international attention as the movement, spearheaded by Grierson, reached abroad to spread the gospel. *Tomorrow* added its voice to the evolving international debate. 'Documentary and Reportage' explored the 'cinematographic origin of the documentary fashion in art' (*Tomorrow* 1935c: 18). While the presence of 'fashion' in the title suggested something transient and fleeting, Rhodes believed that the documentary was here to stay, as it provided a vital means through which audiences could connect documentary (art) to life (lived more fully). In looking closely at the art of filmmaking, Rhodes' cinematic vocabulary had been enriched. To the critically important idea of montage, he now added a broad concept of documentary: 'films which deal with current social struggle, events, scenes and people, photographed without distortion' (*Tomorrow* 1935c: 18) (a curious definition as it overlooks what are inevitably subjective aspects of construction in any documentary).

For Rhodes there were two strands of documented fact, one of which we may call a humanist realism. This strand provided, in the taxonomy of Colin Crisp, 'an unmediated reality offering itself to human experience' (1993: 241). Films that captured life in this authentic way had a 'vitality' that others lacked; they were truer, fresher, and in direct contact with 'reality'. The second strand, social realism, 'implicitly or explicitly rejects any notion of an unmediated or universal truth and sees reality as primarily social and ideological and therefore the site of struggle' (Crisp: 241). There were realities that *should* be shown, truths that needed to be told to power and the realist filmmaker's obligation was to speak out on those matters. Rhodes did not choose between these strands as traces of each can be found in his promotion of the documentary genre.

This second strand often had a left-wing bias, an idea echoed in Rhodes' complaint that documentaries of the type he required, dealing with 'social themes which are of vital importance to us all', would not get made because 'film is so entangled with the interests of big business'. This is Manichean reasoning on Rhodes' part for it implies that documentaries are good or bad according to their sponsors or their politics. Publicly funded documentaries are surely as susceptible to critique as commercial ones. Rhodes was also inconsistent in not questioning the state-sponsored documentaries that Grierson produced at the Empire Marketing Board and the GPO because of their association with the capitalist state. Rhodes' polemic reached higher still when he wrote of the 'conspiracy of silence and suppression' that surrounded depictions of 'man's struggle with man, man's struggle with economic forces' (*Tomorrow* 1935c: 19). His call to arms ended with an appeal that found concrete expression in 1941 with the formation of New Zealand's National Film Unit:

> Even in a small country such as this there is no reason why the attempt should not be made to form an organisation for the production of New Zealand documentary, a valuable weapon in any attempt to remodel society. It is being done elsewhere.
>
> (*Tomorrow* 1935c: 19)

Rhodes' essay helps us to understand why the documentary genre became so important in the 1930s. As film theory, however, his essay is undercut by the unconvincing nature of its principal distinctions. Realism was a central concern of New Zealand culture, but it was seldom theorised in a complex way. Perhaps the lack of filmmaking in New Zealand was one of the reasons for this, since knowledge of the complex processes involved in documentary tends to act as a strong remedy against simple judgements on the grounds of subject matter or explicit political position.

Rhodes returned to the need for local documentary production in 'Keeping it Dark' (*Tomorrow* 1935d: 15). Such production would serve two purposes, one linked with the larger issue of the Popular Front, as an amalgam of disparate leftist forces tactically united against war and fascism, and the second with the need to provide information and analysis as an alternative to the propaganda of the ruling class. In addition to the discussion clubs formed by 'shadowy radicals', Rhodes stressed the need for 'small groups of active workers prepared to devote their energies to certain specific problems' (*Tomorrow* 1935d: 15). He called for the creation of Workers' Art Clubs, 'capable of producing stories, articles, or drawings dealing with New Zealand social themes', and Workers' Film Clubs 'to devise ways and means of producing New Zealand documentary' (*Tomorrow* 1935e: 15). At this point, Rhodes' 'big picture' thinking began to dominate the discussion. Control of the mass media was critical. He felt that radio was an even bigger political threat than either the press or films, as there was 'a very great danger that the air will become a more powerful means for standardising the masses of the people' (*Tomorrow* 1935d: 15).

The Labour Party, too, recognised in radio a powerful means of communication, 'culminating in the Labour Government's 1936 decision that broadcasting be run by the state' (Day 1994: 1). Labour's desire to do this was stimulated by the belief that the privately owned press was politically conservative and therefore unfavourable to its policies. Control of the airwaves meant that 'Radio became a new way for representatives to communicate with the electorate, for rulers to talk to the governed. [A] system of national news broadcasts, prepared through the Prime Minister's Department, was set up, and generally radio was used by the Government to communicate directly with the people' (Day: 4). A massive penetration of radio receivers into domestic space occurred in the 1930s and made the state-owned broadcasting service a major source of entertainment, education and information. Left-wingers were divided between those who saw Labour's firm control of radio as a safeguard against some local form of fascism developing, and those who saw it as a capitalist defence against radical ideas. When the National Film Unit was created, it would come to reflect the same tensions, with left-wing filmmakers such as Cecil Holmes struggling to make 'progressive' documentaries rather than government propaganda.

The Cinema and Education

Another of Rhodes' interesting essays, 'Training in Film Criticism – from School to University' (*Tomorrow* 1936: 22–25), addressed the need for critical media education, obviously an area of particular relevance for him as an educator. Without using the specific idea of 'film culture' he was obviously thinking in similar terms in his advocacy of film production, film criticism, and film education, as mutually reinforcing developments. Rhodes feared the rise of the mass media, seeing in it not an expression of 'folk' or popular culture, but the moneyed manipulation of capitalist exploiters. The task, therefore, was to lay the foundations for the construction of a critical film culture capable of resisting the 'standardisation' of emotion produced by the purveyors of a false popular culture. In educational terms, Rhodes' proposal was ahead of its time.

In the first part of his essay, subtitled 'Who Controls Education?', he explained that the development of a critical awareness of one's social environment was largely ignored by the institutions whose responsibility it had once been: 'Our schools and universities are not producing people capable of applying any standards of criticism they may have learnt to the life they will be forced to live and the influences which will be brought to bear on them' (*Tomorrow* 1936: 22). Students studied Shakespeare and could compose an essay on eighteenth-century comedies, but could this knowledge be used to critique the film comedies of the day? The problem was that whereas education had sometimes concerned itself with the popular art of the past, it did not concern itself enough with the popular art of the present, and yet the vast majority of people absorbed lessons about life from popular art. It was clear that the traditional transmitters of culture (church and school) had lost much of their influence when culture passed into the hands of 'the manufacturers of popular art' (*Tomorrow* 1936: 22).

His second section, 'The Film and its Critics', set out the arguments used by a variety of 'critics' and explained why resistance to the forces of 'standardisation' was needed in education. It was 'worse than useless to talk as though any form of popular art had no bearing on educational methods and objectives, as though the cinema provided entertainment which has no part to play in fixing values or communicating impressions' (*Tomorrow* 1936: 22). The 'immorality' of films lay not in the representation of 'certain acts, gestures, or types of men and women on the screen', but, and far more seriously, 'in a standardised emotionalism which passes for human emotion, and is accepted as such' (*Tomorrow* 1936: 23). The answer, for Rhodes, was one that the liberals in most western societies since the nineteenth century (such as Matthew Arnold in England, Ernest Renan in France, and Wilhelm von Humboldt in Germany) had advocated to guide the working classes towards an active participation in society – an education that adequately armed them for life.

From today's perspective, Rhodes was making a fruitful proposal for media education, though it was based on what today we would describe as an 'inoculation' approach. What was unusual about his attitude was the fact that he at least took film seriously enough to call for educators to pay close attention to it. He found few to share his belief that film, for all its failings, was clearly 'an independent art, as distinct from ordinary dramatic art as dramatic art is from narrative' (*Tomorrow* 1936: 23). Ever the activist, Rhodes noted that those who admitted that the cinema was an escape did not notice that this was an implicit criticism of everyday life, which called for analysis and action.

The crux of his argument against the purveyors of 'pop' culture was that they did not really represent popular taste: 'In other words, for the first time in history, popular art is below the level of popular taste … because it is not really popular art at all but a commercialised substitute brought into existence in the days when the people have no art of their own' (*Tomorrow* 1936: 23). Umberto Eco's Gramscian derived analysis of the same phenomenon is strikingly similar:

> [The masses] way of enjoying themselves, of thinking and imagining, does not originate from below; it is suggested to them instead through the mass media in the form of messages formulated according to the codes of the ruling class … members of the working class consume bourgeois cultural models believing them to be an independent expression of their own class (1995: 45).

This kind of analysis (appearing in early Birmingham School Cultural Studies) has lost some of its conviction today. We are more aware of the 'active audience', and inclined to suspect that the critics' own cultural sympathies prevented them from appreciating the vibrant, energetic, in-your-face flamboyance of pop culture. (Admittedly, Eco himself went on to write more sympathetically of popular culture.)

The tension between art and politics was supposedly reconciled by the Soviet filmmakers, who showed that montage in the service of progressive politics was exactly what the medium had been waiting for. (Rhodes gave no indication of having read other film theorists such as Munsterberg, Delluc, Epstein, Kracauer, Balázs or Arnheim.) It was in the 'Cutting Room' that the artistic principle of the cinema found expression, as 'the photographer-artist weaves his ideas about life into sound and sight' (*Tomorrow* 1936: 24). As editing created the film event, the cinema became more than just a mechanical device. Rather, 'It is art because only the artistic imagination can build up ideas as well as stories out of the separate shots of the camera' (*Tomorrow* 1936: 24). This kind of over-emphasis on montage was typical of much left-wing film criticism of the period; it was of limited use in coming to terms with many aspects of sound-era cinema.

At that time, entry into the pantheon of the arts required each art form to exhibit medium-specific attributes, which was why Rhodes reassured his readers that progress in developing cinematic specificity had already taken place in Europe, thanks to certain films and the publication of small periodicals such as *Close Up, Film Quarterly,* and *Experimental Cinema*. Also, film societies had been established to 'ensure a public for the more interesting film experiments' (*Tomorrow* 1936: 24). Meanwhile, what was being done in New Zealand to inform teachers 'of the real and genuine cinema' in an age where, he claimed, 'minds and emotions are being standardised?' (*Tomorrow* 1936: 24). This speaks to an Arnoldian concept of high art and its dual role as bulwark against the toxic effects of culture in an age of mechanical reproduction and as substitute to a decline in the transfiguring potential of religious belief. Limited as his views were in some respects, Rhodes was ahead of most of his New Zealand contemporaries in his engagement with the medium.

Other Contributions

Debates about the cinema increased in the pages of *Tomorrow*, in response to the arguments about its social and artistic importance advanced by contributors such as Rhodes. Letters to the editor on the subject grew in number, as did the variety of articles and 'notes' written by other contributors. Leading poet A.R.D. Fairburn, whose occasional contributions to discussions on film had hitherto focussed on the idiocies and ineptness of the film censor, now gave voice to more generalised reflections about individual films and the cinema *per se* in the 'Notes by the Way' column he had inherited from Sinclaire. Henry Hayward wrote two lengthy articles, the first of which looked at the churches' relationship with the cinema, while the second concerned itself more broadly with the place of cinema within the community and what could be done to improve the film environment through greater state control of distribution and exhibition. His nephew, the filmmaker Rudall Hayward, contributed an article on film as a social art.[7] A regular film column, called 'Film Digest', appeared from October 1937, and E.S. Andrews, soon to be the first head of the National Film Unit, began writing essays on film in March 1939.

State control was a key topic of serious debate at this time. It was very much on the political agenda after the election of the first Labour Government, with its plan to intervene more directly in the economic and social life of the country in order to alleviate the hardships of the Depression, and to provide New Zealanders with more security. To protect farmers from price fluctuations, it introduced state-guaranteed prices for dairy produce, and later assumed complete control over the marketing of butter and cheese exports. Manufacturers were protected from overseas competition through a system of licensing and by the creation of a new Bureau of Industry. The Reserve Bank was nationalised. Broadcasting, internal airways, and the linen flax industry were also part of the growing list of state monopolies (Sinclair 1988: 275–77). The Government did not neglect cultural production and consumption. A Film Committee was set up in January 1937 to look at ways of improving the public's access to 'films of high quality and standard, which combine cultural and educational features without detracting from the entertainment appeal'.[8] Consequently, there was frequent discussion in *Tomorrow* about possible government moves in the media area.

To point its public in the direction of intellectual film culture, *Tomorrow* published a select annotated list, put together by the Otago Branch of the New Zealand Library Association, of books and periodicals on film now available (*Tomorrow* 1937a: 443). Although, as we have seen, some individuals subscribed to overseas periodicals devoted to the cinema, such as *Close Up*, it is fascinating to learn that some New Zealand public libraries were offering interested readers the following material by 1937: *This Film Business*, R. Mussel, 1928; *Film Technique*, V. Pudovkin, 1929; *The Film Till Now*, P. Rotha, 1930; *Film*, R. Arnheim, 1933; *Film Form*, S. Eisenstein, 1935; *Film Acting*, V. Pudovkin, 1935; *A Grammar of the Film*, R. Spottiswoode, 1935; *Plan for Cinema*, D. Bower, 1936; *Documentary Film*, P. Rotha, 1936; *World Film News*; *Sight and Sound*; and *Film Art*.

Some 20 months after 'Sound Films and Silly Ones' had ceased appearing, 'Film Digest' took its place on 27 October 1937. It consisted of summaries of the opinions of independent Anglo-American film critics who had seen some of the films that would later be shown in New Zealand. In a sense this was an astute development as it exposed the readership of *Tomorrow* to the opinions of seasoned film critics whose writing was informed by the more diverse cultural climate of metropolitan centres; it also illustrates the transnational spread of Anglo-American film cultures in a New Zealand willing to absorb their influence. The practice of collecting favourable foreign reviews became a much-emulated habit that local film societies later adopted as they sought to attract members for their screenings.

The ostensible *raison d'être* of 'Film Digest' was as antidote to the self-serving 'puff pieces' prepared by theatre managers to attract audiences through newspaper advertising. There was as yet no independent film critic in the daily press, 'and only occasionally are men such as Mr. Gordon Mirams encouraged to give candid reviews' (*Tomorrow* 1938: 286). 'Film Digest' took its critical cues from such overseas press as *Time and Tide*, *The Spectator*, *The London Mercury*, *The Observer*, *The Times*, *The World Film News*, *The Christian Science Monitor* and *The New Yorker*. 'Film Digest' also drove home the message articulated by Rhodes about the cultural importance of the cinema in personal, social, and national identity formation. The impact of films on the cultural life of New Zealand children was illustrated in a story concerning a group of 30 Christchurch girls. They had been asked to write a review of any book they had read in the previous four weeks. Only two did so, the others saying that they had had no time or did not like reading. When asked a week later to review any film they had seen recently, 'twenty-seven girls wrote film reviews which were more or less intelligent'

(*Tomorrow* 1937b: 59). The message was that education – as Rhodes had said – needed to include film criticism. 'Film Digest' recommended an American 'twenty-six page study guide prepared for school children on the film of Kipling's story *Captain Courageous*' (*Tomorrow* 1937b: 59). The formative power ascribed to this educational material was considerable, enabling children 'to grow up demanding better films and with the ability to take what good there is in a picture and weave it into their own lives' (*Tomorrow* 1937b: 59).

From April 1938, the 'Film Digest' appeared only monthly, as there were 'not many films worth noticing', and then ended in early December of the same year. *Tomorrow* then opened its pages to a young man of enthusiastic and combative temperament, E.S. Andrews, whose essays on film, beginning in March 1939, enlivened the journal's commitment to understanding the cinema differently. Andrews' participation in the growth of film culture in this country (as critic and producer) has been so little commented on (he has no entry, for example, in the *Dictionary of New Zealand Biography*), and what he said in his columns so reflected the *zeitgeist* of the period that we should end the chapter with a closer look at his work. His career illustrates the importance of being a film enthusiast before becoming a filmmaker. If the Louvre in Paris was Picasso's school, and the *Cinémathèque française* was its equivalent for the 'young Turks' of *la nouvelle vague*, then Andrews' position as film critic for *Tomorrow* was a comparable, albeit less romantic, form of preparation for his leadership of the National Film Unit.

Andrews had been a member of the Wellington Film Society in 1933 and a teacher prior to becoming editor of the New Zealand Educational Institute's monthly *National Education*, in which he also wrote about film, notably documentary. He also commissioned Gordon Mirams to write a series of articles on film appreciation, republished talks (by Grierson, for instance) and texts relating to film and education from such British organs as the BFI's *Monthly Film Bulletin, Sight and Sound,* and the Scottish Film Education Association (see, for example, Mirams 1938: 238–39; Grierson 1939: 242–44; Wilson 1939: 310–11; Miles 1940: 128–29).

The evident gusto of his essays relieved the earnestness of his left-wing views (which perfectly suited *Tomorrow*'s biases). However, being an opinion leader did not come easily to Andrews as the ironic tone of portions of his first essay, 'Previews are Fun', reveals. In part this can, no doubt, be attributed to the distrust that egalitarian New Zealand culture engenders in any who set themselves up as 'experts'. The implication for film criticism was reluctance in many quarters to get 'too technical' because it was felt that knowledge should be accessible to all. This attitude had its counterparts in other ex-colonies. Compare Marcus Cunliffe's essay on 'The Conditions of an American Literature' in which he writes that early American culture and society were sometimes 'socially and intellectually too unitary for [their] own good, or at any rate to nourish a rich imaginative life' (1986: 14). Because of its egalitarian levelling, the United States,

> while cherishing a belief in its progressive moral superiority to Europe, lagged behind culturally, and that this discrepancy placed particular strains upon the American ideology which – mingled as ideologies are with grosser considerations – insisted that knowledge

should be accessible to all, and that claims to professional expertness were 'aristocratic' (1986: 6–7).

Andrews did, however, overcome his uneasiness on this point and developed into an articulate and sophisticated critic. He contributed lengthy articles (five over the year, of two to four pages each), and wrote very much using the first person singular: a voice had been found. More than any one else up to this point, he gave detailed information about cinema technique. He wrote about cinematography, editing, direction, sets, and acting. Not that he neglected the film's narrative, for in the more familiar *Tomorrow* style he added accounts of the story and its morality as seen from a left-wing perspective. Overall, his enthusiasm and commitment to film reflected an interest that was not only theoretical, and not merely practical. Here was a person studying and writing about films with a view to making them. Although his circumstances could not have been more different, his basic situation was similar to that of the young French film critics who wrote for *Cahiers du cinéma* in the 1950s prior to embarking upon the *réalisation* of their desires when they created *la nouvelle vague*. The act of writing about film was for them, as it became for Andrews, the necessary prelude to their *passage à l'acte*.

'Baa Baa Black Sheep', the title of his third article published on 5 July 1939, was held by John O'Shea to have 'very effectively skewered a centennial film on wool growing made by the Government Film Studios' (1996: 16). Andrews' principal complaint was that there was no directorial vision behind 'the collection of pictures which, as stills, would find a place in any photographic exhibition' (*Tomorrow* 1939a: 560). Not only was there no one to tell the obviously competent cameraman what shots to get, the film lacked any comprehensive understanding of the uses of editing in creating a more dramatic impact to the story.

It was now considered acceptable, even mandatory, after the stirring impact British and Soviet documentaries had created, to make dramatic documentaries, and this was exactly what this earnest reviewer advocated. Andrews' analysis of the film involved a mental re-shooting of it, as when he told his readers of the proper way to film the shearers so as to convey the energy and nature of their labour. Clearly this was modelled on Eisenstein:

> The camera should have been close down by the shears, getting an eyeful of the blades gnashing their teeth at each other heaven-knows-how-many times per minute. It should have been closely watching a muscle-rippling forearm guiding the clippers round the sheep, catching something of the beauty of the fleece so deliberately folding itself away from the strangely gaunt body.
>
> (*Tomorrow* 1939a: 560)

Writing during a period when New Zealand–born artists and intellectuals were looking to define themselves in relation to local temporal and spatial coordinates, Andrews' dissatisfaction with the film's commentary signalled his cultural nationalism as he scorned the

> cultural voice and copy-book English [that] finally destroyed what faint smell of the soil might have clung to the picture. New Zealand farmers are not comic-opera yokels … they

can speak for themselves, some of them with deep, rich voices and a wealth of country metaphor.

(Tomorrow 1939a: 560)

Commenting on another scene that he thought might have been an 'exciting little passage' had it had any connection with the story, Andrews' self-conscious use of technical vocabulary introduced his readers, for the first time in the pages of Tomorrow, to some of the terminology used in making films.

> The camera swung smoothly (yes, 'panned') across a middle-distance landscape scene, moving through about 45 degrees from right to left to pick up a figure of a girl on a horse in the background. Cut. Close-up of girl from low-level (nice-looking, too). Cut again. Then the camera swung back the other way to follow the girl riding across the same landscape – a neat though hackneyed pattern.

(Tomorrow 1939a: 560)

Strangely, for someone whose published enthusiasm for Soviet cinema fitted his politics, his review of the powerful anti-Nazi film *Professor Mamlock* (USSR, 1938) was rather subdued and confined itself, principally, to resuming the plot and summarising the story; it was also his shortest, consisting of a single page. In this article, entitled 'Jude…', Andrews took the obligatory swipe at the Hollywood dream factory whose congenital incapacity for realism and honesty meant that even Warner Brothers' *Confessions of a Nazi Spy* (1939), looked 'slick and flimsy beside it' (*Tomorrow* 1939b: 768). He was also mindful of the then contemporary pertinence of 'a film that has some direct connection with the affairs that are overshadowing our daily round of jobs' (*Tomorrow* 1939b: 768). However, he admitted that his exposure to Soviet cinema had been slight, consisting largely of documentaries that celebrated the social and industrial progress in the Worker's State, along with the very occasional fiction film.

It was something of an event to be able to see *Mamlock* at all in September 1939 as one of the cinematographic consequences of the non-aggression pact signed between the Soviet Union and Nazi Germany on 23 August 1939 was that the USSR stopped distributing all films that attacked the German Government and Hitler. In foreign countries, distributors holding the terminable rights to the same Soviet films had the films removed from circulation. In those instances where the rights had been sold outright, however, '[*Mamlock*] continued to be shown for a while, giving courage to the badly shaken anti-fascist forces, disconcerted as it became clear that the Soviet Union was determined to respect the letter of the pact' (Leyda 1983: 356). *Mamlock* was one of three strong anti-Nazi films made by the Soviet Union prior to this. Before the pact, leftists everywhere had been proud of the USSR's courage in so directly challenging Germany. Although *Tomorrow* defended the pact along tactical lines (the Soviet Union was giving itself time to prepare for the eventual clash with Nazi Germany), Andrews made no mention of it in his article. And yet the relative brevity and the muted enthusiasm of his article incline me to think that he was puzzled and perhaps troubled by this reversal in the party line.

'Jude…' was Andrews' last article in *Tomorrow*. The outbreak of the war was the beginning of the end for the journal, which had struggled gamely to continue publishing for almost seven years. Although it was, in the words of the historian, Keith Sinclair, 'a periodical which for a time played the role of the *New Statesman* to the Labour Party', and had campaigned in Labour's favour during the two general elections it won in the 1930s, it found itself increasingly further to the left than the Government would allow. Internal struggles for power within the Labour Party over a successor to Prime Minister Savage became evident when *Tomorrow* published an article by Labour's 'stormy petrel', John A. Lee (then Under-Secretary for Housing), entitled 'Psycho-pathology in politics' in December 1939. This was immediately recognised as an attack on the ailing Savage, who was dying from cancer, although only a select inner circle of people knew this. Lee was expelled from the Labour Party during the annual conference in March 1940. Peter Fraser, the dominant figure in the party, and soon to be elected prime minister by his colleagues after Savage's death, lost little time in leaning heavily on *Tomorrow*. Although no official charges were ever brought against it, a more devious method of suppression was devised: the printers of the paper were advised that under wartime regulations they might be in danger of being prosecuted for publishing seditious material. That warning was sufficient and *Tomorrow* ceased appearing.

In a country already sorely pressed to develop its own high culture, it is obviously regrettable that intelligent comment on the cinema should have thus been silenced. Though its contributors always struggled to reconcile artistic with political priorities, *Tomorrow*'s overall coverage marked a step forward for New Zealand film culture in several respects, and its closure temporarily stalled an intellectual development that was starting to gather momentum. The first Labour Government did, however, engage in significant cultural development, including initiatives in the field of film, as the next chapter documents.

References

Anon. (1935a), 'Letters to the Editor', *Tomorrow*, 16 January.
—— (1939a), 'News from the ZB Stations', *NZ Listener*, 10 November, 1(20), p. 46.
—— (1939b), 'News from the ZB Stations', *NZ Listener*, 22 December, 1(26), p. 52.
Anon. 'Pacifist Objection – Conscientious Objection in the First World War', n.d. [Online]. Available at: http://www.nzhistory.net.nz/war/first-world-war/conscientious-objection/ religious-objection. Updated 15 October 2008. Accessed: 2 September 2010.
Andrews, E.S. (1939a), 'Baa Baa Black Sheep', *Tomorrow*, 5 July.
—— (1939b), 'Jude …', *Tomorrow*, 27 September.

Barrowman, R. (1991), *A Popular Vision: The Arts and the Left in New Zealand, 1930–1950*, Wellington: Victoria University Press.

——— (n.d.), 'Rhodes, Harold Winston – 1905–1987' [Online]. From the *Dictionary of New Zealand Biography*, Te Ara – the Encyclopedia of New Zealand. Available at: http://www. TeAra.govt.nz/en/biographies/4r13/1. Updated 1 September 2010. Accessed: 10 September 2010.

Cunliffe, M. ed. (1986), *The Penguin History of Literature: American Literature to 1900*, volume 8, London: Penguin Books.

Crisp, C. (1993), *The Classic French Cinema*, Bloomington and Indianapolis: Indiana University Press and IB Tauris (London).

Day, P. (1994), *The Radio Years: A History of Broadcasting in New Zealand*, Auckland: Auckland University Press.

Dodd, P. ed. (1982), *The Art of Travel: Essays on Travel Writing*, London: Frank Cass, pp. 64–68.

Dodd, K. and Dodd, P. (1996), 'Engendering the Nation: British Documentary Film, 1930–1939'. In: A. Higson, ed. *Dissolving Views: Key Writings on British Cinema*, London: Cassell.

Dorfman, A. and Mattelart, A. (1975), *How to Read Donald Duck: Imperialist Ideology in the Disney Comic*, New York: International General.

Eco, U. (1995), 'Apocalyptic and Integrated Intellectuals: Mass Communications and Theories of Mass Culture'. In: R. Lumley, ed. *Apocalypse Postponed*, London: Flamingo.

Grierson, J. (1939), 'The Dramatic Factor in Education', reprinted in *National Education*, 1 July.

Hayward, H. (1934), 'Letters to the Editor', *Tomorrow*, 19 December.

——— (1944), *Here's to Life*, Auckland: Oswald-Sealy.

Leyda, J. (1983), *Kino*, 3rd ed., London: Princeton University Press.

Miles, R.S. (1940), 'School Films: Some Practical Matters', *National Education*, 1 May.

Mirams, G. (1938), 'Propaganda in News Films', *National Education*, 1 July.

'Observing Ernest', (1935b), 'Sound Films and Silly Ones', *Tomorrow*, 31 July.

O'Shea, J. (1996), 'A Charmed Life: Fragments of Memory and Eextracts from conversations'. In: J. Dennis and J. Bieringa, eds. *Film in Aotearoa New Zealand*, Wellington: Victoria University Press.

Otago Branch of the New Zealand Library Association, (1937a), 'The Film: A Select Annotated List', *Tomorrow*, 12 May.

Passek, J-L. ed. (1995), *Dictionnaire du cinéma*, Larousse: Paris.

Rhodes, H. W. (1935), 'From Jaegers to Films', *Tomorrow*, 30 January.

——— (1935c), 'Documentary and Reportage', *Tomorrow*, 23 October.

——— (1935d), 'Keeping It Dark', *Tomorrow*, 20 November.

——— (1936), 'Training in Film Criticism: From School to University', *Tomorrow*, 18 March.

——— (1984), *Frederick Sinclaire: A Memoir*, Christchurch: University of Canterbury Publication.

——— (1988), *Kennaway Henderson: Artist, Editor and Radical*, Christchurch: University of Canterbury.

Sinclair, K. (1988), *A History of New Zealand*, Auckland: Penguin.

Sinclaire, F. (1934a), 'Notes by the Way', *Tomorrow*, 3 October.

——— (1934b), 'Notes by the Way', *Tomorrow*, 5 December.

Thompson, F.R. (1934), 'Those Films', *Tomorrow*, 15 August.

Sunshine, J. (1934), '*The Red Ensign* (Or Scoundrels & Co.)' *Tomorrow*, 1 August.

W.B.H. (1937b), 'Film Digest', *Tomorrow*, 24 November.

——— (1938), 'Film Digest', *Tomorrow*, 2 March.

Wilson, N. (1939), 'The Cinema and the Teacher', *National Education*, 1 September.

Notes

1   William Pember Reeves wrote articles on both communism and socialism when he was editor of the *Lyttelton Times* in the early 1900s; Pat Hickey introduced the doctrines and policies of the Syndicalists and a short time later the Federation of Labour, the 'Red Feds', was formed in Christchurch, with branches established on the West Coast by Hickey.

2   The Dodds are summarizing F. Schwarzbach's '"*Terra Incognita*" – an Image of the City in English Literature', in Dodd (1982).

3   WEA Annual Reports, 1938, p. 36.

4   In 1939, the 'commercial' ZB network had a series entitled *Behind the Silver Screen* that looked at the technical production of Hollywood films by the many different studio departments (*NZ Listener* 1939a: 46). Another feature programme, *The Great Goldwyn*, combined 'racy biography, Goldwynian wit and Hollywood history' (*NZ Listener* 1939b: 52).

5   For a modern revision of this argument in terms of cultural imperialism, see Dorfman and Mattelart 1975.

6   Cited by Amengual, B. In: *Dictionnaire du cinéma*, p. 254. My translation.

7   Henry Hayward's article appeared in *Tomorrow* on 16 March 1938, pp. 304–97; Rudall's two months later on 11 May (pp. 443–44).

8   Draft of 'Culture in Films' from the Film Committee, IC 1 27/1/1. Archives New Zealand.

Chapter 4

Public Policy and Private Enterprise

The Labour Party's victory in the elections of December 1935 was a boon to the destitute, the sick and the elderly, and heralded a new era in New Zealand as the Government began to create the world's first comprehensive welfare society in which citizens (rather than consumers) had their well-being safeguarded for life. More vigorous and extensive intervention by the state into the economic and social life of the country came to be seen as natural. The concern for social welfare expanded to include a somewhat paternalistic attitude to culture at large. Of particular interest to this study were the measures taken to offer wider choices with regards to the types of film available in New Zealand and the attempts to 'educate' the public's appreciation of the cinema. The campaign treated the cinema as a vehicle of popular entertainment that needed to become more of a pedagogical tool. This involved moving to a discourse of education rather than a discourse of art, although there were some opportunities for those involved in film art to hitch a ride with education. This was an interesting exercise in social engineering, a state initiative in comparison with the various public and commercial initiatives that dominate other sections of this book.

After documenting the Government's activities, this chapter will also examine the transformation of Natan Scheinwald from wool exporter to film importer, with positive consequences for film culture; and track the début of Gordon Mirams' film column in the *New Zealand Listener* (1939), an initiative that owed much to Labour's cultural activity. My introduction will have particular regard to Mirams' support for the films that Scheinwald imported in the months that preceded the German invasion and occupation of France in May 1940. This chapter will thus explore not only public initiatives based on a suspicion of the commercial film business, but also some fruitful interaction between public and commercial interests.

Institutions and Agents

Appointed to head both state-controlled media – the YA radio network and, later, the *NZ Listener* – was former academic and WEA stalwart, James Shelley, who took up the new position of Director of Broadcasting in 1936. He also became the Chair of a Film Committee set up in January 1937 to investigate how the state might improve the range and quality of films available in New Zealand. The Government saw its mission as regulating or moderating the somewhat sordid activities of capitalism.

An informal conference called to discuss the quality of films available to the public took place on 18 January 1937, under the patronage of D.G. Sullivan, Minister of Industries and Commerce, as the Government worked towards defining a strategy that would enable it to exert some control over the consumption of popular film culture. A detailed account seems justified as the conference was so revealing of the new Government's attitudes and the proposed role of the state in the growth of film culture. Attending the conference, aside from Shelley and the Minister, were J. Robertson (former office holder with the Wellington Film Society and now an MP), W. Tanner (the film censor), R.G. Butcher (General Inspector under the Cinematograph Films Act and committee member of the Wellington Film Institute), and F. Johnson (from the Department of Industries and Commerce). Sullivan reminded the participants of the Government's desire to improve the 'culture of the mass of the people' as well as their economic situation, and alluded to certain 'ideals' that the Government wished to realise (a veiled reference to the idea of nationalising film supply in the country through state ownership).

One view that arch conservatives, paternal liberals, and zealous leftists had in common was a concern over the fact that commercial interests brought into the country only those films that would make money with no regard to the cultural uplift of the 'masses'. The 'better quality pictures', which 'naturally' (as Sullivan felt) originated in England and Europe, did not receive the attention they deserved. Sullivan even felt obliged to 'confess that it was rather an extraordinary type of business as the ordinary standards that guide people in business [did] not seem to apply to the picture business, [which had] its own standard of business morals and outlook'.[1] Several attitudes seemed to lie behind Sullivan's hostility to the film business – a preference for Britain over America, a left-wing suspicion that popular films conveyed right-wing propaganda, and a commitment to high or middlebrow over popular culture.

Sullivan asked each of the participants to express their point of view with regards to the desirability of elevating popular taste and the possibility of getting a better supply of pictures from other sources to offset the preponderance of American films. Shelley was first with his views. The absence of independent film criticism to give guidance to the public was a concern that he was contemplating remedying through the broadcasting service. There was, however, a snag. Shelley did not know where to find such a person who would into combat go, single-handedly, like some latter day St. George, to raise 'the standard of film criticism for the good of the Dominion'.[2] Eventually Shelley did find his critic, and he turned out to be far more than simply a government lackey. But Gordon Mirams' accommodating temperament and Fabian Socialism basically suited the new era's zeitgeist, and while he appears not to have simply tailored his approach to the Government's agenda, he sympathised with the cultural values shared by Shelley and the Labour Party.

The second of Shelley's observations to the Minister concerned the film supply problems that the Christchurch Film Society had encountered while he was president. It was not possible for the CFS to undertake the risk and expense involved in importing films from England. During his American sojourn he had seen *The Road to Life* in Chicago, which was just the type of educational film that should be available in New Zealand. Its Russian origin was immaterial as films ought not to be banned simply because they came from a particular source. Having seen this film in the United States, he wondered why a similar freedom did not exist in New Zealand, 'which is free or supposed to be free'.[3] He also cited the liberty that American universities enjoyed; in Seattle, the University of Washington had shown films from Germany and France and used any profits from such events 'for the advancement of drama classes in the university'.[4] A theatre lover himself, this pragmatic use of film must have appealed to him with particular force; a considerable increase in drama production became 'a hallmark of Shelley's National Broadcasting Service' (Day 1994: 251–52).[5]

As local film societies could not afford to import films, the Government should assume the guise of a beneficent angel of culture, making happen what commerce would not. The Government's role in this regard would not only be to the film societies' advantage but could help to raise the tone of films for general exhibition. Commercial interests, in Shelley's view, underestimated both the intelligence of the public and their capacity for appreciation; they catered and pandered to 'baser' human nature by supplying lewd and violent visual tales. A 'good' film like *Disraeli* (1929) that had done very well for Warner Brothers at the box office demonstrated that there was an unsatisfied public desire for this type of more serious drama. It is clear that the value ascribed by Shelley to such films was less aesthetic than pedagogical and moral. Shelley's emphasis on these two terms was shared by many Labour intellectuals. His attitude had the advantage of 'rehabilitating' the cinema from widespread highbrow disdain but the disadvantage of viewing it in a way that was instrumental and not artistic or film-specific.

If the educational potential of the cinema could be shown, then the Labour Government would be in a stronger position to intervene in the interests of the public. The implied equation was 'state control of film supply equals education'. What needed to be proved before such a radical step could be taken was the existence of a number of 'good' films not released here because of narrow commercial interests. Shelley and Robertson were of the opinion that there were, although they could not support this contention by hard facts and figures. Robertson understood that New Zealand's small population base meant it was not commercially profitable to show minority films to the extent that could be done in larger countries 'with different classes of people, and where there is always a certain section of people that will form an audience to see a picture of [the educational] type'.[6] In an indirect condemnation of America, whose film industry had dominated the world since World War I, he also argued that the cultural values attributed to the cinema in Europe were in short supply in Anglo-Saxon countries, which tended to consider the cinema as mere entertainment. This assertion was, however, belied by the English Films Bill of 1927, for example, which recognised that film was an 'important instrument of propaganda for British culture, British policy and British industry' (*The Economist* 1937). Such legislation was evidence that politicians, as well as media critics and Marxists, were convinced that films were an important vehicle for moral and political ideology.

The Minister had heard of 'thirty or forty first-class continental pictures shown in England [that had] not been shown in New Zealand', and wanted to know what could be done to secure a reliable supply of this type of picture.[7] (English approval was still, it seemed, the highest possible accolade.) R.G. Butcher, General Inspector under the Cinematograph Films Act, replied that so far as English-speaking films were concerned, New Zealand got most of them, and that what did not get shown here was not significantly better. His participation in one of the educational conferences organised by the Wellington Film Institute had led him to the conclusion that it was with children that one had to begin to effect changes in film appreciation, and that schools needed projectors. Related to this idea was the need to build up an educational library of films, and it was Butcher's strong opinion that the Government should undertake this task. The Minister, impressed with Butcher's suggestions, asked those present to constitute themselves into a committee as he wanted to do 'whatever was possible and to use this great and wonderful contrivance for the advancement of the culture of the people'.[8] (The last phrase was typical of the link in Labour philosophy at the time between democracy and improvement.)

When it met again on 19 April 1937, the Committee had increased in size with the appointment of Dr. J.W. McIlraith, Chief Inspector of Primary Schools (representing Peter Fraser, Minister of Education), and R.W. Fenton, Manager of the Government Film Studios at Miramar. The Order of Reference was:

1. To investigate what additional sources of supply of high quality films are available from European countries, which combine cultural and educational features without detracting from the entertainment appeal;
2. What steps of a practical nature can be suggested for the use of motion pictures in schools for educational purposes? In this connection it is desired that the Committee should explore fully the capabilities of the Government Film Studios to produce a proportion of films suitable for this purpose;
3. To explore the feasibility of putting into operation for the greater control of the industry in the national interest, a plan under the provisions of the Industrial Efficiency Act, or, alternatively, the distribution of films under the control of a Department of State;
4. To consider the suggestion that the criticism of films should be included in broadcasting programmes;
5. Any other matter which in the opinion of the Committee is desirable to give effect to the Prime Minister's desire to use the exhibition of films to improve the culture of the people.[9]

This was a remarkably progressive programme – film culture seemed to be on the point of becoming a state priority. This was a moment in political history similar to the debate in 1999–2002 over a possible charter for TVNZ. As on that later occasion, political realities would clash with cultural ideals; and 'entertainment' would prove hard to reconcile with education.

Countries mentioned as providing a percentage of suitable films were Japan, Russia, Germany, and France. Shelley suggested that the language problem could be overcome with the use of captions (i.e. subtitles) in English. (This was a very costly process and many films remained bounded by linguistic barriers.) Robertson pointed out that were they to procure suitable films, their exhibition would prove difficult under the existing commercial operation. The Committee were of the view that the only 'reasonable solution of the present distribution of films in New Zealand would be the substitution of State control'.[10] This controversial solution continued to receive support even at this high level of government. After all, education and broadcasting were in government hands, why not cinema? In today's terms, there had been 'market failure', depriving New Zealanders of a necessary 'public good'.

So far as broadcasting film criticism was concerned, the Committee made recommendations of lasting significance: that the National Broadcasting Service (NBS) be requested to provide film criticism that drew listeners' attention to films of educational and cultural merit; that a review of the selected films be prepared in Wellington and sent out to the other provincial centres at least one week before the dates set down for showing the films; that the NBS employ an 'officer' to do this work and that he work in close liaison with Tanner so as to hear the censor's opinions on films worthy of attention; and, finally, that a publishable version of the reviews be incorporated in a film section of the broadcasting journal, *Radio Record* (the privately owned forerunner of the *NZ Listener*, which was established in June 1939). These were to be 'in the nature of literary articles and more definitely educational in their trend'.[11] (In this discussion, terms like 'artistic', or 'cultural' were always dependent upon educational and moral priorities.)

However, the radical proposals championed by Robertson were judged politically too difficult. State control of film supply did not eventuate and only some of the more modest suggestions were realised. A memorandum to Sullivan, dated 23 September 1937, recommended that the Census and Statistics Department regularly collect statistics from individual theatres and film exchanges regarding attendance, box office receipts, film hire and any other general information so that the Government might deal more knowledgeably with the industry; this useful idea was adopted and such statistics began to be collected in 1938.

The recommendation that Finance Minister Walter Nash look into foreign film supply during his English, European, and American missions yielded no clear dividends. On his trip to Moscow, F. Johnson (Assistant Secretary, Industries and Commerce) and G.W. Clinkard (NZ Trade and Tourist Commissioner in Europe) accompanied Nash to a meeting with the director of Soyuzintorgkino. He suggested that they contact the American and English agencies of the Soviet Union, Amkino and Arcos, respectively, to obtain films for exhibition in New Zealand. Back in London, Johnson contacted Arcos and learnt of the company's recent and impending release of Soviet films. There were not many titles to choose from and there were difficulties facing public exhibition of Russian films, such as the quota system which favoured British films, and the public's preference for films with all-English dialogue. Film societies, whose members looked at film from the point of view of art, were the only reliable audience for Continental, and, very occasionally, Japanese films. This British experience, always an influential precedent for New Zealand, must have seemed discouraging.

However, the New Zealand Trade Commissioner in Canada had more luck with Amkino, which sent a selection later shown to members of Cabinet and a select audience in January 1938 (*Auckland Star* 1938). The documentary and fiction films included in this private screening were *Beethoven Concerto* (1937), *Gypsies* (1936, documenting their transformation into collective farmers), *The Thirteen* (1937), *Happy Youth, Singing Puppets, Dance Festival* and *The Animal's Club*.[12]

A notable feature of this short list was the total absence of those feature films, both silent and sound, that had so enthralled European and American intellectuals at film society screenings. This indicated that film-as-art was not on the Government's agenda, that films had to be broad enough to appeal to 'the people', and that their educational value was of paramount importance. Absent, too, were the 30 or 40 European feature films shown in England that Sullivan had mentioned during the January conference. Pragmatists within Cabinet had had the final say in film supply. The Film Committee's recommendation that a 'film expert', whose job it would be to source films that elevated popular taste, accompany Finance Minister Walter Nash on his missions in 1936–37 was not approved by Cabinet, who entrusted inexpert civil servants to carry out this task. Thus, New Zealand missed out on the possibility of some kind of National Film Theatre (an institution that has been established in the United Kingdom, France, Australia, and other countries).

A Film Committee report, 'Culture in Film', was given to Sullivan in January 1938. Based largely on a report written during Nash's time overseas, its principal focus was the English film industry's responses to American dominance, and the use of films in schools in England and Europe, particularly Fascist Germany. The number of schools equipped with projectors gave a quick indication of the importance that films had for education. Compared to the modest 700 in operation in Great Britain, Germany had 15,000; France, Czechoslovakia, and the United States each had about 10,000, while Italy and Russia made 'extensive use of films in schools'.[13] The German method of regulation for the compulsory showing of 'culture film' in theatres recommended itself to the author(s) of the report, who had studied German film legislation to understand the institutions that carried out the state's intentions. The cultural importance attached to film had seen the creation of the *Reichsfilmkammer*, operating under the *Reichskulturkammer*, who issued certificates allowing the screening of a certain number of films annually.

In addition, the wonderfully named Ministry for Enlightenment and Propaganda authorised the screening of films from countries that Germany approved of. Each programme shown at a theatre had to include a short film whose subject had been chosen by the authorities and approved by the censor, as either artistic, or national and educational, or cultural, or of political value.[14] To ensure uniformity and compliance with the national standards set by the *Reichskulturkammer*, a cultural director supervised their activities in each of the different districts of the Reich. Film producers followed the ideological lead set by the *Reichsfilmkammer* 'and the cinema public is educated to give as much attention to the cultural type as would naturally be given to the entertainment type'.[15]

Ironically, this Nazi model held some appeal for the Committee as it seemed to perfectly match the New Zealand Government's heavy-handed desire to 'advance the culture of the people'. Of the many different English and 'Continental' methods studied in the report, including information on the BFI, the German method of 'encouragement' of culture films was seen as the most effective for 'the peaceful penetration of culture and there is weighty evidence in support of its introduction in the Dominion'.[16] This enthusiasm serves as a reminder of how careful public policy must be once it starts to head down the path of propaganda.

The National Film Library

R.G. Butcher's suggestions to the Minister of Industries and Commerce back in January 1937 at last had a positive outcome when the National Film Library (NFL) began operation in 1942 with Walter Harris at the helm. Harris and the NFL played a significant role in the post-war fortunes of the revived film societies. At a time when educational improvement was a dominant concern of the Government, it is not surprising that this was the aspect of film culture that benefited most strongly; but, thanks to a few individuals with a broader perspective, art was to some extent able to 'piggy-back' on this development. (Synergy is an important aspect of cultural growth.)

Since the history of the NFL has not been well recorded, it seems useful to quickly document it here, along with the story of Walter Harris who deserves greater acknowledgement for his achievements. In 1932, when he was working at the Christchurch Technical High School, he was asked to teach geography even though he had received no training in that discipline.[17] He reflected that, fundamentally, geography was concerned with people in places and their interaction with the environment. Textbooks at the time gave him precious little information about either of those subjects. Harris, therefore, had his students examine Christchurch and its environs simply by going outside the classroom. This method obviously had its physical limits, as one could not access remoter places or foreign countries. Passing in front of the Kodak shop in Colombo St., Harris noted photographs, a small 16mm silent film projector, and a notice that advertised short films for hire or purchase. The manager, G.B. Tomkinson, was sympathetic to Harris' predicament and agreed to come to the school to show black and white films of strangely dressed people inhabiting territories far removed from New Zealand. The success of this initiative, and the generosity of Tomkinson who lent his films free of charge, meant that Harris' geography class came 'alive'. He continued to borrow the projector, thereby allowing his pupils to see more of these stimulating films. Their unusually creditable performance in the Government exam aroused the curiosity of the Education Department who enquired why this school, not noted for its scholarship, had done so well in geography.

In 1936, Harris was appointed lecturer in geography at Christchurch Teachers' Training College and faced a problem comparable to that which had confronted him several years earlier as he contemplated the best means for his teacher trainees to stimulate the interest of their future classes. A variety of physical and visual aids could be used to excite curiosity, but he deemed the best teaching aid to be sound films, which were largely unavailable in New Zealand at that time. However, Harris soon received a visit from Stan Porter, representing Educational Sound Films (Wellington), who demonstrated the efficient Bell & Howell 16mm sound film projector. Educational Sound Films also had a small lending library of films produced in the United States by Encyclopaedia Britannica available for hire. The College principal lent his support to the purchase of a projector and within a short time they were hiring films on a variety of subjects.[18]

Dr. C.E. Beeby, who joined the Department of Education in 1938 and became its director in 1940, 'has referred to a "revivalist" feeling in educational circles during Peter Fraser's time as minister' (Bassett and King 2000: 144). Fraser's evangelical mood of educational uplift was welcomed by teachers who 'marvelled at the "torrent of reform" he released, and for years sang his praises at teachers' conferences' (2000: 144). As Minister of Education, Fraser was quick to see the pedagogical possibilities of films and other visual aids in schools, and quickly adopted a policy of consulting with representative groups. The Auckland Visual Aids Association, who had been asking him for money, was invited to meet him in Wellington, as was Walter Harris. With a limited amount of money available, Fraser wanted to know how it should be spent: on projectors or on films. Told that purchasing projectors was a higher priority as there was a steady increase in the number of 16mm films about, and if a school had a projector, it would find a means to borrow or hire films, Fraser decided that the Ministry would offer a pound for pound subsidy on the purchase of approved makes of projectors, leaving schools to raise their share through local contributions.

The growing interest in developing visual aids to teaching in schools was further encouraged through the financial assistance of the Carnegie Corporation of New York. With its help, the Education Department appointed Museum Education Officers in the four main museums in New Zealand. Senior officers in the Department also decided to appoint someone to develop and encourage more effective methods of teaching. Harris got the job of Supervisor of Teaching Aids and moved to Wellington in April 1941.[19] Increasing demand by schools for both projectors and films was reflected in the annual budget estimates of the Education Department, which contained a small 'visual education' component whose figure increased annually. Initially, visual education was viewed merely as an optional extra. Gradually, over the following decades it would become increasingly valued and integrated into the curriculum (until today when, for example, 'visual language' is an explicit component of English).

Harris now turned his attention to the accumulation of suitable films for school use. This venture began modestly enough with copies of the 35mm and 16mm films the NFU was producing weekly to illustrate New Zealand's activities during the war.[20] Another early player was Sir Harry Batterbee, the first British High Commissioner to New Zealand. (Such consular representatives with an interest in film have often played a key role in enlarging New Zealand's film diet.)

Batterbee was keen on films and had been given a Gaumont-British 16mm sound projector by Queen Elizabeth (the Queen Mother) on his appointment to New Zealand shortly before the beginning of the war. He organised many screenings at his house in Wellington and elsewhere, presenting the films produced by the Ministry of Information (MOI), later the Central Office of Information, to demonstrate the Home Front's part in the war.[21] (Some of the MOI documentary films were being made by New Zealand expatriates such as Len Lye and Margaret Thompson, though there is no evidence whether work by these particular filmmakers was screened back in New Zealand. The NFL did later purchase Lye's animated films and Thompson returned to work for the National Film Unit for a few years.) The small library of 16mm sound films in Batterbee's office was lent free of charge. Harris determined to keep these films, along with those from the NFU, and others, such as those made by Canadian Film Board, in one place. Thus began the National Film Library (1942).[22]

Roughly half of the films in the library were given freely by embassies, high commissions, other government departments and industry, all of whom were glad to have their films distributed to widespread audiences at no charge. The only cost to borrowers was the return postage. What has not yet been mentioned is the purchasing policy of the NFL and Harris' generous vision of film that informed the choices he made. Naturally a great part of that vision included an educational component, but his view of education was broad, deep, and more artistic than a narrow curriculum-based model, as Jonathan Dennis, first director of the New Zealand Film Archive (1981), recalled:

He thought that you bought for the collection the best possible films, primarily documentaries in this instance, and that the best films would have a multitude of applications. You just had to encourage people to use and to see films in a larger way. The film library went out of its way to do a number of things to encourage that. They purchased for the collections a lot of the key documentary films of their times, particularly the British Film Unit films of the 1930s, but also some of the key American films. There were always [many] from the Canadian Film Board which included Norman McLaren's stuff, not simply the more ordinary Canadian ones. For many years the only Len Lye films you could see in New Zealand were the handful of British Len Lye ones that the film library held in their collection. They also, later, bought a lot of the war documentaries [and] had a really marvellous collection of Humphrey Jennings films.[23]

Another useful service proposed by the NFL, so far as film societies were concerned, involved the formal training of projectionists. Damage to films was a worry, especially films that the impecunious Federation of Film Societies bought. Even under good operating conditions, films would be worn out through repeated screenings, but a new film could be ruined at once by a dirty projector or an incompetent operator – that bane of film society audiences whose visual pleasure was interrupted by stoppages. If a borrower wanted a valuable film, such as one bought by the film societies, the NFL would sometimes send out a blank film and ask for it to be run through the projector and returned to the library to ensure that the machine was in good order. People who took the training course were issued with a projectionist's certificate and in this way borrowers became more conscious of the need to care for both films and projectors. Harris noted that these measures reduced considerably the damage done to films.[24]

The post-war revival of independent film societies – at one stage there were as many as 55 all over New Zealand, particularly in small towns – quickly led to a federation of film societies being formed with responsibility for both the purchase and hire of films. This dimension of film society activity developed into a mutually beneficial relationship with the NFL, as Jonathan Dennis explains:

'The Education Department effectively paid for the distribution of film society prints around the country; they paid the freight, the prints were checked and organized according to film library classifications; film library staff dispatched them and checked them upon their return. The pay off for that was that the film society had to make … some of them available to schools should they wish to study them.'[25]

From the NFL's point of view, the reappearance of film societies after the war and their purchase of films that demonstrated the art of the cinema enriched the non-documentary section of the library's collection. Harris recalled that in the early days of the film societies' existence, much of their annual programme was drawn from the library, a practice that continued into the 1980s as Bill Gosden, Director of the New Zealand Film Festival Trust, recalled:

The Film Library continued to acquire films from time to time that were more likely to be distributed to film societies rather than schools. One of the later ones that I can remember is *A Personal History of Australian Surf* [1983]. A great film; a documentary about an Australian who directs lots of plays at the West End and on Broadway. The subtitle of it is 'Confessions of a Straight Poofter' and concerns growing up sensitive in a surfing culture.[26]

Although Harris claimed to treat the film societies no differently from any other educational organisation, the NFL's purchasing of films of particular interest to them, the care it took of their films, and the wider vision he had of the cinema all suggest otherwise. He was in no doubt as to the cultural *bona fides* of the film society movement, as he well knew that many of the societies had developed out of WEA classes or university extension courses, or were affiliated with public libraries and art galleries, offering course that catered to small groups of people interested in film as art. His commitment to film had found a favourable echo in Labour's pragmatic definition of what constituted a 'useful' culture worthy of government support, but his personal supervision of the NFL extended Labour's narrow utilitarian vision. New Zealand's film society movement, made up of unpaid volunteers whose only source of funding was from membership fees, received a considerable, albeit unofficial, government subsidy from Harris' broad interpretation of the NFL's role.

The library had proven its worth as a resource centre but the visionary Harris was also concerned about the long-term life of the NFL's expanding film collection and the many other privately held home movies. The nitrate base of older film stock deteriorated over time and was susceptible to spontaneous combustion. The last of his 'good deeds' involved him in efforts to preserve and to conserve the hundreds of short and feature films – the forgotten celluloid of New Zealand history – that were disintegrating in cupboards and backyard sheds across the country. Harris organised a meeting in April 1956 attended by the Government Archivist, the head of the Government Film Studios and ten other interested people.[27] They agreed that a film archive should be set up and that in the interim the NFL ought to do what it could to safeguard the nation's hidden filmic treasures. A wooden shed was erected at the back of the NFL building and potentially inflammable 16mm and 35mm films stock kept there; anyone holding old 35mm films was invited to send them to the NFL for possible preservation. The NFL's workload did not allow much serious archiving to be done, but interest had been created in the project. (The establishment of the Film Archive is covered more extensively in Chapter 8.)

Ray Hayes, Harris' immediate and chosen successor, faithfully pursued the same vision after the founder's retirement in 1963. By the 1970s, however, under other managers, much of the original spirit had been lost. The last years of the NFL are a depressing object lesson in how such a film institution can self-destruct once it has lost a clear vision of what film culture is about. The machinery lumbered on, 'staffed with people who had no imagination',[28] substituting a perfunctory form of public service for what was once done with care and enthusiasm. The free services provided to film societies came to an end when the NFL was transferred from the Education Department to the National Library. The results of this transfer are sadly remembered today by Bill Gosden:

> They gave away a lot of [the collection] and then they pretended to dispose of it systematically by letting anybody who thought they might have an interest in the films prove an entitlement to them by contacting the original licences, very few of whom would respond to an enquiry about a 'life of print' sale that had happened anywhere from one to 30 years previously.[29]

Jonathan Dennis confirmed this sense of vandalism and noted problems that had occurred when the National Library took charge:

> [The Film Library] had lost its identity by that stage when it was taken out of the Education Department's care and given over to the National Library, who equated this collection with books. Why would they spend hundreds or more dollars on a single print when they could spend the same sum and get 40 books? They constantly equated one with the other. They wanted to issue the films as you would books in a library, whereas films were booked in advance and you would have to allow a certain amount of time, so schools used to book all their films and the dates at which they wanted them throughout the school year. When they found they could no longer do this … schools lost interest. Basically, the Film Library was killed off. The collections were disposed of, and many had been lost by that stage anyway. In its last fifteen or twenty years [the National Library] had narrowed what they were buying to hundreds of Encyclopaedia Britannica prints or something. They had lost any real vision of what they could be by the eighties.[30]

Independent Film Distribution

The 1930s concluded with both a bang and a whimper. The former was *blitzkrieg* as German forces entered Poland, and, later, France. The whimper could be heard in the narrowing corridors of film supply companies as the availability of imports from Europe dried up. This was a blow to film culture as New Zealanders had only just begun to see 'Continental' films again on their screens thanks to the entrepreneurial activity of one man. The coming of the war was, of course, a disaster for the cinema in many other respects also, as many filmmakers would lose their lives and many national production industries would be devastated. The only positive outcome was the cross-fertilisation of film traditions that resulted from the diaspora of filmmakers and film enthusiasts escaping from European anti-Semitism.

Natan Scheinwald arrived in New Zealand in 1931 and worked in Wellington as a wool-buyer until 1937.[31] The collapse of that market caused him to lose a substantial sum of money on a shipment and he needed another revenue source. As a reader of (and occasional contributor to) *Tomorrow*,[32] Scheinwald was aware of the many complaints over the scarcity of alternatives to English and American cinema. There was also now a larger community of refugees from fascism living in Wellington and Auckland willing to pay to see films from Europe.

Scheinwald responded to an advertisement in the *New York Times* for a Russian film called *Professor Mamlock* (1938). This film has been mentioned in a previous chapter, but the story of its importation should now be told in relation to Scheinwald. As there were no import restrictions on films, he bought the New Zealand distribution rights to *Mamlock*. The initial reluctance of theatre owners to screen a foreign subtitled film meant that he had to rent a Wellington cinema himself. This proved a success: 'When I opened, [in October] after advertising the film, the queue outside the Opera House went two blocks down the street' (*Evening Post* 1989).

The leftist zeitgeist of the late 1930s and the presence of European refugees undoubtedly contributed to the warm welcome given to the film in New Zealand, but there were other contributing factors. The original theatrical version of *Mamlock* had already been staged in Dunedin by the city's Left Book Club's drama group. *Mamlock*, although derived from a German play, was a Soviet film that roundly denounced Hitler's brand of fascism and anti-Semitism. Paradoxically, the film's New Zealand release occurred just after the nonaggression pact between Nazi Germany and Communist Russia had been cynically signed. However, the probable key to the film's reception, which made it the financial success it was, came from the pen of Gordon Mirams when he lauded the film in his influential column of film reviews (to be discussed shortly).

Mirams' review of *Mamlock* appeared in the seventh of his weekly *NZ Listener* columns (22 September 1939). In contrast to Stanhope Andrews, whose own review appeared a week later in *Tomorrow*, he referred explicitly to the incongruity of this film and the recent non-aggression pact signed between the Soviet Union and Germany only one month earlier on 23 August:

> The paradox I have mentioned lies in the fact that *Professor Mamlock* was produced in the Soviet Union. In the light of political events, it now makes no more sense than the

Russo-German pact does itself. A cynic might remark that one of Stalin's chickens has come home to roost – and found the perch embarrassingly occupied by an amicable German eagle.

(NZ Listener 1939: 34)

Mirams gave a rapturous review of the film's realistic style as well as praising the direction of it, making light of the Russian dialogue and English subtitles. He also noted that it was the first Soviet film to have been distributed commercially in the United States and that it had even received the 'official blessing of the high-minded Hays organisation': '[T]he action is breathless, and the Soviet cameras, with the relentless realism of a newsreel, have turned the characters into real people and the settings into real places, and have caught the terrifying intensity of mob emotion' (*NZ Listener* 1939: 34). *Mamlock* was, however, also received controversially in the United States, where it was 'banned by authorities in Chicago, Rhode Island and elsewhere for being anti-German propaganda'. (Anon. n.d.)

The unexpected success of the film in Wellington led to a relatively lengthy three-week run and a booking from the nationwide cinema chain that had previously been uninterested in it. This ensured that Scheinwald netted a handsome return from *Mamlock*. It is also evidence that Mirams' reviews, via the national reach of the magazine he wrote for, had a real influence in shaping cultural consumption.

John O'Shea has described Scheinwald as being 'smooth-talking, entrepreneurial and innovative' (1996: 21), and his next venture into film culture confirmed this evaluation: he expanded his operations. His wartime guard duties within New Zealand left him time to continue importing films: *Mayerling* (1936), *Un Carnet de bal* (1937), *Katia* (1938), and *La Charrette fantôme* (1939) were acquired by him prior to the fall of France in May–June 1940.[33] Scheinwald also acquired the lease to a small theatre, which had been used to screen newsreels, underneath the majestic Civic Theatre in Auckland. After renovation, it was re-baptised as the 'Theatre de Paris'. Sheinwald left no one in doubt as to the unusual cultural significance of this venture. Potential patrons were informed that this was 'The intimate house with Continental films for the cultured mind'. His first foreign feature to screen there on 2 March 1940 was Julien Duvivier's *Un Carnet de bal*.

Gordon Mirams informed his readership on 1 March 1940 of Scheinwald's theatre in Auckland, noting that it would operate in a similar fashion to those in London and Australia where revivals of classics would occur alongside new foreign films that would interest, principally, members of film societies. 'I am opening the theatre without lavish celebrations. It is not a pub, but a cultural institution,' Scheinwald declared to Mirams, adding that the reason he was opening in Auckland was because 'Auckland is the largest, most cosmopolitan, most progressive city to start in. … There is also a bigger foreign element' (*NZ Listener* 1940: 19). Films in the second week of operation included *Young Vienna Sings Again* and *Song of Youth*, both featuring the Vienna Boys' Choir, which seemed more likely to attract the middlebrow viewers than cinephiles.[34]

Success in Auckland would have encouraged Scheinwald to open in other centres. Unfortunately, prosperity eluded him. The war in Europe meant an end to European film supply and after showing a few more films – René Clair's *Sous les toits de Paris* (1930); a Czech film, *The Legend of Prague* (1935), advertised as having been banned by Hitler and as the last Czech film made with an English dialogue; *The Charm of La Boheme* (1937), an Austrian version of Puccini's *La Bohème* (for which he incurred the wrath of Peter Fraser, who had persuaded himself that this German language film 'was flaunting Nazism in the face of New Zealand soldiers') (*Evening Post* 1989), and *Fury over Spain* (1937), with its 'Authentic Scenes from the Spanish Civil War', as well as assorted Russian shorts – Scheinwald's lease on the Theatre de Paris was revoked. Scheinwald's temperament may have contributed to these present (and future) troubles, but he may have also been the target of anti-Semitism, the existence of which he had written about in *Tomorrow*:

New Zealand, thanks to its geographical isolation and the restricted immigration, is not flooded with Jewish refugees from Germany – Hitler's Hell. One of the two and a half families who have found their homes in the so-called 'God's Own Country' were not welcomed by some citizens in Auckland a year or so ago when one of the exiles happened to get a position in dentistry. The conflict between Jews and non-Jews (I don't like to use the word Gentile) arises as an economic factor, which must be taken as a basis in establishing the reason for the hatred.

(*Tomorrow* 1935: 14)

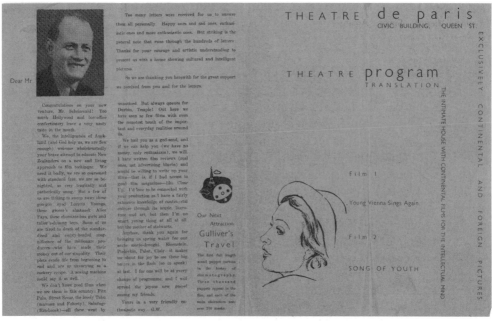

Figure 8: A brochure for Natan Scheinwald's 'Theatre de Paris' in Auckland, 1940. Image courtesy of Sir George Grey Special Collections, Auckland Libraries, Ephemera Collection.

Scheinwald was understating the number of European migrants now living in Auckland, which, while not large, was more significant than he acknowledged here. Jewish refugees tended to cluster in Auckland and Wellington where small Jewish communities already existed; by 1939, there were roughly 300 Jewish refugees living in Auckland.[35] Scheinwald's article, written in 1935 prior to the larger influx of new European migrants, may have exaggerated but he had important points to make. Diversity was not welcomed in New Zealand on several counts.[36] Aside from putting Peter Fraser's nose out of joint, he had also provoked the ire of the New Zealand distributor for Paramount Pictures who was angry that the Russian animated film *The New Gulliver* (1935) – in which Gulliver discovers capitalist inequality and exploitation in Lilliput – had stolen the limelight from Paramount's cartoon version of the same film, which opened two weeks later (*Evening Post* 1989). Scheinwald claimed that further difficulties with Paramount eventually 'resulted in him losing his licence as an exhibitor' in the late 1950s, which forced him out of the country (*Evening Post* 1989).[37]

His relocation in Australia did not, however, bring an end to his problems with the major distributors. 'Although he had a permit to show films on Sundays in a small cinema he rented in King's Cross ... the Theatrical Employees' Union prosecuted him on the basis of a two-century-old English law, the Sunday Hall Act' (*Evening Post* 1989). Fined ten pounds, he also had to endure a two-year boycott by the union, which eventually forced him to sell his home. Thus, war, both the military and the commercial type, combined to thwart Scheinwald in his entrepreneurial approach to the small local markets receptive to 'Continental' films.

Film Criticism Goes National

Gordon Mirams' (1909–66) close association with films had begun as a child when his indulgent and solicitous mother turned to the 'great indoors' of the theatre for a child too frail to endure the usual New Zealand preoccupation with the great outdoors. After gaining an MA from Canterbury University College and a Diploma in Journalism, Mirams joined the culturally inclined Christchurch *Sun*, where a senior reporter advised the 19-year-old 'to specialise in some side-line of newspaper writing, such as football, racing, farming, or high-finance' (Mirams 1945: 180). The movies were not an option, although Mirams had become a member of the Christchurch Film Society in its inaugural year (1933). Nevertheless, his time as a reporter for the paper (1927–35) did see him 'specialise' in supervising the 'puff par' film advertisements placed by the film exhibitors. This allowed him to obtain a regular supply of free weekly passes to the cinema and provided an additional reason for Mirams' cinematic assiduity, as a double pass meant he could take his girlfriend, Ruth Taylor, who later became his wife.

Mirams first became an 'independent' film critic when he worked for the *Radio Record* in Wellington in 1937, attracting a nationwide audience and some repute, as recorded in

Tomorrow's 'Film Digest', where he was described as one of the very few to give 'candid reviews' – a compliment that may have inspired the title of his later weekly film column, 'Speaking Candidly', and book of the same name (*Tomorrow* 1938: 286). The *Radio Record* had positioned itself as a generalist weekly journal concerned with the full range of New Zealand broadcasting. It had also attempted to widen its appeal in tune with what it saw as the home and family orientation of radio: '[The paper] is essentially a home paper– for wireless is a part of the family fireside – and for this reason it retails other news of the entertainment world; the professional stage, the talkies, repertory, gramophone recordings: there is news, too, for women and comments on modern literature' (Day 1994: 173).

As Director of Broadcasting, Shelley had been contemplating the creation of film criticism on the state-run radio network. His weighty 'contemplation' lasted all of two years, finally ending in 1939 with the creation of the quaintly named, literary sounding, 'Leaves from the Diary of a Film Fan'. This radio programme was entrusted to Mirams on 2YA (Wellington) and rebroadcast to other centres over a two-year period. An aversion to impurities of any sort, in refusing to mix the ideals of public broadcasting with the tainted currency of industry, led the YA network to avoid association with any form of commercialism. Hence, Mirams could not include any comment or criticism of contemporary films that might be screened in a theatre in the Dominion, as this could be construed as publicity. There was a double standard at work here because the national stations ran book reviewing sessions, which, in Mirams' opinion, were 'generally so lacking in critical comment that they [were], in effect, nothing much more than publicity for certain books which listeners [were] plainly urged to secure and read' (1945: 18). The social impact of films on the populace might be huge, but the cinema still bore the stains of vulgar commerce, and was thus denied the consideration given to literature. 'Leaves' was obliged to concern itself, therefore, with 'memories of past pictures', about which Mirams was given a free rein to be as uncomplimentary as he wished. Precisely what he did within those limits is unknown as at that time many radio broadcasts were 'live to air' and not recorded.

Although much of the history of New Zealand radio has been lost, it is clear that Mirams' influence on many New Zealanders' perception of the cinema was enormous. Besides writing film reviews for the *Radio Record* (1937–39) under his own name, he also wrote for one of Wellington's daily newspapers, the *Dominion*, under the pseudonym of Roger Holden – the first names of his younger and older brothers. At this stage, his film 'criticism' had to play an elaborate game of 'cat and mouse' with the exhibition and distribution companies who provided the newspapers with important advertising revenue; unfavourable reviews incurred their wrath and threats of advertising withdrawal. This was an improbable occurrence given their need to let the public know of the latest films, but it exerted some influence over newspaper owners and editors who saw films as products to be sold rather than works of art that were appropriately subject to criticism.

After several months on the job, however, Mirams started to include some adverse comments in his reviews, but this was generally tempered by positive remarks about some other aspect of the film. In his review of *The Firefly* (USA, 1937), a musical with the popular Jeanette MacDonald, for example, he judged it 'a most satisfactory piece of entertainment', but wondered whether its musical qualities were enough to make 'a critic overlook other aspects which are not quite so satisfactory'; these he found chiefly in narrative weakness and acting ability. Typically, Mirams redressed the balance in favour of the film by writing that 'these defects … may seem light when balanced against the rich musical offering'. Furthermore, 'the vivid pageantry of [*Firefly*'s] setting and the romantic texture of its story' were also in its favour (*Dominion* 1938: 16). Reflecting later on this balancing act, he wrote that as 'we were all breaking virtually new ground, this experience in honest film comment by a New Zealand newspaper worked reasonably well' (1945: 182–83).

Mirams' public profile, critical acumen, journalistic skills, and Labour Party credentials were sufficient to see him obtain a full-time job as the Chief Sub-Editor of the *New Zealand Listener* upon its establishment in 1939, where he took time out from his editing duties each week to write a film review. He was, for many years, the nation's only paid film critic when he wrote what came to be called his 'Speaking Candidly' reviews between 1939 and 1947, at a time when the cinema was the principal form of entertainment. His readership was huge. As a result of the *Listener*'s monopoly of the weekly radio listings, the magazine was read by all households with a radio. Mirams also lectured on film for the WEA in Wellington, both during and after World War II, and was one of the founders and first president of the renascent Wellington Film Society (1946), which grew out of public interest in the WEA film classes he had given earlier. The wisdom of pooling scarce resources made itself obvious and the disparate regional film societies soon linked up as the New Zealand Film Institute (1947). Mirams was one of the prime movers in this development, becoming its first Chairman.

In the immediate post-war period he wrote his unique book, *Speaking Candidly* (1945), 'at a time when serious and discursive writing about the cinema was rare'.[38] This dealt generally with the habits of the film public in New Zealand and the influence of films on human behaviour. It was well received both here and overseas. The most striking thing about *Speaking Candidly* is the very fact of its appearance in the New Zealand literary landscape at that time; this was the first serious book on film to be written by a New Zealander. Unsurprisingly, it was published by Paul's Book Arcade, *the* serious New Zealand book publishers of the period (Taylor 1986: 1189).

Mirams' book had several key sections. One of the most important for film culture was an appeal for film education in schools. The sociological impact of film was a subject that interested Mirams and many other educationalists (as we have seen with regard to Winston Rhodes, among others). A survey into the 'Reading, Film and Radio Tastes of High School Boys and Girls', conducted for the New Zealand Council for Educational Research by W.J. Scott (published in 1947 as a book), had revealed to the authorities the pervasiveness of film-going as social practice. The cinema, however, was still considered a meretricious form of entertainment that most teachers could not talk about seriously in the classroom. Mirams' concern, shared by many, was that behavioural and attitudinal patterns were being transmitted to children by films in an uncontrolled manner. He did not, in his book, propose any practical pedagogy that would help teachers distinguish between films that were 'good' and those that were 'inferior'. He later addressed these issues, however, in a series of essays written for the Department of Education's *Post-Primary School Bulletin*, whose first volume appeared in 1947.[39]

The importance of European films was a prominent aspect of Mirams' conception of film culture, but, as we have suggested, their scarcity in New Zealand led local film culture to develop incompletely – as a kind of fragmented and diminished mirror of, for example, British film culture. French films had a distinctive individuality that Mirams sought to explain to his readers, attributing the difference to the development of a national cinema, the greater 'artistic' freedom enjoyed by the French director, the absence of a 'star' system, the relatively low cost of French filmmaking, and protective legislation that offered the French film industry some shelter from Hollywood's dominance. Although he did not mention it, the decline of the former French studio giants (Pathé and Gaumont) under the combined onslaught of World War I, the Great Depression, and the conversion to sound had seen the rise of smaller production companies headed by producers willing to take greater technical and creative risks. As Mirams himself noted,

> with little to lose, French directors were able to make continual experiments. As a result they had evolved a technique which was as typically French as that opening shot of the Eiffel Tower which Hollywood seems to stick into every picture that has its setting in Paris. At the same time, their technique was not static: in *The Cheat*, for example, Guitry achieved a remarkable series of innovations' (1945: 135–36).

Perhaps because he was addressing middle-class New Zealand (the YA radio and *Listener* type reader), Mirams almost never analysed the specifics of film technique, so that Guitry's 'remarkable series of innovations' remain both vague and enticing, as do the 'continual experiments' of French filmmakers. Mirams tries gently to nudge his readers towards better films, and is at pains not to be explicitly an intellectual. Having quoted an English critic who wrote of individual film style in such directors as René Clair, Sacha Guitry, and Julian Duvivier, Mirams added his reservation that 'such enthusiasm carries the odour of literary snobbishness', and shifted to a more pragmatic mode, 'but [style] does not explain how so many French films managed to make handsome profits. Purely highbrow pictures never do that' (136). One can both admire his skilful balancing act and regret that New Zealand film culture has always had to pull its punches in deference to the 'common sense' reader.

Aside from French films, Mirams also praised Russian and German filmmakers, although his enthusiasm was primarily for the silent era directors when 'the light of fanaticism [gave] a quality of excitement and daring experiment to those early Russian efforts which shone past all the obvious propaganda' (138). Later films reflected the Soviet Union's decision 'to renounce internationalism in favour of nationalism, seen in such films as *Peter the Great*, *Alexander Nevsky*, and *Suvorov*, which extol the glories of Imperial Russia' (138). German films suffered a comparable innovative decline with the coming of both sound and the Nazis to power, 'and with Hitler came that subjection of the German cinema to almost solely propagandist purposes which would itself have spoilt New Zealand as a market for German films if the language difficulty had not already done so' (140).

Mirams' analysis of the reasons for the greatness of French, Russian, and German silent cinema is in accord with the apparently paradoxical Camusien notion that *l'art vit de contrainte et meurt de liberté* (art is born of constraint and dies of freedom).[40] In the school of hard knocks, adversity is creative: 'it was the devastation of France, and the turmoil of Russia that, more than anything else, were responsible for the vitality, brilliance, and daring experiment of the French and Russian cinema' (235). A respected English critic, C.A. Lejeune, had said as much for the German cinema, too, so the temptation to consecrate this notion was strong: 'Out of material poverty came richness of ideas. Out of devastation came renaissance. … imagination was strong and vivid in Germany in those days… of *Caligari, Waxworks, The Nibelungs, The Last Laugh, Destiny, The Waltz Dream,* and dozens more, each film a full and exciting adventure' (235).

The need for film criticism was a frequent theme for Mirams: 'The movies are not even considered by the newspapers as worthy of being given the same treatment as football or horse-racing, both of which are subjects for expert comment in the average journal' (164). (To this day, no arts culture in New Zealand has been able to compete with the huge amounts of space devoted to football culture.) Mirams noted that informed film criticism would balance the excessive influence star power exerted over people when deciding which film to see: 'An accepted and comprehensive system of film criticism which would provide a large section of the public with the reliable information it needs … would go a good way towards solving this problem' (166).

Practical difficulties included finding at least two critics in each centre (for the morning and evening papers) – 'people with the necessary background of knowledge, experience of film-going, and general cultural standards to write with authority, intelligence, integrity, and liveliness about the cinema' (171) were still thin on the ground in New Zealand, even though Mirams couched his description in general terms (specific film expertise was certainly out of the question). Film criticism would increase throughout the 1950s and 1960s – mainly as a result of film society-led activity – as my next chapter will show.

The vexed problem of film supply and the business of film in New Zealand made up the last key section in *Speaking Candidly*. After describing the 'box-office' mentality that governed the choices made by commercially driven distributors and exhibitors, Mirams fastened on state-sponsored art-house cinemas (described as 'repertory cinema theatre') as an appropriate way to increase the range of films in New Zealand. The analogy he drew was with literary culture:

Large sums of public money are spent on providing rare or expensive books which only a very few persons ever consult, but it is just because they *are* expensive and not otherwise available to ordinary members of the public that they find a place on the shelves. Well, what about the serious students of the cinema?' (222).

How can we reconcile Mirams' anti-bureaucratic streak ('the best censorship, like the best government, is none at all') with his advocacy of the socialisation of film exhibition and distribution in New Zealand? He wrote: 'under socialism the task of bringing pictures to New Zealand, as well as circulating them among the available theatres, might be handled more efficiently than at present, and possibly more cheaply too, through one great clearing-house in Wellington' (226). He was certainly aware of the bureaucratic abuses that such a system might create. However, such a system, 'full-scale socialism', was still 'a good long way off in this country', so he did not have to sort out the details (224). But he did suggest that a 'buffer' would need to be found – one that wedged itself between the individual and the state so that 'State control of material things did not mean state control of the mind as well'. He ventured that institutions such as the University, the Supreme Court, 'and perhaps even the French Academy' might furnish the requisite protection (226). (He was seeking to articulate the 'arm's length' principle that we associate with today's cultural funding bodies or 'quangos'.)

Mirams' book was progressive in many respects, but it had one depressing aspect – a four-page attack on Hollywood as a kind of Jewish conspiracy (56–59). That such sweeping generalisations about the 'money values' and lack of 'social conscience' that supposedly characterised Jewish culture could be published in 1945 is startling evidence to support Natan Scheinwald's suggestion that anti-Semitism was rife in New Zealand. Mirams' apparent racism must, however, be balanced against the generous support he had given to Scheinwald as an individual, and the fact that he had presumably written his book before becoming aware of the horrors of the German holocaust.

Mirams' personal film culture received an enormous infusion during his 1948 sojourn in the French capital when he became one of the first New Zealanders to work at the Parisian headquarters of the newly created UNESCO, in the John Grierson–led Mass Communication Section, where he was First Assistant Film Information Officer for a period of 18 months. Most of the articles he wrote giving his impressions of Paris were written after his return to New Zealand, but he did manage to send back one article, written some three months after his arrival in France, 'The Filmgoer in Paris', which recorded his impressions of that city from a cinephile's perspective. Paris was even then, as it remains today, a Mecca for anyone wanting to improve their knowledge of global cinema production, with numerous small cinemas catering to cinephiles, a network of *ciné-clubs*, festivals of various sorts, thematic retrospectives, and tributes to particular directors and national cinemas.

One of the many films Mirams saw at a *ciné-club* was Carné and Prévert's *Le Jour se lève*, made almost a decade earlier in 1939 when politics, economics, and ideology had pushed French society into a very different mood. Considered to be the zenith of the poetic realist style, which reigned in France for ten years (1936–46), Mirams saw it at a time when Italian neo-realism was supplanting it as the genre, which most excited the critics, especially the influential André Bazin, who saw in it an exciting future direction of film language in the post-war period. Of this development, Mirams' article made no mention, which suggests that he was unaware of it. *Le Jour se lève* satisfied him as fit for adults, and he wrote positively about the film's dramatic maturity, making the inevitable and invidious comparison with Hollywood's remake of the film:

> I am quite sure after seeing the French original, and despite the imperfections of the print, that Hollywood's *The Long Night* can have been only a poor and emasculated imitation. ... The subtle psychological implications of the plot (for instance, the 'villain', played by Jules Berry with a magnificent sense of evil, is here the father of the 'heroine', and the motives which inspire him are consequently a strange mixture of sadism, masochism, and father-love) would be much too adult and 'shocking' for the American censors even if the uncompromising tragedy of the finale were acceptable at the box-office.
>
> (*NZ Listener* 1948: 16–18)

Mirams was stimulated by the prodigious choice of films on offer and regaled his readers with titles that would, for the most part, remain names to be read, not films to be seen and experienced: *Quai des Orfèvres* (France, 1947), *Le Diable au corps* (France, 1947), *Dharti Ke Lal* (India, 1946), *Day of Wrath* (Denmark, 1943), *La Passion de Jeanne d'Arc* (France, 1928), *Vivere in Pace* (Italy, 1947), *Ivan the Terrible* (USSR, 1944), *Paris 1900* (France, 1947), *L'Étrange Monsieur Victor* (France, 1937), *L'Atalante* (France, 1934) and *Zéro de conduite* (France, 1933).

Undoubtedly, this list further whetted the appetite of New Zealand film society members for more 'Continental' films. It may also have stimulated the burgeoning desire of smaller independent distributors/exhibitors, like Ron Usmar and Russell Rankin of New Zealand Film Services, and Eddie Greenfield of Exclusive Films (who followed the example established by Natan Scheinwald), to satisfy a growing mainstream audience eager to see foreign films, particularly French. So extensive was the critical and popular dominance of the films made by Renoir, Grémillon, Carné, and Prévert, to name but the most illustrious representatives of 'poetic realism' (none of which were shown in New Zealand when they were made), that Mirams noted their conquest of England:

> Quietly, steadily, the French have been invading England. Where Napoleon failed, French film producers have succeeded. Two years ago I heard a speaker from Daventry draw attention to the fact that there was hardly a town of any size in England where one didn't come across a theatre showing a French film. And they were doing good business. The language difficulty has been largely overcome by sub-titles in English or by improved 'dubbing' of dialogue (as in Sacha Guitry's *The Cheat*).
>
> (*NZ Listener* 1949: 29)

The remarkable feature of French films was that they were both critical and popular successes. In seeking to account for this situation, Mirams' article drew attention to the influence exerted by and accorded to the director in the French system, which had become rather more individual and 'anarchic' than in either Hollywood or England, after the combined effects of conversion to sound and the Depression had led, as we noted earlier, to the decline and demise of two former production giants: Gaumont and Pathé. The importance of the French director was not an idea native to Mirams, but one that he had pleasure in transmitting to the readers of the *Listener*: 'Because the French pay so much attention to their directors, rather than to their stars, their films have an individuality never encountered in American or British productions, except perhaps in the case of those British films made by Alfred Hitchcock' (*NZ Listener* 1949: 29). The idea of authorship is presented here still in very general terms, but at least there is recognition of the importance of a distinctive style.

John O'Shea, who liked Mirams very much, found him a contradictory character – a 'do-gooder' in the positive and negative senses of that expression, righteous and boring, but on occasion an able public speaker. He was a pacifist, though not a Quaker, who dared to promulgate his views during the war, although his heart condition would have saved him from being sent on any active duty. He was one of a clutch of South Islanders in positions of influence in the capital, yet seen by them as not of their ilk, not quite up to their level, although he aspired to it. As O'Shea later noted of the South Islanders' artistic preferences: 'They were the arts proper, [whereas Mirams] made his regime out of films, [which] at the time were very down market: you lie down with dogs, you get up with fleas, and if you lay down with films, your mind was obviously a bit addled.'[41]

Mirams' anger at not being promoted to the editorship of the *NZ Listener* upon the retirement of its founding editor, Oliver Duff, compelled him to invoke an infrequently used procedure for situations where a Public Service appointment was considered to have been unfairly or incorrectly made. Duff's influence at the appeal hearing, in favour of M.H. Holcroft, was decisive. This was not an easy thing for Duff to do, for they had been friends as well as colleagues. Holcroft later speculated that Duff's reasons for not supporting Mirams in his quest for the top position 'was possibly related to temperament' (1969: 10).

> He was a pioneer in film criticism; his reviews in the *Listener* were influential, and perhaps did more that anything else to banish blurb-reviewing from newspapers. But in spite of wide knowledge of the cinema, historical and technical, the basis of his criticism remained – I believe – an enthusiasm gained in childhood and never quite lost, an abiding delight in pictures for their own sake. It did not weaken his critical faculties, which indeed had been sharpened by overseas travel; but it helped him to stay in love with the cinema even while he explored its faults and helped to build up the rather dreary documentation which surrounds it in the halls of UNESCO.[42]

Underlying the faint praise can be felt Holcroft's patronising attitude to the cinema as an art, seen by implication as one of Mirams' childish enthusiasms. This seems unconsciously to illustrate O'Shea's shrewd summary of a South Island highbrow's patronising attitude to films. As editor of the *Listener*, Holcroft retained the film review column; but had the editorship gone to Mirams, he would have developed the magazine into a far more important vehicle for transnational film culture.

Holcroft assumed editorship of the magazine on 1 June 1949, feeling 'no joy in having to work with a man who had tried to prevent my appointment, and who – I supposed – would resent my presence' (1969: 12). This mutually embarrassing situation lasted until 12 August 1949 when Mirams was appointed to the position of Film Censor to replace the retiring W.A.L. von Keisenberg. To cap things off, so far as his influence on film culture is concerned, he was, for a decade, between 1949 and 1959, a more liberal film censor whose love of film impelled him to introduce a new classification system, the 'R' or Restricted category. This rescued some important films from being banned, and was considered by many overseas commentators to be worthy of emulation in other western countries. The next chapter will comment further on Mirams' cultural activity as it examines the energy liberated at the end of the war to build on the cultural foundations that had been established in the pre-war period.

References

Anon. (n.d.), 'Shadows and Sojourners: Images of Jews and Antifacism in East German Film' [Online]. Available at: http://www.umass.edu/defa/filmtour/sjprofmamlock.shtml. DEFA Film Library, University of Massachusetts Amherst. Accessed: 22 September 2010.

Anon. (1937), 'Policy for Films', *The Economist* 6 November.

—— (1938), 'Film as an Art: Elevating Popular Taste', *Auckland Star,* 28 January.

—— (1938), 'Around the Theatres: Special Reviews of New Films', *Dominion,* 4 June, p. 16.

—— (1989), 'Film Distribution Pioneer Recalls Tough NZ Years', *Evening Post,* 23 November.

Bassett, M. and King, M. (2000), *Tomorrow Comes the Song: A Life of Peter Fraser*, Auckland: Penguin.

Belich, J. (2001), *Paradise Reforged: A History of the New Zealanders from the 1880s to the Year 2000*, Auckland: Allen Lane & Penguuin Press, p. 231.

Day, P. (1994), *Radio Years: A History of Broadcasting in New Zealand,* Auckland: Auckland University Press in association with the Broadcasting History Trust.

Holcroft, M. (1969), *Reluctant Editor: The Listener Years, 1949–67*, Wellington: Reed.

Mirams, G. (1945), *Speaking Candidly*, Hamilton: Paul's Books.

—— (1939), 'Film Reviews: To See Or Not To See', *NZ Listener,* 22 September, p. 34.

—— (1940), 'De Paris Theatrette', *NZ Listener,* 1 March, p. 19.

—— (1948), 'The Filmgoer in Paris', *NZ Listener,* 27 April, pp. 16–18.

—— (1940), 'France Invades the Cinema', *NZ Listener*, 29 March, p. 29.

O'Shea, J. (1996), 'A Charmed Life: Fragments of Memory and Extracts from Conversations'. In: J. Dennis and J. Bieringa, eds. *Film in Aotearoa New Zealand*, Wellington: Victoria University Press, p. 28.

Taylor, N.M. (1986), *The New Zealand People at War: The Home Front*, Vol. 1–2, Wellington: Department of Internal Affairs. Historical Publications Branch.

Scheinwald, N. (1935), 'Why Anti-Semitism?' *Tomorrow,* 20 November, p. 14.

Sigley, S, (2013), 'Imperial Relations with Polynesian Romantics: The Grierson Effect in New Zealand'. In: Z. Druick and D. Williams, eds. *The Grierson Effect: The International Documentary Movement*, London: BFI/Palgrave.

W.B.H. (1938), 'Film Digest', *Tomorrow*, 2 March, p. 286.

Notes

1   Notes of a Conference, IC1 27/1/1. Archives New Zealand.

2   Ibid.

3   Ibid, p. 3.

4   Ibid.

5   The two recording plants owned by the service were kept in almost constant use during 1938–39 when 1157 plays were broadcast, largely from Wellington.

6   Notes of a Conference, p. 3.

7   Ibid, p. 8.

8   Ibid, p. 10.

9   These five points are taken directly from the Minutes of the Committee Meeting.

10   Minutes of a meeting, 19 April 1937, IC1 27/1/1. Archives New Zealand.

11   Minutes, 19 April 1937.

12   Memorandum for D.G. Sullivan, 23 October 1937, IC 27/1/1. Archives New Zealand. Release dates are not available for all titles.

13   'Culture in Films', IC1 27/1/1. Archives New Zealand.

14   Ibid.

15   Ibid.

16   Ibid.

17   I am chiefly reliant on the written reminiscences of Walter Harris himself for much of the detail that follows: 'The Beginnings of the NZ National Film Library'. Alexander Turnbull Library: Harris, Walter, B: MS papers 4158, March 1989.

18   Edgar Swain founded Educational Sound Films. Years later he told Harris that he had been in the Parliament buildings when he saw a Bell & Howell projector screening a sound film for a parliamentary committee. Realising the commercial possibilities, he had cabled Bell & Howell that very evening, with an order for 50 projectors providing he was given the sole agency for New Zealand. They accepted and soon he had acquired agencies for Encyclopaedia Films as well as the films of other 16mm producers such as Gaumont-British. He sold the projectors to schools and universities, and to other government departments, offered a lending library of films, and imported others at a time (circa 1940) when there was not much choice.

19   John O'Shea's 'fragments of memory' incorrectly assumes that Harris' move to Wellington was coincident with the creation of the NFL, in O'Shea 1996: 28.

20   W. Harris, unpublished MS, p. 5.

21   Ibid, p. 4.

22   For a more detailed look at how the establishment of the NFL fitted into British Imperial interests, see Sigley, 'Imperial Relations with Polynesian Romantics: The John Grierson Effect in New Zealand', in Druick and Williams, forthcoming.

23 J. Dennis interview, November 2000.

24 Harris, unpublished MS, pp. 11–12.

25 J. Dennis interview, November 2000.

26 B. Gosden interview, November 2000.

27 Harris, unpublished MS, p. 13.

28 Ibid.

29 B. Gosden interview, November 2000.

30 J. Dennis interview, November 2000.

31 According to an interview that Scheinwald gave in Sydney in the late 1980s.

32 'Why anti-Semitism' was published in *Tomorrow* on 20 November 1935.

33 Mirams' reviews appeared in the *New Zealand Listener* on 6 October 1939, 10 November 1939, 15 March 1940, and 7 June 1940.

34 Release dates for the two choir-themed films have not been found. Auckland's 'Festival of the Arts' also included many filmed operas and ballets that appealed to the cultured in that city from 1953 on.

35 It is undeniable, however, that New Zealand, in 1939, was not used to diversity. 'Aliens', as non-British people were called, 'accounted for only 8000 in a total population of 1,640,000, most of whom had arrived in New Zealand over many years'. Taylor 1986: 851, 878. See also: Belich: 231.

36 New Zealand immigration policy had a lengthy history of discriminating in favour of Britons. Belich attributes this to a New Zealand racial template of weak 'Aryanism'. See pages 223–40 of his book *Paradise Reforged* for a more detailed analysis.

37 It is also possible that anti-Italian sentiment (due to World War II) contributed to the largely negative response that Rossellini's films received in New Zealand; *Rome Open City* (1945) was not successful, and Scheinwald's efforts to screen *Paisà* (1946), Rossellini's second post–World War II neo-realist film, in the late 1940s, encountered resistance from officialdom which did not want to give him an import licence for this film.

38 Obituary by John O'Shea, in *NZ Motion Picture Exhibitors' Bulletin*, 16 December 1966, pp. 8–9.

39 Volume 6 (1952) included 'Our Choice of Films' (no. 9), in which Mirams wanted 'to discover some general rules and principles which will help us to choose the films in which we are most likely to find real enjoyment'. This essay also looked at the major film genres. 'People Who Make Films' (no. 12) combined his reflections on national cinemas with descriptions of key people involved in film production. 'Ideas in Films' appeared in volume 7 (no. 9) and emphasised the explicit and implicit *content* of films in preference to their *form*. Mirams was, as ever, anxious to develop a more critical cinematic awareness in school children.

40 The expression is attributed to Albert Camus who pronounced it during his acceptance speech for the Nobel Prize in Literature (1957), although André Gide also wrote in his *Journal, feuillets 11*: 'l'art naît de contrainte, vit de lutte, meurt de liberté'.

41 O'Shea to Cooke, 8 October 1986.

42 Ibid. Mirams had an abiding interest in toy soldiers and could spend weeks recreating famous battles from the Napoleonic wars.

Chapter 5

Building the Cultural Infrastructure

Generally, the war years represented a hiatus in the development of minority film culture. This hiatus demonstrates anew the importance of film supply as a key ingredient of film culture. Few alternative films reached New Zealand during the war, though the level of mainstream film-going remained high.[1] Films associated with 'enemy' countries, such as Leni Reifenstahl's *Olympia* (1936), were suppressed, and 'New Zealand's tiny group of "enemy aliens", Germans and Italians, received quite harsh treatment. At peak in December 1942, 185 were interned' (Belich 2001: 295). The period immediately following the war saw a step forward in film society activity, as part of a worldwide phenomenon. In England and throughout its declining Empire, on the Continent and in North America, individual film societies emerged from the desolation and privations of war. In France, the opportunity to see American films again served as a catalyst to new kinds of film criticism. In Italy, the film industry re-emerged with the energies of Neo-realism. Whether awareness of a wider world had been stimulated by the war, or it was simply time to catch up with overseas developments, New Zealand saw a strong resurgence in film societies. Around this time, other parts of the country's cultural infrastructure were being consolidated – including a National Orchestra established in 1946, the magazine *Landfall* and the Queen Elizabeth II Arts Council in 1947. The same year would see the creation of a national federation of film societies.

This chapter will trace the work undertaken largely by members of the Auckland and Wellington film societies and, to a lesser degree, the formation of film societies in the two other main cities and smaller provincial towns. I will track the emergence of periods of collaboration between independent distributors and exhibitors of 'minority interest' films and the film societies. I will also describe the moment when a numerically small (although critically acute and organisationally adroit) film culture reached critical mass. More 'challenging' films entered the country through independent film festival organisations, which no longer needed to depend as much as they had done on the favours and support of the dominant commercial exhibition and distribution chains (Kerridge-Odeon and Amalgamated Theatres). This, in turn, enriched the loam in which film culture grew.

The Revival

The technology that assisted the formation of film societies was 16mm, a format that came into widespread use because wartime cameramen needed lighter cameras. Sixteen-millimetre film, cameras, and projection equipment were cheaper and considerably lighter: the celluloid was about one-fifth the weight of 35mm, so print and freight costs were significantly reduced. Another advantageous wartime development was the replacement of cellulose nitrate by cellulose acetate (sometimes called 'safety film'). This was much less prone to catch fire and, when lit, burnt slowly without explosion. Now film societies no longer needed to hire purpose-built cinemas equipped with fireproof projection boxes, nor did they need to pay for a qualified projectionist or fire insurance. Given that film societies had always been financially challenged, the convenience and cost savings associated with 16mm equipment were hugely important, more than compensating for the loss of quality involved in the shift to a smaller format. Although 16mm had less visual detail and a compressed soundtrack that often resulted in distortion, its convenience did much to promote the art of film.

Used in the production of newsreels, documentaries, and educational films, 16mm was also the format for hugely increased libraries of feature films transferred from 35mm as part of Hollywood's war effort. Servicemen throughout the Pacific, for example, were able to rest and relax from the rigours of battle with regular screenings of feature films in military camps and other makeshift theatres. In the intervals of calm amidst the perils of war, Wynne Colgan (later an important film critic and film festival director) organised film screenings for servicemen in the Solomon Islands.[2]

But 16mm films were not only used for rest and relaxation purposes; such 'idleness' did not feel quite right. New Zealand's Calvinist inheritance insisted that entertainment be balanced with something more serious. New Zealand's Army Education and Welfare Service (AEWS), officially established in 1942, grew out of WEA suggestions that 'servicemen should be offered some further education'. There was no stinting of resources for the cultural uplift of servicemen and women once the AEWS was established.

> It enjoyed the full co-operation of all existing educational institutions. The Broadcasting Service [under James Shelley] helped it, especially with group music-making. A large collection of films was available for the use of lecturers. Library services were controlled by trained librarians, and it was possible to maintain recreational as well as study reading
> (Hall 1970: 78–79).

The AEWS screened feature films and documentaries in the larger military camps using 16mm equipment. The success of its adult education programme, and the high quality of the pedagogical material created by its officers (among whom John Reid, who figured prominently in the making of a local film culture after the war) paved the way to an expansion of adult education services for the whole population when World War II finally ended.[3]

After the war, film societies had access to a range of hitherto unaffordable or unavailable films and projection equipment. Gordon Mirams was well aware of this bounty. He was also alert to the initial trepidation felt by the commercial film distributors who feared yet another threat to their revenue stream. They acted as a pressure group upon the Chief Inspector of Films, seeking to have the Cinematograph Films Act applied to 16mm films. The Chief Inspector responded by issuing notice of a conference to be held in September 1945 to consider any dangers to public safety, associated with this film gauge; whether the Film Hire Tax should be imposed; and whether or not its use should be regarded as competitive with the regular industry (*NZ Listener* 1945c: 16–18). In the event, the conference did not take place and the Act was not applied.

Mirams wrote two long and strongly worded articles that explained his opposition in no uncertain terms.[4] Citing *Variety*, 'that queer and colourful but usually authoritative organ of the U.S. entertainment world', Mirams informed his readership that Loew's International, which, among other interests, controlled MGM, had set up a division for the overseas distribution of 'narrow gauge' film (*NZ Listener* 1945e: 18–19). All of MGM's future output would also see a 16mm copy made as a way to reach out to new audiences in areas so remote that distance prevented them from regular cinema attendance. The more flexible attitude in the States meant that local branches of the major Hollywood film distributors had to rethink their strategy. This was surely also a factor in the cancellation of the conference mentioned above. Clearly, some important Hollywood players had decided that it was more profitable to be inclusive, with the re-emergent film societies treated as clients rather than competitors.

In late October 1945, Gordon Mirams invited some enthusiasts of the seventh art to an informal meeting at his house in Brooklyn (Wellington). At the meeting were Gordon's brother, Roger, recently returned from service as a newsreel war cameraman in Italy; Ngaio Marsh, the famous theatre director and writer of detective fiction; Ron Ritchie, who became the treasurer and, later, president of the Wellington Film Society; John O'Shea, and George Eiby, volcanologist, theatre designer and cinephile. In his capacity as film critic at the *New Zealand Listener*, Mirams had often written of films, now he sought to stimulate something more organised: 'It is possible, indeed, that some sort of New Zealand Film Centre or Film Institute, on the lines of those operating in Great Britain, U.S.A., and Australia, may emerge' (*NZ Listener* 1945e: 18–19). The inaugural meeting was also Mirams' way of introducing people that he thought ought to know one another – a classic example of how a culture is built, by bringing together a critical mass of enthusiasts, to see what combustion might occur.

In Wellington, a formal General Meeting was held at the Blue Triangle Hall on 13 December 1945, from which emerged the Wellington Film Institute (WFI), armed with a constitution and elected officers. Mirams became the first president of the post-war WFI and Cecil Holmes (NFU director) its secretary. The WFI described itself (in terms reminiscent of Lord Reith's definition of the BBC's philosophy) as 'an association of people who are interested in the motion picture as art, entertainment and education' (*NZ Listener* 1946a: 28–30). Five months later, in May, Mirams informed his *Listener* readership of various activities, such as regular screenings of 'worthy' films (which tended initially to be largely documentary, drawing heavily on the expanding and free film collections of the NFL and the US Information Service). There were also screenings of much talked-about but previously unseen 'classics' from the silent era (such as *The Cabinet of Dr. Calagari* and *Battleship Potemkin*), and the revival of films that had been released commercially but were 'of particular interest to the student of the cinema'. American titles mentioned were: *The Informer* (1935), *Winterset* (1936), *Fury* (1936), and *Grapes of Wrath* (1940). French films included: *Mayerling* (1936), *Le Roman d'un tricheur* (1936), and *Un Carnet de bal* (1937) (*NZ Listener* 1946a: 30). The Institute also planned to act as a pressure group on important public matters such as censorship.

In May 1946, the WFI purchased three classics from the BFI – 16mm copies of Eisenstein's *Battleship Potemkin* (USSR, 1925), Wiene's *The Cabinet of Dr. Calagari* (Germany, 1919), and Murnau's *The Last Laugh* (Germany, 1924). These were eagerly awaited. Their arrival in September raised an unexpected problem that left the fledgling WFI financially troubled. The BFI had sent the films *par avion*, with the result that a bill of £36, almost the cost of the three prints, had to be paid.[5] These three films were joined by two others ordered from the BFI in April 1947: Hitchcock's first sound film *Blackmail* (UK, 1929) and Pabst's mining tragedy *Kameradschaft* (Germany, 1931).

The much-talked about *Battleship Potemkin* was screened for the first time in New Zealand on 21 October 1946 at the Wellington Town Hall Concert Chamber, some 20 years after its making. This would not be the first time that a seminal film arrived long after its initial incendiary impact in Europe – Jean-Luc Godard's *À bout de souffle* only arrived in 1969, ten years after its explosive début in France. Two short Australian films about Aboriginals, *Walkabout* and *Tjuranga*, accompanied *Potemkin* to a house so full that a repeat screening was later organised at the Paramount Theatre by the Society for Closer Relations with Russia.

In early January 1946, an Auckland group led largely by WEA people established the Auckland Film Society, 'an association of people who are interested in the motion picture both as art and entertainment, and whose object it is to encourage higher public standards of film and protect the interests of consumers' (*Craccum* 1946: 7). Later in the year, similar societies came into existence in the southern cities of Christchurch, Dunedin, and Invercargill. The Dunedin Film Institute seems to have been as energetic as its northern counterparts, judging by its activities.[6] In 1948, there were 13 film societies in Otago (almost as many as the rest of the country combined) receiving monthly programmes (Hall 1970: 128). A significant factor in this rapid growth in Otago was the energetic work of the local adult education tutor: Peggy Dunningham.[7] The aims and activities of these film institutes and societies, whilst not identical, were broadly similar and there was, after initial independence with regard to film purchases, a large degree of co-operation between them.

The general 'pool' of films available to film societies was deepening. Members of the AFS had not been idle while the WFI purchased films, having taken steps to procure their own. The first was Berthold Bartosch's 30-minute animated film *L'Idée* (France, 1932) (*Craccum* 1946: 7), which drew inspiration from the series of 82 woodcuts made by Frans Masereel in 1920. Arthur Honegger wrote the music score. The technique employed by Bartosch is said to have anticipated Disney's multiplane animation. This aesthetically expressive film was also well-suited to the political mood of the times in which it was made as a polemic against exploitation and a cry of hope for the eventual victory of true democracy over brute force (Martin, 1995).

The second of the AFS's films was René Clair's *The Italian Straw Hat* (France, 1928) (*Craccum* 1946: 7). The NFL had, for its part, purchased Cavalcanti's compilation film about the rise of the documentary, *Film and Reality* (UK, 1942) – understood in Griersonian terms – Pudovkin's silent film *Mother* (USSR, 1926), and Flaherty's *Nanook of the North* (USA/France, 1922). From these titles, and those mentioned above, it is clear that film societies were attempting to catch up with the last quarter-century of the films most written about by the overseas (particularly British) champions of 'film as art'. As John O'Shea put it, 'How eagerly we await the screening of those films that have for so many years baffled and thwarted our appreciation and estimation of the cinema. … Years have hallowed the films we await' (*MFB* 1946).

The idea of a New Zealand Federation of Film Institutes was first mooted by the WFI as early as April 1946 when it sought 'to treat with the British Film Institute in the matter of purchasing 16mm prints of important films'.[8] It obviously made good sense for the nascent regional bodies to affiliate and share costs but the impetus to actually do something about it may have been forced on them by the policy of the BFI, always the point of reference for New Zealand film societies. 'What has been done in Great Britain is the model for what is being attempted in New Zealand', wrote Mirams (*NZ Listener* 1946a: 29). The BFI would not supply films to separate societies, nor would it lend films; New Zealand film societies would have to purchase their films outright. The WFI had applied for affiliation with the BFI in the first quarter of 1945 and seems to have been knocked back judging by the response they received from the Deputy Director of that organisation:

In view of the greatly increasing interest which appears to be shown throughout the Commonwealth in film societies I am, quite frankly, wondering whether it would not be possible, now that air services are so much improved for all the Commonwealth Film Societies to co-operate and purchase a number of copies of film for their own use which could be forwarded to one another. In other words, the formation of an Imperial Federation of Film Societies on the lines of the present Federation of Film Societies existing in Great Britain.

(*NZ Listener* 1946a: 28–30)

Such imperial encouragement may have spurred co-operation between the 'Tasman World' rivals of Australia and New Zealand (see Mein-Smith, Hempenstall, and Goldfinch, 2008 for details of the fluctuating fortunes of trans-Tasman relations). Trans-Tasman relations were initially enhanced when the much sought-after *Potemkin* was loaned to Australia at the request of the Sydney Film Society in December 1947, but a minor crisis ensued when the film was damaged while on loan to the Australians. 'A courteous letter asking that they pay the cost of a new copy' was sent.[9] It was a constant problem to keep prints in good condition when they passed through a number of projectors. *Potemkin* and *Calagari* were screened so often that their reappearance became a Film Society joke ('It's *Calagari* this month; it must be *Potemkin* next month!'). In a more positive spirit, one might say they became icons of Film Society membership.

On Saturday 1 February 1947, delegates from the five largest film societies throughout New Zealand took part in a conference in Wellington to discuss the formation of a New Zealand Film Institute (NZFI), which would act as a parent body for the local societies. Present at the meeting were Mr. J.F. McDougall (Auckland), Mrs. McKenzie (Christchurch), Mrs. Dunningham and Dr. Ellis (Dunedin), Mr. Lyttle (Invercargill), Mr. Harris (NFL), and Messrs. Mirams, Holmes, Shankland and Qualter (Wellington). The NFL offered to buy some films recommended by the societies and hoped that the societies would buy others, for example early Chaplin, whose purchase might raise disapproving eyebrows in government circles unappreciative of their educational value.[10]

One practical result of the conference was the establishment of a Working Committee, based in Wellington, to co-ordinate purchases and organise programmes. The days of independent film societies simply purchasing films that appealed to them were numbered. Two years later, in February 1949, at the Annual NZFI Conference (Dunedin), it was decided that ownership of past purchases should be transferred to the NZFI. Film acquisition became the exclusive preserve of the Working Committee of the NZFI as it sought to assert its authority in the interests of a greater collective good. As early as September 1947, although having 'no objection' to the AFS plan to purchase Joris Ivens' 1937 documentary *Spanish Earth* (USA), it was already busy considering purchases for the following year. The films under discussion included Paul Leni's silent 1924 expressionist horror film *Waxworks* (Germany), Walter Ruttmann's *Berlin, Symphony of a City* (Germany, 1927), Christian-Jacque's 1945 version of *Carmen* (France), Lang's *Metropolis* (Germany, 1927), Charlie Chaplin's *The Champion* (USA, 1915), Jean Epstein's 1931 documentary *Mor Vran* (France), Josef von Sternberg's 1930 German classic *Blue Angel*, and D.W. Griffith's acclaimed, if controversial, *Birth of a Nation* (USA, 1915).

This mix of old and new allows us to gauge the varied aims of the NZFI: the revival of older and, in some instances, commercially released films (Lang, Chaplin and Griffith), the presentation of unseen films that had received overseas film society acclaim (Leni, Epstein, and von Sternberg), leftist-inspired documentary (Ivens and Raizman), and Continental productions of 'quality' (Christian-Jacque). The range closely corresponded to what the BFI would have regarded as an educated film taste, though it did not venture into any of the cutting-edge areas that the BFI sometimes explored.

By the end of its first year, membership of the WFI stood at just under 300 and the AFS had around 150. In early 1949, the renamed Dunedin Film Society was proudly claiming its numerical superiority over the other societies. 'With a membership of 450, the Dunedin Film Society, which has existed for only two years, is the largest film society in New Zealand, according to a statement in the annual report' (*Evening Star* 1949). They went from 'Institute' to 'Society' at the same time as Wellington, in May 1947, for reasons that remain obscure but may have been a matter of lining up with the name of the London Film Society and separating out from the New Zealand tradition of Working Men's Institutes.[11]

Developing Discursive Practices

Another of the WFS's ambitions was the publication of a regular film bulletin and the formation of study groups. The Anglo-American connection was strong as this project was to be modelled on comparable publications put out by the BFI and the US National Board of Review. This was, moreover, an ambition shared by the other provincial film societies. Both Auckland and Dunedin were quick to establish a regular publication in which short film reviews mingled with pedagogical articles, as they sought to develop a critical vocabulary that would enable their members to talk more intelligently about the art of cinema. The Auckland Film Society's *News and Reviews* first came out in August 1946 with an article on Fritz Lang's *Metropolis* (1927), screened to members in that month, and a review of Basil Wright's much-admired

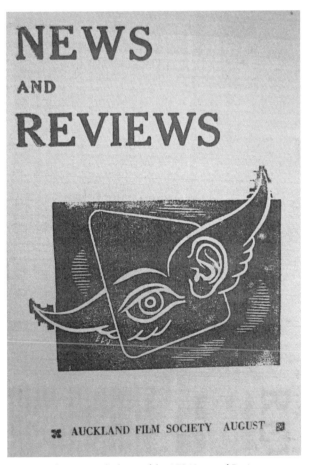

Figure 9: The inaugural edition of the AFS *News and Reviews*.

Song of Ceylon (UK, 1934). *Close Up*, edited by Wynne Colgan, was the resilient successor to *News and Reviews*, appearing for the first time in 1949, and continuing to this day.

Dunedin's *Monthly Film Bulletin*, edited by Ellis, came out in early September. Besides informing readers of the WEA background to the DFS (a past shared by film societies throughout the land), the *Bulletin* also proposed – in a series of short articles – to determine the various technical components of a film and the characteristics that made one better than another. The collaboration between the DFS and the *Otago Daily Times*, probably the result of close community links, saw the *ODT* publish a series of articles 'prepared by the Dunedin Film [Society] as an introduction to the study of the cinema as an art form' (*ODT* 1947b: 2). In one of them, Mr. J.A. Samuel gave a rapid account of the growing mobility of the camera up to the time of Griffith's *Birth of a Nation* and *Intolerance* (1916). Samuel also stressed the importance and artistry of 'cutting' according to the 'Cine-Eye' (an expression he borrowed directly from Soviet filmmaker Dziga Vertov).

Samuel had had some direct experience of filmmaking in 1941 when still a medical student at Otago University. He was identified as a 'film enthusiast' by John Harris, a dynamic librarian at the university who 'commissioned' him to make a documentary that would inform the people of Dunedin about the many services their libraries performed. As Harris later wrote: 'It was far from simple, and problems that we had never thought of kept presenting themselves. We turned to books. We read Pudovkin's *Film Technique*, and other classics' (*New Zealand Libraries* 1941). Apparently certain sections succeeded in presenting a vivid picture of the catalogue as the key to the library. It was also judged effective propaganda for microfilm.

The first of the monthly film bulletins, easily the largest and most informative, was Wellington's. First published in early July 1946, it was discontinued after the AGM of 1953, which decided that the printing costs were too great, being replaced by a subscription to the British *Sight and Sound* – an ironic return to colonial dependency. The BFI was in a generous mood and included 2000 copies of its *Critics' Choice*, as well. *Sequence*, the successor to Wellington's defunct bulletin, began to be published in 1955 – a welcome reassertion of national autonomy. Wellington's *MFB* carried a greater number of reviews though an arrangement with the AFS meant that some were written by Auckland's members because films were often released first in that city before travelling slowly south. From its inception, it ran an editorial in which well-regarded members expounded their considered opinions of the cinema. In the introductory editorial, Mirams bewailed the disappointing nature of the discussions that had so far followed screenings of films.

This was a sentiment shared widely by office holders of the Dominion's other film societies and said something about the mind-forged manacles that continued to inhibit intellectual discussion in New Zealand. The WFS, not content to bemoan this state of mind, initiated small study groups to create an environment for a freer exchange of views. In order for this to work, they understood the need to develop a critical vocabulary. The discourse readiest at hand was that inherited from 1930s left-wing mass cultural critiques – left-wing thought was still strong among leading members of the Society. The one area in which consensus seemed possible was the social impact of the cinema. A sociological approach to the reception of film could draw on various critiques of Hollywood's 'Dream Factory' and its dubious influence on everything from values to clothing and hairstyles. This approach certainly suited Mirams, as later analysis of his work will demonstrate.

During these years there was some more thoughtful discussion of the social implications for film, for example in a public meeting in June 1945, in Wellington, called by the New Education Fellowship to discuss 'The Films in Relation to Children and Child Delinquency'.

M O N T H L Y   F I L M   B U L L E T I N
of the
WELLINGTON FILM INSTITUTE

No. 1   July 4, 1946

Secretary: C. W. Holmes,   Price 3d
21 Hay Street, Oriental Bay.   (Free to Members)

BY WAY OF INTRODUCTION

Nearly all organisations and societies, especially those of a cultural nature, feel the urge at a certain point in their development to put themselves into print, by producing bulletins or newsletters for the benefit of their own members and of interested outsiders. It is a very healthy sign that the Wellington Film Institute, not yet a year old but with a membership already near the 300 mark, has so soon felt sufficient confidence to launch this venture of a regular monthly bulletin.

In doing this we are, of course, merely carrying out one of the primary objects of our organisation. For, to paraphrase our constitution, the Wellington Film Institute is an association of people who are not merely interested in looking at unusual films but whose object is also to encourage higher public standards in the motion picture and to protect the interests of the "consumer" (i.e. the average picture-goer), by supplying reliable information about current cinema entertainment, with particular reference where possible to its suitability for children.

So, while this bulletin will function partly as a kind of notice-board of coming meetings and other events (thus replacing the former circulars), your Executive Committee feels that the Institute's aim of protecting "consumer interests" can best be served by devoting a large part of the available space to competent reviews of current and coming films at the ordinary theatres. Some of these reviews will be gathered from reliable outside sources, but it is hoped that this material will come mainly from the Institute's own panel of film-reviewers.

Figure 10: The first of the Wellington Film Institute's monthly bulletins.

W.J. Scott, a lecturer at the Wellington Teachers' Training College, founder member of the WFS and on its executive committee, chaired the meeting at which Mirams, Stanhope Andrews (NFU), and Walter Harris (NFL) all spoke (*NZ Listener* 1945b: 6–7). F.L. Combs, subsequently president of the WFS, later wrote 'The Cinema and Education' in the *NZ Listener* on 6 December 1946. Scott was commissioned by the New Zealand Council for Educational Research to study the out-of-school cultural habits and preferences of secondary school children (published in 1947 as *Reading, Film & Radio Tastes of High School Boys and Girls*). This was one of the first New Zealand reception studies in the field of popular culture. Scott, an important pioneer in the teaching of modern approaches to education, had been influenced in the 1930s 'by the literary criticism of I.A. Richards and by F.R. and Q.D. Leavis and other members of the Scrutiny group' (Renwick n.d.).

As Vice-President of the WFI, Scott grappled with the uncertain critical status of the medium. His August editorial in the *MFB* expressed his discomfort over the ambiguous nature of the cinema, commingling as it did pleasure (sensuality, eroticism, laughter, and the vicarious delights of trespass) with critical rigour (high moral purpose, political content, social analysis). High art and popular culture appeared to be waging war within his breast. His article accepted as a given the importance of narrative in making sense of life but this created a dilemma for him:

> Like most filmgoers we are really more interested in the story in films than in anything else – in the representations of people performing actions in which we, the spectators, can involve ourselves emotionally. Saddled with critical standards that prevent us from equating value with entertainment, as most filmgoers do, we are rarely able to let ourselves go. Usually we are in the awkward position of feeling that we must not approve of something that we nevertheless enjoy – enjoy because most of us nearly always commit ourselves emotionally to a participation in the fortunes of the hero and the heroine of the film story, even while disapproving of its quality.[12]

Scott's approach illustrated the fact that local intellectuals had still not come to grips with popular culture.[13] The film medium was a central site for this tension. Scott was certainly not uninformed about popular culture but as an educator he had mixed feelings. Many writers about film similarly grappled with guilt feelings as they attempted to reconcile their environment with their 'critical standards' as educators, moralists or political activists. This was a recurrent theme in the 1940s as it had been in the 1930s. An editorial, written by F.L. Combs, a pioneer of adult education, was even less sympathetic:

> Its worst fault is that [film] seeks the greatest common denominator of popularity, and in so doing is callously indifferent to the consequent prostitution of art. The result is that the film serves in a manner more or less specious and synthetic to give the 'lie in the heart' a factitious vitality, and to interpose its silver screen between our civilisation and the living truth. The harm it does can scarcely be exaggerated. Having at its command

an unexcelled medium of verisimilitude it uses it for the purpose of convincingly stating falsities and thus perpetuating them.

(Monthly Film Bulletin 1946)

For Combs, the only solution to this sorry state of affairs was somewhat utopian – 'an educational revolution [that] will give us the film audiences necessary to restore integrity to the artist and make him creatively free' (*MFB* 1946). His sweeping belief that the film medium was failing to become an art seemed based on a curiously romantic conception of writers, painters, and composers as beings untouched by any desire for popularity or the need to make a living. This was hardly an encouraging attitude for local filmmakers. What was lacking in the local debate was any awareness of the Modernist interest in popular culture that had permitted the development of a cinematic aesthetic that encompassed aspects of Hollywood as well as European art cinema. In Berlin, in the 1920s, for example, some sections of the avant-garde had seen American mass culture as a vehicle for the radical modernisation and democratisation of both German culture and German life: 'It stood not only for Charlie Chaplin and the movies, for jazz, the Charleston, boxing, and spectator sports: it represented above all modernity and the ideal of living in the present' (Kaes 1994: 26). It was otherwise in New Zealand where popular culture was still equated with Americanism, voracious capitalism, and the 'prostitution of art'.

The Lecture Hall of the Wellington Public Library was the place for a new venture, 'Tea and Talk', which began in December 1946. In an effort to generate discussion, repeat screenings of notable films were organised. The idea of seeing a film more than once was a radical idea, promoted by the WFI both because it was a precondition for the close appreciation of films, and because the shortage of films made it a necessity. Attendance records seem not to have been kept, but the post-film *soirée* had about it a touch of class. 'The parties and meetings and social gatherings of the early film society were of an extraordinary high tone and I always credited the Ritchies with this. They were determined that everything was going to be done decently, no mucky suppers in chipped cups.'[14]

As had happened in London at the BFI, left-wing sympathy combined with aesthetic enthusiasm to give a special resonance to Soviet films. Eisenstein's *The General Line* (1929) and Pudovkin's *General Suvarov* (1941) were both screened in 1948 under the 'Tea and Talk' rubric, with a young academic, James Bertram, invited to lead a discussion after the second screening of *The General Line* in May.

Collaboration with Business

A Dunedin initiative, watched with great interest by the other societies, was the organisation of a film festival in collaboration with Robert Kerridge's theatre chain. Held in the first quarter of 1947, the festival, which ran for a week, was open to the public. Of particular note

143

was the decision of the DFS to select films, including Hollywood films, based on the reputation of the director rather than the cast, as they believed 'that it is the director who determines the quality of a film' – an early sign of the emergence of the idea of authorship (*ODT* 1947a). During the festival, the public had the opportunity to see examples of the work of René Clair, Walt Disney, John Ford, Harold Bucquet, Frank Capra, and the Marx Brothers.[15] The significance of the festival (apparently the first of its kind in New Zealand) lay in the mutually profitable co-operation between a commercial cinema chain and the film society – beauty and the beast were here reconciled. Kerridge had the organisational machinery, theatres, and contacts with overseas distributors, while the DFS had a niche audience to deliver and a film programme to compose.

Granted, the alliance with a commercial chain meant (as in Dunedin) that many of the films were likely to be American. A large chain would have an output deal with major studios, and this would mean that occasional American films would turn up that seemed too specialised for local cinemas. A festival could provide a useful launching pad. The emphasis on American films also had the advantage of challenging film society prejudices towards such films, though the kind of debate needed to thrash the issue out had yet to happen in New Zealand.

The success of the Dunedin festival prompted other film societies to contact Kerridge with a view to organising something comparable in other cities. A sub-committee of the WFS was set up in September to look into it. This festival, held at the Time Theatre in October 1947, included Chaplin's *The Gold Rush* (USA, 1925), Disney's *The Reluctant Dragon* (USA, 1941), and Carol Reed's *The Way Ahead* (UK, 1944). Some years later, and by arrangement with the managers of Wellington's independent theatres, the Paramount and the Roxy, there were Sunday night screenings of a number of films, which, although imported commercially, either had not received a commercial distribution or had met with limited success. Such films included *The Miracle* (Italy, 1948), *The Raven* (France, 1943), *The Pearl* (Mexico, 1953), and *The Difficult Years* (Italy, 1948), as well as repeat screenings of more successful films such as *Les Enfants du paradis* (France, 1945) and *La Kermesse héroique* (France, 1935).

The immediate post-war period – when the USSR was still seen as a wartime ally – saw greater opportunities for fruitful collaboration between the film society movement and commercial exhibitors to import Russian films, as we have seen. The focus, however, was on French titles. Independent distributor Natan Scheinwald had shown the way in the late 1930s, and led again in 1948 when he organised the first successful European festival, supported by the WFS, of 'Continental' films at the Opera House in a season that ran from 12 November to 30 December. Among the ten French films presented were *La Kermesse héroique* (1935), *L'Éternel retour* (1943), *La Grande illusion* (1937), *Ils étaient neufs célibataires* (1939) and two from the popular Marcel Pagnol, *La Femme du boulanger* and *La Fille du puisatier* (both 1940). With *Behind these Walls* (a.k.a. *Jéricho*, 1945), the astute Scheinwald appealed directly to New Zealanders' patriotism; it was billed as 'a gripping saga of a New Zealand airman's hazardous co-operations with the French underground during the war'.[16]

Other independent film importers, distributors, and exhibitors were also at work offering films from other sources, often from France which, as a national cinema, was New Zealanders' most significant alternative to films from Hollywood and England. An audience for French films had developed, thanks in part to Mirams who had for many years been enthusing about them. The *Listener* ran occasional articles about the film world, such as 'Sixty Miles of Film in Twenty Languages', which stitched together various journalists' impressions of the first real Cannes Film Festival held in 1946 (the French Government had given approval for its creation in 1939 but war had intervened). Of the many interesting details of this article, one in particular should be noted – its praise for Rossellini's seminal neo-realist film *Rome, Open City* (1945), which had been a hit in the United States. 'It is the first example of a new kind of realism from across the Alps, and shows what the best modern European production can be like' (*NZ Listener* 1946b: 30–31).

This article may have served as a catalyst for Eddie Greenfield, an English migrant who arrived here in 1929, after having been publicity manager in Australia for J.C. Williamson Films, to acquire the New Zealand distribution rights. Greenfield had bought the Capitol Theatre in Balmoral in 1934, and eventually owned several cinemas in Auckland, including the Berkeley in Mission Bay, which made up his small Modern Theatres chain. In order to supply his cinemas with 'product', he set up Exclusive Films. As self-styled 'Distributors of World Famous Continental Films' after the war, Greenfield was responsible for introducing New Zealanders to several films of critical and historical importance, of which *Rome, Open City* was arguably the most significant. Other films included *Les Enfants du paradis* (1945), which was both a critical and public success internationally, and Julien Duvivier's *Panique* (1947), his first French film for a decade after Hollywood had lured him there following the success of *Pépé le Moko* (France, 1937).

Aware that film society support was essential to the nationwide reception of his films, Greenfield wrote to the individual societies informing them of his intentions and requesting that they alert their members to the arrival of his films in their towns. The WFS had no hesitation in vouchsafing the first three films to its members but could not promise to recommend others without having first seen them.[17] Greenfield treated some of his films lavishly, creating, for example, a high quality souvenir programme for *Les Enfants du paradis*, which was first released in Auckland in December 1947. 'Continental' or 'foreign' films were associated with high cultural standards (their reputation for being risqué developed later).

The second of the independents was New Zealand Film Services (NZFS). Formed in 1948, this company was the result of a merger between D. Russell Rankin's British Film Imports and Ron Usmar of R.A. Usmar and Company. Born in Christchurch in 1917, Rankin had formed Action Pictures in 1937 with Roger Mirams to import and distribute feature films. Although based in Wellington, the company had been financed by a number of Christchurch businessmen whom Rankin had persuaded to invest in the new venture. He showed considerable business acumen, scoring his first box office hit with an English film, *St. Martin's Lane* (1938), and quickly became managing director of his own company. After the war, the combined passion and acumen of Usmar and Rankin was directed principally towards the exhibition of film from sources other than Hollywood and England. This was because the Kerridge-Odeon and Amalgamated cinema chains had a stranglehold on most of the 'product' from those sources.

The commercial success NZFS later received as New Zealand agents for the English series of populist, very lucrative and very long *Carry On* films (there were 29 between 1958 and 1978), gave them the financial security to vary the range of their films and to play an important role in the establishment of New Zealand's first dedicated 'art-house' cinema in the early 1960s. Rankin and Usmar enjoyed a lengthy association with the film society movement (especially in Wellington) and with Amalgamated Theatres. Close collaboration with the latter gave them access to many of Amalgamated's first-run theatres throughout New Zealand. In many ways they helped to create, service, and form the cinematic tastes of minority film cultures in this country through the 1950s and early 1960s.[18]

Co-operation between the smaller independent film distributors (Sheinwald, Greenfield, Usmar and Rankin) and the NZFI moved ahead. This closeness was assisted by the stupidity of the Motion Picture Distributors' Association (MPDA). The WFS had written to them seeking to hire old films 'for the purpose of reviving them at non-public screenings' (*NZ Listener* 1946a: 30). The MPDA's response showed that they were distinctly out of touch with a growing section of the public and as greedy as ever.

> Your letter was very fully considered at a meeting of this Association yesterday and I was directed to reply stating that instead of screening the old films mentioned for the study of your members, it would probably be better if your members were influenced to attend the theatres at which current films of a similar type were screened from time to time. If your Institute is particularly interested in any film listed in the current year's product, application to this Association would result in information regarding the theatre and screening date being supplied in sufficient time to enable arrangements to see it being made.
>
> (*NZ Listener* 1946a: 30)

At the second conference of the NZFI, held in March 1948, letters were sent to both Scheinwald and Greenfield asking about their conditions of hire to film societies. We have already noted the symbiotic nature of the relationship, each needing the other to advance its cause. Scheinwald's Festival of Continental Film held at the Wellington Opera House later in the year was supported by the local film society. Greenfield screened *Rome, Open City* in Auckland but unfortunately it was not a box office success despite support from the film society (*Craccum* 1948a: 7), and from 'Astra', Wynne Colgan's *nom de plume* as film critic for the Auckland University College student magazine *Craccum* (1948b: 7).

While Greenfield did not import any Italian sequels, this was not the end of Rossellini in New Zealand. When Scheinwald encountered difficulties obtaining an import licence for the second of Rossellini's post–World War II trilogy of neo-realist films, *Paisà* (1946), the WFS wrote to government in October 1949 in support of the film. This was not the first time that the Society had to speak up in support of a film they wished to see, which the Government saw as politically suspect because of its country of origin. Leni Reifenstahl's *Olympia* (Germany, 1936), confiscated from the Consul of the Third Reich at the outbreak of World War II, had languished in a vault in the Prime Minister's Office for over six years until its screening at a Physical Education Summer School in New Plymouth in February 1946. Properly astounded at the way the athlete's bodies had been filmed and edited, other screenings to select audiences were planned. Two days prior to this event, the film was peremptorily removed by the order of the Prime Minister and much pressure needed to be applied before it was re-released. 'The new *Olympia* [was] shorn of 2000 feet of "paganism and propaganda". But even in its truncated form it remains a masterpiece' (*Craccum* 1948a: 7). By the end of the year, it had been seen in secondary schools throughout the country.[19]

Traditional notions of 'high' culture, when applied to the cinema, had encouraged literary and dramatic discussion of films. While these could be thoughtful, they were often compromised by cultural snobbery or a pro-English bias. The paternalism of the 1930s, carried over into the 1940s and 1950s, produced a rash of arguments in New Zealand about the negative effect of films on children, leading to the formation of study groups and public meetings seeking to 'save the young' and promote healthier films produced with that audience in mind.[20]

Meanwhile, *Landfall*, the new literary and arts magazine, invited articles on the subject of film and Mirams was asked to contribute to the first issue. It was to be his only article.[21] Entitled 'Peace – It's Wonderful: A Survey of Cinema since VJ Day', the review was an example of his impressionistic criticism, the expression of his particular taste or sensibility – an approach that can be described as 'neuro-glandular response' (Stam 2000). '*Going my Way* [USA, 1944], in spite of good acting and all the other kind things you can say about it, is basically cheap, and though perhaps not nasty, not far off it' (*Landfall* 1947: 44). Mirams lamented the 'fact' that film standards had not improved, in terms of either production or film appreciation. He added that 'this is the kind of result which produces one of those occasional moods of despondency in which one questions not merely whether one's whole output as a film critic is worth as much as the ink it is printed in, but also whether persons with any pretensions to intelligence are not wasting their time and their indulgence in taking the movies at all seriously' (*Landfall* 1947: 44). He especially bemoaned the rise in depictions of violence and sensuality, when these two activities were used to pander to vulgarity: 'Cheapness and nastiness are the besetting sins also of Mr Rank's *Wicked Lady* [UK, 1945], but here the issue is simpler, for *The Wicked Lady* is not even, I suggest, a well-made or particularly well-acted film. It just goes all out to exploit sex and violence as blatantly as it can; with the result that "cleavage" has once again become a problem to haunt the dreams of censors' (*Landfall* 1947: 45).

It is hard to imagine censors today being very worried about 'cleavage', but this was clearly a hot issue in 1947, for intellectuals too. To buttress his pleas for more serious films, Mirams invoked an English authority, Roger Manvell, familiar to YA listeners through the 'Art for Everyone' series produced by the BBC in which he had discussed 'The Things Which Really

Make a Good Film'. Dr. Manvell was film critic for the *Times Literary Supplement* and author of a popular Pelican book entitled *Film* (*NZ Listener* 1945a: 6–7).

Mirams believed that World War II was largely responsible for the decline in standards that now saw 'eroticism, violence, and sadism [forming] the basis – sometimes separately but usually in combination – of by far the largest single class of films made since the war ended' (*NZ Listener* 1945a: 46). He cited several examples of what the French film critic, Nino Frank, had recently identified as *film noir*, cynical American crime dramas with lashings of sex and visual style: *Cornered* (1945), *Confidential Agent* (1945), *Deadline at Dawn* (1946), and *Dark Corner* (1946). For Mirams, these films exalted 'the social and moral irresponsibility of the ruthless individualist. Indeed, this current adulation of toughness in the cinema becomes, with repetition, not merely a trifle boring but even perniciously anti-social. Or, to put it bluntly and perhaps to exaggerate a little, the spiritual climate of many of our new films is basically fascist' (*NZ Listener* 1945a: 47). Walt Disney's cartoons were included in the sweep: 'Donald [Duck] has all the makings of a fascist, if he isn't one already' (*NZ Listener* 1945a: 48). This was a provocative suggestion that later cultural critics would develop in detail (Elliot 1993; Roth 1996).

The final trend noted in his survey, and, for Mirams, the 'healthiest and most promising', was the emergence of a cinema that drew its 'subjects from real life and treats them with imaginative realism' (*Landfall* 1947: 46). This suggests that Mirams was alert to the neo-realist winds of change that had begun to blow in some Italian filmmaking. I have stressed his moralism to illustrate the extent to which he was a man of his time, and to suggest the positive and negative sides of his work. Distaste for popular culture makes sense in an age when cinema attendance was at an all-time high, and Hollywood studios were churning out films in a manner that was likened to a production line. We can also appreciate the effort involved in creating a high culture in New Zealand, having to push popular culture aside to make space for something more 'serious'. By today's standards, however, his moralism seems excessively earnest and limited by a kind of political correctness that sometimes ignores the stylistic energies of films or their subversive and carnivalesque aspects. Like most other critics of the period, he did not stray far beyond the explicit aspects of content.

There was, in so many of the critiques that circulated in this period, a marked suspicion of mass art's appeal to the emotions (Carroll 1998). For Mirams, the task of the film critic was to balance two things – a defence of the potential of the cinema and a strong critique of its everyday practice. His sense of the power of the medium implied a corresponding need for vigilance. One of the clearest examples of the social and political basis of his crusade was his address to the conference of the Royal Society of New Zealand in 1947, on 'The Cinema as a Social Influence'. This expressed his intimate conviction that films played a vital and formative role in society. He cited extracts and conclusions from J.P. Mayers' *Sociology of Film*, a 1947 critique of mainstream film culture similar to the pessimistic analysis of the Frankfurt School for Social Research, an intellectual trend now more commonly called critical theory, which has had widespread influence on many critics' conceptions of the effects of mass art on culture, and the individual's relationship to society, as mediated through mass art works: 'The spiritual dictatorship of the modern cinema is more powerful than the dictatorship of Hitler because it is less obvious, hidden in the vast machinery of the modern large-scale industry.'[22]

An echo of the myth of audience passivity was heard in *Landfall* in June 1947, when a young Canterbury College academic, J.G.A. Pocock, then Assistant Lecturer in History, examined the changing relationship between the spectator and the actor brought on by the introduction of sound. Pocock, who would go on to an illustrious academic career in the USA, argued in the *Landfall* article that the critical faculties of the spectator had been significantly diminished as the 'screen's hypnotic and illusive powers were greatly heightened; it was thus possible to develop the spectator's sense of emotional participation in the events presented to him until it quite outstripped his power of criticism and his sense of being separate from them' (1947: 134). The mass audience thus endured 'standardised vulgarity, the lowest-common-factor conventions, the false catharsis and the escape into glamour and unreality' (134).

Today such critiques of popular culture have at least in some areas been qualified by awareness of the spectator's 'negotiation' of meaning in seeing a film; reception is now acknowledged to be an active, locally specific process. Film theory has also challenged the assumption that popular culture is simply a matter of emotion. This assumption, common among intellectual critics in the 1940s, echoed an old Platonic theme: 'Plato's arguments against the arts are premised on the way in which he thought that drama and painting address the emotions of spectators. Plato's central argument hinged on his conviction that the emotions are irrational in the sense that they undermine the rule of reason, both in the individual and, in consequence, in society' (Carroll 1998: 250).

Media theory has also made problematic any notion of direct negative influence. While the popular media reflect and refract mainstream attitudes – else they would not be popular – they do not necessarily cause them to come into being. Greater openness to commercial popular culture is a characteristic trend of our age. People of Mirams' and Shelley's stamp reflected the 1940s and 1950s, inspired as they were by paternalistic notions of social improvement. The intellectuals had a pastoral role to play as shepherds of film taste. One is reminded of Kendrick Smithyman's poem from this period about a man of faith, clearly intended to describe one role model for the New Zealand intellectual: 'Wayward I could sing for its born people, being/ one knows no faith in them, being perversely of them. /It takes me, makes me, taxes me, and I shall not/turn from its service. Yet shall I be true priest!' (1960: 275).

This calling seems to have had broad general appeal among the educated, and, more particularly to James K. Baxter, one of the country's most promising poets in the 1950s. During a New Zealand Writers' Conference, organised by the English Department of Canterbury University College in 1951, the precocious Baxter stole the show with his address on 'Recent Trends in New Zealand Literature'. In it he declared that the poet was to be 'a cell of good living in a corrupt society' who must attempt both by his writing and his example to change it (cited in Barrowman 2003: 319). This was a challenge that our next individual rose energetically to meet.

The Perils of Passivity

'By 1946, John Reid, a conservative young Catholic academic critic, was complaining about the generally irreligious influence of American social fiction on New Zealand writers of the 1930s and 40s'. Laurence Jones' article (1994), from which this quote is taken, addressed the influence of American literature in New Zealand, but there are obvious reasons to relate the analysis to Hollywood. During World War II, Reid served in the AEWS and had access to the growing number of essentially educational documentaries that the NFL, under Walter Harris' enlightened direction, was collecting. Film was a lifelong interest for Reid. He was twice president of the NZFI (1949 and 1950), and once of the AFS (1950), and 'a notable film reviewer for the *Auckland Star* from 1954 to 1961' (Smith 2003: 123). With the support of Bishop Liston, editor-in-chief of the scholarly *Catholic Review: A Monthly Review Devoted to the Arts, Science and Culture* (1945–49), Reid wrote a series of essays on film for that periodical and contributed film criticism to other magazines (such as *Landfall* and *Comment*). He also participated regularly as a tutor for the Winter Film School in Wellington upon its establishment in 1954, until his untimely death in 1972.

Reid was one of a small group of New Zealand academics who were very alive to questions of local culture building. Though close in age to the generation of Allen Curnow, Colin McCahon, or Douglas Lilburn, he was distanced from what we might call the '*Phoenix* group' by his more traditional attitudes to religion, politics, and lifestyle. Nevertheless, he was just as passionate in his commitment to nation-building, and he serves as a reminder that cultural nationalism had other aspects and other styles.

Reid's sense of the need to 'thicken' middle-class culture in New Zealand at that time made him intolerant of small sects promoting an erudition that he saw as exclusive. In his view, the chief group that the NZFI should set out to influence was the middlebrow: 'The type who reads Charles Morgan and J.B. Priestly, and the better detective stories. ... The high-brow either belongs to a film society or is wedded to something else; the low-brow, not irredeemable, is a couple of stages away yet.'[23] There was a negative aspect to Reid's approach, strategic and public-spirited as it was. The 'three harmonies' of Belich's 'Great Tightening' thesis can help us to locate intellectuals like Reid within a particular cultural field, making him one voice in a chorus.

The 'great tightening' was the social and cultural aspect to the 'recolonial' order (1880s–1920s) that forged closer political, ideological, and economic connections with 'Mother England'. During this phase, a 'protein bridge' bound New Zealand farms to London markets: roughly 90 per cent of New Zealand's primary produce was sold there. The interest Belich's ideas hold for this investigation into film culture is found not only in the explanation for the close links with England, but also in the cultural and social transformations that economic and technological change wrought in the New Zealand psyche. The massive moral, social, and racial integration that was then developed 'tried, as it were, to harmonise, homogenise and even pasteurise New Zealand society. They harmonised acknowledged differences, suppressed and camouflaged others, and purified and laundered both form and content' (2001: 121).[24]

The approach of public intellectuals like Reid was more sophisticated than simple 'harmonising, homogenising, and pasturising', but their focus on middlebrow culture did involve some unfortunate tradeoffs; and what was originally a strategic decision came at times to seem a temperamental moral choice, excluding more specialised possibilities. Knowledgeable as he was about film, Reid had little time for the technical subtleties of cinematography, montage or *mise en scène*. His presidential address to the NZFI held in Auckland in 1949 gave fair warning. To stress 'artistic qualities' betrayed an insecure desire to impress, a result of the cinema's recent emergence from 'a brash and naïve entertainment to technical smoothness and something approaching seriousness'.[25]

Neither did he favour the sociological approach to films that he saw in the documentary work of Grierson and Flaherty. He thought (with some justice) that Cavalcanti's *Film and Reality* (1942) would be better called 'Film and Realism', as it was only 'one form of interpreting reality as a creative individual sees it'.[26] There were other notions of reality, including Catholicism, which seems to have been the intellectual centre of his analysis. Reality was, for Reid, 'the whole of life, all the dimensions, including the kind of realism the documentaries show, but including much else besides, the spirit and human values of *homo sapiens*, as well as his social preoccupations'.[27]

In film (as in life), the values that Reid was most interested in promoting were announced at the 1949 NZFI Conference, and could be seen in the films he then cited: Pagnol's warmly humanistic and wry series of films set in southern France, including *The Well-Digger's Daughter* (1940) and *The Baker's Wife* (1938); Maurice Cloche's reverent, and honoured, film *Monsieur Vincent*, which won an Oscar in 1947 as the Best Foreign Film; Emilio Fernandez's *The Pearl* (Mexico/USA, 1947), a morality tale warning of the false rewards and real troubles that material wealth brings; *Odd Man Out* (UK, 1947), Carol Reed's taut character study of an idealist symbolically crucified; Luigi Zampa's neo-realist *Vivere in pace* (Italy, 1946); and *The Search* (Swiss/USA, 1948), Fred Zinnemann's semi-documentary film on the plight of World War II orphans, with its sober meditation on the damage wrought by war.

The element that united them all, for Reid, was *caritas* – love. Not Hollywood love, nor 'the somewhat neurotic love and death-wish passion of *Les Enfants du paradis*, but love of man for man, for his home and children, the common bond of suffering which breeds love'.[28] Reid was looking to establish a Christian metaphysics of film that transcended the technical and the sociological aspects, which were not enough in themselves to make film an art. This was a time when local film culture was looking for new ways to understand film; and Reid was influential because of his confident approach which drew upon an impressive store of cultural capital. At its best, this pointed towards the kind of Catholic-influenced film aesthetics circulating in France; but at times, it narrowed to a campaign on behalf of positive Catholic role models. The cinema's job was to provide the general public with heroes and heroines: 'An audience prefers *affirmative* resolutions; they desire their *ideals* dramatised. The death of a hero, if he dies for an acceptable ideal, is not tragedy. The death of a protagonist, if he dies because he lives counter to an ideal, is affirmative', asserted Reid in his address to the 1951 NZFI Conference.[29] The best films provided lessons in living through a skilful blend of drama and didacticism. And he could cite many examples of great literature that displayed a similar moral value.

One of Reid's missions involved alerting his 'congregations' (secular and religious) to the morally perilous dangers of a certain type of cinema and a certain type of uncritical film appreciation. In his 1948 series of essays for the *Catholic Review*, Reid helped to provide Catholic leaders with the intellectual means to resist a variety of secular ills disseminated by commercial films. The titles of his essays give a broad idea of his concerns: 'Catholics and the Cinema: (1) The Influence of Films; (2) Catholic Film Action; (3) Censorship and the Children's Film; (4) What is a Good Film?; and (5) The Practice of Film Criticism.'[30] I propose to briefly trace his intellectual or philosophical objection to mainstream cinema as an instance of debased art with pernicious consequences for its consumers, locating it as a local expression of an intellectually fashionable discourse.

Reid saw Hollywood creating a new mythology to replace the ailing Greco-Judeo-Christian one. A fascination with superficial appearance informed its productions. It valorised being 'pushy', smartly dressed, wealthy, and nonchalant about sexuality, while Christian virtues of humility, chastity and love were forgotten. Reid developed a wide-ranging analysis of the harm done to a putatively passive cinema audience.[31] He saw passivity on the rise as 'one of the most destructive elements in modern commercial culture'.[32] Although his critique came primarily from a Christian perspective, Reid's remarks about spectatorial passivity in front of the silver screen bore a curious similarity to Marxist attacks on popular culture. Both operated within contemporary assumptions about reception that acknowledged the power of the film transaction but not its complexity.

Reid was well aware of modernism but – like many New Zealanders – he had little sympathy for its extreme forms. For him this was not a fragmented or absurd world in which isolated individuals struggled to create sense and meaning through their actions. There was no God-shaped hole in human consciousness, as Sartre had proclaimed. In reviewing Clouzot's celebrated film *Le Salaire de la peur* (1953), Reid acknowledged its cinematic virtuosity: 'Skilful direction and camera work, forceful acting and ... exciting story [would] ensure its popularity with everyone who likes thrills of the seat-clutching kind' (*Auckland Star* 1955: 2). Despite these attributes, Reid could not call the film 'a great picture, in the strict sense, since health is absent from it. Its shining shell surrounds soft existential pulp' (*Auckland Star* 1955: 2).

In another article, he wrote that 1955 had been notable for the quality of the many foreign films, 'with comedies and operas happily outnumbering those featuring post-war gloom and existentialist self-pity' (*Auckland Star* 1956: 6). Health was an important element in his aesthetic, a key concept, to balance the extreme individualism and 'materialistic cancer of our day' (Smith 2003: 121). So too was the need for social cohesion, the effort 'to weld society together again as a dynamic unit' (2003: 121) - a project reminiscent of Belich's 'three harmonies'. In these terms Reid saw his job as providing constructive criticism of cinema and radio as powerful modern influences.

Reid's film reviews were a later successful instance of a subject very much on the agenda of the NZFI's programme of activities. To enrich the public's appetite for film with various critical herbs and spices, the NZFI approached the major regional papers throughout 1948. At the 1949 NZFI Conference in Dunedin, John O'Shea reported that the papers not already publishing film reviews were amenable to the idea 'provided that a suitable person could be found'.[33] However, it was not until November 1954 that John Reid started his regular film column in the *Auckland Star*. Entitled 'Films of the Week,' Reid's column appeared prominently on page two of the newspaper, several pages ahead of the Hollywood gossip about stars and films that the paper had also printed from the 1920s at least. Perhaps this owed something to Reid's status as lecturer in English at the University of Auckland, and to the ambitious cultural scope of his film criticism, as well as to his ability to entertain and enthuse readers. For seven years he put his energies into this film column until Wynne Colgan became his chosen successor.

An earlier, although less widely read strain of weekly film criticism had started to appear from 4 July 1946 in *Zealandia*, a Catholic weekly newspaper, first published in 1934 by the Bishop of Auckland. A British Catholic digest, *Context*, provided the model for *Zealandia*'s reviewing. A principal ambition of this weekly was the formation of a Catholic film public with 'higher' critical standards that might exert pressure 'in the important matter of securing a production of worthwhile films' (*Zealandia* 1946). Not that its reviewers were mere ideologues. Robert Allender, who began *Zealandia*'s 'first experiment at independent film reviews', had lectured on film appreciation for the Auckland Adult Education Centre (*Landfall* 1948).[34] His first article began with an analysis of documentary filmmaking; his second considered the generic attributes of melodrama. Both articles stressed the importance of the director to the making of a 'good' film. His first review praised John Ford's direction of *They Were Expendable* (1945), while his second noted how well Billy Wilder had handled *Lost Weekend* (1945).

The rapid rise and enthusiastic spread of the post–World War II film society movement throughout the Dominion encouraged another experiment. On this occasion, the medium was the YA radio network. James Shelley was still at the helm of the renamed New Zealand Broadcasting Service (1946), which now ran both the YA and ZB stations (Day 1994: 277–79). The film 'experiment' was launched at 7.15 p.m. on 16 June 1948, when the NZBS broadcast *Footnotes to Films*, a half-hour fortnightly programme made by 'serious' enthusiasts from Auckland and Wellington. This experimental programme was designed to give foreknowledge of films released in Auckland and Wellington that wound their way south after having exhausted audiences in the north. Once this would have been considered improper – too close to advertising – but now it was viewed as a public service.

Auckland reviewers were to concentrate on British and Continental films, since these had their first release as a rule in that city, while Wellington handled American films. Each city had three reviewers. In Auckland, members of the AFS were at the forefront. J.F. McDougall, tutor-organiser of the Auckland Adult Education Centre, AFS Chairman and contributor to *News and Reviews*, the monthly film bulletin of the AFS, even had his photo in the *Listener*. Maurice Lee, another tutor-organiser with the WEA, committeeman of the AFS, and proselyte of the merits of visual education (who organised many factory lunchtime screenings of essentially documentary films) was the second. The threesome was completed by Ron Bowie, already known to 1YA (Auckland) listeners for his broadcasts on films in 1YA's Winter Course Talks. Bowie was a filmmaker who had produced documentary films such as *Industrial Auckland*, led an Adult Education class on film appreciation, and was also a contributing author of a correspondence course on the same subject (*NZ Listener* 1948a: 25).[35]

The triumvirate in the capital consisted of John O'Shea, Hubert Witheford and C.K. Herbert. Herbert was a freelance journalist and poet, secretary of the WFS and had participated in a WFS-sponsored amateur group's filming of a Frank Sargeson short story, *The Great Day*. O'Shea was Chairman of the Working Committee of the NZFI and editor of the WFS monthly bulletin. He was exceptionally well-informed on films but his strong opinions, combined with a tendency to stammer, made him a brave choice for the NZBS. Witheford was better known in local circles as a poet but had also written an article on war films published in *Landfall* and was a friend of O'Shea's. In the first of the *Footnotes to Films*, O'Shea and McDougall discussed 'the importance of informed film criticism' (*NZ Listener* 1948a: 25).

An anonymous Dunedin commentator received the first programme favourably: '*Footnotes to Film* is an extremely welcome addition to the 4YA programmes. The listener who "never goes to the pictures" must surely be in a very small minority nowadays, but, if he exists, I advise him to listen to this feature. … [C]riticisms and reviews of forthcoming films are not so much a feature of his everyday life that he can afford to miss hearing what other intelligent filmgoers have to say' (*NZ Listener* 1948b: 12). British film culture was introduced when a six-part BBC programme, 'Pictorial Parade', was heard on the YA network from April 1948.

Radio as an instrument of liberal cultural improvement was further combined with raising the standards of film appreciation when 1YA and 1YC offered their weekly reviews. They were 'of varying quality', wrote John Reid in his appraisal of them. 'The better 1YA reviewer is Wynne Colgan, whose comments show a keen appreciation of film values, are up-to-date and not too "arty"' (*NZ Listener* 1949a). Reid's appraisal of the 1YA film reviewers drew a vigorous response from Beatrice Russell of Auckland, 'a keen lover of films', who took exception to his masculine bias. She agreed that Colgan did a good job during these morning sessions but found that 'the women broadcasters are not only giving us excellent reviews, but that their views are more reflective of feminine viewpoint than Mr Colgan's can hope to be' (*NZ Listener* 1949b).

This wave of film reviewing reflected a new energy in public broadcasting, giving local enthusiasts a chance to talk about favourite topics. At the same time, the educational impulse remained extremely strong. These developments were in line with the vision of the future of broadcasting that Shelley had published in 1947, which saw devolution of authority from the centre and the inclusion of local performers over the airwaves. 'However the local broadcasts were to remain those selected by Reithian standards. Performers who most closely approximated the traditional high cultural standards in both content and performance would be entitled to broadcast from the more powerful stations' (Day 1994: 293–94).

This was a combination of outreach and uplift that opened the door a little further for film. Once again, however, moral issues loomed large. Film culture had so far been dominated by moral, religious or political priorities, and still rare indeed were aesthetic (film-as-film) perspectives or 'experimental' approaches of the type that had energised some of the most innovative thinking about film in other countries.

The main problem in the development of New Zealand's film culture was its emergence in an environment characterised by uniformity and narrowness rather than depth, a culture in which specialised, alternative interests and viewpoints had seldom reached critical mass. By the early 1950s, there were roughly 30 film societies in New Zealand with a combined membership of about 1500; in 1957, there were approximately 56 film societies with around 3000 members.[36] Reid used the NZFI Conference in 1952 to make a few telling remarks about the progress, influence, and importance of the film society movement in the course of its still short existence. He could not, however, repress the need to denigrate those who sought in film-art the exploration of new forms of thought and feeling, and who attached too much importance to experiment and technical vocabulary: 'I regard them as pernicious ... because they widen the gulf between modern manifestations of the artistic impulse and the general public, which is one of the greatest problems of the twentieth century.'[37]

Growing the audience remained the priority. Reid spoke of the very positive contribution in raising standards of film appreciation that the Auckland Film Society had made in that city, bringing together various pieces of the film culture jigsaw:

Before the Film Society existed, there was no radio film criticism, little newspaper criticism, no reporting or revival cinemas. Now 1YA and 1YC regularly broadcast frank radio film criticism and discussions, given either by members or associates of the Society, and inaugurated by the Society; three newspapers present copious weekly reviews, again a large part done by Society members; two cinemas present 'classic', foreign and revival films, many on the advice of the Society; several 'discarded' films have been released. ... Several public lectures, reported fully in the press, have been given to Auckland Societies and Training Colleges; a course on film was included in the last English Teachers' Refresher Course.[38]

It was clear that 'a wider and deeper critical interest in film should be produced in Auckland since the Society was founded.'[39] By the end of the 1940s, the film medium was receiving serious middlebrow attention from various quarters and in an increasing number of publications. The range of films offered to mainstream and minority publics was growing in the late 1940s and throughout the 1950s, through a combination of film society activity and private enterprise. Another important figure, however, drawn to the *visually* expressive possibilities of the medium, was less happy with the state of film culture. John O'Shea, who went on to make three feature films himself in the 1950s and 1960s (the only ones to be made in the country), saw journalistic film criticism as it appeared in the nationally distributed *NZ Listener* as lacking honesty (propaganda passing itself off as truth or common sense). We shall return to O'Shea in the next chapter after a discussion of the rise of film festival culture.

References

Anon. (1946b), 'Sixty Miles of Film In Twenty Languages', *NZ Listener,* 13 December, pp. 30–31.
———— (1948a), 'Footnotes to Film', *NZ Listener,* 11 June, p. 25.
———— (1948b), 'About Films', *NZ Listener,* 30 July, p. 12.
Anon. (1949a), 'Radio Reviews', *NZ Listener,* 14 October.
———— (1949b), 'Letters to the Editor', 11 November.
Anon. (1947a), 'The Film as Art: Work of the Institutes', *ODT,* 1 March.
———— (1947b), 'The Film as Art: Techniques of Production', *ODT,* 5 March, p. 2.
———— (1948), 'Notes on Contributors', *Landfall,* December.
———— (1949), 'Dunedin Has Most Members of N.Z. Film Societies', *Evening Star,* 11 March.
Allender, R. (1946), *Zealandia,* 4 July.
'Astra'. (1946), 'Mainly about Movies: *Olympia*', *Craccum,* 8 October, p. 7. 'Astra' was Wynne Colgan's *nom de plume.*
———— (1948a), 'Last, Loneliest, Laziest', *Craccum,* 1 July, p. 7.
———— (1948b), 'Death at Karangahape Road', *Craccum,* 26 July, p. 7.
Barrowman, R. (2003), *Mason: The Life of R.A.K. Mason,* Wellington: Victoria University Press.
Belich, J. (2001), *Paradise Reforged: A History of the New Zealanders from the 1880s to the Year 2000,* Auckland: Allen Lane and Penguin Press.
Carroll, N. (1998), *A Philosophy of Mass Art,* New York: Oxford University Press.
Combs, F. (1946), 'Art, Truth and the Films', *Monthly Film Bulletin,* (3:5), September.
Day, P. (1994), *The Radio Years: A History of Broadcasting in New Zealand,* Auckland: Auckland University Press.
Eliot, M. (1993), *Walt Disney: Hollywood's Dark Prince,* Secaucus, NJ: Birch Lane Press.
Fields, M. (1945d), 'The Films Which Children Like', *NZ Listener,* 12 October, pp. 10–11.
Guttmann, A. (1998), 'The Appeal of Violent Sports'. In: J. Goldstein, ed. *Why We Watch: The Attractions of Violent Entertainment,* New York: Oxford University Press.
Hall, D. (1970), *New Zealand Adult Education,* London: Michael Joseph.
Harris, J. (1941), 'Books in Dunedin: The Making of a Film', *New Zealand Libraries,* (4:10), May, pp. 123–24.
Jones, L. (1994), 'Colonial Like Ourselves: The American influence on New Zealand Fiction, 1934–65', *Australian and New Zealand Studies in Canada,* Dec.(12), pp. 112–22.
Kaes, A. (1994), 'Cinema and Modernity: On Fritz Lang's *Metropolis*'. In: R. Grimm and J. Hermand eds. *High and Low Cultures: German Attempts at Mediation,* Madison: University of Wisconsin Press.
Langlois, S. (1997), 'Images that Matter: The French Resistance in Film, 1944–1946', *French History,* 11(4), pp. 461–90.

Manvell, R. (1945a), 'Most Popular of the Arts', *NZ Listener,* 27 April, pp. 6–7, 46–8.

Martin, M. (1995), *Dictionnaire du cinéma*, Paris: Larousse, p. 52.

Mein-Smith, P., Hempenstall, P. and Goldfinch, S. (2008), *Remaking the Tasman World*, Christchurch: Canterbury University Press.

Mirams, G. (1945b), 'Films and Children', *NZ Listener,* 22 June, pp. 6–7.

—— (1945c), 'Films, Fires and "Unfair" Competition', *NZ Listener,* 31 August, pp. 16–18.

—— (1945e), 'More About 16mm', *NZ Listener,* 19 October, pp. 18–19.

—— (1946a), 'Taking the Cinema Seriously: Film Societies Here and Overseas', *NZ Listener,* 10 May, pp. 28–30.

—— (1947), 'Peace – It's Wonderful', *Landfall*, 1(1): 44–6.

—— (1947–48), 'The Cinema as Social Influence', *Transactions and Proceedings of the Royal Society of New Zealand*, vol. 77, Dunedin, p. 343.

O'Shea, J. (1946), 'On Waiting to See a Movie', *Monthly Film Bulletin,* (6:1) December.

Pocock, J.G.A. (1947), 'The Screen and Its Spectators', *Landfall*, 1(2): 132–36.

Reid, J. (1955), 'Films of the Week', *Auckland Star,* 4 June, p. 2.

—— (1956), 'Films of the Week', *Auckland Star,* 7 January, p. 6.

Renwick, W. (n.d.), 'Scott, Walter James 1902–1985' [Online]. From the *Dictionary of New Zealand Biography, Te Ara – the Encyclopedia of New Zealand*. Available at: http://www.teara. govt.nz/en/biographies/5s8/1. Updated 31 July 2003. Accessed: 15 October 2010.

Roth, M. (1996), 'A Short History of Disney-Fascism: *the Lion King*'. In: *Jump-Cut: A Review of Contemporary Media,* 40, pp. 15–20.

Smith, D.I.B. (2003), 'John Reid'. In: N. Tarling, ed. *Auckland Minds and Matters*, Auckland: University of Auckland Press.

Smithyman, K. (1960), 'Journey towards Easter: Part One'. In: A. Curnow, ed. T*he Penguin Book of New Zealand Verse*, Harmondsworth: Penguin, p. 275.

Stam, R. (2000), *Film Theory: An Introduction*, Malden, MA: Blackwell.

Taylor, N.M. (1986), *The Home Front: The New Zealand People at War*, Historical Publications Branch, Department of Internal Affairs, Wellington: Government Printer, chapter 14, 'The American Invasion', pp. 621–61.

Notes

1 American and British films were plentiful in New Zealand during World War II and the arrival of large numbers of American servicemen after May 1942 had a significant impact on local social life, including the advent of Sunday entertainment. For an in-depth account, see Taylor 1986.

2 W. Colgan interview, April 1999. One of his other vivid memories from this period – during his posting to the Far North as a member of the Signal Corps – was attending a cinema in Kerikeri that unofficially segregated its audience along a racial divide: Māori had to watch the film from the ground floor, while European New Zealanders occupied the upper level of seating. Merata Mita documents a similar situation in her essay in *Film in Aotearoa New Zealand*. Colgan's confirmation is valuable, as Mita's claim has been challenged.

3 For a fuller account of the AEWS, see chapter 4 of Hall's book.

4 The first appeared in the *Listener* on 31 August 1945, 'Films, Fires and "Unfair" Competition'. The second, published in October, brought readers up to speed with the changing nature of the film industry's attitude towards 16mm film.

5 *Monthly Film Bulletin*, no. 5, WFI, 6 November 1946, p. 4.

6 Similar documents may exist in Christchurch and Invercargill, but I have been unable to verify this.

7 Ron Ritchie to Peter Cooke, 28 September 1986, unpublished MS.

8 Notes from the General Meeting, 12 April 1946. The New Zealand Film Archive.

9 WFS Executive Meeting, March 1948. The New Zealand Film Archive.

10 In fact, the societies purchased some extremely early Chaplin (such as the pre-tramp comedy *One A.M.*).

11 To avoid any confusion, I will hereafter refer to all post–World War II film institutes as film societies.

12 *Monthly Film Bulletin*, no. 2, WFI, 1 August 1946.

13 Later critics would see aspects of mass culture as highly significant; such texts offered levels of analysis other than pleasure or enjoyment. Moreover, in the light of findings emerging from ethnographic research and the cognitive sciences, new conceptions of the 'active audience' emerged.

14 Eiby to Cooke, 28 September 1986. Unpublished MS. Margaret Ritchie became honorary secretary of the WFI and negotiated the importation of the films it wanted to screen, a role she continued to exercise until her death in the late 1960s.

15 H. Bucquet (1891–1946) had had a fruitful run of 'B' movies produced by MGM. *On Borrowed Time* (1939) was the example included in the festival.

16 *Jéricho* was one of a number of French films about the French Resistance made in the immediate aftermath of World War II as people felt the need to document what had happened, celebrate the victory, and allow national unity to be rebuilt in the spirit of *fraternité*. For a more detailed account of these films, see Langlois 1997.

17 WFS Executive Meeting, November 1947. The New Zealand Film Archive.

18 The success of New Zealand Film Services should not obscure the activities of other companies that sought to 'cash in' on the burgeoning art-house or foreign language film market. Kerridge-Odeon established International Film Distributors in 1952 and imported 35mm films. Photographic Wholesalers NZ Ltd., a division of Kerridge-Odeon, not only imported cameras and photographic equipment, but also had a library of 16mm features and shorts from many leading studios. In the late 1960s, the library became a separate entity: Sixteen Millimetre NZ Ltd. The pioneering New Zealand film-maker, Rudall Hayward, formed Modern Films in the early 1950s which had, reputedly, the largest 16mm library of foreign films in the country; he also established Film Classics (NZ) Ltd., sometime in the 1950s, to import and distribute such films as *Ivan the Terrible* and *Quiet Flows the Don*. These were important sources for film teachers as well as film societies. Video technology (VHS) supplanted 16mm in the early 1980s and many film libraries were liquidated. (For this information, I thank local film historian David Lascelles.)

19 Joris Ivens' short film *Indonesia Calling* had similarly been blocked by the Labour Government. Made in 1946 when Indonesian nationalists and Dutch soldiers were still engaged in military conflict, the Government held it up at the Censor's Office throughout the latter part of 1947, and the WFS was still complaining about the delay in February 1948.

20 Mary Field, associated with the Rank Organisation, was in the forefront of this campaign during the 1940s. 'The Films Which Children Like' was the title of a BBC Pacific Service talk given by her in its 'Arts for Everyone' series, broadcast over the YA network in October 1945 (*NZ Listener* 1945d: 10–11).

21 Late in 1947, Mirams resigned his presidency of the WFS in order to take up a position in Paris as First Assistant Film Information Officer in the Mass Communication Section of UNESCO.

22 As quoted in Mirams: 343.

23 Reid's presidential address to the 1952 NZFI Conference. The New Zealand Film Archive.

24 Ibid, p. 121.

25 NZFI Conference Papers, 1949. The New Zealand Film Archive.

26 Ibid.

27 Ibid.

28 NZFI Conference Address, 1949. The New Zealand Film Archive.

29 His italics.

30 *Catholic Review*, (1) vol. 3, no. 11, pp. 649–59; (2) vol. 3, no. 12, pp. 713–24; (3) vol. 4, no. 3, pp. 180–90; (4) vol. 4, no. 4, pp. 230–41; (5) vol. 4, no. 6, pp. 364–74.

31 In the 1930s and 1940s, one of the principal intellectual arguments against mass art works was that their reputedly standardized production and diffusion led to their standardised reception and consumption – partaking in some mysterious and total communion. In the immediate post–World War II period the 'standardisation' argument was bolstered by the 'passivity' argument popularised by Clement Greenberg's seminal article 'Avant-garde and Kitsch', originally published in *Partisan Review* (Fall 1939). Greenberg maintained that kitsch art involved 'unreflective enjoyment' and 'passive spectatorship'.

32 'Catholics and the Cinema: (1) The Influence of the Films', *Catholic Review*, 1948, 3(11): pp. 649–59. The logic of this line of thought led to the idea that sadistic and sensationalist elements would come to feature more prominently in film as an increasingly passive (and jaded) people sought stronger stimulants. This was not a new point of view. The harmful effects of popular entertainments had been noted from ancient times. See, Guttmann 1998.

33 NZFI Conference, February 1949. The New Zealand Film Archive.

34 Allender also wrote on film for *The Arts Year Book*.

35 Bowie later moved to Wellington to work for the NFU.

36 12th Annual Meeting of the Council of the NZFI, Christchurch, January 1958. The New Zealand Film Archive.

37 J.C. Reid, President's Address, NZFI Conference, Dunedin, 1952. The New Zealand Film Archive.

38 Ibid.

39 Ibid.

Chapter 6

Happy Together: Education, Networks, Festivals

This chapter tracks the emergence of an increasing number and variety of discursive and non-discursive practices that contributed to the development of film culture. The former are seen in the appearance of magazines and university extension film courses that contributed to the development and dissemination of novel ways of imagining and talking about the cinema, while the latter make their presence felt in the form of 'art-house' cinemas, independent distribution networks, and film festivals. In one sense, these practices are tributaries of reconstructed national film industries, which are recovering from the destruction caused by World War II and exporting their work to an expanding global audience, one made up, moreover, of a growing number of people with higher education and more willing to encounter cinematic modernity.

We have noted that the aftermath of World War II brought various initiatives to develop and deepen cultural life in New Zealand. One such was the creation of the Auckland Music Council in 1948, an association of the many musical societies set up by cash-strapped enthusiasts, which organised the first Auckland Festival, 'a modest undertaking of performances by local artists and societies with a visiting soloist' in August 1949 (Simpson 1961: 139). The exclusively musical nature of this festival soon expanded to include the exhibition of work by the Auckland Society of Arts, plays, and poetry readings. This extension led to a name change in 1952, and the Auckland Festival Society was born (Simpson: 139). Although located geographically within Auckland, this was not merely a regional event as the NZBS broadcast many of the performances throughout the country (Simpson: 139). (It is interesting to note that the 30 years for which the Festival was active (1952–82) have since largely disappeared from historical memory, and the creation of a new Auckland festival in 2003 was constantly being referred to as the first of its kind.)

'Festival' films began to be programmed, on the advice of AFS members, as an integral part of the festival from 1953. Their inclusion in the festival's programme can be interpreted in at least two ways. One explanation sees the cinema accorded the same status or respectability as that given to the more established artistic media. Granted, this meant admission to a kind of upper-middlebrow rather than highbrow ambience; for in the 1950s even the visual arts were still largely contained within the representational/figurative tradition – modernism was slow in finding expression and acceptance. The films favoured at first were those whose dramatic or literary associations accorded with notions derived from theatre and literature.

A more prosaic explanation for the inclusion of film in the Auckland Festival was the need for the potentially loss-making Festival to sell more tickets. Its income came principally from ticket sales to the various events, with some additional funding given by the Auckland City Council and the Arts Union fund controlled by the Department of Internal Affairs (Simpson: 140). The cinema section of the Festival, initially an inexpensive event as many of the films selected had already been brought to New Zealand by commercial distributors, ended up subsidising 'nobler' live performances such as opera and ballet. Table 6.1 reveals that cinema was generally as popular as the other arts represented in the festival in terms of attendance.

The films were mainly at the upmarket end of American films, but there was an increasing presence of European films as the decade wore on. At first, many came to the screen through Eddie Greenfield's company Exclusive Films.[1] *Bicycle Thief* (Italy, 1948) was at the 1954 festival. Akira Kurosawa's *Rashomon* (Japan, 1951) was shown in 1957. The film committee was not sure how Auckland audiences would respond to this 'exotic' film, and so warned them that they 'may find the mood and timing of the film strange, but these are small defects when compared with the force and vitality of the acting. This alone is a revelation.'[2] In 1958, of the seven films presented, audiences could see *Rififi* (France, 1955), *Si tous les gars du monde/Race for Life* (France, 1955), *Le Marriage de Figaro* (France, 1959), and *L'Oro di Napoli/Every Day's a Holiday* (Italy, 1954). Of the 12 films at the 1959 festival, eight were foreign language, including *And Quiet Flows the Don* (USSR, 1957), *Smiles of a Summer Night* (Sweden, 1955), and *Nous sommes tous des assassins* (France, 1952). Satyajit Ray's *Pather Panchali* (India) was shown in 1960 with five other foreign language films. A novel aspect of that year's festival was the introduction of a programme of locally made 8mm films.[3] In 1962, a programme of locally made 16mm films was added.

It was a successful combination to screen the works of recognised directors of European art cinema (some classics and some new arrivals) alongside opera films and British or American literary adaptations. Bergman made an early entry into the festival in 1959 and

Table 6.1: Attendance figures Auckland Festival of the Arts

Auckland Festival	1958	1959	1960	1960
Concerts and recitals	19,914	18,463	18,448	18.3%
Theatre and poetry	3459	19,631	5266	5.2%
Ballet	*	*	10,342	10.2%
Opera	15,000	*	12,259	12.2%
Exhibitions	17,634	34,239	32,897	32.8%
Films	**19,720**	**22,724**	**15,108**	**15%**
Church service	500	300?	300?	0.3%
Social Committee Projects	5143	6688	6028	6.0%
Total	81,745	102,200	100,648	100%

was regularly screened thereafter; others included Antonioni (*La Notte,* Italy 1961) and Visconti (*Rocco and His Brothers,* Italy, 1960), both in 1963; and Fellini (*8½,* Italy, 1963) could be seen in 1965, while maverick American filmmaker John Cassavettes' *Shadows* (USA, 1959) appeared in the 1966 festival. These were the forerunners of a remarkable new generation. In addition, the Festival audience finally got to see the second part of Sergei Eisenstein's *Ivan the Terrible* (USSR, 1958).

By creating the Festival in 1952, Auckland had stolen a march on the rest of the country. The first arts festival in Dunedin did not begin until 1954 and was coincident with the celebrations that accompanied a royal visit. Wellington's first festival of the arts began seven years after Auckland's in February 1959. Purporting to be 'a festival for all', Wellington's attractions were not confined to the arts proper but sought to cater to all ages and tastes: 'it ranged from classical music to jazz, from drama to films, from opera to variety, and from cricket to boxing' (Simpson: 141). No New Zealand festival in those days could specialise in high culture. The organisers of this festival had a two-fold aim: to foster an interest in the arts and to put Wellington on the map (Simpson: 141). An artistic map of New Zealand was being drawn.

New Zealand's fourth provincial capital, Christchurch, had not been idle. To it goes the honour of having organised this country's first International Documentary Film Festival, which screened about 75 films from October 16 to 28, in 1950 (*NZ Listener* 1950: 6–7). That Canterbury was celebrating its centenary year was one reason for this extraordinary event. The National Film Unit's (NFU) *Canterbury is a Hundred* (1950), which portrayed the growth of the province with local repertory members playing the parts of the pioneers, was but one of the NFU entries to the festival; the others were *Centennial City* (1949), *Journey for Three* (1950),[4] *Prelude to Aspiring* (1949), *The Coaster* (1948), and *The Railway Worker* (1948). The Christchurch Film Society organised the festival, which was modelled on the successful International Festival of Documentary Films first held at Edinburgh in 1947. Billed as the first festival of its kind in either New Zealand or Australia, it attracted films from 15 countries.

Forsyth Hardy, John Grierson's great friend and eventual biographer, who had spearheaded the Edinburgh Film Guild's work in organising its festivals, acted as technical advisor to the Cantabrians. Like the Reithian vision of public broadcasting, documentary offered a way for film to 'instruct' and 'educate' as well as 'entertain'; and it was also associated with worthy political aims. To make this explicit, the *Listener* reprinted part of Robert Flaherty's message to the 1949 Edinburgh Festival, which enjoined the power elites 'to recognise what a great instrument lies ready to their hands – that documentary is of all mediums, not only the most widely understood, but the most convincing. Seeing is believing. If ever we are to have peace and understanding in the world, what medium could more effectively develop it?' (*NZ Listener* 1950: 7).

One of Christchurch's 'not-to-be-missed' films was Paul Haesaerts and Henri Storck's much praised semi-experimental *Rubens* (Belgium, 1948), a sometime didactic, sometime lyrical exploration of the life and paintings of the Flemish baroque artist, which had won a prize at the Venice Film Festival and been acclaimed in Edinburgh. Notes supplied by the CFS assured spectators that the film employed techniques that brought 'the spirit of the painter's work to the layman, and does it in a way which creates a real emotional understanding of the value behind Rubens' pictures' (*NZ Listener* 1950: 7). Because he was writing for the *Arts Year Book*, a periodical devoted to the arts, whose readership was culturally articulate and not narrowly puritanical, the review of the film went a little more deeply into those techniques:

[The film] projected something of the sweep and largeness of gesture without capturing the sense of lubricity, the tumultuous rape of the senses. The use of animated lines and twin shots in a single frame meticulously exposed the painter's formal obsessions; yet, so amorously did the camera nuzzle the canvas that the effect of the painting was lost in the proliferation of detail while the tizzy of camera arabesques, disallowing time to focus properly, superimposed a false movement on the pictures. ... In short, the virtues were legion, but the attention to detail rather exhausting and myopic (Walshe 1951: 117).

The review represents a rare attempt to acknowledge formal aspects, but suffers from a lack of appropriate technical terms ('the tizzy of camera arabesques'). It is ultimately more interested in the subject matter (Ruben's art – particularly his nudes) than in documentary form or strategy. However, the fact that *Landfall* and the *Arts Year Book* were commissioning such articles was another indication of the cinema's promotion from popular to higher culture in the post-war period.

The Christchurch Documentary Festival was a huge success, possibly the best-attended event of the celebrations organised by the Arts and Cultural Committee of the Canterbury Centennial Association. 'Soundly organised, spiced with informative programmes, it was completely booked out for most of its run from October 16 to 28, slightly crimping receipts and furrowing brows in the local stucco dream-palaces' (Walshe: 120). Brows would not need to be furrowed again, however, until three years later, in 1953, when the Second International Documentary Film Festival was again held at the Civic Theatre in Christchurch in October.

Another example of the strong critical interest in the documentary genre was the essay 'Documentary Film in New Zealand', an overview of that genre written by an Auckland academic, M.K. Joseph, for the 1950 edition of the *Arts Year Book*. New Zealand's film production in the 1940s had been almost entirely documentary, a fact that led Joseph to quote Gordon Mirams' appreciation of New Zealand's potentially distinctive contribution to film culture: 'The documentary is the only branch of film production in which this country has any chance of making a contribution of real value' (1950: 12). Joseph quoted Grierson's well-known definition of documentary film as the 'creative treatment of actuality' and virtually paraphrased the comments Grierson had made during his visit to this country in 1940. In Joseph's words: 'Documentary begins when it shows, not the country itself, but how people belong in the country and what they do with it' (1950: 16).

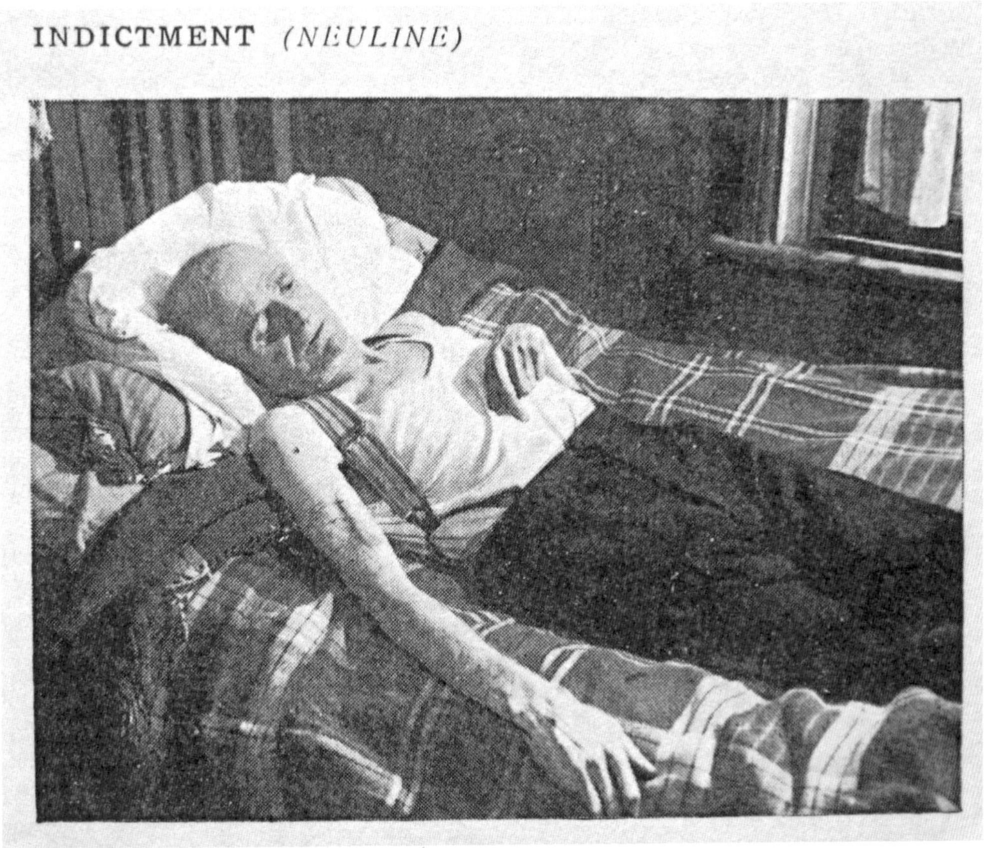

INDICTMENT *(NEULINE)*

Figure 12: A still from Neuline's film (1950) about the need for social housing.

If one reads between the lines of Joseph's essay, he appears to be doing his best to encourage the Griersonian side of the NFU, which was already losing out to the bureaucrats who wanted more tourism and more government propaganda. It is to Joseph's credit that he recognised the good work being done by a small independent company: '[The film] *Indictment* (Neuline) was unusual in this respect: sponsored by the Auckland City Mission, it movingly dramatised the conditions under which old-age pensioners live' (1950: 17). For Joseph, this film was 'a rare bird' that showed 'the seamier side of our social problems'. He acknowledged that the NFU still produced some hard-hitting films such as *Backblocks Medical Service* (1948), but social criticism in local films, which were mostly commissioned projects, was scarce.

Joseph's perspective on documentary was thoughtful but derivative. He also made a point of stressing moral, thematic aspects and disapproved of the experimental or aesthetic tendency in documentaries such as Walter Ruttman's *Berlin: Symphony of a Great City*

(Germany, 1927). A principal element in his disapproval of this film (and others like it) was that they seemed more concerned with their proper form than with any relation to society at large. A poet, novelist, and English lecturer, Joseph (1914–81), who was a colleague of John Reid, shared some of the latter's views on the type of film culture needed for New Zealand. Considering how little specialised discussion was published during this period, one suspects that his (and Reid's) talk of film society members as aesthetes was more a stereotype than a reality.

Joseph wrote about films in *Here and Now* (1949–57), which published a good deal of film criticism. His first article for that monthly periodical – whose editorial board he was on – was entitled 'Down with the "Arty" Film', and expounded the error of concentrating on 'means' rather than 'ends':

> Like other, more academic bodies, [film societies] have been concerned with the question of means – camera, lighting, cutting, and so on – and have safely avoided the question of ends. The result has been a certain cult of secondary virtues, and a fostering of the "film-society film". … What really matters, in the end, is the dignity and absurdity of man.
>
> (*Here & Now* 1949: 29)

While Joseph's film writing was thoughtful and detailed, it was symptomatic of the level of cultural life in New Zealand that an intellectual such as he felt the need to attack 'arty' attitudes and had no difficulty in separating the form of a film from its content. There appeared to be no debate about the ways in which content was constructed in ways specific to the medium – surely a primary rather than a 'secondary' issue in film criticism. Joseph would have been unlikely to make such a confident distinction when writing or lecturing about poetry. A few 'arty' or experimental films did reach New Zealand, but they tended to be too alien for New Zealand viewers. One such was the Auckland Film Society's screening of *La Coquille et le Clergyman* (France, 1927) by Germaine Dulac. At its original 1927 screening in Paris at the Studio des Ursulines, noted for its support of the avant-garde, it had provoked controversy because of disagreements as to whether it deserved to qualify as a Surrealist film. Its reception in Auckland in the early 1950s was somewhat different, as Colgan recalls:

> We few, we happy few. And all so solemn. Mesmerised by *The Seashell and the Clergyman*, all Freudian sexual symbolism, with characters leaving rooms in reverse on their heads. And none of us questioning. 'Ssshhh, this is Art'. Then somebody bold enough to whisper, 'Could it have been reeled backwards and inside out or something?' It had![5]

Documentaries *about* art were more accessible than pure examples of the 'art film'. Interest in films of this kind shown at the Christchurch festival had been particularly strong. Mirams wrote a tie-in article for *Design Review*, a new quarterly magazine published in Wellington by the Architectural Centre. He was well placed to write such an article, having recently returned from his job with UNESCO in Paris with memories of the work done by that

Down with the 'Arty' Film
BY M. K. JOSEPH

IT SEEMS UNGRATEFUL, at this date, to say a word against the film societies. In this country, they have been until very recently our only means of escaping from the routine of the Queen Street cinemas and the tyranny of the current Hollywood-Elstree film; and in all countries they have been schools of cinema, the forming grounds of critics, encouraging an informed approach to film and slowly building up that historical conscience which alone makes criticism possible.

There has been so much to learn that we can hardly reproach the film societies if they did not manage to teach us quite enough. Like other, more academic bodies, they have been concerned with the question of means—camera, lighting, cutting, and so on—and have safely avoided the question of ends.

"big" picture; and it is a sign of the times that the Academy, one of London's repertory cinemas, has been showing two American "B" features, Ray's *They Live By Night* and Tetzlaff's *The Window*. Yet it is a poor film-industry that never brings off a big picture. That is a symptom of Hollywood's current weakness, and we look forward only lugubriously to *Mourning Becomes Electra* and the Bergman *Joan of Arc*.

Minor excellence is not enough. British films can show at least some sizable successes. If *Hamlet* and *Oliver Twist* were comparative failures, it was by comparison with the success of *Henry V.* and *Great Expectations*. And to fail lamentably in making *The Red Shoes* is perhaps in the long run worth a gaggle of gangsters and a wilderness of westerns—Powell and Pressburger have made almost a habit of significant failure.

Break The Rules

The only rule for a good picture at present would seem to be that it breaks the rules. Where the vast majority of pictures are sexually motivated, the hero of *The Search* is a small boy re-

Figure 13: M.K. Joseph denounces medium-specific film criticism as pretentious.

organisation to foster awareness of films on art. UNESCO had organised a conference of art films in Paris, produced 'an authoritative brochure entitled *Films on Art*', and hoped to form an International Federation of Art Films 'as a permanent body charged with fostering this branch of the cinema' (Mirams 1950: 39). Realising that he was one of the very few New Zealanders to have seen a number of such films, he was duty-bound to enlighten his fellow New Zealanders about this new development in documentary film.

He tempered the widespread enthusiasm for *Rubens* with the warning that its length was excessive and its technical innovation rather repetitive once the shock of novelty had worn off. He also dwelt at surprising length on the question of censorship because the paintings in the film depicted men and women in various stages of undress: 'I don't know just how some of the solid burghers of Christchurch and their wives and families (or for that matter those of any New Zealand city) would accept the camera's frank and detailed scrutiny of the ripe nudes in which the artist Rubens delighted' (1950: 39). Mirams was the New Zealand censor at that stage, and referred to himself ironically in the third person when he added that the nudes were 'another headache for the Censor, poor fellow, and doubtless he can find a way to overcome it' (1950: 40). Writing about films during this period provides many examples of the contrast between sophisticated European mores and provincially prudish New Zealand, as do the controversies that erupted around a number of art exhibitions, such as a Henry Moore show at the Auckland City Art Gallery.[6]

Mirams' article is interesting not only for the information it provides, but also for what it unintentionally reveals of the times and the man (so acutely aware of the conservative context in which he wrote, and seemingly accepting of many of its attitudes). He ended with some typical moralising, a pious hope that Art be 'safe', its beauty bright, and its 'message' edifying. This is the theme that characterised so much intellectual discussion in New Zealand – an eagerness, but nervousness, about finding the right films to educate a raw country:

> It is probably very true that the main reason why more people do not appreciate good art and good design is not because they are, in general, insensitive to beauty, but because they do not get enough chance to see it and understand it. But now, just as the radio has done much to bring music to the people, so the cinema is beginning to do the same for the pictorial and plastic arts. That is why the present development of the art film overseas is so worthwhile, why the securing of such a film as *Rubens* for the Christchurch Festival is so much welcomed (1950: 41).

The educated viewer (and certainly reviewer) can never simply relax and allow his or her intellect and imagination to interact with the film – there is always a novice or unsympathetic local viewer looking over one's shoulder – like 'the rest of the bus listening united in one unspoken sneer' as Bill Pearson summed up the local situation around this time in 'Fretful Sleepers' (1952). Consequently for the reviewer there is always educational (or political, or moral) work to be done. To revel in an unusual film for its own artistic or sensuous qualities would run the risk of indulgence.

The breakthrough – in film criticism as in filmmaking – came from John O'Shea. In 1950, *Design Review* asked O'Shea to write two articles 'on the fundamentally visual nature of the cinema'. In the first of them, he excoriated two *Listener* reviewers: John Maconie, who wrote under the pseudonym 'Jno', and P.J.W. 'Between them they have murdered many a film' (O'Shea: 130). The two had assumed responsibility for Gordon Mirams' column in the *Listener* when the latter had become New Zealand's film censor in August 1949. O'Shea wrote: 'My animosity is reserved for those writers who split off the literary and dramatic contents of a film, pillory them, and lead the public to believe they are film critics by making an occasional reference to the film's visual qualities' (130). His ire had been roused upon reading Jno's review of *Saraband*: 'a brilliant example of what irritates me so – the patronising interest of a literary gent who seems incapable of *seeing* a picture' (130). His chief complaint was that the qualities that marked the cinema as being a distinctive art (which for O'Shea were essentially visual qualities) were either skipped over lightly or not mentioned at all. His passion for this issue was a singular one in New Zealand where criticism of 'film as film' had yet to make any significant impact. What then did O'Shea find of interest in *Saraband*, a film he freely admitted to be unexceptional in other respects?

> Its merits lay in those very pictorial qualities, which Jno omitted to mention, in the elegance, fidelity and artistry with which it reproduced the ornate, rather heavy period atmosphere of the Hanoverian Court. The film was a series of quite attractive pictures. Not a series of unified pictures, not cinema. The pictures remained static and cinema should develop its effect by the conscious arrangement of pictures in motion (131).

The interest O'Shea's critique holds for us today, aside from showing his developing conception of the cinema's specificity, resides in the desire to have the cinema appreciated for qualities it had mostly been denied in this country; in this instance an attention to the way *mise en scène* constructed meaning through the web of relationships it articulated in the frame. That his critique should appear in a publication devoted to examining the conscious application of design to objects – houses, furniture, clothing, and utensils that had been largely devoid of design in the land of the *bricoleur* – was an appropriate context.

He returned to the attack in the second of his articles, 'If Those Eyes Could Only See...', enlarging his visual analysis through the symbolic and narrative use of colour. He cited Rouben Mamoulian's use of it in *Blood and Sand* (1941) 'to intensify the final, brilliant, sun-lit scenes of death and passionate despair in the bull-ring' (1950b: 10). The visual impact of this scene was due, he thought, principally to the editing, but 'Colour lent emphasis to the special arrangement of the pictures'. This identified two other tools by which meaning and pleasure were created formally. John Huston's film, *We Were Strangers* (USA, 1949), also demonstrated for him the power of camera angles and camera movement: 'Liberal hesitancy and fear, and working class treachery were graphically indicated not solely by the expressive faces of the Senators but also by the angles from which their faces were photographed and the varying speed at which the camera moved from one face to another' (1950b: 10).

His close reading of another scene highlighted the visual and auditory methods used to construct temporal and spatial rhythms, to drive the narrative and generate emotions.

> Hence, while the car is driving slowly through the streets, its engine quietly throbbing, Huston has used mainly long and medium shots with some closer tracking shots. At the

sight of the police, the sound track accentuates the roar of the accelerating motor and the sequence is thereafter filled with the sound of shots, horses' hooves, the shrieks of the crowd. The visual tempo is also accelerated. Close shots of the car, close-ups of its driver and of the two men in the back. ... At the end of the sequence there is a dissolve to a long and sustained shot of a quiet scene in which some of the principal characters of the film are introduced (11).

Rare in local film discussions at the time, here is a description that uses five technical terms precisely and shows a keen awareness of the filmmaking process. Such detail is used with an appropriate sense of context to develop an understanding of the filmmaker's shaping of a sequence, and his general narrative and expressive strategies. O'Shea's article is important, too, for its understanding that genre films, where iconic figures re-enact familiar patterns of coded human behaviour, afford directors a measure of creative licence to work on their *film style*. 'The Western, for instance, is such a staple diet of the mass audience that directors, especially John Ford, have felt free to rhapsodise cinematically on its established themes and have made such good films as *Stagecoach, Blood On The Moon, Red River, My Darling Clementine*' (O'Shea: 11). Film noir was another genre in which directors 'try to transcend the limits of their formulated themes'. Robert Siodmak's *noir* gem, *Crisscross* (USA, 1948), was singled out for close analysis, even though O'Shea felt it necessary to point out that it 'barely deserves inclusion. In many ways it was a deplorably vicious, degenerate and sadistic film' (O'Shea: 11).

This last comment sounds so like Gordon Mirams in his role as defender of bourgeois decorum that I am tempted to speculate that O'Shea's guilty pleasure in the film's thematic and erotic charge required this switch to moral defensiveness. Is this another example of the reader over the shoulder so vividly described by Bill Pearson? It is interesting to note that Mirams was at that time the country's film censor, and we may speculate further that, in the attitudes he represented, he acted as a kind of internalised super-ego even for a sophisticated viewer like O'Shea. What is most striking, however, is the extent to which O'Shea breaks away from the typical moralism of the period (shared by Mirams, Reid, Joseph, and many others) in his appreciation of film style:

In this sequence, the hero ... sees his wife ... in a seamy dance hall. He has been separated from her for some years. He sees her across a crowded dance floor. Oblivious of his presence, she is 'giving' herself to the frenzied rhythms of the dance band's 'Afro-Cuban' number. The music gets louder, shriller, more frantic as the sequence progresses. Shots of the band and the soloists are interspersed with shots of Lancaster watching his wife dancing. Long shots of Lancaster and his wife give way to mid shots, then closer and close-up shots as the sequence reaches a climax of passionate, tense frustration. No words are spoken and neither Lancaster nor Yvonne de Carlo have to 'act' during the sequence. Yet the inner currents of their earlier life together, their emotions and characters are conveyed with precision and economy (1950b: 11).

O'Shea's two articles reveal the gulf that separates someone who loves the cinema to such a degree that he seeks to penetrate its every secret in order to fully understand its nature, and someone who is constantly worrying about the response of the public or their moral and spiritual health. In the former approach, critical writing about film can never simply distinguish between content and style (the two are interrelated and equally important). Such critical attention serves two apparently paradoxical purposes: to be less in the cinema's thrall (to ask 'How did this happen?' creates a distance) *and* to worship it more ('I *love* the way that was done. I'll try it myself one day').

The reviews demonstrate there was at least one person in New Zealand, at the beginning of the 1950s, trying to discover the medium-specific qualities of the art. Each film that advanced those qualities, in howsoever small a degree, was 'defining a specific idiom of the cinema; and the cinema draws a little nearer to finding its own particular style of perceiving and illuminating subject matter which it shares with other arts' (O'Shea: 11). But several years would elapse before the infrastructure was created to support this insight, firstly in the form of WFS Film Schools, and secondly in O'Shea's first venture (with Roger Mirams) into feature filmmaking.[7] The quotation above would provide a valuable insight into several scenes in *Broken Barrier* (1952) in which similarly no words would be spoken.

Magazines and Film Classes

In this chapter, which must brush with broad strokes the emergence of many new aspects of film culture, I have briefly noted the emergence of a number of magazines (such as *Landfall*, *Here and Now*, and *Design Review*). Other sources that appeared towards the end of the 1940s need to be at least mentioned here in the hope that more detailed analysis can be given them in the future. New outlets for occasional film discussions included the university student papers: *Craccum* in Auckland, *Salient* in Wellington, and *Arachne* produced by the Victoria University College Literary Society (another 'spasmodical' in the vein of *Phoenix* and *Oriflamme*). Insisting it was 'not a student magazine', *Arachne* managed to produce three issues prior to folding in 1951, one of which contained an article by Peter Alcock, 'The Gleaming Lens', promoting the idea of a New Zealand film school where both theory and practice could be studied in order to train filmmakers (McEldowney 1998: 668). This represented a radical departure from the ideas of film societies whose members seemed more concerned about the formation of audiences than the production of films (even though a few members were involved in documentary-making). The inspiration for Alcock's idea was French – the *Institut des hautes études cinématographiques* (IDHEC), established late in 1943, which Alcock noted in his text.

The inevitable shadow that falls between an idea and its realisation – in this instance the notion of a film school in New Zealand – would stretch for many years. The first tentative steps towards the teaching of film production began at the University of Canterbury School of Fine Arts in 1964, when the retirement of the lecturer in textiles gave the University an opportunity to extend its teaching into moving images. This change followed an earlier decision that had led to the creation of a graphic design section within the School of Fine Arts in 1962. M.V. Askew was appointed to this position.[8]

Askew had many students pass through his classes in film and television production including Vincent Ward.[9] By the end of the 1960s, the Elam School of Fine Arts at Auckland University had a similar programme taught by photographer Robert (Tom) Hutchins. Very short-sightedly, however, the University refused to support Hutchin's attempts to expand his programme into a full Film School. Nevertheless, there were a number of notable graduates such as cinematographers Leon Narbey and Rodney Charters.[10] Despite the pioneering work of Askew and Hutchins, the teaching of filmmaking was slow to develop.

Writing about film gradually changed as the 1950s progressed. Dennis Garrett illustrates the contemporary mixture of influences. These were first apparent in an article he wrote for the Victoria College student newspaper, Salient. Garrett's article, 'Philistines and Pharisees', sought to create a middle zone of film culture, within the increasingly bourgeois arena of artistic appreciation. The task for anyone writing seriously about film was where to position film in relation to the two extremes of specialised and popular culture. Garrett espoused typical assumptions about the 'standardised' passive spectator absorbing and reproducing a 'false consciousness' and his discourse involved a binary distinction between physical 'appetite' and 'spiritual' rigour:

> The philistine majority has no particular attitude which could be called appreciation. Having learned in early childhood that sustenance is regularly provided and that no critical standards are expected towards either the provision or the source, the majority accepts regularly and uncritically the film fare provided. It averages its eighteen annual trips to the theatre in much the same spirit as it once imbibed its four-hourly feeds. … The dissenting film minority … is chiefly marked by a dislike of anything liked by the majority … marked above all by passivity. It wishes to be passively entertained, passively titillated, passively overwhelmed. … In reaction to this, the typical minority view becomes that realism, fantasy, poetry, and technical novelties are good in themselves (1953).

Despite familiar clichés of this kind, the article carried signs that thinking about the cinema in New Zealand was becoming more vigorous and diverse. No longer were overseas sources the only reference point for film 'appreciation'. Local texts on films and the cinema were now sufficiently numerous and critically dense enough to circulate among the small number of film society members and to influence their opinions. To this circulation should be added the vociferous debate in the letter columns of the Listener. Wynne Colgan took 'Jno' to task for his merciful review of The Best Years of Our Lives (USA, 1946) and supported an earlier irate Letter to the Editor that had taken exception to Jno's condemnation of The Long Night (USA, 1947), a remake of Marcel Carné's more celebrated Le Jour se lève (France, 1939). C.K. Herbert complained of the poor review given to Behind these Walls/Jericho (France, 1945). Jno defended himself by suggesting (with some justice) that 'Europhiles' tended to exaggerate the intrinsic worth of 'Continental' films while basking in easy anti-American rhetoric.

Film reception is not an exact science – it changes according to one's temporal and spatial location – so that controversies are inevitable and healthy. Frameworks of knowledge play a significant part in reception, too. Jno's framework of knowledge differed from that shared by many film society members who placed more weight on European (and English) values. Many film historians today, however, consider *The Best Years of Our Lives* as one of William Wyler's best, if not his best film, on various levels. Anatole Litvak's remake of a French classic, meanwhile, has not aged well and suffers invidious comparisons. New Zealand cinephiles were grappling with the problem of how to compare European with American films in a way that did justice to both; in the same way they were struggling to reconcile new with traditional values.

Garrett's particular dilemma – how to reconcile the new ideas of film art with a culture that had always distrusted elitism (sometimes for worthy egalitarian motives) – was shared even by established critics such as John Reid, whose presidential addresses to the NZFI conferences of the early 1950s were roundly applauded and widely approved. Reid had tapped into something deep within the psyche of middle New Zealand. The country at that time was in some respects an unfriendly environment for the emergence of specialised forms of aesthetic taste. Reid's solution to the tension between populist and elitist was essentially to define a middlebrow aesthetic of film, but this involved the loss of energies that resided at the two extremes.

Garrett (1953) 'solved' his personal dilemma by combining aspects from both Reid and O'Shea's approaches to the cinema. But his method had an Achilles heel – he wanted to talk about 'effective' directing but could not bring himself to use the 'cursed' language of 'the extreme film aesthete who has a battery of the technical jargon in which it is meet and right that any film be discussed'. Even such apparently anodyne words as 'panning' and 'tracking', used to describe camera movement, were belittled as 'considerations left to the juvenile few'. This essentially moral repudiation of a film-specific language sounds strange to contemporary ears, yet it was deeply embedded in New Zealand's anti-intellectual culture. It left critics bereft of a precise discourse.

The conservatism of literary/theatrical influences still hampered film criticism even in France. François Truffaut had, some months earlier in the same year (1953) written his incendiary article, 'Une certaine tendance du cinéma français', in which he excoriated a prestigious group of French filmmakers and the critics who admired them. Published in early 1954 in *Cahiers du cinéma*, this article exploded like the polemical bomb it was intended to be, and marked the first stage in an assault upon the *cinéma de papa* and the critical values that underpinned it. One of the aims of the present work is to track the emergence in New Zealand of similar ideas about the *politique des auteurs* and to note the somewhat different inflections they received due to the particular features of New Zealand's cultural development.

The problem was that critics now spoke of 'film as art' but were not allowed to use or develop specific discourses relevant to this idea. For specialised language, a film critic had to turn to established art forms such as the theatre. But the application of theatrical terms to film had been discredited in France before and during World War I (Abel 1975).

The Winter Film School

Dennis Garrett's time as president of the Wellington Film Society (1952–55) saw the establishment of the long-running and influential annual Winter Film School, which first began over Queen's Birthday weekend (early June) in 1954 and continued until 1981, when falling numbers and rising costs finally brought it to a halt. The first School, which attracted over 30 people and was held at Victoria University in Wellington, was a joint venture between the WFS and the Regional Council of Adult Education. The first two Schools featured John Reid as one of the tutors. 'Film Appreciation in General' examined the literary sources of *The Browning Version* (UK, 1951), *The Red Badge of Courage* (USA, 1951), and *Orpheus* (France, 1950). Co-tutoring the first film school were O'Shea and Mirams, completing a line-up that represented the 'top team' of New Zealand film criticism at this time. Ron Bowie, who was then working for the NFU in Wellington, co-tutored the second (1955) Winter Film School. Entitled 'The ABC of Film Appreciation', it analysed one 'good' film and one 'not so good', with *The Asphalt Jungle* (USA, 1950) and *In a Lonely Place* (USA, 1950) as yin and yang. Knowledge of Reid's cinematic eschatology would suggest *In a Lonely Place*, a 'bleak, desperate tale of fear and self-loathing in Hollywood' (Ankeny n.d.), as the 'not so good'. In subsequent years, the School would continue to be the leading event of its kind, a showcase for emerging critics, new trends, and overseas visitors (such as Chaplin expert Harry Geduld).[11]

Another venture overseen by Garrett was the creation of the Current Film Criticism Group and the Film Appreciation Group, which eventually merged to form a Film Discussion Group. A perennial complaint at all such events was the reluctance of audiences to participate, instead deferring to the 'experts'. For example, a session attended by some 40 people to see and discuss Antonioni's examination of the barren inner lives of the post-war rich, *L'Avventura* (Italy, 1960), caused John Blennerhassett, who led the discussion, to note that 'very little comment [was] contributed by the audience'.[12] The characteristic shyness or reticence of New Zealand audiences (often commented on by overseas visitors) was intensified by the arrival of the new wave of European 'art films' for which many local viewers lacked either context or discourse. Still, the discussions remained popular. The WFS Annual Report of 1957 recorded continued growth, and meetings throughout the 1960s had fairly regular attendance figures of 30 or so people. Some of the other films discussed included the landmark Italian neo-realist film, Guisippe de Santis' *Bitter Rice* (Italy, 1948), Flaherty's *Louisiana Story* (USA, 1948), and Truffaut's *Les 400 coups* (France, 1959). And 60 perplexed people turned up to hear someone explain Resnais and Robbe-Grillet's conundrum, *Last Year at Marienbad* (France, 1961).

Garrett's energetic leadership of the WFS saw membership and film-related activities increase. A notable one-off event, the screening of Josef Von Sternberg's *The Blue Angel*

(Germany, 1930), in the latter half of 1953, was made possible by Mirams' creative reinterpretation of a censorship decision made in the 1930s. As Chief Film Censor, he decided that the original restriction banning the screening of the film did not apply to film societies, as they had not existed when the decision had first been made. The film attracted many people, and helped membership to leap from 235 in 1952 to 533 in 1953. This rise was carried on into 1954, which saw 543 people join the WFS before dropping off again significantly. By the end of the decade there were only 248 members. The 1960s saw no real improvement in the number of people joining the WFS, with an average of approximately 340 annual subscribers, although the mid 1960s did see a short spike in membership to over 400.[13] Seeking to address this erosion in a more durable manner, the WFS looked at the provision of extra activities and more promotion. This was obviously a motivation for running the discussion groups.

One of the reasons for the gradual decline in membership could be honourably attributed to the film society movement's very success – a point made by the societies themselves. Their 'mission' to introduce exotica into an aesthetically impoverished land by making 'foreign' films more popular to audiences, encouraged commercial interests to become more active in this niche market. In narrow-minded New Zealand, André Bazin's perception had real significance: *Le cinema substitue à notre regard un monde qui correspond à nos désirs.* (The cinema replaces our gaze with a world that corresponds to our desires – my translation.) But to ascribe these developments in film culture solely to the activity of film societies would be too much of a single-factor explanation. It was true that film societies, together with film critics like Gordon Mirams, had promoted 'foreign' films, especially French and Russian ones, because of their artistic and historical significance to the development of the cinema, but this knowledge should not eclipse the achievements of people in the film business such as Natan Scheinwald, Eddie Greenfield, Ron Usmar and Russell Rankin. Individually and collectively they also played a significant part in the growth of film culture, introducing minority interest films to local cinema audiences because it was good business. New Zealanders had been eager, especially at the end of World War II, to escape the narrow confines of these islands, and films offered significant alternative experiences.

Commerce and Co-operation

In 1955, the film society movement in New Zealand was encountering familiar obstacles to the satisfaction of its desires. The vexed question of how to procure a sufficient range and quantity of films was again on the agenda. Independent distributors and exhibitors and film societies were now in close competition for the same type of film, and commercial screenings of foreign films had increased enormously.[14] In 1957, the NZFI lamented the fact in its Annual Report when it noted that 'less than ten films were imported from other than the UK or USA five years ago, nearly 100 last year. Since 16mm copies are not available for us when the 35mm commercial rights are sold, the Institute takes what the commercial distributors do not want. Though we must welcome commercial distribution, it makes our task more difficult'.[15]

The NZFI was caught between a rock and a hard place. Controversy could be courted by making more challenging choices from the wide range of films produced throughout the world, but this would have meant a significant sea change in thinking. The *raison d'être* of the film society movement would have moved from middle-class 'improvement', to a more vanguard position, screening films that challenged the prevailing social and artistic order, and also questioned cinematic modes of narration and representation. There had been controversy enough in the championing of Russian films during the 1930s, but the post-war period had embraced the idea of quiet reform rather than revolution. It was not until the late 1960s that younger film festival and film society organisers, more in tune with the values of the burgeoning counter-culture, began to redefine priorities – traditional forms of entertainment and uplift gave way to experiment and controversy. The discourse would change from that of F.L. Combs, president of the WFS, who remarked in 1949: 'Notwithstanding the difficulties [in film supply], I am convinced that our Society and its fellows have a valuable task to perform – that of *upholding cultural and social standards* in an art over which merely commercial influences have an excessively strong hand'.[16]

The film societies did attempt to work with independent commercial interests. The most significant of these independents was New Zealand Film Services (NZFS), the company operated by Usmar and Rankin. An obvious advantage of this arrangement was that the NZFI was no longer as dependent on the vagaries of supply or the haphazard initiative of well-meaning members travelling to London on holiday. A certain Mrs. McKenzie was one of the last to perform this duty. During her overseas trip in 1952, she made contact with some British distributors, 'which produced such notable films as *Orphée* and *Jour de fête* for our programmes'.[17] Although Special Sunday night screenings became a regular feature at the Paramount Theatre from early 1957, Robert Kerridge, who rented the building from the Wellington City Council until November 1959, had no special relationship with the film society (Lascelles 1997: 45). When he vacated the theatre, it was renamed Paramount International by the new leasee, Syd Bridgeford, who thereby signalled his programming policy. New Zealand Film Services became his major supplier (Lascelles: 46).

The pragmatic decision to work with friendly commercial exhibitors and distributors was also made necessary by government import controls, which limited the purchasing power of the Institute. (It is hard to explain to young people today just how regulated the country was, particularly in terms of overseas transactions, prior to 1984.) In 1959, the Institute had applied for an import licence totalling £450, but had been granted one of only £80, thereby reducing the funds available for the hire of films.[18] A sign of things to come was given when Wellington organised its first Festival of the Arts in 1959. The WFS, in collaboration with Kerridge, selected the films that were shown at the Roxy Theatre. This was an opportunity to showcase films from many countries, with four each from France and Italy, three from the UK, and one each from Japan, Switzerland, West Germany and Sweden. Charlie Chaplin's first feature-length film, *The Kid* (USA, 1921) was revived, as was the initially under-appreciated *Sweet Smell of Success* (USA, 1957) with its striking black and white cinematography by James Wong Howe.

The WFS continued to broaden the range of cinematic offerings for its members through an arrangement with the managers of the Roxy and the Paramount cinemas. Monthly screenings of (mostly) foreign films occurred throughout the winter months of 1961. The Roxy's impressive programme included *Casque d'or* (France, 1952), *La Strada* (Italy, 1954), *Ugetsu Monogatari* (Japan, 1953), and *Hiroshima mon amour* (France, 1959). Russell Rankin, meanwhile, was supplying the Paramount and announced in 1961 that future screenings would include *Orfeu negro* (France/Brazil/Italy, 1959), *Mein Kampf* (Sweden/West Germany, 1960), *Marcelino, pan y vino/The Miracle of Marcelino*, Italy, 1955), *Celui qui doit mourir* (France, 1957), *Les 400 coups* (1959), and *Les Sorcières de Salem* (France/East Germany, 1957).[19]

There had been earlier attempts to 'sell' foreign films to Wellington and Auckland audiences but such attempts had broken down after a comparatively brief period.[20] However, by early 1962, the success of the Sunday screenings was such that Rankin offered very generous terms to the WFS – no charges for film or theatre hire, and the profits were to be shared. Success with the initiative prompted Rankin to suggest further programmes, and, 'if this could be arranged in Auckland also, he would be prepared to bring in films which would not normally be available in this country'.[21] Thus was born Auckland's first dedicated 'art-house' cinema: the Lido in Epsom, which was controlled by the Moodabe brothers who owned the Amalgamated chain of cinemas, with theatres throughout the country. A salient feature of the Sunday night shows was the fact that 35mm copies of films were shown in standard theatres, in contrast to the 16mm prints projected monthly by the film society movement in places not specifically designed to be cinemas. The visual and aural improvement in viewing films in these conditions proved so popular that a semi-autonomous body was established within the WFS to handle this activity alone. The time was propitious, with Europe producing an astonishing series of innovative films.[22]

The Cinema Group met from April 1963 until March 1966 when it was disbanded; competition from other sources (Amalgamated had set up a Wellington Lido to emulate its successful Auckland cinema in March 1964), and a growing acceptance amongst the general public of 'unusual' films persuaded NZFS to withdraw its support. Their agreement with the Moodabes gave them access to the many 'first-run' cinemas controlled by Amalgamated. Consequently, they no longer needed to rely as heavily as they had on the smaller film society circuit. In a very real sense, the success of the venture led to a marked drop off in membership of the WFS, which had soared to over 400 in 1964 when the Cinema Group was doing very good business. An appraisal of the 1963 season noted that 'There is an obvious public demand for unusual films'.[23] And, in a self-congratulatory mood, they added that it was 'only through the auspices of the Cinema Group that the public have the opportunity of seeing top class films'.[24] Over 200 people had joined this group, which made it a financial success as well.

Some of the films shown through this group included *Umberto D* (Italy 1952), Vittoria de Sica's last neo-realist work; Jean Cocteau's final chapter in the trilogy that charted the poet's progress (his own) amidst mankind, *Le Testament d'Orphée* (France, 1960); one of René Clair's late films, *Les Belles de nuit* (France, 1952); and Max Ophuls *Madame de …* (France, 1953). Fresh from a recent trip across the Tasman Sea where he had seen Roman Polanski's first feature-length film, *Knife in the Water* (Poland, 1962), George Eiby suggested that the Cinema Group show this Polish film. In fact, it received a commercial release. European films were becoming hot properties.

A figure of undeniable prestige and exotic appeal had already begun to make an impression on film culture in New Zealand. Docking discreetly in Wellington in July 1958, she trailed in her wake the sparks of distant European stars. Her arrival was soon the talk of Wellington's small film society movement and it was not long before she began to be heard expressing opinions on film throughout the Dominion. Alexander Fry, a colleague of Catherine de la Roche's at the *Listener*, remembered that:

> At a time when European films were at their exciting best she knew everybody who was anybody in making them, and names such as Balcon and Lean and Korda dropped naturally into her conversation. … One or two of my *Listener* colleagues – better read than I – had to curb an impulse to genuflect when she entered a room.
>
> (*Evening Post* 1997)

Clearly, her reputation as a film critic with the BBC had preceded her arrival. Reflecting on her career later, she recalled that when she had tried to get assignments from the BBC to cover the first Cannes Film Festival in 1946, she was asked why the British public should care about a programme of highbrow films in the south of France when they kept away from that sort of thing at home (1988: 53). By 1949, parochial British attitudes had softened. The festival circuit flourished and de la Roche travelled to Berlin, Venice and Cannes on a regular basis, covering these events for a variety of publications such as *Picture Post, Tribune,* and *The Times.* In 1953, she covered Sweden's inaugural Festival of the Arts, which included a film section. Sweden was benefiting from a liberal censorship that allowed more candid representations of sensuality, as in Bergman's *Summer with Monika* (1951), in which an unabashed Harriet Andersson displayed her breasts. Her coverage of the festival led her to the Stockholm Film Institute, where she discovered the new censorship classifications in New Zealand. Gordon Mirams, prime conductor of these more liberal tunes amidst the conservative hubbub of the 1950s in New Zealand, replied encouragingly to her enquiry about the possibilities of finding work, thereby facilitating her eventual arrival.

De la Roche's career illustrates the extent to which British film culture had developed since the war. Her many writings included essays in the *Penguin Film Review.*[25] She co-wrote, with Thorold Dickinson, *Soviet Cinema* (1948/1972), and also published monographs on *René Clair* (1958) and *Vincente Minnelli* (NZ, 1959, France 1966). She was then a highly experienced freelance media journalist and cinephile, comfortable with both the spoken and the written word. She had, moreover, a colourful (if somewhat mysterious) past involving her links with British writers and bohemians, and a fashion sense that instantly distinguished her amongst the pearls and twin sets or the grey-flannel suits symbolic of Wellington. John O'Shea, who would become a close friend, wrote that: 'Her appearance in Wellington in the later 1950s was unexpected and memorable. Suddenly in our midst was a multi-lingual figure, both exotic and unfamiliar, part of Europe's literary and film world, as much at ease on the Copacabana and the Côte d'Azur as she was in the glitter of London' (O'Shea: 8).

Even before her physical arrival in the country, plans were afoot to provide her with employment.[26] She was hardly off the boat before she found herself commissioned by National Radio to give talks of 15–20 minutes in the 'Mid-Century Cinema' series on general film subjects, some of which were then reprinted (in abridged form) in the *NZ Listener*; one such was 'The Film Heroine Today' (*NZ Listener* 1959: 8). Other topics included new audiences, censorship, heroes, the new wave, and cinema in a changing society (de la Roche 1988: 113). She lectured for the WEA, participated in the Winter Film Schools, and gave talks to the WFS. At the end of an early talk she gave to the latter, Max Riske, then president of the society, thanked her for her 'new attack'.

In April 1961, the *NZ Listener* announced that another radio programme devoted to the cinema was soon to be heard on the 'highbrow' YC network. Entitled *Cinema*, this half-hour monthly magazine consisted of 'interviews, reviews, discussions, sound tract excerpts, news – anything connected with the films', and ran from May 1961 to December 1962 (de la Roche: 122). Now a member of the New Zealand Broadcasting Service, she was responsible for the programme format and orchestrated its various parts.

Taking part in the *Cinema* programmes were many of the usual suspects associated with the Wellington Film Society: John O'Shea, Ron Ritchie, Gordon Mirams, Dennis Garrett, and Walter Harris, as well as those who had either written on film, such as Graham D'Oyly Rhind, a leader writer on *The Dominion*, or were involved in making them, such as Oxley Hughan of the NFU.

One of the programmes focussed on 'Film Pioneers in New Zealand'. Assembled over a period of several months, it contained interviews with pioneer New Zealand filmmakers, such as Cyril Morton, Jack Welsh, Rudall Hayward, and Stanhope Andrews, as well as some of their friends. These filmmakers had never received their fair share of critical attention. De la Roche, with her training in overseas film culture, saw clearly that such a programme was needed. Other subjects included the development of film criticism in New Zealand, the influence of films on youth, horror films, and Gordon Mirams' work with UNESCO in Paris. One programme even featured a recorded discussion that took place among members of the WFS at the end of a lecture on film (*NZ Listener* 1961: 21). The topics explored by de la Roche were not new but she obviously brought a confident approach to the series. Rather than simply concentrate on overseas subject matter, she worked hard to use local material, and to link New Zealand with overseas film culture.

Sadly, there are no known recordings of the programmes. Media archiving was in its infancy and film was a particularly vulnerable topic. One can only hope that recordings will one day surface as the programmes would provide a unique historical record of New Zealand filmmaking and film culture.

At the Art-house

Although the Paramount in Wellington played an important role in screening foreign language films in the first few years of the 1960s, its influence was less durable and geographically more constrained than that of Amalgamated's Lido 'circuit'. Russell Rankin had been directly responsible for supplying the Paramount with films (Lascelles 1997: 51) and his death in October 1966 hastened the decision to cease supplying films to the theatre, which led the Paramount to close on 21 December 1966. Prior to that, however, the screening of films from Sweden, Italy, France, and Russia, among other countries, had received additional support from the second largest film exhibition and distribution company in the country: Amalgamated Theatres. Their Regent Theatre in Epsom (Auckland) – renamed the Lido in the final months of 1962 – can be called the country's first dedicated 'art-house' cinema.

Meanwhile, the advent of television was having a devastating effect on the cinema business. In 1960–61, when television began to broadcast in Auckland, Christchurch, and Wellington, there were 4808 licensed television sets. By 1964, television had reached 50 per cent of New Zealand households and the number of licensed sets was 305,410 (Anon. 1966). Just prior to the advent of television in New Zealand, there had been 545 cinemas and 40,632,000 admissions; six years later those figures had fallen to 312 and 19,606,000, respectively (Dennis and Bieringa 1996: 209). The downturn in cinema attendance was, at least initially, not felt so strongly by the specialised audience that frequented the Lido, which 'brought in as much cash as a city cinema', a remarkable feat for a suburban theatre (*NZ Herald* 1964). Similar developments occurred (as we have seen) in Wellington, and in Dunedin where the State International (now demolished) played an important formative role and, presumably, in Christchurch where Amalgamated also had theatres. To quote a former Dunedinite, Bill Gosden, the State 'would have been programmed by whoever was programming the Lidos: same programme, same films, same kind of ambiguous line between the continental art movie and what to the censor was synonymous with naked women and a suggestion of pre-marital sex, all very dangerous stuff'.[27]

Filmmaker Bruce Morrison 'remembers the "duffle-coat" days of the early 1960s, when debate centred around various "underground" figures such as Lawrence Ferlinghetti, Jack Kerouac, the writers of *Evergreen Review* and *Paris Review*, and the French existentialists – heady arguments to a background of jazz music' (Horrocks 1985). He also remembers the impact of the new European films:

> Foreign films, as they were called, only came out in one theatre, the State Theatre in Dunedin. It was the time of *400 Blows, Fahrenheit 451, Dolce Vita* those sorts of films. ...

And Bergman was in midstream at that time making all of those black and white films: *Seventh Seal, Wild Strawberries*; all of which I saw. I saw early Fellini and Roberto Rossellini and various other people; *Bicycle Thief, Rome, Open City* and a number of others that were more in a documentary style. … You couldn't see them anywhere else. That was my source of film education at that time.[28]

Although the creation of a few art-houses was hardly a solution to the loss of the mainstream audience, it was the only growth area in the cinema business. Suburban theatres were entering an agonising twilight zone as the shadow of television fell across them. Although not decrepit, the Regent had not had much money spent on maintenance, and it was doing little business. What did Amalgamated have to lose in re-branding it as the Lido? And however strange it may have appeared to commercial minds, there was a growing public willing to pay to see subtitled films. Moreover, Michael Moodabe Jr., the youngest and more artistically inclined of the three Moodabe brothers who ran Amalgamated, had a real affection for the Lido: it became 'his baby'. He baptised it, and commissioned an inventive Auckland artist, David Kennedy, to design a logo. Moodabe recalls the marketing strategy:

We printed an inexpensive programme that the people could take away. We hit the universities as much as we could. At that stage there were a lot of young people coming back from overseas, having done their OE, and lamenting the fact that they couldn't see that type of movie anywhere. We gradually built up a "core audience". It was hard going. There wasn't big money to start with, and then it depended on the picture.[29]

The first of the films shown was Rossellini's *General Della Rovere* (Italy, 1959), a 'well-wrought drama' based on a true story that won the New York Film Critics' Circle award for best foreign film and the Catholic Film Office Award at the Venice Film Festival of 1959. The film that proved the commercial viability of the Lido was not, however, a 'well-wrought drama' but a softly biting French satire, parodying some of the perils of materialism: *La Belle Americaine* (1961), one of the rare French examples of American burlesque (Passek 1995: 188). It played for 14 weeks at the Lido. It seemed that the ideal Lido film combined French culture with accessibility, and if possible a touch of the *risqué* – audiences were eager for a taste of sophistication.

If many of the films screened at the Lido were made by a new generation of filmmakers, many of the audience belonged to a new generation of local movers and shakers. The term used internationally is the '60s generation', but in New Zealand, this generation did not emerge clearly until the late 1960s and early 1970s. During the 1960s, however, they could be found frequently at art-house films – this was an important part of their education. From this group (born in the 1940s) would come not only new forms of film criticism but new styles of film and television programme making. One of these future creative figures was Michael Stedman (CEO, Natural History NZ Ltd, one of the world's largest producers of

Figure 14: Logo created for the Lido in 1962.

wildlife and factual programmes), who recalled the heady flavour of the period in Dunedin. Stedman remembers his first years in television, when he began working there in 1965:

> Film was very much part of the fabric of television here. People thought of television as being an extension of film and owing its origins to it. I think that there was a similar feeling in Wellington. I can't speak for Christchurch or Auckland. It was just assumed that

everybody would see every film that was on in the city and that everybody would go to festivals. … And in their spare time people were making movies. I was an editor but I also shot quite a lot of film when I was associated with Capping Reviews and we played around with various styles. … I think there was then, more so than now, a fascination with the moving image and an endless quest to find things that had been written about film.[30]

Stedman still has a pile of old British *Sight & Sound* magazines. His emphasis on film is a useful counterbalance to the widespread assumption that New Zealand television took its bearings primarily from radio. That assertion may have been true for top management, but young staff members such as Stedman were caught up in the film fever of the period.

The traditional conception of New Zealand's most southern provincial centre, Dunedin, as conservative and homogenous was belied by its seething diversity, its cultural underground tendencies, and its student anarchism (it is a major university town). The late 1960s saw an upsurge in literary magazines and early hippie activities. European films were an integral part of this ferment. Stedman, who saw his first 'serious' films at the State, recalls the impact that festivals had on the burgeoning film culture, Dunedin seemed to be in the grip of an audio-visual feeding frenzy.

I remember once going to see seven Bergman films one after the other. This left me with one large Bergman film, which was not a good experience. … those festivals became oases in a desert of Hollywood indifference. The discovery of things like *montage*, film technique, and film grammar … I discovered that you could learn more from looking at crappy films than at good films. As an example, I remember *To Sir With Love*, I saw that eleven times because it had a montage in the middle of it when all the kids visited the museum and it was a very interesting part of the film. I was really interested in the structure of that.[31]

A veritable festival fever broke out in the latter part of the 1960s. An increasingly exotic virus spread throughout the land, infecting the body filmic, with its strange tongues speaking many languages. The Bergman festival was but one of an increasing number of generally foreign film festivals on the art-house circuit. Other festivals included a season of westerns entitled 'Tribute to a Bad Man', held in Wellington in September 1965 – and westerns were as much a part of the new generation's film culture as European art movies (as we see from later New Zealand films such as *Utu*, 1983). Indeed, one of the distinctive features of the hippie culture that emerged locally in the late 1960s would be the relaxed way it combined intellectual with popular culture – rock music and comics alongside art movies; with the two sides combined in *Blow-Up* (UK/Italy/USA, 1966) and *Zabriskie Point* (USA, 1970), among other films.

Bergman's success awakened interest in Swedish cinema, three earlier examples of which flickered onto the screen in Wellington in September 1966: Mauritz Stiller's 1919 feature, *The Treasure of Arne*; and two films by Bergman's mentor, Alf Sjöberg, *The Road to Heaven* (1942), and *Only a Mother* (1949). The next port of call for the curious was Czechoslovakia. Six films from this country, brought in by NZFS, were shown in Auckland, Wellington, and Christchurch at Amalgamated theatres. The 'liquorice all-sorts' principle of film programming, designed to cater to different heights of brow, was in evidence: three comedies, a romance, and two wartime dramas. *A Blonde's Love* (1965), directed by Milos Forman, was one of the six that made up the festival. It was one of the many European films to display a more open-minded attitude to sex than the uptight films Hollywood was still turning out for its rapidly vanishing family audience. Following the Russian invasion of Czechoslovakia in 1968, which ended the Prague Spring's effort to create 'communism with a human face', Forman went first to France and then to America, where he enjoyed both critical and popular success. (By then, Hollywood had been forced to take more interest in the European new wave.)

So many films were now being screened that serious filmgoers began talking of the need for a more selective kind of festival. The next chapter will track this development, as well as citing some of the cultural outcomes of the 1960s ferment, as the duffle-coat brigades (born in the 1940s) and later the more colourfully-clad legions of Sgt. Pepper (born in the late 1940s or early 1950s, the so-called 'baby-boom' generation) began making films and talking about them in new ways.

References

Abel, R. (1975), 'The Contribution of the French Literary Avant-Garde to Film Theory and Criticism (1907–1924)', *Cinema Journal*, 14(3), 1975, pp. 18–40.

Ankeny, J. (1950), 'Overview', *In a Lonely Place* [Online]. Available at: http://www.allmovie.com/movie/in-a-lonely-place-v24617. Accessed: 10 May 2000.

Anon. (1950), 'Festival of Films', *NZ Listener*, 29 September, pp. 6–7.

——— (1961), 'Monthly Magazine on Cinema', *NZ Listener*, 28 April, p. 21.

——— (1966), 'Recent Growth'. In: A.H. McLintock, ed. *An Encyclopaedia of New Zealand*. Available at: www.TeAra.govt.nz/en/1966/broadcasting-and-television/8. Updated 22-Apr 09. Accessed: 7 June 2012.

Campbell, G. (1979), 'Vincent Ward: Living on Celluloid', *NZ Listener*, p. 22.

D. W. L. (1964), 'Good Films Made Best Holiday Season', *NZ Herald*, 1 February.

de la Roche, C. (1959), 'The Film Heroine Today', *NZ Listener*, 3 April, p. 8.

——— (1988), *Performance*, Palmerston North (NZ): Dunmore Press.

Dennis, J. and Bieringa, J. eds. (1996), *Film in Aotearoa New Zealand*, Wellington: Victoria University Press.

Fry, A. (1997), 'Writer from Europe's Stage and Screen World', *Evening Post*, 15 May.

Garrett, D. (1953), 'Philistines and Pharisees', *Salient*, September.

Grant, B.K., Fox, A. and Radner, H. eds. (2011), *New Zealand Cinema: Interpreting the Past*, Bristol (UK) and Chicago (USA): Intellect Books.

Joseph, M.K. (1949), 'Down with the "Arty" Film', *Here & Now*, October, p. 29.

Horrocks, R. (1985), 'New Zealand Film Makers at the Auckland City Art Gallery: Bruce Morrison', Auckland: Auckland City Art Gallery.

Joseph, M.K. (1950), 'Documentary Film in New Zealand'. In: E. Lee-Johnson ed. *Arts Year Book*, 6, Wellington: Wingfield Press, pp. 12–17.

Lascelles, D. (1997), *Eighty Turbulent Years: The Paramount Theatre, 1917–1997*, Wellington: Millwood Press.

McEldowney, D. (1998), 'Publishing, Patronage, Literary Magazines'. In: T. Sturm, ed. *The Oxford History of New Zealand Literature in English*, 2nd ed., Auckland: Oxford University Press.

Mirams, G.H. (1950), 'Art and the Cinema', *Design Review*, Sept–Oct.

O'Shea, J. (1950a), 'Saraband for Blind Critics', *Design Review*, May–June.

—— (1950b), 'If Those Eyes Could Only See', *Design Review*, July–Aug.

—— (1999), *Don't Let It Get You*, Wellington: Victoria University Press, p. 43.

—— (1988), 'Foreword', *Performance*, Palmerston North: Dunmore Press, p. 8.

Passek, J-L. ed. (1995), *Dictionnaire du cinéma,* Larousse: Paris.

Pearson, B. (1952), 'Fretful Sleepers: A Sketch of New Zealand Behaviour and Its Implications for the Artist', *Landfall,* 6(3), pp. 201–30.

Simpson, E.C. (1961), *A Survey of the Arts in New Zealand*, Wellington: H.H. Tombs.

Walshe, J.W.B. (1951), 'International Documentary Film Festival'. In: E. Lee-Johnson ed. *Arts Year Book,* 7, Wellington: Wingfield Press, pp. 117–21.

Notes

1   W. Colgan interview, April 2001.

2   1957 Auckland Festival Souvenir Programme, p. 59. Made in 1950, *Rashomon* won the Golden Lion at the Venice Film Festival in 1951 and sparked renewed interest in non-Western films.

3   1960 Auckland Festival Souvenir Programme.

4   *Journey for Three* was the most ambitious of the NFU films in terms of length and narrative structures. It was the first feature-length 'story' film the Unit produced, with influences as diverse as British documentary, Italian neo-realism, German 'alpine' cinema and Hollywood. See 'Rites of Passage in post-WW2 New Zealand Cinema: Migrating the Masculine in *Journey for Three* (1950)', in Grant, Fox and Radner 2011.

5   W. Colgan, 'Shhhh! This is Art', 28th Auckland International Film Festival Programme, p. 166.

6   See: *When Art Hits the Headlines: A Survey of Controversial Art in New Zealand*, Wellington, National Art Gallery, 1987.

7   Whether or not O'Shea ever felt inclined to denounce the pioneering film reviewing of Mirams with as much vigour as he displayed in 'Saraband for Blind Critics', we shall never know. By 1952, he was in the process of making *Broken Barrier* with Roger Mirams. (Gordon had introduced him to his brother when this latter was looking for a writer.) Upon completion of the film, O'Shea embarked upon an uncertain career making films. Gordon Mirams, Chief Film Censor, took him on as his assistant, which allowed him to study films

very closely, and also, on occasion, involved some re-editing. Elia Kazan's *On the Waterfront* (1954) was one such assignment. 'The visuals in the meat packing plant were judged too violent and had to be reduced – so I got to cut a few bars out of Leonard Bernstein's own toccata-fugue as someone was hung on a meat hook. No one noticed the cut!' (O'Shea 1999: 43).

8 Personal correspondence with M.V. Askew.

9 Ward began his studies in practical filmmaking in 1974, when he directed his first film, 'a typical first-year-at-art-school topic, something about Plato and the nature of reality' (*NZ Listener* 1979: 22). His fifth film, *State of Seige* (1978), became internationally successful with television sales in many European countries. He made this in collaboration with Timothy White who has gone on to a notable international career as film producer. The film also beat 140 other student films from around the world to win a Golden Hugo at Chicago in 1979.

10 R. Horrocks interview, April 2002. Horrocks began teaching Film Studies at Auckland University as an academic subject in 1975, and a number of filmmakers passed through his course.

11 Other early Winter Film School topics included: 'Humour, Satire and Wit in Films (1956), 'From Stage to Screen' (1958), 'The Film as an Art Form' (1959), 'The Film with Social Purpose' (1960), 'Film Adaptation' (1961), 'From Idea to Actuality' (1962), 'The Film in Britain Now' (1963), 'The Musical' (1964), 'Shakespeare on Film' (1966), 'Myth and Reality' (1967), 'French Film and Reality' (1968), 'Violence in Film' (1969), 'Joseph Losey, the Director and his Films' (1970), 'Censorship and the Cinema' (1971), 'Horror on Film' (1972).

12 Wellington Film Society, Minutes of the Executive Meeting, June 1963.

13 Statistics from George Eiby Papers, Alexander Turnbull Library, 92-204-11/08.

14 Hollywood and British films were, in contrast, not 'foreign'.

15 NZFI Annual Report, 1957. The New Zealand Film Archive.

16 WFS Annual Report, 1949. The New Zealand Film Archive. Emphasis added.

17 NZFI Annual Report, 1957. The New Zealand Film Archive.

18 WFS Annual General Meeting, 1959. The New Zealand Film Archive.

19 Executive Meeting, July 1961, WFS. The New Zealand Film Archive.

20 Natan Scheinwald and Eddie Greenfield are the most obvious examples. According to John Reid's informants, the South Island was 'considered by most distributors as a dead loss for Continental films.' And his polemical verve was in evidence when he emphasized how regionalism affected local film reception: 'While the most moronic British comedy will often run for months in Christchurch, and Hollywood rubbish like *The Miracle* break records there, a great film like *Pather Panchali* falls flat with a dull thud in the Cathedral City.' *Comment*, Autumn 1961, p. 18.

21 Executive Meeting, WFS, September 1962. The New Zealand Film Archive.

22 J.C. Reid had noted in 1961 that a solution to the irregular arrival of 'Continental' masterpieces would be the 'establishment in each main centre of a comfortable, small-capacity prestige theatre devoted to really outstanding foreign movies, a "sure-seater" that by its quality product and appointments would gain a certain snob status.' But he was not at all confident that this would happen soon: 'It seems that Auckland, with its increasingly

cosmopolitan citizenry and its population of 420,000 has no immediate prospect at all of regular Continental films while cities of half its size elsewhere in the Commonwealth, and Sydney, a few hours across the Tasman, feature the newest and most "difficult" of the foreign productions.' *Comment*, Autumn 1961, pp. 17–18.

23   Cinema Group Minutes, August 1963. The New Zealand Film Archive.
24   Ibid.
25   No. 1, 1946, 'Recent Developments in Soviet Cinema'; no. 2, Jan. 1947, 'The Moscow Script Studio and Soviet Screenwriting'; no. 3, Aug. 1947, 'Scenic Design in the Soviet Cinema'; no. 5, Jan. 1948, 'The Soviet Cinema and Science'; no. 7, Sept. 1948, 'The Mask of Realism'; no. 8, Jan. 1949, 'That "Feminine Angle"'; no. 9, May 1949, 'No Demand for Criticism?'
26   Minutes of Meeting, WFS, 19 June 1958. The New Zealand Film Archive.
27   B. Gosden interview, November 2000.
28   B. Morrison interview, June 1999.
29   M. Moodabe interview, January 2000.
30   M. Stedman interview, December 2000.
31   Ibid.

Chapter 7

Nouvelle Vague: Film Culture Meets Counterculture

The deaths of Russell Rankin and Gordon Mirams, occurring respectively in October and November 1966, symbolised the end of a phase in the development of film culture. Both men had made significant contributions, the first by building a niche market supplying foreign language films to film society members and, gradually, to a wider art-house public; the second through his pioneering film column, 'Speaking Candidly', in the *New Zealand Listener* and his position as film censor (1949–58). Business acumen and a burgeoning appreciation of film, not necessarily as art but at least as a serious social arena, had collaborated in the formation of an expanded film taste. They and other members of their generation, their jobs done, left the scene, and now a younger generation of New Zealanders, having benefited from their activity, was ready to take film culture to another level.

Bob Dylan's song, 'The Times They Are A-Changin', first released in January 1964, was a portent of things to come:

Come gather 'round people
Wherever you roam
And admit that the waters
Around you have grown
And accept it that soon
You'll be drenched to the bone. [...]
For the times they are a-changin'. [...]
Come mothers and fathers
Throughout the land
And don't criticize
What you can't understand
Your sons and your daughters
Are beyond your command
Your old road is
Rapidly agin'.
Please get out of the new one
If you can't lend your hand
For the times they are a- changin'.[1]

The song was ahead of its time, particularly for New Zealand; but some of the European films of the early 1960s had also served as an early warning. Middle-class taste came under more direct attack as the so-called 'Sixties generation' began to emerge. There was, therefore, intergenerational strife, often the expression of broad cultural mutation. These developments were highly relevant to film as Roger Horrocks recalls:

> The first thing one has to say to qualify that is that in New Zealand they weren't really the Sixties generation; they were the early Seventies generation. That generation, born mostly in the mid '40s, profoundly changed New Zealand culture. Film was one of their major art forms along with comic books. I think the [1969] Festival, although it attracted the foreign language communities which had always been the mainstay of the film society movement, was really a young adult event. They were the driving force. If you start a festival in 1969, you are perfectly poised to take advantage of the upsurge of the '60s and '70s generation.[2]

This chapter will track changes and conflicts of this kind as they occurred in the 1960s and early 1970s. First, however, it is important to place them in the general New Zealand context. The economic and social stability of the 1950s and 1960s, which had characterised mainstream New Zealand society and led to certain kinds of cultural conservatism, criticised by intellectuals like Bill Pearson in his seminal essay, 'Fretful Sleepers' (1952), was being strongly questioned by the late 1960s. James Belich has argued that New Zealand in 1960 was a 'tight society', which did not tolerate diversity: 'It was homogenous, conformist, masculist, egalitarian and monocultural, subject to heavy formal and informal regulation.' His thesis then describes a 'domestic process of decolonisation'; a period of great internal change occurring between 1960 and 2000, which 'interacted very closely with external decolonisation: the disconnection from Britain, and the opening-up to the world' (2001: 463 and 465). Opening up to the world involved an incremental receptiveness to dissent and difference, elements of which were to be found in film, both European and Anglo-American, seen at festivals, film societies, and the art-house.

Cultural change was thus a complex phenomenon involving external and internal synergies. That which had hitherto been on the margins moved closer to the mainstream. The innovations of the late 1960s and early 1970s evident in the hire and programming of more contemporary and contestatory films, was a continuation of the practice begun in the previous decade when more foreign language films were shown through the art-house circuit. It was, however, the fact that there were things to react *against*, a traditional set of practices (however recently developed) that made the new wave more radical; while the film arguments were often about films imported from other countries, those films served as an expression of changing attitudes, values, and interests within New Zealand.

There were several factors that contributed to change, some of which I have already introduced: the rise of the young adult audience (given importance by the shift of the 'family' audience to television); a championing of politically contestatory and art-house foreign language films by 'a generation born in the 1940s whose enthusiasm for films had been fuelled by the European New Wave directors such as Fellini, Bergman and Resnais' (Horrocks 1992 and 1996: 61); a new intellectual or avant-garde dimension in minority film culture as it became a vehicle/flagship of the counterculture; pressure for a liberalising of film censorship which no longer reflected the tastes of the young adult public; a new wave of young New Zealand filmmakers working outside established institutions; the beginnings of the teaching of filmmaking and film studies at tertiary (as well as adult education) level; and the popularity of a new kind of film festival that catered to those tastes. What would the interaction between these various changes mean in terms of New Zealand film culture? Let us consider the last item on my list first, since to some extent it predates (and arguably, is one of the catalysts for) the later and more radical trends.

The Auckland International Film Festival

Emboldened by the successes of the several small and largely commercially motivated film festivals that proliferated during the 1960s, and frustrated by their dependence on the two local cinema chains of Kerridge and Amalgamated, certain members of the Film Committee of the Auckland Festival Society began to entertain a grander scheme: a stand-alone Auckland International Film Festival capable of offering a broader and bolder selection of world cinema. Wynne Colgan, one of the prime movers, remembered the negotiations:

I told my people on the Film Committee in 1968 that I felt we should get on the bandwagon here [in organising a film festival]. I went to see Kerridge who received me warmly, as per usual. He smiled benignly when I said that I felt we were ready for an international film festival, and said, 'Oh, you can try it once but you won't be back for a second'. So it began. The other chain, Amalgamated, had the best person in Michael [Moodabe] Jr., who knew movies. [His brothers] Royce and Joe just had dollar signs.[3]

Although still working under the umbrella of the Auckland Festival Society, and screening at Kerridge's cinemas, the first festival was held several months after the Auckland Festival of the Arts. Preparation for it began in earnest in 1968. The launch date was set for September the following year. The cost of going round the world to locate films was out of the question, but it was possible to share costs with an Australian festival, picking up some of their films to screen soon after in New Zealand. One or two members of the Auckland committee could travel to Australia to make the selection. There were three possibilities – Sydney, Melbourne, and Adelaide. In a spirit of rivalry, each festival imported films independently of the others and attempted to gain exclusive titles.[4]

The large established festivals in Sydney and Melbourne showed no desire to join forces with Auckland but it was quite the opposite with Adelaide, under its director, Eric Williams. In Colgan's words:

Here, it seems, is an organisation most akin to our own, one moreover which its director convinced me, over an evening of drinks and hard talking, followed up with a car ride to the airport a few days later, is anxious to join with us in promoting something like an *Anzac Film Festival*.'[5]

In the course of its tenth festival, in 1968, Adelaide had screened 55 films, 24 of them feature length. To help attract entries from many different countries, they offered a prize worth A$6000 in 1968. The competition with Sydney and Melbourne helped to give an edge to Adelaide's selection of films – politics was a strong thematic interest, as was an emphasis on new directors. Colgan recalled that 'Adelaide was heavily into Russian films as Eric Williams was very much into left-wing politics.'[6]

Impressed by the organisational ability of the Australian festival and the amiability of Williams, whose day job was with the Australian equivalent of the WEA, the Film Committee of the Auckland Festival Society confirmed the link-up with Adelaide. Both organisations stood to benefit from the economies of scale involved – they could share expenses and offer filmmakers exposure in two countries. (The strongest incentive for filmmakers to offer their films to a festival is the prospect of attracting interest from distributors who will then offer a commercial release in that territory – or in this case, territories.)

The Auckland Film Committee was naturally nervous about the venture. A considerable sum of money was at risk and Sir Robert Kerridge was not the only member of the film business to be sceptical. In Colgan's words, was Auckland ready for 'a season of exotic fare?'[7] Adelaide was not significantly larger than Auckland in terms of population, but Auckland could not rely to the same degree upon the support of ethnic minorities. In the event, the Adelaide/Auckland International Film Festival did better than expected. The budget was helped by the fact that the committee's work was unpaid and members of the Auckland Film Society worked as volunteers. The logistics of film shipments, censorship, and screening made it a very busy fortnight. Accustomed to films running for weeks, projectionists were horrified at having to deal with one or two new films each day. Despite a degree of chaos, the event was an unmistakable success.

Fourteen feature length films were shown in Auckland against Adelaide's 25 (some were simply not available for the Auckland date). Half of the shared films were from Eastern 'bloc' countries which were then going through a 'golden age' of film production. Opening night of the film festival saw the projection of *Hunger* (Denmark/Norway/Sweden, 1966), an appropriately symbolic choice that signalled the voracious appetite of the New Zealand film public, still famished despite the steady trickle of foreign language films occupying the art-house cinema screens from the early 1960s. Eleven thousand people attended the 12-day cinematic smorgasbord (and bought 16,000 tickets) (Colgan 1969). An article by Colgan noted that the times really were a-changin', foreign film fever had reached a younger audience, often university trained.

For 12 days at a Queen Street cinema there were beards, bare feet and jeans (and jalopies at the kerbside) for the Auckland section of the two cities' festival. On the first night black

Figure 15: The cover of the brochure for the independent Auckland/Adelaide International Film Festival in 1969.

ties and cocktail gowns seemed somehow incongruous. The official opening by an MP flanked by a group in national costume (the film *de jour* was the Scandinavian *Hunger*) assumed briefly the air of an election meeting when a claim was made that the occasion marked a 'great leap forward' for New Zealand audiences. Clearly the audience had come for pictures not pleasantries.

(Colgan 1969)

The first signs of film fever, noted in Chapter 5, were associated with the 'duffle coat' generation born in the first half of the 1940s. The new wave – with 'bare feet and jeans' – was the group associated with the 'sixties counterculture', typically born in the late 1940s or early 1950s. Film was as important a medium for them as it was for the group immediately before them. The young adult audience was now reaching critical mass. John Reynolds (teacher, filmmaker, and scholar), one of the young adults that made up the majority of festival-goers, recalled the stimulation that the Auckland international film festivals provided in the early 1970s:

You were always trying to find something different. Swedish films, of course, Bergman and people like that, and they were always packed. I mean it wasn't a little handful of devotees; the place was jammed, mostly with people in their 20s and 30s who were looking for other ways of making films or other filmmakers' views of the world. I think that had a big influence.[8]

Wynne Colgan concurred: 'It was the young people who made the festival a success. They had an enquiring mind. It became an expected event in the year, which is when it became important, I think.'[9] Colgan's testimony also bears witness to the increasing internationalisation of New Zealand that accompanied technological advances in transport; wide-bodied jet aircraft carried thousands of young New Zealanders on their important overseas experiences (OE), which often had a radicalising effect on them. In Colgan's opinion, 'it was the demand of a younger generation that had travelled which resulted in the film festival ... They wanted more than Hollywood.'[10] Clearly this was a significant factor, though the internal cultural changes should not be underestimated, particularly as it was the two groups described above (the duffle coats and hippies) that would together establish a new film industry in New Zealand.

Auckland's festival tried to be as resolutely contemporary as possible. Of the 14 films in the first festival, seven were made in 1968–69, five in 1966–67 and one each in 1965 and 1963. The last was an Italian film, *The Engagement/I Fidanzati*, directed by Ermanno Olmi, a filmmaker 'known for making realistic films about the lives of average people that are infused with an almost austere subtlety and rare ambiguity that is sympathetic yet not overly sentimental' (Brennan n.d.). Olmi's rather bleak film can be seen as an example of the organisers' desire to represent the important strains of the art of film rather than assault the audiences with only controversial counterculture films. The international nature of the festival was in evidence with 18 different countries represented, with four of the films co-productions involving two countries.

The new waves of filmmaking in Eastern European countries were well-represented: Jan Nemec's Kafkaesque nightmare *Report on the Party and the Guests* (Czechoslovakia, 1966), Jiri Menzel's *Capricious Summer* (Czechoslovakia, 1967), Miklós Jansco's *The Red and the White* (Hungary/USSR, 1967), Mircea Drogan's *The Column* (Romania/West Germany, 1968), and Andrzej Wajda's *Everything for Sale* (Poland, 1968). Many of these filmmakers went on to important careers and influenced at least one filmmaker in New Zealand (Geoff Steven, about whom I will soon speak).

Films by recognised *auteurs* were also in evidence, Satyajit Ray and Robert Bresson being the most prominent. Noboru Nakamura, a 'disciple' of Yasujiro Ozu, had filmed *Springtime* (Japan, 1965), from an original story by the master himself. With great prescience, the Festival included David Cronenberg's just-completed first feature-length film, *Stereo* (Canada, 1969), adding some 'shock' value. *Stereo* was written up in the festival brochure as 'an off-beat satire on the psychology of sex'. Such a film was a sign that Auckland was now, for the first time, on the cutting edge of counterculture filmmaking.

Proving that the organisers of the festival had correctly felt the winds of change, each subsequent festival brought an increase on the 11,000 people that attended the inaugural festival – 19,000 in 1970, 30,000 in 1971, and 38,000 in 1972: a phenomenal growth curve (*New Zealand Herald* 1972: 6). The 1970 July festival included an interesting mix of new and unseen films: Bresson (*Mouchette*, 1966), Welles (*Falstaff*, 1966), Chabrol (*Les Biches*, 1968), Imamura (*A Profound Longing for the Gods*, 1968), Jansco (*Confrontation*, 1969), and Cronenberg (*Crimes of the Future*, 1970). Roger Horrocks, a University of Auckland English lecturer and a member of the Festival organising committee, began to run a week of free public screenings (as a platform for Adelaide's 16mm films) at the university. This also served as an outlet for material that was considered too experimental or bizarre for cinema screening – Werner Herzog's first feature film was shown in one of these seasons. Usually held in the week before the main season, these 16mm screenings helped for many years to build interest in the Festival. Guest speakers, such as film censor Doug McIntosh, filmmakers Rudall Hayward and John O'Shea, and critic Catherine de la Roche were invited to speak during this 16mm season.

The dynamic of festivals – to keep astonishing as well as delighting its audience – ensures that censorship stakes continue to be raised.[11] One of the Auckland organisers defined the appeal of the early festivals in this way:

> The first phase of the Festival's history needs to be understood as a time when (1) There weren't many art-house films being screened in Auckland, so the festival was like an emergency package that we received once a year; and (2) All through the 1970s, New Zealand film censorship was extraordinarily severe. The festival offered the rare opportunity to see films that were really 'edgy'. The success of the art-house cinemas was in part due to 'culture' and in part due to sex.[12]

In its third year, having now deleted Adelaide from its title, the Auckland International Film Festival featured works by French 'new wavers' Godard (*La Chinoise*, 1967) and Rohmer

(*Ma nuit chez Maud*, 1969), as well as Bresson (*Une Femme douce*, 1969), and Resnais (*Je t'aime, je t'aime*, 1968). The erotic shock factor saw the arrival of a heavily cut Japanese film directed by Yoshishige Yoshida, *Eros + Massacre* (1969), described in the film festival brochure 'as one of the most original films of the modern cinema. It juxtaposes scenes from 1916 with scenes from the present, as a young couple become fascinated with the story of a group who tried 50 years ago to work out the connections between sexual freedom, women's liberation and politics'. The programme also included Pasolini's 'blasphemous' *Theorem* (1968), hailed as 'unquestionably one of the most *moral* works of modern cinema'.

On behalf of the Festival, Horrocks sent lengthy justifications of films to the censor's office. He also tried to enlist the support of local film reviewers. He was not always pleased with the response. For example, the censor still banned *The Inferno of First Love* (Japan, 1968), a film the festival had hoped to screen in 1969. Horrocks sent his defence of the film to Don Lochore, the *Herald* film reviewer as well as a member of the Festival Committee. This defence gives us a sense of the kinds of censorship issues that characterised this period, often in films about troubled adolescents that horrified and baffled older viewers:

> This film attempts to grapple with serious problems, and does so with remarkable imaginative energy. Most impressive is its study of the disturbed feelings of an adolescent boy, his loneliness, curiosity, and disturbing encounters with sex. This is a subject that has often been dealt with frankly in the novel, but seldom convincingly in a film. ... Technically, the film is an important experiment in 'immediacy', the attempt to involve the viewer so intimately in a scene that he seems to be experiencing the events, rather than merely watching them.[13]

The reviewer's help was not forthcoming. After apologising to Horrocks for having been able to watch only the first 30 minutes of the picture, which he found 'boring – not pornographic', he went on to say that he had heard that 'the film presents a catalogue of perversions' and that he would not support any challenge to the censor's decision.[14]

Born in 1941, Horrocks' role on the committee was to represent a younger, more provocative film taste. He had been known earlier as a critic of the Auckland Festival of the Arts, which he accused of being too conservative. His opinion of the film section of the festival was disparaging. 'The Film Festival could also be planned more coherently. We might have, say, a festival of Bergman, or of Fellini, or of the French new wave films, or the American new wave films. This year's programme was disorganised and disappointing' (*Craccum* 1962: 10). It is to the credit of Wynne Colgan (and the advocacy of John Reid) that the committee decided that the best way to deal with its harshest critic was to co-opt him. Horrocks became a member of the pre-International Festival Committee for several years, and then of the Festival Committee proper for its first ten years.

The festivals of the early 1970s brought the new German cinema and the Brazilian *cinema nuovo*. The 1972 Festival screened films by Herzog (*Fata Morgana*, 1971) and

Fassbinder (*Why Does Herr R. Run Amok?*, 1970). Wenders' film, *The Goalkeeper's Fear of the Penalty* (1972), was shown the following year. *Memories of Helena* (1974), *The Rogue's Trial/A Compadecida* (1969), *Macunaima* (1969), and *The Gods are Dead* (1970) represented the Brazilian contingent. Other notable films from that Festival included Godard's *Weekend* (France, 1967), Buñuel's *Tristana* (Spain/Italy/France, 1970), Tati's *Trafic* (Italy/France, 1971), Pontecorvo's *The Battle of Algiers* (Italy/Algeria, 1966), and Jodorowsky's *El Topo* (Mexico, 1970). In total, 27 films were screened from 13 countries. The sense of cultural crusade provided deep satisfaction as audiences engaged in spirited debate. 'It was very clear that the Festival was making a difference to film culture. We had visiting filmmakers, and critics such as Roger Manvell and Albert Johnson. Johnson was from the San Francisco film festival, and while in New Zealand he saw *State of Siege* [1978] by Vincent Ward, then a student at Ilam [School of Fine Arts]. Johnson was so impressed by it that this was the start of Ward's international reputation.'[15] The screening of Ward's film occurred in 1978.

The successful establishment of a full-scale Auckland International Film Festival was a remarkable achievement for which Wynne Colgan must take much of the credit as he led the organisation so efficiently through its early difficult years. The selection of films for a festival is always difficult to analyse because it reflects a number of different factors – the tastes of committee members (one or two of whom would fly to Adelaide each year to view and select Auckland's quota), but also the availability of films, financial considerations (such as financial assistance by Embassies), censorship issues, and so on. In general, the Auckland festivals did reflect the growing force of the new cultural politics in the number of controversial films that challenged censorship and audiences. This was evidence of changing attitudes internationally as well as locally. The next section of this chapter will look beyond the Auckland festival at similar censorship battles elsewhere in New Zealand.

Youth Culture and Film Censorship: 1930s Redux

The notion that New Zealand society suffered from an excessive 'Puritanism' had been a constant theme of cultural critics. Robert Chapman's 'Fiction and the Social Pattern' and Bill Pearson's 'Fretful Sleepers' are two classic expressions of this theme, from the early 1950s. Sexual restraint was not the only concern of Puritanism but it was certainly an integral part of it, and this aspect shaped a particularly strict approach to film censorship, applied even to film society films. During the volatile political years of the 1930s, censorship had also been a matter of politics. In the infamous court case of 1933, WFS members of the capital's political and cultural elite had to testify in favour of the serious artistic and educational merit of the Soviet *Road to Life*, a film the censor had banned.[16]

During periods when liberals worked as censors, they would do their best to assist film societies, but they had limited room for manoeuvre within the regulations. Even so, Gordon

Mirams' liberal attitude was selectively applied. He favoured an 'art cinema' that appealed to a cultural elite and was more tolerant of sexuality than he was of violence in popular films that appealed to a different audience. He was, for example, alarmed at the rise in the number of 'youth' pictures that featured violent and anti-social behaviour in young people, now described as juvenile delinquents. *The Wild One* (USA, 1954) and *Rebel Without a Cause* (USA, 1955) were much talked about examples of the genre of the emerging youth picture and he banned them both. *Rebel* was later released, on appeal, with an R16 certificate, against Miram's better judgement (Watson and Shuker 1998: 44).

Youth culture was on the rise during Mirams' time as censor and New Zealand's 'tight society' was ill-prepared to deal with it. One of the main seedbeds of youth culture was found (to the alarm of adults) to be secondary schools. 'For the first time, most adolescents spent a substantial and significant chunk of their lives surrounded by other adolescents. Before this watershed, on leaving primary school, most adolescents returned to the family or went out to work – both sites dominated by adults' (Belich 2001: 507). There was significant growth in the number of secondary schools to accommodate the post-war baby boom in the period between 1945 and 1970: 'At almost 1.5 million, [the 'baby-boomers'] are roughly twice as numerous as the pre-boom generation of 1920–45, and are more numerous than the post-boom generation of 1970-95' (Belich: 489).

While Hollywood was coming to terms with the fact that it no longer had a monopoly on family entertainment, New Zealand censors were trying to come to terms with the fact that Hollywood films were no longer the 'safe' family entertainment of yore. Instead of a single dominant entertainment package with broad appeal, there was a growing awareness in Hollywood of the need to address niche markets. As Thomas Schatz has noted,

> By and large, films were now appealing to a more limited portion of the public. Thus movies were 'targeted' for specific, specialised tastes. There was a growing 'exploitation' market for teenage drive-in crowds, 'blaxploitation' and martial-arts films for inner-city theatres, cross-country car-crash films for rural audiences, and so on (1983: 24).

As previously mentioned, television arrived rather late in New Zealand in 1960,[17] and it did not really develop mass appeal and wide household penetration until the mid-1960s.[18] Consequently, the cinema was still the primary source of family entertainment throughout the 1950s and early 1960s, and censorship operated on this assumption. But as we have just seen it was otherwise in Hollywood, which was already trying to make some films relevant to new audiences. The controversy surrounding the 'youth' films of the mid-1950s shown in this country is to some degree attributable to this cultural mismatch – an expression of chronological/technological delay. A growing youth culture (in both countries) was not content with dramas that showed them behaving as adults would like them to behave. 'The adolescent audience preferred representations that portrayed youngsters as rebels engaged in behaviour that offended adults' (Watson and Shuker: 43). A moral panic developed in the 1950s as adults grew increasingly concerned about young people's behaviour and a burgeoning youth culture that they neither understood nor liked, one influenced by America and its mass cultural productions. Rock and roll, comics and films were seen as dangerous.[19]

In the period that concerns us here, the 1960s and very early 1970s, the censor was a man with a much more conservative outlook. Doug McIntosh took up the position of Chief Censor in 1959 upon Mirams' return to Paris and UNESCO, and remained in office until his death in 1976, becoming (in the eyes of his critics) increasingly out of touch with contemporary cinema. Where Mirams had been obliged to confront the issue of screen violence, McIntosh had to deal with increasing sexual content in films. 'Between 1957 and 1970, the proportion of cuts for violence fell from 80 per cent of the total to just 33 per cent. Those for sex increased from 17 to 33 per cent. Such things as foul language made up the balance of excisions,' on which McIntosh maintained a hard line (Christoffel 1989: 28). The overall percentage of cut films remained roughly similar, about 37 per cent (a very high proportion by today's standards).

Of particular concern was that censorship often rendered a scene, or, indeed, an entire film, incomprehensible, or made even more offensive the depiction of certain events that were now deprived of their dramatic/narrative motivation. 'William Dart in *Landfall* … made much the same point with respect to *Bonnie and Clyde* (1967) and *In the Heat of the Night* (1967) where removing the motivation for violence meant that the violence which followed was gratuitous' (Watson and Shuker: 46).

Lindsay Shelton, who became the programmer of the WFS in 1969 and was a prime mover in founding the Wellington Film Festival in 1972, remembered another example of the censor's lack of concern for a film's integrity (or, by implication, for the art of film):

The worst example of cutting was a Swedish film called *The Bookseller Who Gave Up Bathing* [1969]. It was a charming nineteenth century tale of a bookseller who marries: he's been lonely and sad and [then] meets a woman with a past. They get married and are very happy. She brings, as her trousseau, a huge sideboard, and one day when his wife is out he looks at the sideboard and discovers a hidden drawer. Inside it there are some pornographic photographs showing his wife's past. The censor said to me: 'These are pornographic photos; they're against public order and decency so I'll have to cut them'. So the New Zealand audience that saw this film saw a guy with an idyllic marriage until one day he looked at a sideboard and everything fell apart.[20]

Horrocks publicly protested the censor's treatment of a number of festival films when he banned *A Married Woman* (France, 1964) and *Inferno of First Love*: 'If an art gallery received an exhibition of paintings with areas cut out of them, there would be a heated controversy. Yet many films come here in a mutilated condition, and there is often not a word of protest' (Horrocks 1971: 14–15). In the case of *One Flew Over the Cuckoo's Nest* (USA, 1975), first screened by the Auckland Festival, there were approximately 50 cuts to remove the word 'fuck', thus giving parts of the film an avant-garde style of staccato editing.

Some of the censor's difficulties may be traced to the Cinematograph Films Act 1961, which required him simply to consider the decency or indecency of a film, or any part thereof. Indeed, this act and its provisions descended directly (and largely intact) from the original Cinematograph Film Censorship Act, first passed into law during World War I in 1916. The sweeping powers given the censor were in some measure due to the anxieties generated by that war, which allowed the censor to ban any film which in his opinion 'depicted any matter that was against public order or decency' or was considered 'undesirable in the public interest' (*NZOYB* 1990: 326).

In contrast, the censoring of books, magazines, sound recordings, and comics was governed by an Indecent Publications Act that had been liberally reformed in 1963. The Tribunal was encouraged to consider the 'dominant effect of the book or sound recording as a whole', and the 'literary or artistic merit' of the work. McIntosh had no such guidelines. And it would not be until 1976 that the Cinematograph Films Act was brought more into line with the Indecent Publications Act.

McIntosh had already acknowledged Bergman's *bona fide* connections with high culture, as reported by William Dart: 'We do know, with Bergman, that we are dealing with the work of a serious artist – nothing in a film of his is just there for sensationalism' (1970: 70). This recognition was not, however, sufficient to protect *Persona* (Sweden, 1966), and several other Bergman films, from the censor's knife: 'Yet in 1968 we find *Persona* (R16 with only scanty screenings to art-theatre audiences) crassly mutilated. And the same thing happened with *The Silence, Wild Strawberries, Smiles of a Summer Night, The Seventh Seal, The Virgin Spring*' (Dart: 70). McIntosh was not uniformly insensitive to films with high culture associations, but some curious logic was at work in his decision in relation to the film version of James Joyce's *Ulysses* (UK/USA, 1967). The word 'fuck' disturbed McIntosh but he was sensitive to the cultural status of the novel and did not want to ban the film. He therefore hit upon what seemed to him the inspired solution of showing the film uncut to gender-segregated audiences.

> Thus an amused world (the decision was reported in *Playboy* … the Sydney *Daily Mirror* and the English *Daily Express*) learned that while in most cases the cinemas screened the films to males one day and females the next, there were times when it was shown to both sexes at the same time and physical separation was imposed. For example, in Motueka, women sat upstairs and men downstairs; at Otago University, a rope was run down the middle of the audience.
>
> (Watson and Shuker: 48).

Such a practice may have provoked gales of laughter in the readerships of those overseas papers but locally 'there was little major outcry over the segregation requirement' (Guy 1992: 16). Nevertheless, the criticism may have dissuaded McIntosh from making other attempts to treat 'serious' films selectively.

It was his practice to cut nudity and bad language automatically. His justification lay in treating the cinema as no different from any other public place. He held 'that repetition of [swear] words in a public place was a criminal offence, and that screening a film with those words was thus committing a criminal offence which he could not permit' (*NZOYB* 1990: 326). There were many precedents outside the cinema. For example, in 1972, visiting Australian feminist Germaine Greer was prosecuted for saying 'bullshit' and 'fuck' (albeit in a serious context) at a public meeting in the Auckland Town Hall (King: 1988: 45), and the same year, hippie activist Tim Shadbolt was prosecuted for saying 'bullshit' (which he later made part of the title of a book, *Bullshit and Jellybeans*).

The counter-argument was that the cinema was not a public place because viewers voluntarily purchased tickets. Initially this argument was not accepted. Under increasing pressure in the 1970s, McIntosh occasionally relented:

> In 1971 *Blow-Up* was approved for public screening despite its display of female pubic hair, as also was *Women in Love* despite its display of male frontal nudity. In 1972 *Clockwork Orange* was granted a first ever R20 classification and approved for screening despite what many regarded as an abhorrent portrayal of mindless rape and murder.
>
> (Guy: 16).

Rights were again put to the test in 1972 when the New Zealand Federation of Film Societies (NZFFS) not only appealed the censor's proposed cuts to the Swedish film *I Am Curious – Yellow* (1967) but also made representations to the Minister of Internal Affairs about reforming the Cinematograph Films Act 1961. The censor had objected principally to the scenes that depicted the female character sitting astride the male character; Lena removing her panties; and another scene which hinted at the possibility of oral sex (Watson and Shuker: 49). The film was virtually a manifesto of hippie or counterculture values, and its free-wheeling style had a great deal of freshness at the time. The sexual freedom of the central character was presented not merely as hedonism but as a kind of 'make love not war' politics.

Lindsay Shelton, Bruce Mason (a well-known dramatist and actor), and Peter Munz, a historian at Victoria University, appeared in front of the Appeal Board to defend 'an important film intended for showing to a group of serious film-goers'.[21] Of equal concern was the fact that the censor was not required to explain the rationale for decisions or indicate where the cuts had taken place. This secrecy irked: 'A departmental officer had the audacity to say that the public is not entitled to know what the Censor, a public servant, does on its behalf.'[22] By a majority decision, the Appeal Board upheld the Censor's decision to cut *I am Curious – Yellow*.

The 'censorship' problem remained anomalous until 1976 when two things happened – a new Act was passed that brought film into line with book censorship, and McIntosh died, to be succeeded by his deputy Bernie Tunicliffe. Effectively, it was accepted that the cinema was not a public place and that the censor was not required to be a champion of 'public order and decency' (as the previous Act had implied). Legislative change came not a moment too soon for the film community, which had seen New Zealand's censorship grow increasingly out of touch with international trends and the films of the *Easy Rider* (USA, 1969) generation.[23]

A new wave of young filmmakers had joined film society lobbyists as outspoken critics of censorship – they were understandably concerned that the banning of New Zealand films could hurt the nascent industry financially. 'When Tony Williams returned from the Cannes Film Festival in 1976, he reported that New Zealand had gained an international reputation as having the most draconian censorship system outside the Iron Curtain' (Horrocks 1992: 62).

The 1976 Act did not eliminate censorship battles but it removed some of the heat. Not that everyone supported the new act – Patricia Bartlett and the Society for the Promotion of Community Standards (SPCS) staged a strong rearguard campaign. A 49,000-signature petition calling for stricter censorship was presented to Parliament by Bartlett and others in September 1970 (Christoffel: 31). McIntosh apparently felt he was steering a sensible middle course between two pressure groups. The censorship battle, however, had one positive aspect for film culture – it forced its spokespeople to sharpen up their arguments for film as an art worthy of serious consideration alongside books.

A representative of the new kinds of Auckland festival-goer mentioned earlier was Geoff Steven (born in Auckland in 1946). He was soon co-opted onto the committee of the Auckland Film Society by Horrocks, who recognised certain affinities. Steven represented the arrival of the hippie counterculture onto the filmmaking 'scene' in Auckland. His main interest was filmmaking. Besides founding Alternative Cinema, which not only shared equipment but also published a monthly magazine from 1972, he later joined the executive of the NZFFS. Steven's involvement in the growth of film culture in this country is important for a number of reasons. As a filmmaker he experimented with cinematic codes of narration and representation, and as a film activist he made submissions to parliamentary select committees advocating more support for filmmakers. Alternative Cinema was Auckland's equivalent to Wellington's Pacific Films in the sense of being a training ground for younger filmmakers.

Steven had had a varied background, which included student political protest and work as a fashion industry photographer.[24] There was a trans-Tasman connection, too, as Steven screened underground films produced by the Sydney Filmmakers' Co-op, *inter alia,* whose guiding spirit was Albie Thoms, a figure 'who relentlessly proselytised for avant-garde filmmaking and personally engineered the development of a synergic support network for production, distribution and exhibition of films outside the industrial aegis' (Zuvela 2003).

Steven's interests reveal the maelstrom of convergent influences associated with the counterculture both in New Zealand and overseas. Less established art forms, such as comics, films, and rock and roll, featured prominently, as younger people expressed their contempt for the old and their optimism to remake the world and to express their ideas in fresh ways. Steven went on to have an important (if controversial) career in film and television production. What his early career illustrates – like that of many other local filmmakers of the period – is the importance of both the counterculture and the expanded range of films available in New Zealand, as catalysts for the growth of a new film industry in the 1970s. It is another example of the way in which the different ingredients of film culture can interact to produce an effect of synergy.

Another kind of 'mover and shaker' was Lindsay Shelton (born in 1938). He came to the cinema as a suitor dissatisfied with his relationship with film's older companion, the theatre, and as a journalist with a regular job in the younger medium of television. He discovered the existence of the Wellington Film Society, which he considered 'well-kept secret' because every year its brochure looked the same and it was only distributed in a couple of places. 'It had had a membership of between 200 and 300 every year since it had been started. Its image was as a really conservative and secretive organisation with a very small programme.'[25] Shelton would substantially transform both these aspects.

We need to understand the general state of the WFS (still the central organising body of the NZFFS) in order to appreciate the important changes that were soon to occur. In September 1968, the Discussion Group could only muster 14 people to see Guiseppe de Santis' landmark neo-realist film, *Bitter Rice* (Italy, 1948). As important historically as this film was, it certainly did not speak to the 'baby boomers' of the late 1960s. Ron Ritchie,

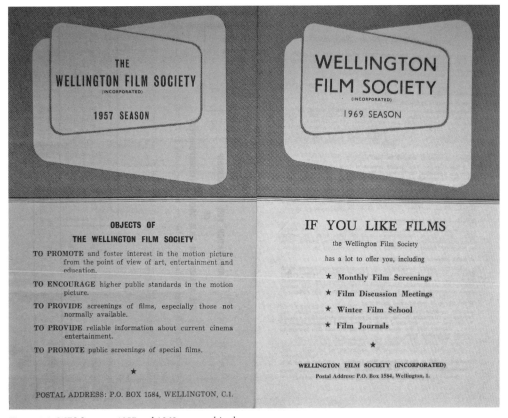

Figure 16: WFS Seasons, 1957 and 1969, no graphic change.

stalwart of the WFS, committee-man for over 20 years and president since 1967, stressed, at the 1968 AGM, that 'some new blood would be good'. Subscriptions in that year were down and screenings of films were in danger of being cut back to two per month in an effort to reduce expenditure. At the AGM of 1969, Shelton questioned the selection policy of films for the 1969 season, remarking that only three had been made in the 1960s, the latest being 1966, and that they were all European in origin with nothing from the United Kingdom or the United States of America.

In July 1969, Maurice Askew, of the Little Film Society associated with Canterbury University, which had a membership of some 400, voiced similar concerns about programming. The general feeling of the Little Film Society was that they should secede from the NZFFS in order to negotiate directly with distributors who held a commercial film catalogue. This represented a serious threat to the very existence of the Federation. Although the Canterbury committee decided, in September, to remain with the Federation, its dissatisfaction was symptomatic of a general mood around the country.

The film society movement seemed to have run out of steam and was in danger of becoming irrelevant to the lives of a younger generation. Endeavouring to halt the gradual slide, Shelton,

Figure 17: WFS 1971 season, a graphic illustration of change.

who had now joined the executive, offered to arrange some publicity for the WFS through the pages of Wellington's *Evening Post* as well as pushing an article about the Society into the Saturday edition of the *Dominion*. As a journalist, Shelton had good connections and reported back to the executive committee on a successful publicity campaign in May 1969. Recognising his good work, he was elected vice-president at the AGM in 1970. The membership decline had not only been halted; there was, in fact, a significant increase, with total membership standing at 531, compared with 378 in 1969, 410 in 1968, and 470 in 1967.

Much of the turnaround was attributed to the pulling power of one film, Hiroshi Teshigahara's avant-garde psychological drama, *Woman of the Dunes* (1964), which had generated much discussion. What the *Blue Angel* had done for the film society movement in 1953, when Gordon Mirams lifted the censor's 1930s ban, *Woman of the Dunes* did for the WFS in 1970 – it rekindled interest in the Society as provider of hard-to-see art films with an air of novelty, a socio-political edge, and/or a controversial erotic aspect.

Shelton, who now controlled the programming and hire of films for the WFS and, via the NZFFS, the rest of the country, had an understanding of the new energies. He wanted to redefine the objectives of the film society movement and may usefully be situated within the 'process of decolonisation' (1960–2000) that saw a 'coming-out' of difference and dissent, and a 'coming-in' of new differences. In contrast to earlier Film Society leaders (such as John Reid), Shelton had no intention of gradually enlarging traditional taste through his programming policy. He was not worried about the need to earn respectability for the film medium. During his presentation of the WFS's Annual Report for 1970, he took advantage of the occasion to recall a forgotten truth about the fundamental difference between the aim of commercial cinema, to entertain, and that of the film society: to court controversy. A fresh wind was now pulling the sails of the good ship Cinema into uncharted waters, and a brazen captain was at the wheel.

For many New Zealanders, an overseas experience (OE) is a transforming and important one. It is interesting to note how important Shelton's London experience was for his understanding of film culture – in some ways a road to Damascus experience. It is also to the credit of Ron Ritchie that he recognised Shelton's energies and decided that here was the 'new young blood' required by the WFS. As Shelton recalled of his OE: 'there was a commercial set-up for screening films called the New Cinema Club [in London], run by Derek Hill. … I spent [time] looking at a lot of his films and I suddenly discovered that there was this very wide range of amazing films that weren't coming through commercial sources.'[26]

The transformation of the WFS did not entail severing all connections with the past. A primary provider of films for the NZFFS had been an independent English distribution company, Contemporary Films, run by Charles and Kitty Cooper, who had the foresight to acquire the rights to many films produced on the periphery of Anglo-American empire and made it possible for them to be seen.

A secondary source, it later transpired, was not as legitimate. But this illegality had positive consequences, as Shelton recalls: 'I was given new prints of all [Kenneth] Anger's films from a guy in London who I thought was legitimate because he had access to the original negatives ... but I don't think he really had the right to do the sales.'[27] Jonathan Dennis, who later became a key figure in New Zealand film culture (his contribution is described in the next chapter) and a friend of Anger, was encouraged to join the WFS, which he did in 1972, upon seeing the 1971 season which included an Anger programme comprising *Eaux d'artifice* (1953), *Scorpio Rising* (1962–64), and *Invocation of My Demon Brother* (1969). Although two of the films looked back to an earlier wave of the counterculture, they were still highly relevant to the energies of the early 1970s in their sexuality, drugs, and music. In some respects, the films were deliberately provocative with their references to black magic, Nazism, and gay sexuality. Ironically, *The Wild One* (banned by the New Zealand censor) figures prominently in *Scorpio Rising*. The Anger package brought the energy of the American underground to the Federation's permanent collection and generated huge interest, not all of it positive.

What different film societies thought about the year's films became a regular feature of the Federation's quarterly newsletter, *Newsreel*. These comments were consulted by film society committees as they planned programmes for the coming season. They serve today as roughly hewn yardsticks that allow us to gauge the reception of these films in those parts of New Zealand with a film society, the number of which was also on the rise in this period.[28] Comments on the Anger programme revealed a healthy diversity. In Hamilton, 'the audience dwindled as the programmes proceeded. *Scorpio* and *Invocation* in particular fell pretty flat – subject matter "old hat" to both young and old' (*Newsreel* 1971: 4).

Scorpio Rising may have seemed old hat in its allusions to the 1950s Beat Generation, but there was a new spirit reflected in the films for those who could recognise it. Response to films at this time was often a matter of whether one was 'on the same wavelength', and rational debate seemed almost a waste of time if a viewer had failed to feel 'the vibe'. Anger had been taken up by the hippies as a valued forerunner, and he was a personal acquaintance of rock stars such as Marianne Faithful and Mick Jagger. *Invocation* made direct reference to the Vietnam War, and the films were full of drug allusions for those in the know. Drugs were one of the main areas of difference between the older and younger generations. McIntosh cut any drug references he noticed, but it was a running joke among young adult viewers that the censor was often so unfamiliar with the subject that outrageous scenes would sometimes slip past him unawares.

With films like these the film society movement as a whole was reinvigorated. Membership in Wellington grew from its previous high of 530 (1970) to over 900 (1971), at which it had to be capped, with a substantial waiting list. The following year membership rose to 1200. Two years later it peaked at 2500, making it one of the largest film societies in the world. This was the moment when the film society shifted gears, going from pure volunteerism to nascent professionalism. Rosemary Hope was employed full-time to run the WFS, the federation of film societies, and the festival in Wellington. A similar growth occurred in Auckland, with membership doubling between 1971 and 1972, rising from 300 to 600 (*Newsreel* 1972: 2).[29] Shelton recalls the excitement that accompanied the upsurge in membership of the WFS during the early phase of his presidency and the advertising that played its part in the process:

'we worked very hard to distribute [the brochures] all over town. The copy's great, really persuasive, full of references to international reviews saying the films were important,

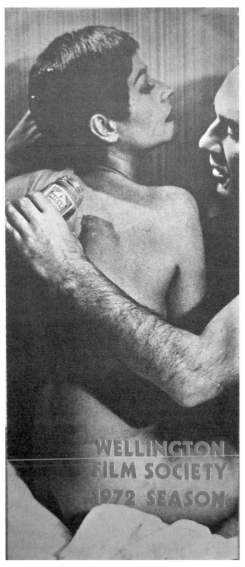

Figure 18: The graphically rich WFS brochure in its 1972 season.

and I think the first paragraph for that brochure is fairly well directly lifted from the New Cinema Club in London.'[30]

The attractive force of the films was not the only reason for this phenomenal growth around the country. In Wellington's case, it also involved a more aggressive promotional policy; a graphically bold WFS brochure; recent articles and television reports on the subject of film censorship; and the desire to be part of a burgeoning cultural challenge to ossified middle New Zealand. (Film culture was perceived as one of the major sites of cultural revolution.)

Maintaining the excitement of the 1971 season was Nagisa Oshima's *Diary of a Shinjuku Thief* (Japan, 1968), whose title referred to Jean Genet's novel, *Diary of a Thief*, as Oshima's way of signalling his many and varied intellectual and artistic debts to France. *Diary* was another of his 'scandalous' attacks on the 'taboos' of modern Japan. The censor allowed this film to be screened uncut to film society audiences. Reception of the film was prepared by an extensive series of reviews that appeared in the January 1971 edition of *Newsreel*. There was a short extract of an interview (translated from French) with Oshima conducted by *Cahiers du cinéma*; a film review by the actor and playwright Peter Harcourt, and comments of a preview panel to which the Federation had shown the film in Wellington in December 1970, which included the following: 'As a subjective experience it demands the fullest participation from its audience. Whether you like it or not, it is a significant film'; and 'I found the excessive use of the hand-held camera distracting. ... but an interesting example of what we normally don't get an opportunity to see' (*Newsreel* 1971: 5).

Comments made by different societies in smaller towns revealed a stronger puritan strain than was evidenced in the capital's preview audience. People in Nelson found it 'An extremely poorly executed and ill-conceived film by western standards and affords nothing to enhance the reputation of the Japanese film industry.' While in Timaru, 'Some members after reading the preview notes refused to come to such a film and said they would not remain members if we screened such films. Others say we have gone sex mad. However, it is better than having a passive membership who just sit and look' (*Newsreel* 1971: 5).

That last comment was an interesting one. Typically, the conflict within film society circles over films of this kind was between two notions of seriousness – a more earnest, older view that was likely to see sexualised films as 'commercial' or 'populist pandering' rather than 'serious' (the true goal of film appreciation being to make a case for its artistic seriousness, as sustenance for the spirit); and a younger, more radical view that associated seriousness with *épater la bourgeoisie*. When the conflict was articulated in formal terms, it involved a preference for 'well made' films, with conspicuous skills, versus a preference for free-wheeling, non-linear types of film (with innovative use of hand-held camera, unusual forms of editing, and so on).

This generation gap (sometimes associated with a big city/provincial gap) brought to the boil an old tension that had always existed within the 'field of foreign films' – some people were drawn to such films as a form of high (or upper-middlebrow) culture; some were loyal to them because they represented their home country and language; some were tantalised by their 'adult' approach to sexuality; and still others wanted to be startled by their enigmatic modernity. The new films of the 1960s and early 1970s were likely to alienate the first two groups. Foreign language communities did not want their cultures represented by sexual licence or drug-taking; and many older members wanted cultural uplift not controversy. One member of the Wellington panel that had reviewed Oshima's film made the generous comment: 'I did not fully understand this film … but I think it could be of significance to younger members and should be available to them.' Another said: 'It typifies so much that is vigorous about cinema today. The "old" cinema is dead (or exists on TV) and the young people who will find this exciting will start approaching film societies to take advantage of what they should be offering. Brava Oshima' (*Newsreel* 1971: 5).

Younger or more radical cinephiles would enthuse about society films that included critiques of racism, support for sexual liberation,[31] opposition to the Vietnam War, experimentation with drugs,[32] resistance to patriarchal 'oppression', and romantic ideas of communes – as represented, for example, in the emblematic *Easy Rider*. A Wellington member summed up what a younger generation expected of a bold contemporary film: 'A terrifying sociological and sexual statement that makes [the] film experience a total one' (*Newsreel*: 5).

Shelton's success in securing more contemporary and controversial films was assisted by the cultural agencies of various foreign governments whose embassies and legations promoted their respective national cinemas in an admirably broad-minded way. The French were particularly active, as Bill Gosden (Director: New Zealand Film Festival Trust) recalled of a later period: 'Those films cost us nothing, and the film society movement in those days had a very effective distribution circuit'. It was a very logical choice for those foreign government agencies to place their films with it.[33]

The Wellington Film Festival

Shelton's introduction to the cinema had been both rapid and productive but he was learning that not all the films he wanted to programme for the NZFFS were available in the 16mm format used by the film society movement. His desire to screen a broader range of contemporary cinema from around the world led to the creation of 'The First Wellington Film Festival', which screened films in 35mm. Held at the Paramount Cinema between 28 July and 3 August 1972, it neatly followed the 4th Auckland International Film Festival (July 14–27). Auckland's festival had gradually increased the number of films presented, from 14 to 17 in its first three years of operation; by 1972, however, the number of films jumped to 27, more than three times the number shown in Wellington (8) during its inaugural festival year. Of the eight films shown in Wellington, five had come from Auckland. At least two of the other three came from contacts Shelton had made with the organisers of the Sydney Film Festival who were now less reluctant about sharing films with their neighbours across the Tasman.[34]

Initially the two New Zealand film festivals worked closely together, but even in Wellington's inaugural season there were signs that tastes and perhaps objectives diverged – Wellington had more Australian films, for example. (It is, of course, a natural process for festivals to seek to develop a distinctive identity.) It was not only a question of size that accounted for the much broader range of films offered by the film committee in Auckland; and it was significant that whereas Auckland called itself an *International* Film Festival, Wellington chose not to. In 1972, films from 15 countries were presented in Auckland, and although Western Europe was heavily represented with 15, there were six films from Central and South America, one a piece from Japan, Egypt, Algeria and India, and two from Eastern Europe.

Wellington's festival was more tightly focussed, with a more pronounced Western European flavour. The only exceptions were an independent American film by Dalton Trumbo, *Johnny Got His Gun* (1970), and a co-production between Italy and Algeria, *The Battle of Algiers* (1966). France was represented by Rohmer (*Le Genou de Claire*, 1970) and Malle (*Le Souffle au coeur*, 1971); Buñuel represented himself (not Franco's fascist Spain) with *Tristana* (1970), and Italy's Mauro Bolognini was there with *Metello* (1970), 'shot in beautifully misty colour which enhances the beauty of Florence'.[35]

In 1973, Auckland showed 28 films from 17 countries, though this was reduced in 1974 to 21 films from 14 countries. By way of contrast, in 1974, Wellington screened 13 films from nine countries, with three coming from the United States of America, two apiece from France and West Germany, and the rest of the selection showing a strong Euro-North American preference: Belgium, Canada, Czechoslovakia, Switzerland, the United Kingdom, and the USSR. It took some films from Auckland but also made more use of Shelton's excellent contacts to tap other sources.

Auckland was thrown into crisis in 1979 (the 11th Festival) when the Auckland Festival Society intervened and fired its organising committee. Unsympathetic observers saw this as an attempt by an arts festival close to bankruptcy to exploit the film season more vigorously as a cash cow to subsidise traditional forms of art that were losing money. The 1979 organising committee cancelled the usual pre-Festival activities (talks and 16mm screenings) and moved the film festival back to its earlier and subaltern role of handmaiden to the 'arts proper'. The new organising committee, for example, made greater use of films already in the country instead of sourcing them from overseas, thus eroding some of the film festival's hard-won cultural authority and independence. (The evolution of local film festival culture and this particular event is examined in more detail in the next chapter.)

In February 1979, an editorial in *Alternative Cinema* assessed the state of New Zealand's film culture. On the one hand, 'Two important ingredients have been added in the last two years – a feature-film industry (though still very modest in size), and a New Zealand Film Commission.' On the other hand, film culture remained at a rudimentary stage; there was, for example, 'no adequate archive, no training school, and no National Film Theatre'. Film education was 'almost non-existent, and there is almost no detailed film criticism, only hastily written "reviews"'. This mostly negative assessment managed to end on a note of optimism: 'New Zealand film culture is small but it is fortunate enough to have a reasonably good atmosphere. There is a lot of friendly contact between different people and groups [filmmakers, critics and educators]' (Horrocks 1979).

From an activist's point of view, there was indeed much still to be done; but as this chapter has shown, the decade of the 1970s did succeed in carrying the local film culture to a new level. To reinforce this positive assessment, I will end the chapter with a brief overview of the film culture we have seen developing over the course of the 1970s.

Some Conclusions

The most dramatic news of the decade was the emergence of a new *filmmaking* scene. Short films, more adventurous than the routine tourist and industrial projects made by the National Film Unit, began to appear in the 1960s. This activity built up to the emergence of a feature-film industry in 1977. *Sleeping Dogs* (1977) was the first 35mm dramatic feature film to be made in New Zealand since 1966. Few features had been made in the country since 1939. Most importantly, the production of features became an ongoing process after *Sleeping Dogs*, with an average of four per year. The industry was sustained by funding from the newly created New Zealand Film Commission (1978).

It is notable that the creation of the new industry was very much the work of the generation born in the 1940s, though John O'Shea played a key role as mentor to many of them. In the case of directors such as Bruce Morrison, Geoff Steven, and Tony Williams, exposure to European art films during the 1960s was an important part of their education. Although the economics of the New Zealand situation strongly encouraged filmmakers to take a mainstream, commercial approach to storytelling, the features made by this group were clearly influenced by the hours they had spent in art-house cinemas or at film society or festival screenings. For example, Steven's two features, *Skin Deep* (1978) and *Strata* (1982), were both influenced by East European cinema. Indeed, *Strata* was co-scripted by Ester Krumbachova who had been prominent in Czech cinema during the 1960s.

Assisted by a QEII Arts Council grant, Williams travelled to France in 1967 to become an unpaid 'student observer' on the sets of two films directed by Alain Resnais. The films Williams made in the 1970s contained reminders of Resnais' style, for example in their use of long tracking shots. All three directors shifted closer to the mainstream in subsequent filmmaking, but continued to speak passionately about the importance of their exposure to new conceptions and styles of filmmaking during the 1960s and 1970s.

The 1970s also saw the emergence of avant-garde filmmaking in New Zealand, along with the rediscovery of Len Lye as an ancestor. Though still scarce, the experimental work emerging from university art schools and Alternative Cinema broadened the tradition of local filmmaking (see Horrocks' essays 1982a, 1982b, 1992; see also Rumsby 2003). Another important development was the arrival of the first video recorders at the end of the 1970s – a crucial new tool for both the making and study of moving images.

The second key aspect of the late 1960s and early 1970s was the expansion of *film availability* through the emergence of full-scale annual film festivals. There was a revitalisation of the film society movement. Along with the continued growth of art-house cinemas, these developments ensured a steady supply of innovative films. Some of the more unusual overseas films still fell through the cracks, though universities and film co-ops caught a few of the more specialised examples.

Film education was growing, albeit slowly (Horrocks 1999). It had long been established in adult education, and was now gradually becoming a part of teaching in high schools (particularly in English). The most dramatic developments were in the universities. Film studies and/or filmmaking courses were taught by Maurice Askew at Ilam (whose early students included Vincent Ward and Timothy White), Robert Hutchins at Elam (whose early students included Rodney Charters and Leon Narbey), Roger Horrocks in the English Department of Auckland University (whose early students included David Blyth, Alison Maclean, Sam Pillsbury, and Ray Waru), and Russell Campbell at Victoria (who was involved in the political work of Vanguard Films and the establishment of *Illusions*).[36] Discussion in these courses explored a wide range of film history and aesthetics, represented by textbooks such as *Film Theory and Criticism*, first published in 1974 with Gerald Mast as editor. (This was used at Auckland as a text for many years as it evolved through various editions.) Robin Scholes, who taught for a couple of years at Auckland in the mid-1970s, contributed the knowledge of new developments in theory that she had gained in London. (She then left teaching to begin an impressive career as a film producer.)

The combined effect of the above developments was to ensure that films were talked about – at least occasionally – in detailed aesthetic terms. Granted, the particular interests of the newest generation of film buffs seemed often to be somewhat narrowly focused on sex, drugs, rock and roll, and revolution – which were as much a distraction from aesthetics as the focus on socialism had been in the 1930s. The personal memoir included in my Introduction provides anecdotal evidence that 'serious' film culture was still marginalised. A certain amount of luck was involved in stumbling across it. Nevertheless, there were corners in which it existed, and it did so with a growing vitality. The idea of 'auteur' was now established to the point where it was invoked in cinema advertising (and not only for directors as well known as Hitchcock). There were at least a few *cinéastes* on the scene who were aware of the critical ferment that had accompanied *la nouvelle vague* – they had read Bazin, Truffaut on *la politique des auteurs*, and perhaps Andrew Sarris on 'auteur theory'.

One of the most interesting developments to emerge from the 1960s in New Zealand was a new attitude of openness to popular and high culture, seeing them as complementary rather than opposed. The American Pop Art of the 1960s, the growth of interest in 'cult movies', and the new sophistication of 1960s rock music made a sharp division between popular and high art no longer possible. To mention just one example of the new sensibility that emerged in New Zealand during the 1970s we may turn to a 1975 documentary film directed by Tony Williams, *Lost in the Garden of the World*. With funds provided by Pacific Films, the Arts Council, and TV1, Williams and his team travelled to the Cannes Film Festival to interview filmmakers. His choice of interviewees was a deliberately provocative juxtaposition between Steven Spielberg, Martin Scorcese, Werner Herzog, and two 'cult' directors, Paul Bartel (*Death Race 2000*, USA 1975) and Tobe Hooper (*The Texas Chainsaw Massacre*, USA 1974).

The poetic, free-wheeling documentary that resulted from this trip was a celebration of cinema and authorship in all its forms, contrasting the openness and vitality of the festival with New Zealand's lack of support for filmmakers and the harshness of its film censorship. The documentary was clearly intended as a manifesto of film culture, passionately embracing not only the best of Hollywood (Spielberg and Scorcese) but also the American independents (Hooper and Bartel) and a European auteur (Herzog). Considering the long battles fought in New Zealand over the evils of Hollywood and popular culture, Williams's broad, excited perspective was something very new for New Zealand. Television reviewers were disconcerted by it, but this was a film aimed at a 'new generation' (see Horrocks 1977).

In general, then, various barriers were in the process of being dismantled (the fence between high and popular culture, the limited knowledge of filmmaking, the antipathy to specialised film analysis, and the over-protective censorship policies) so that film culture could now develop vigorously on all fronts, as the next chapter will show in tracing the evolution of international film festival culture and the establishment of the New Zealand Film Archive.

References

Anon, (1971), 'What Societies Thought About This Year's Films', *Newsreel,* 5, October, pp. 4–5.

———— (1972), 'More Increases in Membership', *Newsreel,* 6, Autumn, p. 2.

———— (1990), *NZOYB,* Wellington: Government Printer, p. 326.

———— (1990), *NZOYB,* Wellington: Government Printer, p. 340.

Belich, J. (2001), *Paradise Reforged: A History of the New Zealanders from the 1880s to the Year 2000*, Auckland: Allen Lane and Penguin Press.

Brennan, S. (n.d.), 'Ermanno Olmi: Biography' [Online]. Available at: http://www.allmovie.com/artist/ermanno-olmi-p105064. Accessed: 10 May 2000.

Christoffel, P. (1989), *Censored: A Short History of Censorship in New Zealand*, Wellington: Research Unit, Dept. of Internal Affairs.

Colgan, W. (1969), 'Full Film Fare', *NZ Listener,* 24 October.

Dart, W. (1970), 'Film Censorship in New Zealand', *Landfall,* 24, pp. 70–71.

Guy, L. D. (1992), 'The Cinematograph Film Censorship Debate in New Zealand, 1965–76', unpublished Master of Arts research essay (History), University of Auckland. Republished in *New Zealand Journal of Baptist Research,* 3, (1998), pp. 19–39.

Horrocks, R. (1962), 'Auckland Festival of the Arts', *Craccum,* 28 June, p. 10.

———— (1971), 'Film as Art, Film as Business', *NZ Listener,* 24 May, pp. 14–15.

———— (1977), 'Surviving in Films: The Career of a New Zealand Film-maker', *Islands,* 20, December, pp. 144–45.

———— (1979), 'Editorial', *Alternative Cinema*, February, p. 4.

———— (1982a), 'Twenty Years of Experimental Films', *Art New Zealand*, 24, pp. 40–45.

———— (1982b), 'An Essay about Experimental Films that Ended Up as an Essay about New Zealand', *Parallax*, 1, pp. 78–87.

———— (1992/1996), 'Alternatives: Experimental Film Making in New Zealand'. In: J. Dennis and J. Bieringa eds. *Film in Aotearoa New Zealand,* Wellington: Victoria University Press, pp. 55–88.

———— (1999), 'The Late Show: The Production of Film and Television Studies'. In: M. Peters, ed. *After the Disciplines: The Emergence of Cultural Studies*, Westport, Connecticut: Bergin and Garvey (Critical Studies in Education and Culture series), pp. 175–86.

King, M. (1988), *After the War: New Zealand since 1945*, Auckland: Hodder and Stoughton in association with Wilson and Horton.

Lochore, D. W. (1972), 'Watching Films: Festival Success', *New Zealand Herald,* 5 August, Section 2, p. 6.

Pearson, B. (1952), 'Fretful Sleepers: A Sketch of New Zealand Behaviour and Its Implications for the Artist', *Landfall*, 6(3), pp. 201–30.

Rumsby, M. (2003), 'A Place Near Here', *Illusions,* 35, Winter, pp. 15–20.

Schatz, T. (1983), *Old Hollywood/New Hollywood: Ritual, Art and Industry*, Ann Arbor: UMI Research Press.

Watson, C. and Shuker, R. (1998), *In the Public Good? Censorship in New Zealand*, Palmerston North: Dunmore Press.

Zuvela, D. (2003), 'The Ubu Moment: An Interview with Albie Thoms', 25 July [Online]. Available at: http://sensesofcinema.com/2003/27/albie_thoms/. Accessed: 10 October 2010.

Notes

1 From *The Times They Are A Changing*, Columbia Records, 13 January 1964.
2 R. Horrocks interview, May 2002.
3 W. Colgan interview, April 2002.
4 Memo to the Film Committee, Auckland Festival Society, 21 May 1968, private papers of Roger Horrocks.
5 Ibid.
6 W. Colgan interview, April 2002.
7 Ibid.
8 J. Reynolds interview, 22 February 1999.
9 W. Colgan interview, April 2002.
10 Ibid.
11 May 2002, the Auckland International Film Festival was embroiled in a 'scandal' when a self-styled Society for the Promotion of Community Standards (led by David Lane) objected to the sexual and violent content of two of the proposed films at the eleventh hour. Lane demanded a review of the Classification Office decision relating to *Y tu mamá también* and *The Piano Teacher*. Only hours before the opening night of the festival, the organisers heard that the injunctions had been denied.

12 R. Horrocks interview, March 2002.

13 Private papers, R. Horrocks. Horrocks was involved in the development of film culture in Auckland from the early 1960s when he was a student at the University of Auckland and wrote lengthy film reviews for the student newspaper *Craccum*.

14 Letter from Lochore to Horrocks, 26 August 1969; Private papers, R. Horrocks.

15 R. Horrocks interview, March 2002.

16 See Chapter 2 for details about the court case.

17 'The TV networks went into business in 1948 and by 1955 the medium had "saturated" roughly eighty-five percent of the homes in America' (Schatz: 18). Instead of 'going to the movies', a new social ritual developed, 'watching TV'. 'By 1960 the average American was spending roughly twenty-five hours a week watching television' (Schatz: 18).

18 There were 4600 television licences in 1961. By 1966, this number had exploded to 500,000 (*Official Year Book* 1990: 340).

19 The Mazengrab Report (1954) was an official response to youthful rebellion. It found that 'improper sexual behaviour among children was extensive'. Other signs of corruption were seen in the Parker-Hulme incident of 1954, when two Christchurch schoolgirls, believed to be lesbians, killed one of their mothers when she tried to separate them. (This was the subject of *Heavenly Creatures* (1994), the later film by Peter Jackson.)

20 L. Shelton interview, November 2000.

21 Chairman's Report, January 1973, p. 3. The New Zealand Film Archive.

22 Ibid, p. 4.

23 *Easy Rider* (1969) had most of its main drug sequence cut by the New Zealand Censor.

24 G. Steven interview, May 2000.

25 L. Shelton interview, November 2000.

26 Ibid.

27 Ibid.

28 The Federation added four new film societies in Reporoa, Wanganui, Masterton, and Pahiatua to its list of 18 established societies in 1971.

29 The Auckland Film Society was also changing character as younger cineastes took over executive roles.

30 L. Shelton interview, November 2000.

31 Assisted by the introduction of contraceptive pills in January 1961.

32 Marijuana was also grown in large quantities for the first time in New Zealand in the 1960s.

33 B. Gosden interview, November 2000.

34 Shelton has written about the Festival during his tenure as director here: http://www.nzff. co.nz/wellington/the-birth-of-the-wellington-film-festival.

35 From the 1972 Wellington Film Festival brochure.

36 The first academics to teach film at Victoria University between 1974 and 1981 were Philip Mann and then David Carnegie, who convened successive courses on film analysis, into which a production component was incorporated from the beginning. (I thank Trisha Dunleavey for this information.)

Chapter 8

Between Spectacle and Memory

L ooking at the historical development of film culture in New Zealand, one can identify key moments of growth and transformation as the various pieces that constitute a sophisticated film culture take shape and form synergies – a combination of discrete elements creating an effect greater than the sum of its parts. As we saw in the last chapter, energies released as a result of the 'counterculture' and external decolonisation (disconnection from Britain) were ingredients of a heady brew responsible for reinvigorating alternative exhibition venues (represented by the film society movement), independent distribution networks, and local film production throughout the 1970s. In the decades that followed, individual and institutional initiatives led to an extension of the film festival phenomenon and the creation of the New Zealand Film Archive; signal developments in the growth of film culture that this chapter will document. Combined with university film studies courses and the establishment of the New Zealand Film Commission (1978), they represent the culmination of a long revolution to establish film as art, as culture, and as industry.

Film Festival Expansion[1]

One of the functions of film festivals in New Zealand has always been to provide foreign language films. New Zealand has many small immigrant communities – small because the overall size of the population is small – and the Festival is one of the few opportunities they have had to see a film in their first language. For such publics, language is still a reason to go to the Festival. There are, however, new complexities: it is easier to purchase DVDs and Blu-ray discs from overseas for the 'home theatre'; video streaming sites, such as MUBI, have appeared; there are some nationally-based DVD rental stores (for example, Indian and Chinese); and some national film festivals have become established (such as the annual Italian and French festivals).

In the last chapter, I noted the creation of the first independent international film festivals in Auckland (1969) and Wellington (1972). As with the introduction of television, New Zealand was slower than Europe, North America, and Australia in developing its variant of an international cultural phenomenon. To take Australia as an example, Melbourne and Sydney had established film festivals in 1951 and 1954, respectively, while Adelaide began its own in 1958. (The remarkable International Documentary Film Festival, held in Christchurch, New Zealand in October 1950, which might have inaugurated a broader feature film festival, had no immediate successor.) As film festivals began to spread over the entire globe in the 1980s (de Valck 2007: 68), members of the Wellington Film Society, who also ran that city's annual film festival, had cause to worry about the future of their increasingly popular event. The principal reason for their concern in 1983 was the way in which the separate Auckland International Film Festival (AIFF) was conducting its affairs.

As with many other film festivals, New Zealand's had come about as singular ventures independently of the other, 'existing as temporary entities and discrete exhibition sites' (Iordanova 2009: 25). An ad hoc arrangement governed relations between the two organisations, which consisted principally in sharing films and the significant costs associated with bringing them to the country and submitting them to the censor for festival approval. One of the several specificities of film festival culture in New Zealand is that its degree of professionalisation was modest when compared to similar overseas events. In contrast with overseas film festivals, volunteers ran the Auckland and Wellington versions for many years. In 1982, ten years after its successful debut, Wellington had one full-time paid employee (it now has four and they programme the nation's 14 film festivals), who also co-ordinated both the local film society and the New Zealand Federation of Film Societies. Moreover, the film festivals relied to an unprecedented and anomalous degree on ticket sales for revenue – some 90 per cent of the New Zealand Film Festival Trust income still derives from them.[2]

It was otherwise overseas: 'Few film festivals raise more than 20 per cent of their income from box office, most much less than this. Most of the funding comes from the public sector or sponsorship' (Cousins 2009: 156). On the occasion of Wellington's tenth film festival in 1981, founding director, Lindsay Shelton, wrote that it was organised 'entirely by voluntary effort – the film festival, unlike most other similar events, has had no financial support from any civic or national body as it has expanded to its present substantial size' (Shelton 1981: 3). In 1983, the president of the WFS reported on a fleeting visit to the capital of Ken Wlaschin, then director of the London Film Festival, who was 'extremely impressed with our Festival but quite unable to understand how we could survive without outside funding. We share his amazement. Major festivals of the standard and standing of the Wellington Film Festival all receive funding from their cities or government'.[3]

To return to the source of friction that agitated office holders of the WFS, organisers of the WFF, in their dealings with the programmers of the Auckland International Film Festival. Between 1980 and 1983, the number of films the Auckland and Wellington festivals shared began to fall (from a high of 33 – out of 50 films screened in Wellington – in 1981, to a low of 23 – out of 48 – in 1983).[4] This represented a very serious threat for the ongoing financial viability of Wellington's event. Had it not been for the fact that 1983 was a record year in terms of ticket sales, the festival would have operated at a loss.[5] This dire state of affairs led to the formation of a sub-committee charged with examining the financial relationship with the Auckland Festival Society. Previously, Auckland had taken roughly 50 per cent of the films Wellington proposed, but in 1983 this had dwindled to only 20 per cent.[6] There were, too, other causes of major concern. Programming differences between the two festivals emerged more starkly – something noted in Chapter 7 when the Auckland Festival Trust removed two prominent members of the AFS from the committee that programmed the films screened during the AIFF.

According to Roger Horrocks, who had been one of the Festival organisers for the first ten years:

> The initial team ran the Auckland International Film Festival for the first ten years according to their original philosophy; then there was a management upheaval. The Auckland Festival of the Arts, which was legally the 'umbrella' organization, was in financial strife, whereas the Film Festival had been making some money. The general Festival then took over the Film Festival, removed two members (including myself) from the organizing committee, and put its representative (Max Archer) in charge. I believe that its reason for doing so was to enable it to use the Film Festival as a cash cow to help to fund other Festival activities. There were certainly members of the Auckland Festival who regarded traditional artistic activities (such as classical music) as more important than film, and therefore saw this cross-subsidization as perfectly appropriate. I did not, and so I was given my marching orders. The "money-making" Film Festival (with a greater number of commercial titles) ran for the next four or five years; but the strategy did not save the Auckland Festival of the Arts which finally closed its doors. Fortunately, Bill Gosden then intervened and rescued the Auckland Film Festival which recovered its artistic emphasis and became the Auckland outlet for the Wellington Festival.[7]

Horrocks's account has received support from Gosden:

> The Auckland Festival Society ran the Auckland film festivals as a profitable venture to pay for live arts events of a fairly middlebrow nature and Max Archer … the artistic director of the AFS, was quite blunt about being commercially motivated. … What was happening in Auckland was that they were screening some fairly disreputable films – I mean they were showing some David Hamilton films and ignoring others; Louis Malle's *My Dinner with André* [USA, 1981] was programmed to screen once on a Wednesday morning.[8]

Committee members in Wellington railed against the 'exploitive' turn that the Auckland festival seemed engaged in and were also shocked that Auckland's private arrangement with Amalgamated Theatres gave them access to films (such as those by Robert Altman) they would not share, which were then toured nationally as a separate mini-festival by Amalgamated. The egregious nature of these developments prompted the WFF to note that:

> We are the only Film Festival in the country interested in 'Film Culture' and our survival is entirely dependent on the support of those who share our interest. The Auckland Film Festival – which is programmed, most successfully, to raise money – has turned down twenty of the features we made available to them this year. Without financial assistance for these films from Auckland we find ourselves, more than ever, out on a limb. Perversely

perhaps, this enforced increase in independence is exciting in terms of the extra clarity it lends to our identity (Auckland can afford to look upon us as tatty eccentrics who turn up the occasional winner), but in terms of our financial security ... It's ironic that what we consider our strongest Festival in years is also our most financially precarious.

(Gosden 1983: 3)

Action was clearly needed to ensure the continued viability of the WFF and it came in the shape of Larry Vella, then managing director of Kerridge-Odeon, the largest cinema exhibition chain in the country, who initially offered to take the whole WFF and screen it in competition with the AIFF at the Kerridge-owned St James Cinema in Auckland. However, he eventually brokered a three-way deal between himself, Amalgamated, and the WFS. This resulted in Max Archer, film programmer for the Auckland Festival Trust being divested of programming responsibilities, which went to Gosden, now director of the WFF.[9] It seems that Archer's instrumental view of films (they should make money in order to pay for the Festival Society's live performances) was out of step with the new zeitgeist – film was a form of art to be appreciated in its own right. He had, for instance, turned down 'a phenomenally successful film' in 1983 called *Liquid Sky* (USA, 1982), which had quite perplexed Richard Warburg, the Australian distributor of this film, who also played a role in convincing Vella that Archer was not the programmer required to take advantage of the director-led films being made internationally.[10] Warburg was the distributor for a number of key films, for example, Fassbinder's, which may have influenced Vella's decision to back the WFS programmed film festival.

As a result of these negotiations, from 1984 to 1993, the AIFF alternated between the Civic (owned by Amalgamated) and the St James (owned by Kerridge Odeon), with each company sharing a percentage of the ever-increasing box office as film festival culture continued its growth, providing temporary exhibition sites for new films and larger audiences; a phenomenon in keeping with the increasing importance of 'experiences' and 'spectacle' in the contemporary cultural economy (Pine II and Gilmore 1999). For the WFS, it was a plus, too, as they had access to the catalogues of both companies in composing their programme; anything that might have local distribution was theirs for the asking. This considerably strengthened both the selection possibilities and the Wellington festival, which now accessed films previously denied to it by Archer's intransigence.

A year later, at the 13th WFF in 1984, of the 52 films screened, some 47 were also seen in Auckland, a marked turnaround. Wellington's centrality (a hub position both politically – as the nation's capital – and geographically) ushered in a new era in national programming and allowed for an expansion of film festival culture (other cities and towns were progressively added), a phenomenon echoed globally as film festivals mushroomed,[11] leading to the establishment of an international film festival circuit, which, as our indigenous example demonstrates, needs to be understood 'as being materially and discursively constructed through the negotiation of varied, and sometimes conflicting, motivations of stakeholders' (Rhyne 2009: 20).

Programming the Nation

In her study of European film festivals, Marijke de Valck (2007) notes three main developmental phases. The first encompasses the period 1932–68, from the establishment of the first recurring film festival in Venice to the events of May 1968, which disrupted the festivals in Cannes and Venice, and led in the early 1970s to a reorganisation of the initial film festival format (film festivals used as national cinema shop fronts). Her second phase showcases the rise of the independently organised festivals 'that operate both as protectors of the cinematic art and as facilitators of the film industries', while the third (taking shape over the 1980s) shows signs of increasing professionalisation and institutionalisation.

The second and third phases have the most local resonance, except that the non-competitive New Zealand festivals do not, as some of the Australian ones do, act as facilitators of the film industry.[12] This means that the NZIFF retains a cultural agenda-setting aspect or remit that was, for the 1980s and much of the 1990s, a sometime combative one inherited from the cultural struggles occurring in the 1970s. Produced discursively via the selection process, this agenda was structured following a predominantly thematic or *auteur* optic rather than a nationalist one (although new 'waves' of emergent national cinemas are still routinely followed – Rumanian cinema, for instance, has attracted recent festival attention). The fact that the cinema was now considered part of high culture and the film director an *auteur* ensured that film festivals became sites where such discursive formations were both produced and heard (de Valck: 62–3).

At a local level, themes that emerge in the programmes of the early 1990s, for example, are active interventions in the debates animating the community at different times: a 'community' that could also have an international dimension to its reach in allowing, for example, various marginalised social formations to be represented. Gay rights, battles with censorship, female directors expressing a feminist politics, indigenous rights, and the value of screening challenging documentary films at a time when television in New Zealand had lost its public service model in favour of a commercially driven 'ratings' model, were issues addressed in the selections made by the film festival director in constructing the annual programme. There was an avowed cultural mission to shake festival audiences from complacent (mainstream) values and to give cinematic prominence to hitherto less visibly evident sections of society.

In the 1991 programme, for instance, the director was 'pleased that we're screening a record number of films directed by women – and that the Festival is able to accentuate this by turning spotlights on two of them'.[13] In 1992, the 'openly and specifically gay visions realised in this year's programme amount to a new way of seeing'. The increased visibility of gay artists in the era of AIDS created a new 'queer cinema', in which 'the need for positive gay images has been impatiently jettisoned by many gay filmmakers, along with any attempt to pander to mainstream acceptability'.[14]

In 1993, on the occasion of remembering the censor's banning of *Henry, Portrait of a Serial Killer* (USA, 1986) a year earlier, the director rued the fact that even film festival patrons endorsed the decision and noted a tightened censorship environment: 'The

Parliamentary select committee has reported back on the Government's new censorship bill and recommended that the extent and degree to which a film *tends to demean* any person be added to an already needlessly explicit list of grounds for rejection.'[15] The position of censor had become increasingly politicised and required 'the additional imprimatur of the Minister of Women's Affairs'. Another source of disquiet was that the censor was not obliged to publicly disclose the reasons for her (or his) decisions. In an ironic twist, Gosden noted that 'At least we were told why *Henry* was banned – and had the consolation of three irreconcilable views of the film from the three censorship authorities required to give a written account of it.'[16]

At the 23rd WFF in 1994, approximately 34 of the some 110 films screened were documentaries, which allowed the programmer to note the festival relevance of this genre at a time when,

> driven by ratings and dominated by ludicrously self-important commercials and promos, television in New Zealand is amongst the least edifying there is. With few exceptions, the best documentaries in the world are considered too obscure to "rate" on New Zealand television, which is why every year the Festival is in a position to field such a rich collection.[17]

The 'edification' that such films provided was clearly appreciated as it did nothing to impede film festival growth, which has been on an upward trajectory since the first was established in Auckland in 1969.

The lack of a public service television channel has also reinforced the need for a Festival. New Zealand's television environment has been exceptionally commercial and populist in its orientation. There have, however, been a few changes since Gosden made those remarks. The free-to-air Māori Television Service (which could now be described as a public service network), established in 2004, screens some 'foreign' films. Also SKY pay television offers the Rialto channel, which is like a 'film festival' channel. New options of this kind will gradually expand (especially through the Internet), but because New Zealand is a small country, this will happen more slowly than elsewhere.

Today, all film festivals are going through a period of major upheaval as part of the media shake-up brought about by the Internet and digital media. Other forms of distribution, both legal and illegal, are eroding the function of a festival to be able to provide films that would not otherwise be seen. In New Zealand, however, the main Film Festival still feels like an important special annual event, but its administrators are no doubt keenly watching overseas developments.

Festival Professionalisation

I would like now to trace the transformations of the film festival as temporary exhibition site requiring a sporadic supply of content. The NZIFF is a national, rather than a city, event, which is another of the specificities of film festival culture in New Zealand. From a programme of between 150–170 features presented in the two northern cities of Auckland and Wellington, approximately 75 features – plus shorts – are selected for two southern festivals in Dunedin and Christchurch, both of which were founded in 1977. Following these festivals, a selection of up to 30 films travels to 12 provincial cities, beginning with the university towns of Hamilton and Palmerston North (Festival History n.d.).[18]

Partly the expansion emerged from an arrangement whereby Blue Angel Films, which had a circuit of many towns in which they exhibited an international selection of films, approached the NZIFF Trust to sell that package.[19] This allowed the NZIFF to extend its own programme into those smaller towns. Another exhibition platform run by the NZIFF is the World Cinema Showcase, now in its 13th year of operation. A feature of this Cinema Showcase, which takes place in April and May, is that film selection results from close collaboration between the independent cinema exhibitors in Auckland, Wellington, Christchurch, and Dunedin, and the NZIFF. These temporary venues enable the screening of films that would not otherwise be selected for commercial distribution in a country with a total population of some 4.4 million people (in 2012), thereby enriching the range of cinematic visions available.[20] The more accessible of the films thus showcased may even be picked up for wider release, as happened in 2011 with Mike Leigh's *Another Year* (UK, 2010), Jean Becker's *My Afternoons with Margueritte* (France, 2010), Francois Ozon's *Potiche* (France, 2010), and Xavier Beauvois' *Of Gods and Men* (France, 2010) – French national cinema has long had an appreciative audience in New Zealand.

Another of the distinctive features of the NZIFF is that it has evolved to present as broad a selection of films as possible in order to satisfy a variety of audiences. In the absence of a national film centre, or *cinémathèque* – an institution charged with regularly programming an array of different types of filmmaking, including *auteur*, experimental, and national cinemas, to new audiences – the NZIFF has become the annual de facto surrogate or simulacrum that, try as it might, cannot accomplish over 15 days what a properly endowed *cinémathèque* could in the course of a year.[21] While 'simulacrum' may sound derogatory, this designation should not be understood as dismissive of the varied programmes put together by the NZIFF, which have often been of an exemplary cinematic breadth, depth, and variety, with many challenging contemporary films from established and emerging national cinemas, revivals of silent cinema (for example, Victor Sjöström's *The Wind*, USA 1928), *auteur* retrospectives (Maurice Pialat), thematic selections ('Scary Women'), experimental (Sadie Benning), and animated films ('Disney's Unseen Treasures, 1929–50').

To pursue the quasi-*cinémathèque* function of the NZIFF, let us note that in 1992 it introduced audiences to an 'Archival Programme', curated by Jonathan Dennis, first director of the New Zealand Film Archive, consisting of four films by Murnau (*Faust*, 1926, *Nosferatu*, 1922, *Sunrise*, 1927, and *Tabu*, 1931), the first two of which were projected with live piano and percussion accompaniment. This programme grew the following year with films by Buster Keaton (*The General*, 1926, *Sherlock, Jr.*, 1924, *The Navigator*, 1924, *Steamboat Bill, Jr.*, 1928, *The Cameraman*, 1928, *One Week*, 1920 and *The Playhouse*, 1921), pioneering stop-motion animator Ladislaw Starewicz, former Dziga Vertov Group co-founder Jean-Pierre

Gorin (*Poto and Cabengo*, 1980, *Routine Pleasures*, 1986, and *My Crasy Life*, 1992), and Orson Welles (*Macbeth*, 1948, *Othello*, 1952, and *The Trial*, 1962).

In 1994, the archival programme mutated into 'Special Programmes' (still run by Dennis); a richly varied one featuring Czech surrealist animator Jan Svankmajer's short films and his second feature film – *Faust* (1994), Starewicz's first fully animated feature film *Le Roman de renard* (1929–30), new computer animation, a Ross McElwee retrospective (*Charleen*, 1980, *Backyard*, 1984, *Sherman's March*, 1986, and *Time Indefinite*, 1993), a homage to the westerns of John Ford (*The Searchers*, 1956, *Fort Apache*, 1948, *She Wore a Yellow Ribbon*, 1949, and *My Darling Clementine*, 1946), two silent films by Raymond Longford – *On Our Selection* (1920) and *The Sentimental Bloke* (1919) – and a selection of animated films by Tex Avery and Chuck Jones. The 1995 specials included three films by Gustav Machaty – *Erotikon* (1929), *From Saturday to Sunday* (1931), and *Ecstasy* (1933) – 11 documentary films Humphrey Jennings made between 1934 and 1949, of which *Listen to Britain, Fires Were Started*, and *A Diary for Timothy*, and six experimental films by Maya Deren, including *Meshes of the Afternoon* (1943), *Meditation on Violence* (1948), and *Ritual in Transfigured Time* (1946).

The 'Live Cinema' section of the programme grew to include orchestral accompaniment of at least one silent film (the others typically had a pianist and Neil Brand made several visits sponsored by the British Council). In the 2001 season, Timothy Brock's restored score of Dimitry Shostakovich's original composition for *The New Babylon* (USSR, 1929) was played.[22] Chaplin's *City Lights* (USA, 1931), Pabst's *Diary of a Lost Girl* (Germany 1929), Wyler's *The Shakedown* (USA, 1929) and, more contemporaneously, *Des Rives* (France, 2001) by Yann Beauvais and Thomas Koener completed the live cinema section, while the restored version of Von Stroheim's *Greed* (USA, 1924) and three Bud Boetticher westerns (*Seven Men from Now*, 1956, *The Tall T*, 1957, and *Ride Lonesome*, 1959) made up the special programmes in that richly diverse 2001 festival season.[23]

Institutionalisation and professionalisation of the film festival circuit inform the third phase of the global film festival phenomenon (as identified earlier in the study made by Marijke de Valck). While film festival culture in New Zealand retains site-specific features (an audience-focussed national event filling a variety of functions in the absence of a *cinémathèque*), it is also part of a transnational network of loosely linked film festivals. In terms of calendar events, the NZIFF closely follows the completion of the world's most prestigious international film festival, held in mid-May in Cannes. It also has close links with the Melbourne International Film Festival (MIFF)[24] – again because of calendar harmonies, which mean that certain costs can be shared (such as the substantial freight charges which have not diminished in any significant sense with the advent of digital projection – hard drives replacing 35mm celluloid prints).[25] Both MIFF and NZIFF advertise the fact that they are able to source many of their films from the two most prestigious sections at Cannes: films in Official Competition and those chosen to appear in the equally select *Quinzaine des réalisateurs/Director's Fortnight*. The home page of the 2011 NZIFF proclaimed that the 'haul of films' direct from Cannes was the Festival's best and biggest ever, including Palme d'Or winner Terence Malick's *The Tree of Life* (USA).

Figure 19: A live performance of *Nosferatu* at the Civic Theatre in Auckland. Score by Timothy Brock. Auckland Philharmonia Orchestra conducted by Marc Taddei, 31 July 2011. Image courtesy of THE EDGE.

According to Paris-based Sandra Reid – now in her 16th year with the NZIFF – and the festival's official programmer since 2001, the organisation has a very good reputation among international producers and distributors, which enables it to secure a good number of titles featured at Cannes. This ability derives from services the NZIFF provides, for example, a report on audience reaction and attendance, 25 per cent of the box office,[26] clear lines of communication, years of reliable service, and the knowledge that the festival represents the only exhibition possibility in New Zealand for many of the films.[27] This enviable reputation extends into the internal organisation of the Cannes Film Festival, which has an accreditation system for representatives of various media and press organisations that prioritises who gets to see what, where, and in what conditions. Only the top credentials give access to all areas and premiere screenings. Cannes' ranking of the NZIFF means that Reid can see all the films in competition. Although not one of the four full-time paid employees of the New Zealand Film Festival Trust,[28] she is a professional film festival programmer with a specialised skill set closely aligned to the evolution and growth of the international film festival network – a clear marker of institutionalisation and professionalisation.

The cultural value of the New Zealand film festivals was now officially recognised in the form of both corporate and public sponsorship. The merchant bankers Fay Richwhite began an 11-year association in 1988, while the New Zealand Film Commission (NZFC) and the Arts Council (later renamed Creative New Zealand) contributed public monies for the first time in 1995. To this day, the NZFC remains the principal public sponsor as part of its obligation to support festivals, 'which provide the public with a diverse selection of feature film programming to encourage informed debate and which give opportunities to new talent'.[29] In exchange, the NZIFF does its best to showcase New Zealand films (both feature-length and short), often opening the festival with a 'world premiere' of a New Zealand film.[30] In 1996, other sponsors' logos (both cultural and commercial) began to appear in the festival programme. European government–funded cultural organisations, such as the British Council, Goethe Institute, and the *Alliance Française*, provided not films alone but also grants to have filmmakers attend the festival – adding to its glamour and prestige – and making the audience 'experience' of it a more singular event.

Corporate sponsorship of the NZIFF, which still relies principally on ticket sales for revenue, has been fragile. The fact that the festival is a national rather than a city phenomenon means that corporate sponsors need to have a national profile; this significantly limits the number of eligible companies. Aside from Fay Richwhite, the only other major sponsor has been New Zealand Telecom, which acquired national naming rights over four festivals between 2004 and 2007. This was also the last time a lavish souvenir programme was printed – the NZIFF now uses the Internet and new social media, such as Twitter and Facebook, to communicate more regularly with those that sign up to receive its missives. The ready accessibility of information about films and filmmakers on the Internet meant that the extensive notes gleaned from film festival files, and edited into a substantial number of pages in the souvenir programme, became redundant.[31]

Another of the consequences attending the loss of the souvenir programme has been that the festival director's voice has become more diffuse. Instead of an annual oration, in which festival themes were identified, calls to various battles made (saving the Embassy Theatre from destruction being one such),[32] and the state of world cinema diagnosed, there are sporadic emails informing those on the list of the results of the festival just past, upcoming event alerts, and the travails of a festival director.[33] This use of new media represents a deliberate attempt to make the festival more enduringly relevant to the lives of those for whom such spectacular exhibition represents an important calendar 'event'. This development is yet another way the metropolitan consumption of cultural artefacts enhances the value of living and working in a world-class city for an increasing number of well-paid professionals.

Once an arena of contestation in which a variety of political issues were articulated via the selection process and programming, the film festival more recently has added another plank to its already variegated platform; one that furnishes commoditised products for the international consumer culture of the metropolis. (A development also apparent in museal and art gallery practices, in which curated shows travel to a variety of global cities.) The multi-faceted commoditised nature of the NZIFF (needing to be many things for audiences throughout the nation) became clearer still when an entity originally called the 'Incredibly Strange Film Festival' (ISSF) – an unashamedly eclectic concoction of cult and exploitive cinema – became an official mini-festival within the international film festival proper in 2004, under the rubric 'That's Incredible Cinema!'

The brash entrepreneurial talent of the original ISFF was initially expressed as a form of subculture in 1994, deliberately seeking to shock elements of what was deemed an overly censorious New Zealand middle- and upper-middle class culture.[34] With its loud espousal of seemingly antithetical aesthetic and moral values, the mercurial talents of its founder Ant Timpson initially injected a steady stream of exploitation cinema into the optic nerves of its diehard fans. That this 'bad' cinema should later create a space for itself within a festival that had constructed itself around notions of the *auteur* and the art-house demonstrates that aesthetics, politics, and cultural value were in ferment, experiencing a period of febrile hybridisation in New Zealand: a small and still young settler society whose arts infrastructure is being established.[35] This is not to ignore earlier Māori settlement, which began in the thirteenth century (Wilson n.d.), but film culture here is seen, initially at least, as having European antecedents.

The bold assertion, indeed celebration, of lurid sensationalism and erotic arousal associated with the early incarnation of the ISFF 'matured' as the annual festival grew, culminating in 2001 when it became the Incredible Film Festival (IFF) and filled the 2300 seat Civic Theatre. It now programmes what it calls 'populist genre fare' sourced from around the globe, and seeks to remain true to its founding anarchic spirit: 'Say hello to mayhem. Films in this section have been selected to arouse, terrify and outrage.'[36] The commoditisation of film festival culture signalled earlier would seem to find here its clear manifestation as the 'festive' functions of spectacle and experience in contemporary culture displace the earlier conjunction of film with high art and a forensic-like cinematic inquiry of sociocultural,

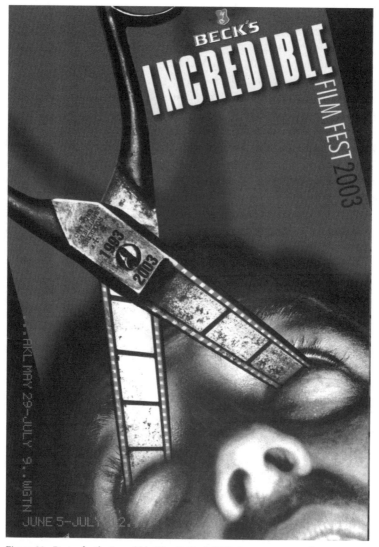

Figure 20: Poster for the Incredible Film Festival, 2003. Image courtesy of Ant Timpson.

socio-political, and socio-economic phenomena in post-industrial capitalist societies – as seen, for example in films by the Dardenne brothers, Jean-Pierre and Luc.

Having said that, the Festival's advocacy of 'film as art' is as important today as it has ever been because of the strength of corporate capitalism and consumerism. Since 1984, New Zealand has been reshaped by a series of governments according to the overall philosophy of neoliberalism. In terms of everyday experience, this has reinforced the idea that films are consumer goods, to be enjoyed as entertainment, or as a social activity, or as offering the pleasures of fantasy and daydream. The idea of film as art has no accepted place in this paradigm. The Festival therefore serves an important function not only by importing films but also by assembling them under the banner of 'film culture' or 'film as art'.

As the pre-eminent art form of industrial capitalism, the cinema has a historic role via its system of representations. For critics like Jean-Michel Frodon, this involves the creation of singular spaces that allow individuals to participate in critical debate. The function of such debate is multiple: to articulate a relationship between the real and the imaginary, the collective and the singular; to question the specificity of the medium of cinema and its relationship with multiple realities; or to engage audiences in urgent debates about what it means to be a citizen in contemporary post-industrial capitalist societies (Frodon 2006).[37] In its start-up and growth phase throughout the 1980s and 1990s, the NZIFF path was in synch with such a vision of film as art (a precondition enabling the debate). However improbable it may seem, the incorporation of the 'Incredibly Strange' strand could yet encourage audiences to engage with the medium specific qualities of the cinema and its representation of multiple realties; the programme is nothing if not eclectic.[38]

Such an extension of 'specialised' and 'thematic' programming is another intervention in cinema culture and may contribute to (unwittingly perhaps) or provoke debates about aesthetics, politics, and cultural value – the purpose of a recent conference in Australia entitled 'B FOR BAD Cinema'.[39] The verve with which 'Incredibly Strange' seeks to shock, however, resembles a desire to *épater les bourgeois*, a strategy that Jean-Michel Frodon would probably find insufficiently compatible with the type of engagement he so adroitly advocates.

Creating a Memory Site

In *Les Lieux de Mémoire/Sites of Memory* (1984–1992), Pierre Nora argues that a nation's identity is rediscovered as a result of reconfiguring the rationality that makes up its *mileux de mémoire/memory realms*. The work conducted under Nora's direction (seven volumes that seek to identify the 'memory sites' that have constructed French national identity since the Middle Ages) was driven by the knowledge that memory today no longer functions as it once did. Memory sites come into existence because memory realms are no longer directly, personally, and intimately experienced by people living in a condition of modernity, in societies subject to constant change and accelerating history. In Nora's view, the 'acceleration of history' brings us face to face with 'the enormous distance that separates real memory – the kind of inviolate social memory that primitive and archaic societies embodied, and whose secret died with them – from history, which is how modern societies organise a past they are condemned to forget because they are driven by change ...' (1996: 2).

One consequence of this fundamental sundering is the advent of a 'commemorating era' and the importance of places (museums, archives, monuments) that maintain the vestiges of ritual and the 'sacred' in an increasingly disenchanted world. Modern memory, for Nora, is essentially archival, reliant on 'the specificity of the trace, the materiality of the vestige, the concreteness of the recording, the visibility of the image' (1996: 8). Inasmuch as collective memory is no longer intimately experienced as interiority, memory needs to distinguish itself via various prosthetic attachments (places), whose tangible role it is to remind us 'of that which no longer exists except *qua* memory – hence the obsession with the archive that marks an age and in which we attempt to preserve not only all of the past but all of the present as well' (1996: 8). It is appropriate then that the final section of this study traces the establishment and evolution of an important 'memory site': the New Zealand Film Archive, an eminently transnational phenomenon that experienced a period of accelerated global growth in the 1980s (Huston 1994: 3). With the advent of the Archive, the final significant institutional component in the nation's increasingly sophisticated film culture was manifest.

Founded in March 1981 as an autonomous charitable trust, the Archive came into being at a time when the country was coming to terms with the combined powerful processes of internal and external decoloniation. As the United Kingdom shed its waning Commonwealth connections in order to invest its future in the European Economic Union, New Zealand was forced to wean itself from the strong material and symbolic attachments to the 'Mother Country' and commence several fraught journeys: it sought new markets for its goods and services; rapprochement with its Asia-Pacific neighbours; and embarked on a delayed identity quest.

National identity found cinematic expression with the local success of *Sleeping Dogs* (1977), Roger Donaldson's film of C.K. Stead's novel, *Smith's Dream* (1971). As his name suggests, Smith is an 'Everyman' faced with a series of difficult choices, much like the nation itself. The film's commercial success and critical acclaim clearly spoke to these broader concerns, but it also contributed to the State's decision to provide funding and institutional support for a fledgling film industry when it established the New Zealand Film Commission (NZFC) the following year. Arguments advanced to persuade government to nurture an indigenous film industry included import substitution, job creation, and the construction of a national identity. Alan Highet, Minister of the Arts, addressed the last point explicitly in a speech he made in Parliament when introducing the legislation to create the Film Commission: 'We need our own stories and our own heroes. We need to hear our own voices' (cited in Shelton 2005: 25).

Re-examining the past so as to understand the present (as well as projecting itself into a future of its own making), the decision to create a film archive needs to be seen in the light not only of modernity and 'accelerated history', but also of these more specifically local macro social, economic, and cultural forces. It also, and just as much, needs to be seen as the result of the work of committed individuals and small 'ginger' groups who appreciated that film was fragile, expensive to store, and could be dangerous. 'Nitrate can't wait' became the evocative international rallying slogan that galvanised energies towards the end of the 1970s and can be seen as the discursive mode that informed and constituted the 'heroic' phase in the history of the NZFA.

The first director of the Archive, Jonathan Dennis, was well suited to the task of bringing the embryonic institution into the limelight. A former actor and assiduous Wellington

Film Society member, he became imbued with the idea that film in New Zealand had to be saved from imminent disappearance.[40] His immediate awareness of the dire condition of the nation's film heritage was, according to his own recollection, a result of meeting Clive Sowry, an employee of the National Film Unit (NFU) who had developed a personal interest in the Unit's collection and spoke to Dennis of the 'Shelley Bay bunker'. Together they catalogued nitrate film held in an old World War II army bunker in Shelly Bay on the Miramar Peninsula in Wellington. Their discoveries included such precious silent features as *My Lady of the Cave* (1922), *Rewi's Last Stand* (1925), *The Te Kooti Trail* (1927), and *The Bush Cinderella* (1928), four films made by pioneering local filmmaker Rudall Hayward.

Prior to the advent of the Archive, film conservation and preservation in New Zealand was, as in many other countries, hardly a priority, hardly on the 'heritage' radar.[41] Lindsay Shelton recounts how he and Doug Eckhoff (then Head of News and Current Affairs with TVNZ) would produce a review of the year on television in the 1970s by simply taking original 16mm footage and recutting it to suit their story; ordinary and unconscious vandalism that demonstrates how little consideration was given to archiving the nation's visual history.[42] That conservation and preservation were among Sowry's personal 'hobbies' was completely fortuitous, a felicitous happenstance. He knew that some NFU films had already been damaged; knew that nitrate-based films needed duplication and preservation; knew that the master copy of the films needed to be handled infrequently; and also knew that a copying programme was required to begin preserving those films showing signs of decay. Such awareness, however, was not widely appreciated. Initially, while at the NFU, he was an autodidactic archivist – teaching himself what needed to be done to preserve film. In a gesture redolent of antipodean *bricolage* culture, he paid his way to Canberra (at the end of a self-funded club rugby trip to Brisbane in 1977) and spent a week there visiting the Australian National Film Archives.[43]

Both Sowry and Dennis were the recipients of small grants given by the QEII Arts Council in 1979,[44] which allowed them to study preservation practices in the United Kingdom. Dennis' sojourn at the National Film Archives followed Sowry's but both visited several European archives; were observers at separate annual conferences of the International Federation of Film Archives (usually known by its French acronym FIAF); and, particularly in Dennis' case, began the important task of establishing personal relationships with other archivists, thereby joining an international network. As we saw in the section tracing film festival culture, Dennis took good advantage of such a network.

That they were able to do this reflected in part the awareness of the cultural importance of film of a few committed people, for the most part based in Wellington, who had access to small sums of public money. When the Archive was finally established in 1981, its Board membership was thoroughly based in the capital. David Fowler, former manager of the NFU, was its Chairman, veteran filmmaker John O'Shea was the Minister of the Arts representative on the Board, which also comprised the Chief Archivist from National Archives, and members representing the Film Commission, the Federation of Film Societies, the NFU, the Education Department, the Broadcasting Corporation, and, later, members of the independent film industry.

Structurally, the Archive has a six-member Board elected by a Convocation (electoral college) comprising between 12 and 20 members. The Convocation is a self-perpetuating body that elects itself. It meets twice a year, receives the Annual Report, and has a community-mandating oversight role (representing Māori and filmmakers). This brings us, briefly, to an aspect of 'post-colonial' history. At an institutional level, biculturalism became prominent in the mid-1980s (symbolically reflected in the attribution of a Māori name for the Archive in 1985: Nga Kaitiaki o nga Taonga Whitiahua/Guardians of Treasured Images of Light)[45] but during Dennis' tenure as director it was a passionate, personal, and rhetorical position, with no visible manifestation in the structure of the Archive. Redressing this discrepancy was an early priority for the current CEO, Frank Stark, when he became director in 1992, with both Board and Convocation membership reflecting a 50/50 split; the Board's bicultural makeup is strictly enforced while the Convocation's is more loosely observed. The Archive's constitution comprises three documents: the procedural formal structures of the Trust, a Kaupapa largely formulated by Barry Barclay (2005),[46] and the Treaty of Waitangi in three versions. There is now a structured relationship with various iwi – eight of whom have signed a memorandum of understanding regarding the manner in which images relating to that iwi are stored and used.[47]

The Archive's bicultural commitment preceded the Government's and, according to its CEO, is not a reflection of it, but rather an independently held position. Stark holds the view that at a fundamental level (and in the eyes of the world), the unique component of New Zealand screen culture is Māori-based.[48] Such a view has affinities with cultural entrepreneurialism and marketing strategies that 'brand' New Zealand in distinctive ways.[49] To speak only in terms of film, successive governments have deployed 'indigenising' strategies to sell New Zealand and its varied products to the world since the 1920s, with Peter Jackson's *Lord of the Rings* trilogy and *Hobbit* prequels being the most recent avatars of this need to differentiate the nation's goods and services in an increasingly competitive international moving image market. Stark's perspective, therefore, may be interpreted as catering to an orientalising view of New Zealand as exotic 'other'. It also insufficiently recognises how secondary (European) and tertiary (Asian) migrants have shaped (are shaping) the singularity of the nation's international screen image quite as much as the primary (Polynesian) migrants.[50]

The transnational character of the Film Archive may be read in the Deed establishing the Archive as an autonomous charitable Trust, modelled on the aims and objectives for film archives in Australia, North America, and Europe:

1. To collect, preserve and catalogue film materials;
2. To provide premises and facilities for preserving, storing, consulting, viewing and displaying film materials;

3. To provide access to material held by the Archive consistent with overriding preservation and copyright requirements;
4. To issue publications, screen archive films and by similar means encourage and promote public interest and awareness in film materials, film history and culture, preservation matters and film archives generally (*NZFA Newsletter* 1981).

The second of these aims provides an insight into an important aspect of the Archive's relationship with the diverse communities it sought to connect with in New Zealand. Rather than simply being an institution that preserved and conserved film, the Archive would actively promote itself as an 'embodied' site where memory would be commemorated via a screening programme. The Archive's Travelling Picture Show – making old films remain 'living objects'[51] – began in 1983 when it travelled to the Taranaki Museum and presented four films made in New Plymouth in 1912 (*NZFA Newsletter* 1984). This commemorative function was noted as being especially poignant when the Archive travelled to distant Māori communities so that the ancestors captured on film could be 'returned' from whence they came.

An account of one such excursion to Koroniti Marae on the Wanganui River appeared in the February 1987 newsletter of the Archive. Films made in the 1920s by James McDonald (on behalf of the Dominion Museum ethnographer Elsdon Best) during expeditions to Gisborne and the East Coast region, Rotorua, Ruatāhuna and the Whanganui River region were among the first that the Archive began restoring.[52] Their historical and cultural value meant that they were in high demand and the Archive began touring them in 1985. After recounting the reactions, ranging from hilarity to silence, that accompanied the projection of *He pito whakaatu i te Noho a te Māori i te awa o Whanganui (Scene of Māori Life on the Whanganui River,* 1921), the writer noted that:

> Far more profound and moving is the direct communication which the films open up between the living and the dead. The children in the film are identified as the brothers and sisters of the elders amongst us. The adults are their parents, aunties and uncles. [...] After the film some of the elders talk to the group about the effect the films have on them, of seeing people they still feel spiritually close to on the screen, of the inheritance they have received, and the traditions they want to pass on... We all feel touched by the greatest gift our ancestors have handed down to us, their love, and their abiding presence with us.[53]

What Sharon Dell, Māori Materials Subject Specialist at the Alexander Turnbull Library, is describing here is the almost spontaneous safeguarding of memory by a minority people in modern society; an enclave whose 'commemorative vigilance'[54] acts as a bastion against the sweep of history, which would consign their protected collective identity to yesteryear. More problematically, it is also another European positioning of Māori as stamp and seal of 'the authentic'; traditional memory may have vanished as intimate everyday experience among peoples subject to modernity but here, at least, Walter Benjamin's 'angel of history', with his face turned towards the past, contemplating the storm of progress that 'irresistibly propels him into the future to which his back is turned, while the pile of debris before him grows skyward', seems to want 'to make whole what has been smashed' (Benjamin 1940).

Born in Poverty

The Archive began modestly. Using a NZ\$33,000 establishment grant from the Film Commission, Jonathan Dennis, its sole employee, used cramped office space and facilities provided by the Federation of Film Societies. Kodak gifted some black and white film stock to make a few safety copies of the old films, and IBM donated a typewriter. When the Minister of Internal Affairs accepted the Chief Archivist's recommendation that the Archive become an Official Repository under the Archives Act, it inherited nearly one million feet of film from various government agencies, such as the Education Department and the Ministry of Public Works, whose disparate collections could now be said to be 'centralised' (although the Archive was initially bereft of its own storage space). A second employee was hired later in 1981 to begin repairing film.

For many years, much energy was devoted to raising funds, as the Archive, not being a government agency, had no guaranteed revenue stream. Dennis was an ardent advocate and zealous publicist on behalf of the body he now ran. As a slogan, 'nitrate won't wait' was effective in the campaign he waged to alert Wellington's political and cultural elite of the dire condition of the nation's film heritage. His voice was heard regularly on national radio and in the press where he leavened the gloom with good news, such as when *Venus of the South Seas* (1924) or a copy of Gustav Pauli's *The Romance of Hine-Moa* (1926) were located and returned from the National Film Archive in London, or when the Archive's Museum of Cinema was opened in November 1982 by the Minister of the Arts following the first of several relocations into larger spaces as the collection grew.[55]

As a campaign, 'nitrate won't wait' was successful in raising the Archive's public profile and several 'one off, never-to-be-repeated' grants came its way through sympathetic government ministers. The first such was in 1983, when Alan Highet provided \$50,000 for the Film Preservation Programme. The Film Commission gave \$55,000 the following year, which also saw Television New Zealand and the Lottery Board make contributions.[56] Philanthropy and corporate sponsorship are not marked features of the arts infrastructure in New Zealand and so it has usually been governments that have (often reluctantly) assumed the responsibility of investing in the nation's cultural heritage. Peter Tapsell, the new Minister of the Arts in the fourth Labour Government (1984–90), reinforced this practice in 1986 when he authorised a \$103,000 grant, which, when combined with \$115,000 from the Film Commission and \$100,000 from the Lottery Board, made this an especially generous year (*NZFA Newsletter* 1986: 1).

This support can be attributed not only to the Archive's growing national profile but also to its international reputation. In 1985, it gained full member status to the FIAF and presented a major New Zealand Film Season at the Pacific Film Archive in Berkeley, California (*NZFA Newsletter* 1985: 1). A Panorama of New Zealand Cinema hosted by the *Cinémathèque française* followed in 1987. While the Fourth Labour Government embarked on a series of major social and economic reforms, it also, typically, supported culture and national identity. Former university historian Dr. Michael Bassett, then Minister of Arts and Culture, had a particular sensitivity to the work the Archive was engaged in (having used its resources for his own research) and made 1988 a special year by allocating an extra 'one-off-never-to-be-repeated' grant of $40,000 and ensuring that the Lottery Board increased their grant to $200,000 for that financial year. He noted that the Archive

> is to moving images what art galleries are to paintings, or libraries to books. Yet it is inconceivable to think of either books or paintings of great cultural importance to New Zealand being allowed to rot away before our eyes, as has already happened with many early films and tapes ... Preserving and making available New Zealand film as a part of our culture is something this government sees as important.
>
> (*NZFA Newsletter* 1988a: 2)

The Minister's words were not idle ones. The following year he announced an increased grant of $400,000 from the Lottery Board to the Archive (*NZFA Newsletter* 1989: 1).

The year 1989 was arguably the high water mark of Dennis' directorship of the Archive. After almost a decade in the job, which he largely defined and developed, the collection had grown to some 10,000 titles (stored in seven separate locations), including rare silent films from New Zealand's past which would otherwise almost certainly have been lost.[57] However, the public sector had not escaped the major social and economic reforms of the Labour Government and the refashioned environment seemed less conducive to someone possessing Dennis' singular skill set. The first decade of the Archive's existence had seen it operating in 'heroic' mode – there was a crisis (to which the international slogan 'nitrate won't wait' gave vivid voice) and an urgent need to preserve nitrate-based film from disappearance. Dennis was the 'saviour' in the sense that it was important to first find film and then start to preserve it. In this he constructed a very effective narrative. What was left of the nitrate era was secured, as was government support.

The heroic myth, however, was also limiting in that it did not encourage the Archive to do what current CEO Frank Stark believes was required to create an 'intergenerational' structure for the organisation. (Dennis was skilled in creating a series of personal rather than structural or institutional relationships.) As a general rule, archives have a quiescent function that relies on mundane processes rather than heroic action. Under Dennis, only a small portion of the Archive's now considerable collection had been accessioned, which means looking into a cardboard box of material, examining each film (sometimes on a light table) to establish what the film is, and then cataloguing the information so that the material could be filed and then retrieved when required. Major titles such as *The Adventures of Algy* (1925) and *Venus of the South Seas* (1924) had taken the majority of the Archive's usually stretched resources. There was, therefore, a lot of outstanding archival work to be done.

One consequence of public sector reform (circa 1989–90) and the Archive's enhanced status was that tensions had arisen between the Board and Dennis, whose model of stewardship (one person leading the organisation), representative of his tenure, was judged insufficient to lead the Archive into a 'new' world of public sector service and the sort of organisation the Board wished the Archive to become.[58] In 1990, the Board accepted his (unwilling) resignation. A roughly two-year interregnum period followed his departure before the Archive's current CEO was appointed in late 1992. In that time, significant developments took place.

One of these involved establishing a collection management regime – one of those slightly dull (non-heroic) archival tasks. The retrospective accessioning and cataloguing of non-film documentation was a massive task that led to the temporary closing of public programming and preservation. For roughly 18 months, most of the Archive staff members were thus engaged in readying the move into new premises and proper vaults. The second of these developments involved seeking a suitable new location, as the Archive was obliged to move following urban development. The Board eventually purchased the John Chambers Building in downtown Wellington. Built in 1918, the building was stylistically advanced for its time and remarkably modern in design, occupying a dramatic and highly visible wedge-shaped site. Its three levels allowed staff and collections to be united in one location and also enabled the Archive to begin a more substantial public screening programme in 1995, following a successful fund-raising campaign to create a cinema (shared with a commercial exhibitor who operated it in the evening) and exhibition space. The hope was that this building would provide office space and storage for a 20-year period; an overly optimistic time frame, as would soon be revealed.

The Last Film Search (1993–2000)

This seven-year long programme was designed to discover films held by individuals throughout the nation. Generously funded by the BNZ – the Archive's first long-term sponsor[59] – the Archive went on the road, region by region (looking for 'lost nitrate') and turned up a rich series of non-theatrical films. Stark argues that this campaign significantly modified the public's perception of the Archive – away from a narrow range of nitrate features into a broader – and more accessible – archival organisation.[60] It is possible that the Archive was something of a world leader (in terms of timing) in its interest in amateur (or orphan) film, which had been seen as inferior to the artistic canon (or hierarchy) that had underpinned archival collection, conservation, and preservation from the 1930s. Through the Last Film Search, the Archive became a more solidly national institution, forging relationships with a variety of cultural agencies, such as regional museums and art galleries, as well as individual film buffs. More than 7000 titles were collected over those seven years with the various BNZ branches acting as collection points (*NZFA Newsreel* 2010: 5).

The success of the Last Film Search and an agreement signed with New Zealand on Air in 1997 to make the Archive the official repository of the National Television Collection (NTC) created an unexpected but familiar problem: storage. The expected 20-year plan for the John Chamber Building was now in tatters. By 2002, the film and video collection had grown to roughly 85,000 titles (a seven-fold increase over a decade) and now serviced a national audience of some 150,000 users annually, significantly above the fewer than 10,000 in the mid-1990s (*NZFA Newsreel* 2002).

There were other issues, too, notably about the seismic security of a building constructed in 1918 and the too-close proximity to the National Museum of New Zealand (Te Papa o Tongarewa), which opened in 1998. With its striking post-modern architecture, vast collections, and generous funding, the waterfront-located Te Papa was a beacon whose brilliance made the Film Archive's street presence seem drab by comparison.

The long-standing accommodation problems were solved with the purchase of a new home in central Wellington: a six-story structure built in 1970 that combined strong construction standards with large, uninterrupted floor space. The CEO declared that it gave 'very safe storage for the collections as well as a great site for developing and presenting our new public programmes' (*NZFA Newsreel* 2002). This latter remark indicated the Archive's desire to be part of the street life of the community. Whereas the old building had been black with few windows, the new one was white with large ground level windows and a façade that suggested multiple viewing opportunities. People could see it as a user-friendly space (with a café and viewing facilities – with 23,000 titles), free and open to the public.

The exhibition strategy changed, too. There was a move way from the large 'didactic' show, such as *Te Māori* in 1986, which required a lot of curatorial work to put in place, towards a smaller series of thematic shows that focussed on artists and their interaction with film and video. The intention was not to let this aspect of the Archive's activities dominate the viewer experience. The opening of the Archive's Mediaplex in 2004 enabled this changed exhibition focus, with its new public access facility, providing a coffee bar/on-line mediacentre, research library, video gallery, and 120-seat cinema. One of the first exhibitions was Phil Dadson's 2005 solo performance for the opening of the BODY chapter of 'Tapping the Pulse', a survey show of his film, video, and related works from 1971 to 2004. Another was 'Light Piercing Nerve: A Performance by Abject Leader', in June 2009. Brisbane-based artists Sally Goulding and Joel Stern used 'analogue film and manipulated archival footage alongside Stern's caustic soundscapes to create expanded cinema performances' (*NZFA Newsreel* 2010: 11).

While the new Taranaki Street location had 75 per cent extra vault space, it was never the intention that this building be used primarily as a storehouse for the Archive's ever expanding collection, much of which was not kept in rooms capable of controlling temperature and humidity, a serious flaw in the Archive's asset management programme noted in at least two reports; an internally commissioned one written by Jim Lindner (an American preservation and digitisation consultant) whose April 2009 report noted that 'the reality is that many parts

Figure 21: The Film Archive in Taranaki Street, Wellington. Image courtesy of the Film Archive.

of the collection are in jeopardy due to lack of adequate and proper storage ... The collection is simply too large and important to be kept the way it currently is'.[61] The second report (presented by Professor Roger Horrocks in October 2009) was conducted on behalf of several of the Archive's principal funders: NZ On Air (NZOA), the Film Commission, Te Māngai Pāho,[62] and the Ministry for Culture and Heritage. Parts of this review will be addressed in the following section. In response to the reports' criticisms and in order to meet international archival requirements concerning conservation, the Board commissioned the construction of a purpose-built storage vault, with about four kilometres of shelving, to be erected in Plimmerton on land purchased in 2009. On current rates of collection growth, the new building, which opened in January 2011, is expected to meet the Archive's storage needs for the next five to seven years, with scope for further expansion beyond that, when required.[63]

In the wake of Lindner and Horrocks' reviews, a project called 'Saving Frames' was devised and launched. One substantial component of this multi-faceted project was the provision of the aforementioned storage vault in Plimmerton (some 15 kilometres north of Wellington) capable of maintaining the film and video collections at a constant temperature. Of the Archive's three core functions – to collect material, to make it available and to preserve it in good condition for the future – the second review was of the opinion that preservation had suffered in comparison with the Archive's other activities, and that a serious preservation backlog existed. This was especially the case with regards to many of the New Zealand feature films of the 1970s and 1980s, considered to be at risk as a result of insufficient care. The poor and worsening condition of many of these 'classic' films, whose historical importance resides in the fact that they represent the 'new wave' of indigenous filmmaking, was embarrassingly discovered by the filmmakers and the Film Commission in 2008 during a 27 feature film retrospective of New Zealand cinema at the Era New Horizons Film Festival in Wroclaw, Poland.

An ambassador expressed similar consternation about how the country was presenting itself overseas following an invited survey of New Zealand films in Israel in 2009.[64] In responding to the criticism, the Archive noted that in many instances good quality prints and printing intermediaries of some of these films had never been deposited with them. Lindsay Shelton has also stated that the Film Commission never provided funds to ensure that such prints would be maintained in a condition that enabled both proper preservation and the provision of projectable copies for such important cultural events as film festivals.[65] These objections notwithstanding, the fact is that more than 40 per cent of the Archive's collection was not adequately conserved.

Among the second review's several recommendations, one in particular is apposite here: it called for the emergency provision of $1 million to cover the preservation of 'at least a dozen key New Zealand feature films'.[66] In the event, the Archive received another special one-off payment of $2 million in its 2010 budget from the Minister for Arts, Culture and Heritage. The conservation brief was extended, as well, to cover the preservation of 'iconic films from the last 110 years, in all genres and formats' to ensure they were kept safe and accessible for future generations (*NZFA Newsreel* 2010: 9). In practical terms, although Saving Frames concentrates on films from the 1970s and 1980s, the aim is to have all 25,000 films benefit in some way. At a minimum, this involves visual inspection; dusting and rehousing 20,000 in new plastic cans and relabelling. At the next level, some ten per cent (or 2400 films) will be selected for cleaning and repair of damaged sections, and 2000 of these conserved films will have a digital copy made in order to make them accessible. A further 300 films will receive serious preservation work, including photochemical or digital transfers to create preservation material and projectable copies, with much of the work being done in collaboration with the internationally renowned post-production facility, Park Road Post. At the top end, some eight to ten films will receive full restoration treatment, beginning with the sound version of *Rewi's Last Stand* (1940). Saving Frames is a major four-year project whose full impact will be felt across the Archive and contribute to a significant increase in the sustainability of its collection. The shelf life of thousands of films will be enhanced as will their screen and on-line presence.

Roadmap for the Future

The 2006 New Zealand Film Archive Capability Review made it clear that a digital technology programme needed to be implemented (*NZFA Newsreel* 2007). To that end, the Archive acquired digital hardware in July 2007 to begin the lengthy and time-consuming task of migrating its collection from an analogue to a digital platform. With significant financial support from NZOA, the 150 square metre media laboratory built to handle this work opened in early 2008, giving the Archive 'a robust base for a sustained programme of digitisation just as an international consensus emerges on digital standards for moving image archives' (*NZFA Newsreel* 2008). The Lindner report indicated the strategic and material direction the Archive should take in developing its digital infrastructure, which presents significant challenges in terms of cost and size. One fundamental principle is that master files should be lossless, which is to say that all information from the original analogue file should be present in the digital one. Lindner's expertise in the migration of archival film and video material to digital form has proved as useful to the Archive as it had to the Australian National Film and Sound Archive and the US National Audio Visual Conservation Centre, operated by the Library of Congress, and should ensure that the Archive adheres to best practice as it participates in the complex worldwide shift to digital technology.

A further salient consequence of the 2009 Horrocks review was that previously disparate sources of income from a variety of public sector organisations, such as NZOA, Te Māngai Pāho, and the Film Commission, were amalgamated and administered by the Ministry for Culture and Heritage. This revenue restructuring meant that the CEO no longer devoted as much time to raising funds, with further benefits accruing from the amalgamation, such as lowered reporting and compliance costs and, importantly, enhanced strategic planning. The Archive still operates at arm's length from government, thereby maintaining its tradition of proud independence, but it now has more time to implement its core functions, neatly divided into collection, protection, and connection.

Although established relatively late in 1981, the New Zealand Film Archive has become an important 'memory site' that commemorates national culture. In the space of 30 years, it has grown considerably from 'a staff of one located in shared, cramped offices to a thriving organisation with nearly 50 staff, secure premises and a collection of more than 130,000 films and videos, supported by a documentation collection' (*NZFA Newsreel* 2008: 5). The Archive accumulates an ever-swelling number of fragments, reports, documents, sounds and images: tangible remnants or signs of what once was. They replace, stand in for, or are otherwise surrogates for vanished traditional or social memory. It may be, as Pierre Nora has noted, that, as complex memory sites, Archives function, materially and symbolically, as if they might 'some day be subpoenaed before who knows what tribunal of history. The trace negates the sacred but retains its aura' (1996: 9). While awaiting history's judgement, future generations of New Zealanders will come to know the nation's audio-visual heritage as a form of collective commemoration.

References

Anon. (1981), 'At Last', *NZFA Newsletter*, (1), October.
—— (1984), 'The Film Archive Travelling Picture Show', *NZFA Newsletter*, (8), April.
—— (1985), 'FIAF and The Film Archive in San Francisco', *NZFA Newsletter*, (12), September, p. 1.

———— (1986), 'The Financial News', *NZFA Newsletter*, (15), August, p. 1.

———— (1988), 'Nitrate Won't Wait', *NZFA Newsletter*, (19), March, p. 2.

———— (1989), 'Lottery Support', *NZFA Newsletter*, (20), October, p. 1.

———— (2002), 'Moving House', *NZFA Newsreel*, (49), July.

———— (2007), 'Capability Review Update', *NZFA Newsreel*, (57), Winter.

Barclay, B. (2005), *Mana Tuturu: Māori Treasures and Intellectual Property Rights*, Auckland: Auckland University Press.

Benjamin, W. (1940), *On the Concept of History* [Online]. Available at: http://www.marxists.org/reference/archive/benjamin/1940/history.htm. Accessed: 8 December 2011.

Callanan, V. (2010), 'Saving Frames', *NZFA Newsreel*, (61), December, p. 9.

Cousins, M. (2009), 'Widescreen on Film Festivals', in D. Iordanova and R. Rhyne, eds. *Film Festival Yearbook 1: The Festival Circuit*, St. Andrews (Scotland): St. Andrews Film Studies in collaboration with College Gate Press.

de Valck, M. (2007), *Film Festivals: From European Geopolitics to Global Cinephilia*, Amsterdam: Amsterdam University Press.

Festival and Awards Programme, (n.d.) [Online]. Available at: http://www.nzfilm.co.nz/IndustrySupportAndTraining/FestivalsAndAwardsProgramme.aspx. Accessed: 8 July 2011.

Festival History, (n.d.) [Online]. Available at: http://www.nzff.co.nz/festival-history. Accessed: 8 July 2011.

Frodon, M. (2006), *Horizon cinéma: l'art du cinéma dans le monde contemporain à l'âge du numérique et de la mondialisation*, Paris: Cahiers du cinéma.

Gosden, B. (1983), 'Introduction', 12th Wellington Film Festival brochure, p. 3.

Huston, P. (1994), *Keeper of the Frame: The Film Archives*, London: BFI.

Iordanova, D. (2009), 'The Film Festival Circuit', in *Film Festival Yearbook 1*.

Māori Dictionary – Te Aka Māori-English, English-Māori Dictionary, (n.d.) [Online]. Available at: http://www.maoridictionary.co.nz/. Accessed: 14 December 2011.

Moullier, B. (n.d.), 'The Role of the FIAPF in the Coordination and Regulation of International Film Festivals' [Online]. Available at: http://www.fiapf.org/intfilmfestivals_role.asp. Accessed: 12 July 2011.

Nora, P. (1996), *Realms of Memory*, New York: Columbia University Press.

Pivac, D. (2010), 'Thirty Crowded Years', *NZFA Newsreel*, (61), December, p. 5.

Pine II, B. and Gilmore, J. (1999), *The Experience Economy: Work Is Theatre & Every Business a Stage*, Boston: Harvard Business School Press.

Rhyne, R. (2009), 'Film Festival Circuits and Stakeholders', in *Film Festival Yearbook 1*.

Shelton, L. (1981), 'Introduction', 10th Wellington Film Festival brochure, p. 3.

———— (2005), *The Selling of New Zealand Movies*, Wellington: Awa Press.

Sleigh, T. (2010), 'Making Tracks: Tributes to Mark Williams', *NZFA Newsreel*, (61), December, p. 11.

Stark, F. (2008), 'Digital Media Matters', *NZFA Newsreel*, no. 59, Winter.

Timpson, A. (Oct 2008), 'Uncut & Untamed' [Online]. Available at: http://www.incrediblystrange.co.nz/tv/intro/. Accessed: 12 July 2011. For more information, see http://www.incrediblystrange.co.nz/festival/history/.

Wedde, I. (2005), *Making Ends Meet: Essays and Talks 1992–2004*, Wellington: Victoria University Press.

Wilson, J. (n.d.), 'History: Māori Arrival and Settlement' [Online]. *Te Ara – The Encyclopedia of New Zealand.* Available at: www.TeAra.govt.nz/en/history/1 Updated: 3 March 2009. Accessed: 6 June 2012.

Notes

1. Ticket sale figures (1998–2011) obtained from NZIFF range from a low of 193,904 (1999) to a high of 250,903 (2006). In 2011, 215,000 tickets were sold; a solid figure given the Festival competed for disposable income (in a time of economic insecurity) with the Rugby World Cup, which New Zealand hosted that year.
2. B. Gosden – Director, New Zealand International Film Festival – interview, November 2010.
3. Turner, R. (1981), 'Introduction', 10th Wellington Film Festival brochure, p. 2.
4. I have compared films from the festival brochures for Auckland and Wellington to arrive at these figures.
5. 'Amended Minutes of a Wellington Film Society Inc Festival Sub-Committee Meeting, 1 February 1984', p. 2. The New Zealand Film Archive, D4621, MA0989, Manuscripts: Film Society Records, NZFFS, 1946–1995, Box 4 WGTN Film Society Minutes 1975–1978/84.
6. Ibid.
7. Private communication, December 2010.
8. B. Gosden, interview, November 2000. Another source of information is *Craccum*, the Auckland University student paper. A somewhat guarded account by Roger Horrocks appeared on p. 22 of the 19 June 1979 issue. He pointed out that Wynne Colgan had 'retired' and the rest of the committee had been 'disbanded' and that 'some serious disagreements' had been at issue. The new management had done away with the pre-Festival activities and the traditional '5 for 4' concession tickets. He added that the new organisers appeared to be saving money by picking up a large number of its films from local distributors, and he also questioned other programming decisions, which he saw as being made by 'non-specialists'.
9. The Auckland Festival Trust received a percentage of the AIFF takings for a couple of years but eventually the Auckland Festival of the Arts disappeared.
10. B. Gosden interview, November 2010.
11. In 2004, the International Federation of Film Producers Association (FIAPF) estimated that between 700 and 800 festivals existed (Moullier n.d.).
12. There is, for example, no New Zealand equivalent of the Melbourne International Film Festival's 37° South Market and Accelerator – Industry and Public Partner Events, which aims to stimulate film production, *inter alia*.
13. The female directors thus highlighted were Kira Muratova and Su Friedrich. From 'Introduction', 20th Wellington Film Festival, 1991, p. 4.
14. 'Introduction', 21st Wellington Film Festival, 1992, p. 4.
15. 'Introduction', 22nd Wellington Film Festival, 1993, p. 2.
16. Ibid.
17. 'Introduction', 23rd Wellington Film Festival, 1994, p. 2.

18 The other cities are Gisborne, Greymouth, Hawke's Bay, Kerikeri, Masterton, Nelson, New Plymouth, and Tauranga.

19 B. Gosden interview, November 2010.

20 In the 2011 programme, audiences could see such films as 2010 Cannes Palme d'Or winner *Uncle Boonmee Who Can Recall Past Lives, Rubber, Restrepo, Of Gods and Men, We Are What We Are* and *White Meadows.*

21 The New Zealand Film Archive is another insufficiently endowed substitute that partially positions itself as a *cinémathèque* alongside the more traditional roles associated with film preservation and conservation.

22 In 2011, the Auckland Philharmonia Orchestra played Tinothy Brock's score for *Nosferatu, a Symphony of Horrors.*

23 A varied programme still informs the selection process of the NZIFF. The 2011 brochure is divided into several thematic sections: Big Nights & Special Presentations, Worlds of Difference, For All Ages, Animation, New Directions, Go Slow, Sporting Life, At the Barricades, Inside Stories, Framing Reality, Music, Portrait of the Artist and Incredibly Strange.

24 In 2011, MIFF took place between 21 July and 7 August, while AIFF began a week earlier, running from 14 to 31 July.

25 Over 50 per cent of the films screened during the 2010 NZIFF were on hard drives according to festival director, Bill Gosden.

26 This is a practice becoming more widespread with the advent of the 'festival film', basically (and somewhat tragically) a film not seen in cinemas outside the international film festival exhibition circuit.

27 S. Reid interview, July 2010.

28 A non-profit, registered charitable trust that runs the festivals.

29 Of the NZ$192k budgeted by the NZFC for festival support in 2010, some $85k was awarded to the NZIFF, according to the director, Bill Gosden (Festivals and Awards Programme n.d.).

30 In 2011, Florian Habict's *Love Story* (2010) opened the Auckland Festival.

31 Escalating printing costs and the absence of a sponsor also contributed to the demise of this very useful service.

32 The third instalment of Peter Jackson's *Lord of the Rings* saga, *The Return of the King* (2003) had its world premiere at the Embassy Theatre in Wellington.

33 The NZIFF has had only two directors, both of whom have been men – the second's tenure has lasted 30 years, making him something of a rarity in terms of directorial longevity.

34 After a sojourn as a teenager in Los Angeles had exposed him to cult material on television, Timpson's return to New Zealand was a shock: 'But coming back to NZ for a now converted cult movie maniac was depressing as hell. Remember this was when NZ was in a pre-vhs puritanical vice like grip from moral crusaders like Pat[ricia] Bar[t]lett and a nervous nanny for a Chief Censor' (Timpson 2008).

35 Large-scale European occupation only dates from the mid-nineteenth century.

36 NZIFF (Auckland) brochure, 2011, 'Incredibly Strange', p. 74.

37 Frodon seeks to redefine the place that cinematographic art occupies in the new audio-visual landscape created by digitisation and globalisation.

38 Films from East Asia, Europe and North America make up the Incredibly Strange programme in 2011, with such titles as *The Woman, Knuckle, The Last Circus, Cold Fish* and *Hobo with a Shotgun*.

39 'B FOR BAD Cinema: aesthetics, politics and cultural value', Inaugural Centre for Film and Television Studies Conference, Monash University, Melbourne, April 15–17, 2009.

40 L. Shelton interview, November 2010.

41 The celebrated Henri Langlois was a poor conserver/restorer of films, which were kept in a lamentable condition with many losses. See: Borde, R. (1983), *Les Cinémathèques*, Lausanne: Editions l'Age d'Homme, pp. 122–23.

42 L. Shelton interview, November 2010. Doug Eckhoff was also the last Chief Executive of the National Film Unit prior to its disestablishment, and is a current Film Archive Board member and the Convocation President.

43 C. Sowry interview, November 2010.

44 QEII Arts Council (Queen Elizabeth II) is now called Creative NZ. The name change reflects an assertion of cultural independence, although the Queen is still the country's Sovereign and acts (symbolically) as the Queen of New Zealand.

45 Māori became an official language in 1987 with the Māori Language Act.

46 A kaupapa is a set of values, principles, and plans which people have agreed on as a foundation for their actions. Film-maker and writer Barry Barclay (1944–2008) – director of landmark productions *Tangata Whenua* and *Ngati* – was a campaigner for the right of indigenous people to tell their own stories, to their own people. In 2004, he was made an Arts Foundation Laureate, and in 2007 a Member of the New Zealand Order of Merit. His book, *Mana Tuturu*, guided the Archive in its actions over films with strong Māori content.

47 Iwi: extended kinship group, tribe, nation, people, nationality, race – often refers to a large group of people descended from a common ancestor (*Māori Dictionary – Te Aka Māori-English, English-Māori Dictionary*, n.d.).

48 F. Stark interview, November 2010.

49 *See* Wedde, I. 'Introduction', *Making Ends Meet*, p. 10, for a discussion of cultural entrepreneurialism and commodity values, such as "uniqueness", in respect of national branding exercises for world markets.

50 In that regard, one has only to mention Peter Jackson and Jane Campion as distinct Pakeha (New Zealanders of European, primarily British, descent) creators of cinematic figures that express the local at an international level. More recent Asian New Zealand creators include Roseanne Liang and Stephen Kang. Stark's view may also be read as being more prevalent and more germane within the political atmosphere of the capital city, Wellington, where institutional adherence to government policy is the norm.

51 Jonathan Dennis remembers this expression following his meeting in Paris with Mary Meerson, Henri Langlois' partner and co-conspirator at the *Cinémathèque française*.

52 Early McDonald films also included *Te Hui Aroha Ki Turanga: Gisborne Hui Aroha* (1921) and *He Pito Whakaatu i te Noho a te Māori te Tairawhiti/Scenes of Māori Life on the East Coast* (1923).

53 The New Zealand Film Archive/Nga Kaitiaki o nga Taonga Whitahua Newsletter/He Panui, (16), February 1987, p. 4.
54 The expression is Pierre Nora's.
55 The Archive now occupied the entire top floor of the Wakefield Building in central Wellington and could open its doors to the public, weekdays 11 am–3 pm.
56 TVNZ gave $15,000 while the Lottery Board gave $3000 towards the purchase of a Steenbeck viewer for film cataloguing and research. The Lottery Grants Board has since become a substantial annual funder of the Archive, which now receives some 30 per cent of its budget from this source. The Archive is one of only four statutory bodies to be so treated – the others being the Film Commission, Creative NZ, and Sport and Recreation NZ.
57 'Background', *The Film Archive 15 Year Report*.
58 At that time the Board included representatives of government agencies that were ceasing to exist, for example, the Broadcasting Corporation and the Department of Education. The details of Dennis' resignation are too complex to recount here. However, by his own admission, Board members 'grew to resent' his unorthodox ability to get results the Board had not sanctioned through his personal relationships with various ministers of the crown. Oral history: Dennis, J. (2000). New Zealand Film Archive, AUD 0672 & 0673.
59 In order to understand why the Bank of New Zealand (BNZ) entered into such a generous (and unusual) sponsorship arrangement with the Archive, I should point out that the National Australia Bank purchased the BNZ in 1992. Trans-Tasman relations are deep, abiding, complicated and rife with sibling rivalry (to employ a family metaphor) so the corporate logic at work in deciding to sponsor the Last Film Search may have a lot to do with re-establishing grassroots connections with New Zealanders. The BNZ is one of New Zealand's oldest trading banks and has been operating in the country continuously since 1861.
60 F. Stark interview, November 2010.
61 J. Lindner, 'Initial Assessment and Digital Infrastructure Roadmap for the New Zealand Film Archive', 2009, p. 3.
62 Te Māngai Pāho is a Crown Entity established to make funding available to the national network of Māori radio stations and for the production of Māori language television programmes, radio programmes and music CDs.
63 Capital development is very much in the hands of the Board. Not being a government department confers certain advantages, one of which is speed in making decisions. The $850,000 required for the purchase of land and construction of the vault came primarily via several charitable trusts.
64 NZ Film Archive: Review of government agency funding arrangements and service delivery, October 2009, p. 11.
65 L. Shelton – Marketing Manager of the Film Commission (1979–2001) – interview, November 2010.
66 NZ Film Archive: Review of government agency funding arrangements and service delivery, October 2009, p. 4.

Conclusion

Film culture, like any form of culture, is a multi-faceted dynamic process of interconnecting elements – cultural, social, and economic. The complexity of this web of relationships was suggested by a diagram in the Introduction (page 2). Thus, film culture, like any good film, is a hybrid process and product. At its optimal (and ideal) level of operation, the various components make up a richly variegated culture with the characteristics of articulate debate about films, a strong sense of history, an international awareness, a willingness to engage with ideas (at the level of theory, philosophy, and aesthetics), and the ability to generate original conclusions – the characteristics that we associate with forms of 'high' (highbrow or intellectual) culture. Tracing the interaction of the varied components of this kind of transnational film culture in New Zealand has documented one aspect of cultural or intellectual history in a relatively small, former colony of the British Empire, situated on islands in the South Pacific, thousands of kilometres from the perceived centres of highbrow culture. What is particularly distinctive about this history is the recentness of its development. A general intellectual culture has had to be constructed in New Zealand, in a pioneer society, in circumstances that were frequently uncongenial. The slow growth (or building) of a film culture is in some respects a microcosm of this larger project, involving some of the same movers and shakers.

Inevitably, such a development happened more rapidly and strongly in older European cultures (most notably in France). I hope, however, that I have also told positive stories about the smaller victories that accompanied the spread of intellectual film culture in this younger country. 'Young' is of course a complex descriptor because the country had older Māori traditions. But film culture is seen here as an outgrowth of European culture, part of the imagining of a post-colonial 'New Zealand' culture. (This is not to ignore the fact that Māori writers and filmmakers – such as Barry Barclay and Merita Mita – subsequently played an important part.) There has been a revivalist, and celebratory, aspect to this narrative as it has resurrected the names of individuals and institutions involved in this development, many of them long forgotten. My account has also examined the varied contexts in and around which filmic and written texts, individuals and institutions, have interacted. The aim has been not only to illuminate historical processes but also to document all this work, often 'behind the scenes', and not previously acknowledged.

The New Zealand Environment

There are certain structural elements common to most modern societies that have sought to develop an intellectual film culture. The making of such a culture typically involves the emergence of film critics (with an awareness of history and aesthetics and an interest in detailed analysis); the formation of an audience receptive to unconventional forms of style, structure, and subject matter; and the growth of related organisations such as film societies, 'art-house' cinemas, and film festivals. Filmmaking is not an essential ingredient, although some understanding of the technical aspects of production is required. The manner and pace in which these common structural elements are developed will vary from country to country, shaped in major ways by the particular patterns of economic, political, and cultural growth in each of them. In most instances, therefore, history and geography will provide a more or less unique blend of these elements. The work of the cultural historian is to identify and explain both commonalties and differences. The points that made the development of a 'high' (or intellectual) culture in New Zealand difficult included:

- a small population size and geographical isolation;
- commercialism dominant in many cultural areas (because public funding and private sponsorship were slow to develop);
- a colonial society of pioneers whose class background and focus on material progress made high culture a low priority for them;
- a troubled social and political history (shared by many other countries) involving depression and war;
- a strong strain of egalitarianism which involved a distrust of anything that resembled elitism;
- Puritanism and a strong regime of censorship, often associated with religious groups;
- suspicion of non-British foreignness in many quarters;
- suspicion of popular culture in educated society;
- suspicion of some aspects of modernity;
- a 'brain drain' (many talented New Zealanders emigrated).

Clearly, the interaction between these tendencies was complex. For example, a suspicion of popular culture did not cancel out a suspicion of high culture or a strong strain of egalitarianism – rather, the combined result was an affirmation of middlebrow culture as the dominant arbiter of taste. Although these tendencies did not impact solely on films (other aspects of high culture such as modernist art were subject to their effects), they certainly created obstacles for film culture. There was also a specific problem in that film culture as a whole seemed a direct competitor to older forms of high culture. Generally, New Zealand's political and cultural elite did not experience the same enthusiasm for films that they experienced for modern literature, theatre, painting, sculpture, opera, and poetry (whose cultural authority had evolved over time). Although attitudes to film evolved, there was no critical mass of the local intelligentsia that welcomed art cinema as an integral element of high culture as happened among the modernists in France. Such supporters in New Zealand tended to be somewhat isolated – Winston Rhodes was one example.

Meanwhile, the general context was a difficult one. As Wystan Curnow (1973: 157–58) puts it: 'any discussion of New Zealand's high culture will have to dwell on failures, inadequacies and possibilities rather than on achievements'. Curnow's lament was written prior to the changes associated with 'Rogernomics' but in many respects his complaint is still relevant.[1] Certainly, any history of the growth of intellectual culture in New Zealand needs to acknowledge the sense of *difficulty* expressed by so many of the participants. James Belich (2001: 335) cites an example: 'In 1944, Frank Sargeson, the leading literary nationalist in fiction writing, described his home town of Hamilton as "The Grey Death, puritanism, wowserism gone most startlingly putrescent." Literary visions of the mainstream New Zealand society of the 1950s were not much better.' 'The Expatriate Game' is the title of Belich's eleventh chapter in his general history of New Zealand from 1880 to 2000. The title of the chapter refers to three different responses to the prospect of cultural life in this young country in the first decades of the twentieth century. The first was physical exile. The most talented New Zealanders simply left (such as the writer Katherine Mansfield, the painter Frances Hodgkins, and the filmmaker Len Lye). Internal exile was the fate of those who remained. One group accepted the situation and integrated into society; another was neither happy nor integrated. However, almost everyone made some effort to adapt, with the desire to work within the local community being reinforced by the commitment that many had to socialism. But this was easier for some than for others. Some fitted in successfully to their churches, universities or government departments; others remained restless and unfulfilled giving a sour tone to much New Zealand cultural life. As Belich (2001: 336) has reductively noted,

> The problem was that they were deeply alienated from the society they wished to fertilise. For its part, that society was not keen on being led from the putative wilderness by prophets who described it as "The Grey Death". The literati disliked mainstream society because it disliked them, and it disliked them because they disliked it. From the 1920s to the 1960s, and perhaps beyond, New Zealand literati writhed in this unhappy trap.

In practice, however, most intellectuals did find a niche of some sort; and it is thanks to them that the country's cultural institutions gradually developed.

A more positive view of the phase (1920s–60s) in which 'New Zealand literati writhed' would argue that cultural development is a gradual process – a long revolution. High culture's partial success is in having acculturated the middle-class incrementally, *à la* Matthew Arnold. Even Sargeson, from whom Belich has quoted a particularly negative comment, was steadily at work helping fellow writers and helping to build a tradition. By the 1960s, for instance, an audience had been created whose artistic appreciation combined with its disposable income to provide for 'the establishment of a [local] market for writing and art' (Pound 1992: 27).

Film societies and their organisers participated actively in this enculturation process, too, as the creation of art-house cinemas in the early 1960s and the growth of film festivals attest, changes that I have explored in some detail.

John Reid's morally serious and socially engaged film criticism in the *Auckland Star* for seven years (1954–61) was an instance of Arnold's 'civilising' cultural mission. If there was a downside, it was the tendency for such cultural champions to concentrate too much on the middlebrow audience. Hence, Reid avoided difficult aesthetic modes of criticism (which required a willingness to examine the specificity of the film medium). Arguably, the creation of a middlebrow audience was the first priority – but critics such as Wystan Curnow have subsequently argued that this strategy actually delayed the development of an uncompromising highbrow culture. My history has offered evidence to support both positions. Because film is an expensive medium, it urgently needed a critical mass of (middlebrow) viewers; but intellectual approaches to film did develop slower than one might have expected.

Another complicating factor was the highly negative attitude of intellectuals towards the growth of popular culture, with film inevitably tarred by that brush. Marxism made this antipathy more intense because it saw Hollywood films as capitalist propaganda. This often led to harsh (and peremptory) value judgements when applied to particular instances. Indeed, a striking feature of this study has been how insistent was the need to establish a hierarchy of aesthetic value (to put the rapidly growing 'mass' consumer culture in its place), and how rarely critical methods of a high cultural type were applied to the cinema (as a powerfully expressive medium combining form and content in ways unique to film). Literary scholar Bill Pearson recalls contemporary critical attitudes:

> People didn't think about criticizing film then except in the sense of saying that it was lousy or that there was a good show on at the Regent, and that sort of thing, without analysing why. It was entertainment. Occasionally an unusual film would come along that people couldn't understand which would lead them to say that it was boring. One such was screened in Dunedin in 1940 with Sacha Guitry. It was French and didn't follow any of the Hollywood formulas so people didn't understand it. I remember seeing *Citizen Kane* in 1942 in Greymouth, and was really taken by the film, believing that it did what novels and films should do. For me, it seemed to represent that modernist ideal of an unillusioned presentation of modern life. I'd recently been reading Dos Passos, his *U.S.A.* [1938] trilogy, and this just seemed to me to be a film translation of him, especially the brief biographies of prominent figures and industrialists. But people went along expecting the Dream Factory to provide some comforting formulae.[2]

Films were simply not expected to be a focus of thoughtful analysis. An unholy alliance between establishment and Marxist attitudes attacked the cinema directly. Hollywood was seen by both as contributing to the weakening of the moral fabric of society (through the encouragement of various promiscuities), the debasement of artistic values (through mass-produced entertainment), the 'standardisation' of reception on the part of 'passive' cinema audiences, and the promotion of consumerism. The terms changed as the cultural reach and standing of the cinema improved over time, but the disquiet that such a popular medium produced remained constant, and was sometimes given a pseudo-scientific or philosophical basis, for example when the culture industries were analysed by the Frankfurt School in the 1920s and 1930s, firstly in Germany, and then in the United States, by such theorists as Max Horkeimer and T.W. Adorno (1972 and 1991), whose work called attention to the industrialisation and commercialisation of culture under capitalism.

A key issue in the growth of film culture is the nature of the discursive practices that surround the medium. In most instances, discourses developed overseas in richer contexts were simply imported and reproduced without transformation. Typically, these were seen as internationally applicable, analytical 'tools' that attempted to identify or isolate the 'essence' of the medium. One thinks of Clifton Firth's enthusiasm for Soviet theories of montage (as the key driving force of film), and J.G.A. Pocock's condemnation of the cinema's 'hypnotic' powers that stripped audiences of intellect and individuality. It is difficult to discern any local inflection or adaptation of these conceptions of film. But although many ideas were imported, there were some conspicuous gaps in the growth of New Zealand film culture that deserve explanation. One of the material reasons is simple (and one I shall emphasise): many of the films that had most interested overseas critics arrived late or not at all. Problems of film distribution and exhibition are crucial to understanding local reactions to such overseas critical writing as was available. More generally, these networks – or infrastructure – can be seen as profoundly important to the evolution of discursive practices by local film critics. This is a dimension of media studies that tends to receive less attention than others such as production and reception.

Peculiarities of distribution and exhibition combined with the local cultural configuration to give New Zealand film culture some distinct properties. There seems to have been no echo of the enthusiasms that gripped overseas critics of the 1910s and early 1920s. More intensive research may eventually uncover connections; but I have found, for example, no mention of Vachel Lindsay's *The Art of the Moving Picture* (1915), which was an early attempt to improve the prestige of moving pictures. Early French contributions to film theory and criticism, such as those of René Clair – whose films were celebrated by A.R.D. Fairburn – are also conspicuous by their absence. Modernist material reached New Zealand in those years, but the network was so fragile that what arrived was to some extent a matter of accident. When international debate and enquiry into the aesthetic specificity and value of film did arrive in New Zealand in the early 1930s, it would seem from available evidence that at least two distinct sets of ideas about film were conflated in a short (and politically heated) space of time.

Internationally, the pioneers of film criticism had attempted to identify the ways in which the cinema was more than a mechanical recording device by noting the ways in which the camera *added* to reality, drawing attention to features that might escape one's attention in everyday life. Cinema's use of the close up was of decisive importance in this regard, capable of transforming a commonplace reality into something exceptional; rapid cutting, later theorised by Soviet filmmakers as a complex source of artistry and political meaning, also demonstrated the way in which the filmic event was *created*. Soviet theories entered New Zealand via London by way of periodicals (including, surprisingly, the avant-garde *Close Up*) and were compatible with the strong strain of left-wing politics among local intellectuals.[3] The idea of film as art (particularly editing) combined with the idea of film as politics. This was the first important discourse to make its presence felt in New Zealand film culture.

The second was associated with the documentary genre. In contrast to 'aesthetic' approaches, documentary sought to reveal the real, sometimes to instruct and delight, but increasingly in order to galvanise public opinion, usually in support of a liberal humanist agenda, against the social injustices that had become painfully obvious in the Depression. The powerful influence of documentary on New Zealand film culture was encouraged both by distribution (a wide range of such films reached the country, on 16mm if not on 35mm) and by the prevailing cultural attitudes (reflected, for example, in the strong realist values that informed much New Zealand literature).[4] The fact that Britain was a strong centre of documentary production and theory was also an advantage. This sense of 'close to home' was demonstrated by British documentary pioneer John Grierson's visit to New Zealand in 1940 to advise on the State's use of film. The 'creative treatment of actuality' that Grierson advocated found a receptive ear; the general temper of the country, distinctly down-to-earth and egalitarian, helped documentary to become strongly established.[5]

It was one of the consequences of the strength of realist and political influences that more distinctly aesthetic approaches to film criticism struggled to find expression in New Zealand. 'Art for art's sake' has seldom been seen as enough – it needs to be linked to education, truth or progressive politics. In other parts of the world, modernism encouraged a stronger respect for 'pure' or abstract artistic qualities, and an understanding that content could not easily be separated from form. That is, formal or aesthetic qualities were not simply 'icing on the cake'. The challenge lay in revealing ways in which form *is* content, and not merely in a narrowly 'formalist' spirit that took no account of human concerns.

Film aesthetics involves an awareness of the history of film style and the ways in which it has developed as a result of (1) technological advances (the progressive improvement in film stocks, camera lenses, sound and lighting equipment, colour, widescreen, special FX, etc.); (2) the resolution of craft problems in the translation of the filmmaker's ideas onto the screen (through *mise en scène* and narrative); and (3) the development of useful theoretical concepts and historical categories. Each of these aspects impacts on film reception in various ways, either separately or in combination. This leads to analyses of style, form, point-of-view, authorship, filmic discourse, and so on. It is useful to point out that the emergence of a real interest in film style in New Zealand was first heard in the voices of two people who wanted to *make* films. Stanhope Andrews and John O'Shea both needed to develop their understanding of the ways in which particular effects were achieved on the screen and in the minds of viewers because they sought to replicate them in their own work.

The development of aesthetic discussion of films was further slowed down by the absence of a filmmaking community with any critical mass. Other forms of high culture (poetry, painting, music, and literature, for example) had a reasonable number of practitioners and in these fields there were many close personal links between creators, critics, editors, and readers. Although the small size of the community could encourage critics to pull their punches, there was at least an exchange of views of benefit to everyone with an interest in local work. This type of relationship was virtually non-existent in local film culture. New Zealand had many film-goers and film 'fans' but few *cinéastes* or filmmakers. In the period from 1939 to 1976, only five 35mm feature films were made by New Zealand filmmakers: *Rewi's Last Stand* (1940), *Journey for Three* (1950), *Broken Barrier* (1952), *Runaway* (1964), and *Don't Let it Get You* (1966). One man (John O'Shea) made three of them. Rudall Hayward, who made the first, also made a 16mm feature, *To Love a Māori*, in 1972.

Despite these brave efforts, film culture lacked a strong dimension of production. Ideally, theory is in dialogue with *practice*. A significant part of the 'art' of cinema, the understanding of technical and stylistic devices used by a filmmaker to obtain certain cognitive and emotional effects, was absent from most local writing about films; nor was there much interest shown in the evolution of the cinematic apparatus from a historical or aesthetic point of view. We have seen that there was also direct resistance to any display of technical or specialised knowledge on the grounds that it tended to intimidate or repel the sought-after middlebrow audience. 'Serious' film criticism was expected to perform a modicum of textual analysis, but this was generally of a literary type, such as discussion of theme and moral implications. The alternative was political analysis, again focussing on explicit content and implicit ideology. This approach was developed in the 1930s in the pages of *Phoenix* and *Tomorrow* and continued into the 1960s. If film-specific aspects (camerawork, editing, lighting, etc.) were mentioned, it was generally in the form of brief comments with vague, value-laden adjectives, rather than precise technical or aesthetic discriminations.

The gradual development of detailed and technical analysis (by critics such as O'Shea) represented a profound change of focus. A shift away from educational, moral and political priorities began to occur when John O'Shea's criticism was informed by his commitment to filmmaking. With a few such critics, New Zealand at last had the beginnings of a film-specific approach in which *style* was as important as theme. O'Shea's production company, Pacific Films, was the training ground for many New Zealand filmmakers of the 1960s and 1970s. In the early 1960s, he taught a course on the French *nouvelle vague* at one of the Winter Film Schools organised by the Wellington Film Society, and had widespread personal influence (for example, through his screenings at home or at Pacific Films).[6]

Another gap in discussion was the experience of filmic pleasure. While reviewers were discouraged from becoming too serious – the editor of the *Auckland Star* told Wynne Colgan (a film reviewer in the 1960s) that he was to write for the milkman (although Colgan deftly disagreed) – they were also not supposed to be frivolous. Early reviewers who had taken pleasure in 'entertainment' were given short shrift. The anonymous scribes of the Auckland Film Society who had defended some of Hollywood's pleasurable products in the late 1920s fell out of favour. 'Observing Earnest' of *Tomorrow*, writing in the mid-1930s, was chided for being 'too lenient' with Hollywood. Filmic pleasure was suspect for three reasons: it was politically dubious in the eyes of the left because it was a bait laid by commercialism and capitalism; it was morally unacceptable to Puritans because of its associations with filmic sensuality; and it was suspect to the high-minded middlebrows who were struggling to raise New Zealand out of the swamp of mindless entertainment and lowbrow simplicity. Obviously, films – like television in later years – were watched and enjoyed by many of the same people who spoke disparagingly about them, but there were not yet public discourses in which filmic pleasures could be acknowledged, explored, and discussed frankly. (Overseas *la politique des auteurs*, and the new 'pop' and 'cult' critics of the 1960s, would open up the possibility of such discussion.)

Education was an important arena for the development of film culture. The very successful Winter Film Schools, which began in 1954, were held in conjunction with the Regional Council of Adult Education and helped to advance an 'artistic' appreciation of film, albeit one coloured by the dominance of literary and theatrical modes of appreciation. Changes in the national education system had both positive and negative aspects since the system promoted the use of films but did so on its own terms. New Zealand's first Labour Government had an almost evangelical fervour in its educational crusade to reform and modernise schools, beginning in the mid to late 1930s under the inspirational direction of Peter Fraser (Minister of Education) and C.E. Beeby (Director of Education). Both men shared a vision of continuing education as a democratic right.

Particularly valuable to the growth of film culture was Labour's establishment of the National Film Library (1942) under Walter Harris (a lifelong friend of Beeby's) whose primary role was the provision of visual teaching materials to schools and adult education organisations.[7] Film societies also qualified for support from the NFL whose infrastructure greatly aided their spread in the post–World War II period. There were many other ways in which film became an educational tool, such as the purchase of 16mm projectors for schools and the series of articles that Gordon Mirams wrote for the Ministry of Education's School Publications Branch. These were admirable initiatives and are deserving of further research (and we shall return to the subject later in this Conclusion, with some comments on individual educators). At the same time, there was a limit to the extent to which they advanced New Zealanders' understanding of film *as film* – films were intended to be 'teaching aids' for other subjects.[8]

Christianity was an important shaping force on film culture as it was on education. Beeby, for example, was a Methodist lay preacher from the age of 17 (Renwick n.d.).[9] This often took the form of a keen sense of morality and earnest work ethic. The downside was a strong strain of puritanism (reflected in film censorship), a fear of hedonism, and a tendency to conformism, summed up by James Belich (2001: 121) in his conception of the Great Tightening of New Zealand society from the 1920s, which 'harmonised acknowledged differences, suppressed and camouflaged others, and purified and laundered both form and content'. This is obviously not a direct description of film culture, or of Christian culture at large, but it suggests the difficulties of the general environment. The 'puritans' of New Zealand society did much that was beneficial – education in New Zealand advanced greatly, and an attention to hygiene saved lives.[10] But the excesses can also be regretted. The cinema was often considered a pernicious ill that undermined the moral and physical well-being of society. Film criticism, when it emerged, was necessarily aware that such a culture was reading over its shoulder.

As an outpost of Great Britain, with some American and Australian influence, New Zealand's cultural elite was not particularly attuned to continental film theory and criticism. There was little direct contact and language was an obstacle. As an example of this: significant advances in film criticism were made in the 1950s, mainly in France, in theorising the re-emergence of a film style associated with Erich von Stroheim, William Wyler, Jean Renoir, and Orson Welles, involving attention to staging in depth, deep focus photography, and long takes, sometimes with fluid camera movements or an elaborate choreography of figures in front of the camera. This style devalued the critical orthodoxy that editing was cinema's primary signifying system. The Italian neo-realist theoreticians and filmmakers, and the film criticism of André Bazin, were associated with it. Such a theory did not reach New Zealand at the time, or if it did – by way of English commentaries – it aroused little interest. Those neo-realist and innovative Hollywood films that were seen here were read in limited terms (as Pearson's earlier comment illustrates). Distribution problems kept other films away from New Zealand screens. Bazin was a realist and a Catholic, but his way of viewing films built upon decades of sophisticated aesthetic perception of film not available in this country.

One of the striking aspects of the history of New Zealand film culture is the extent to which it was focused on London. Australia appears not to have had any significant influence until the 1960s and 1970s (when the Auckland Film Festival linked up with Adelaide, and there was increasing contact between members of the new 'sixties' generation who had an interest in film). The exceptions were in the field of filmmaking, with Australian filmmakers such as Raymond Longford working in New Zealand and the young Rudall Hayward undertaking his filmmaking apprenticeship in Australia during the silent period. But even in film production, contacts were sporadic until the 1970s (when Tony Williams, Pier Davies, and a number of others started working in both countries, and Roger Donaldson shifted to New Zealand). There has always been movement of writers and academics between New Zealand and Australia, but it is difficult to identify any particular impact that this made upon film culture.

Even though Gordon Mirams and John Reid were both impressed and influenced by French film culture (Mirams more by the films themselves than by French film criticism), neither appear to have engaged with the contributions that Bazin and his younger colleagues at *Cahiers du cinéma* were making to a fuller understanding of film. Bazin's emphasis on the revelatory powers of the medium, the power of the long take, and the art of *mise en scène* would have been (in one sense) a way to combine realism with aesthetics, and it could have provided critics such as Reid with the opportunity to relate moral concerns to issues of filmic style. New Zealand critics did occasionally refer to French critics (even, in Reid's case, to some not yet translated),[11] but there were few direct lines of communication with France, and what there were tended to connect with middlebrow rather than highbrow or avant-garde sources. Mirams actually lived in France on two occasions (in the late 1940s when Bazin was especially active, and again in the early to mid-1960s when the *nouvelle vague* was attracting much French media attention – so he must have been aware of it).

Another prosaic explanation for the lack of discussion in New Zealand of these new developments in European filmmaking and film theory was their remoteness from New Zealand, reinforced by the failure of local distributors to pick up many of the key films. Occasionally ideas can gain purchase in a culture separate from the texts associated with them, but the ideas involved in this case were not high on the agenda for New Zealand viewers – at least not for a few years yet. Modernism had a delayed arrival in New Zealand – local writers and artists picked up some aspects early in the century, but others had to wait. One of the surges would come in the 1960s, when a new generation of young, duffle-coated intellectuals began to display a heightened interest in international forms of modernism, including cinema.

Until then, *la politique des auteurs*, and its validation of the director as the creative genius organising the events presented on screen, did not receive the critical attention here that greeted it overseas. Auteur theory was especially important in bridging the divide that separated high culture from popular culture in European and American critical discourse; shockingly, the 'young Turks' writing for *Cahiers* had declared that some Hollywood studio filmmakers were *auteurs*, authors in the full romantic sense.

Cultural Growth

What else can be said of the film culture that emerged from this environment? This section will focus more directly on the growth of film culture as a historical process. But first, we need to remind ourselves of an important distinction. Film culture can be seen in two ways: as a subculture of the larger culture of people who like films, which (like any subculture or fan culture) has its own clubs, icons, discursive practices, and so on. Or we can see it as a type of intellectual or high culture. This study has traced both histories.

If we see film culture in the second way, we bring certain expectations to it. To be a member, it is necessary:

- to have some knowledge of high culture (the arts and general intellectual history), preferably international as well as local;
- to have an understanding of the specific medium of film, including its history;
- to be able to operate at the level of ideas and to have some knowledge of film theory;
- to be active (not merely a passive consumer) by developing ideas or making films;
- to be willing to deal with complexity, obscurity, and the unfamiliar.

These expectations – especially the last two – distinguish high culture from middlebrow journalism or reviewing or mainstream discussion. At best, middlebrow culture includes some knowledge of high culture, but tends to be derivative.

Creating a space for high culture to exist within a somewhat raw and pragmatic environment raised a number of issues of strategy, the most difficult being the question of a middlebrow culture that sometimes seemed an ally and sometimes a rival. The growth of the middlebrow audience and education of its aesthetic sensibility was the context for the work of many pioneers such as John Reid. At the end of World War II, New Zealand was prosperous, unemployment almost non-existent, and wages were rising; this set of unprecedented conditions continued for a further 20 years. In these conditions, middlebrow film culture developed broader support, but it had so many prohibitions and inhibitions (censorship, moral earnestness, political rectitude, anti-formalism, etc.) that arguably it was not a good conductor of ideas. In European countries, there is a more fully developed process of transmission from one cultural level to the next.

Ideally, high culture is the source of ideas that constantly trickle down to middlebrow culture, which is interested in receiving them. In New Zealand, most of the high culture ideas that became associated with films were borrowed from literature. Much film discussion was swamped with earnest ideas about morality, politics, education, and so on. Where highbrow activity did occur in film circles, it was sometimes shrill, displaying signs of dogmatic assertion and manifesto-making. There was sometimes more than a hint of contempt for a society that could not provide the diversity that its 'internal exiles' called for. Such striking of poses was understandable but it did not help ideas to ripple out from within the small circle of initiates to take root in the wider society.

I have tracked film culture as both a subculture and as an intellectual culture on the assumption that one provides the context or infrastructure for the other. The first has required a sociological or cultural studies approach; the second has involved intellectual history. I have a strong personal interest in the second development, being grateful for the interpretive strategies developed over time by patient and enthusiastic film critics that have provided me with many new insights, and I have been fascinated to observe the historical process at large that has led to the development of film societies, festivals, art cinemas, filmmaking, and university film courses. What has struck me above all is the difficulty of that process, a difficulty related not only to the general problems of high culture in New Zealand but also to problems specific to the medium of film. Film thus provides an interesting case study of the process of climbing the cultural ladder from fairground attraction to university or art gallery. The special difficulties of the medium are twofold. Firstly, film is an expensive medium. With only one print of a film generally available, there were real problems of access (VHS, DVD, the Internet, and Blu-ray only made their gradual appearance from the 1970s). This is a very different situation from print culture. The NFL's founding director and enlightened prime mover, Walter Harris, was constrained both financially and ideologically in the variety of films he could purchase. Secondly, the making of feature-length sound films was very expensive and so, with a few exceptions, this activity developed late in New Zealand. The country did not have a system of subsidies or other government support to nurture a national cinema (as in England, France, and Germany from the late 1920s).

There were also particular social difficulties in New Zealand with its small population (which creates problems of critical mass for an expensive medium like film) when the distribution and exhibition industries operate for profit. The first Labour Government's attempts to broaden film distribution foundered and came to nought. New Zealand was also a relatively isolated country not only in terms of the distribution of films but also in terms of the distribution of ideas. (It was quite a surprise to discover, in the course of doing research, a small local audience of filmbuffs reading *Close Up, Experimental Cinema*, and *Film Quarterly* in the 1930s, but many other publications appear not to have reached New Zealand. *Sight and Sound* was one of the few journals regularly available in public libraries and on subscription.) Much film culture was neither British nor American but 'foreign', and the reception of Russian, German, and Italian films all suffered by being associated with historical enmities (Communism and two world wars). Furthermore, films were subject to strong forms of state censorship and general opprobrium on the part of the articulate middle class; the film medium was associated to its detriment with popular culture (and American popular culture at that).

For these reasons, it is not surprising that film culture as a form of high culture developed much later in New Zealand than in other countries and that its growth was shaped by the local political and cultural environment. My study has drawn attention to the difficulties that attended the development of an intellectual film culture, which was itself part of a broader project to build high culture, and the patient work of many people who contributed collectively to the creation of a (sub)culture. One of the most interesting results to emerge from this account of film culture's growth, for me, has been an appreciation of its place within a complex, constantly changing field of cultural forces.

Film reception is, to a large extent, local. Clifford Geertz (1983: 4) has implied as much (albeit indirectly) in the course of his anthropological work:

> To an ethnographer, sorting through the machinery of distant ideas, the shapes of knowledge are always ineluctably local, indivisible from their instruments and their encasements. One may veil this fact with ecumenical rhetoric or blur it with strenuous theory, but one cannot really make it go away.

To better understand film culture's growth in New Zealand, it is useful to keep Geertz's admonition in mind. The viewing of Cuban revolutionary films by an Auckland hippie group was a very different matter from viewing such films, say, in Paris in 1968, or in the Dominican Republic, or in Miami. This is not to suggest that their New Zealand reception was any less important or influential. By the 1970s, New Zealanders were making films such as *Test Pictures* (1975), *Te Matakite o Aotearoa/The Māori Land March* (1975), *Landfall* (1977), *Sleeping Dogs* (1977), *Angelmine* (1978), and *Skin Deep* (1978), revolutionary in their own (New Zealand) way. What strikes me as under-readings in the discursive practices of local film culture may be viewed by more sympathetic historians as idiosyncratic elements in the development of a distinctive film culture.

Every film culture takes on a slightly different configuration as a result of its geographical and cultural position, and in a positive sense its very peculiarities and gaps can provide the basis for original discoveries and distinctive strengths. In the case of New Zealand, it may be argued that the very practical, commonsense aspects of its film culture have produced a particularly strong understanding of the documentary genre (though not a very adventurous documentary filmmaking practice). On the other hand, the limited availability of films is hard to see as anything but negative, and the delayed impact of *auteur* theory meant that New Zealand film culture was slow to overcome the division between 'art films' and 'popular films', with discussions still being encumbered by old-fashioned notions of morality and cultural status. There is a danger of 'cultural cringe' in stressing the superiority of French over New Zealand film culture, but problems of isolation and thinness cannot easily be interpreted as signs of originality.

One way to understand the field of forces in which film existed in New Zealand is to identify the main conceptions, each giving rise to particular forms of discourse. The following were particularly widespread. Many educated New Zealanders saw film as the new popular medium: a form of entertainment (or 'mere entertainment'); a booming business (or 'crass commercial operation'); a purveyor of American attitudes (or 'political propaganda'); and, finally, a bad moral influence.

In contrast, this study has been concerned to watch for the emergence of different conceptions of the cinema, arguing the 'seriousness' of the medium by seeing it as artistic (the '7th art'); part of (or linked with) 'culture' (high culture); original or experimental (not stereotyped and predictable); complex (not simple or simplistic); politically progressive (not hegemonic or reactionary); specialised and diversified (not necessarily a part of homogenous mainstream culture); having educational value; having moral value (like other forms of 'great art'); and real, realistic, or truthful (not merely escapist daydreams). The emergence of each form of defence, and the discursive practices associated with it, can be traced historically and located socially (as I have attempted to demonstrate). Although each involves a different priority, they have in some cases reinforced one another and worked together to build the case for film.

In terms of social organisation and activities, a list can be compiled, though it is difficult to arrange the items in precise historical order. My study has tracked the emergence and growth of:

- film societies (which had their beginning in New Zealand at the end of the 1920s but came into their own in the post–World War II period);
- adult education institutions that gave courses in 'film appreciation' (beginning with the WEA in the 1930s), often conducted by university lecturers from a department such as English;
- discussion of film in small magazines associated with the creative or intellectual communities (*Phoenix, Tomorrow, Landfall, Here and Now*, etc.) that began publication in the 1930s;

- film reviewing on the YA radio network and in the *New Zealand Listener* in the late 1930s (under James Shelley as Director of Broadcasting);
- film introduced into education via the educational reforms of the first Labour Government (1935) and the growing interest in 'visual education';
- the founding of the National Film Unit (1941) and the National Film Library (1942);
- new technologies (16mm films and projectors) which allowed films of interest to minority film culture to be purchased and projected at reduced cost (especially after World War II);
- new patterns of independent distribution and exhibition (via Natan Scheinwald in 1939) developing 'niche' audiences from the late 1940s (Modern Films, New Zealand Film Services, etc.);
- the inclusion of a film season within new city arts festivals in the early 1950s;
- regular film reviewing in the daily newspapers from 1954;
- the boom in European art cinema in the 1950s and 1960s, leading to the emergence of 'art' cinemas (such as Auckland's Lido in 1962);
- the introduction of television as the site of family entertainment (1960), leading to (1) a decline in the cinema business, but also (2) the growing importance to cinema of the young adult audience adventurous in its tastes;
- the rise of the counterculture in New Zealand, giving strong support to certain forms of innovative or unusual film (late 1960s and early 1970s);
- the appearance of annual international film festivals in the main New Zealand cities (from 1969);
- a more positive attitude to popular culture by intellectuals influenced by the 1960s counterculture, Pop Art, and other cultural tendencies;
- the emergence of a new wave of local filmmakers (from the late 1960s);
- the creation of a New Zealand Film Commission (1978);
- the expansion of film and media teaching and research in universities (from the 1970s);
- the creation of a national Film Archive (1981);
- media studies and screen media arts taught in high schools (1990s).

These elements add up to the social infrastructure that underpins film/screen culture in New Zealand. Presenting the points in 'shorthand' in these lists should allow us to appreciate the presence of a cultural dynamic, a Long Revolution that has seen film culture in New Zealand develop from a position of scarcity to one of relative plenty ('relative' because the range of films and the contexts of history and theory are still limited in comparison with some overseas centres). There have been persistent problems such as a small and relatively homogenous population; the absence of institutions such as a National Film Centre; and continuing resistance to forms of art and discussion regarded as pretentious or not politically progressive. Such factors have always influenced the style of minority film culture in New Zealand. Despite such constraints, the list represents a gradual filling-in of the pattern of film culture, with a 'multiplier effect' or synergy operating between the various pieces. Not that this narrative proceeded in a perfectly straightforward way – there were many setbacks and complex overlaps.

In understanding cultural growth, it is important to build a model that is dynamic and multi-dimensional – in the manner of a 'rhizome' (Deleuze and Guattari 1980). Hence, my lists of bullet points should be understood not as a series of static items but as different ways to track an energetic process. Trends interact, collide, and combine. What makes the process particularly complex is the way external forces join internal forces. A partial list of relevant developments external to film culture might include:

- the availability of new technologies;
- a quantitative rise in the number of people with higher education;
- a loosening of import controls to allow private enterprise greater latitude, which encouraged film distribution and exhibition entrepreneurs to operate in the niches that the mainstream ignored;
- improved telecommunications and air travel to ensure a more regular flow of films, people, and information;
- a long post-war period of political stability and economic prosperity.

That such a broad range of factors had an influence serves as a reminder of the complexity of culture, the dangers of prediction, and of the inadequacy of any single-factor or binary explanation. For example, the development of film culture depended upon both local and international developments, and both commercial and non-commercial initiatives. The development of a film culture in New Zealand has required a mix of public policy and 'grassroots' activism. The State has, at different times and in particular historical contexts, been both a blocking agent and a facilitator. As an instance of the former, we have only to recall its treatment of the Wellington Film Society in 1933, prosecuted for screening an uncensored Soviet film (*The Road to Life*). But Janus can look in two directions at once. The State's more beneficent face was revealed after Labour's election to office in 1935, when the Government oversaw the establishment of public institutions that sought to improve film reception (albeit in a middlebrow way). The key concern was to *educate* a broad band of the burgeoning middle class – the type of person that listened to the YA radio station and read the *Listener*.

In a small country like New Zealand, the 'market' would never have provided enough films without some help from public funding and volunteer organisations; but commercial entrepreneurs (such as Natan Scheinwald, Eddie Greenfield, and Ant Timpson) also made important contributions to the development of the culture. Clearly, also, the growth came about through the efforts of both organisations and exceptional individuals. It is necessary, therefore, for anyone researching culture to employ a 'thick' form of description. Any attempt to separate out from this confluence of activities one factor that purports to be the principal element risks simplifying the complex environment in which culture is seeded, nurtured, and harvested.

To develop the horticultural metaphor a little further, the 'garden' of film culture required the application of seeds and fertilisers (intellectual ingredients) to terrain prepared and tended by informed and enthusiastic gardeners (agents and institutions). The terrain exhibits geological and climatic variables whose specificities go some way to explaining the existence of regional variance in the growth of film culture even in a small country like New Zealand. (A particularly energetic 'gardener' can be responsible for an abundant crop – as was the case in Southland, for example, where Peggy Dunningham was the adult education tutor for the WEA in the late 1940s.) At the same time, large changes in the weather (on a national or international scale) inevitably influence regional developments.

This study has not looked in detail at the development of film production in New Zealand. Rather, I have focused on the arrival and development of the ideas that influenced the discursive elements of film culture. In a few cases (such as Stanhope Andrews and John O'Shea), filmmakers have – as we have shown – played an important part in the film society movement. After the 1960s, the connections would be more numerous, as a new film industry emerged, led in some instances by those who had frequented art cinemas in the 1960s. In addition to the directors, some film society stalwarts (such as Lindsay Shelton and Roger Horrocks) became involved in industry funding or policy organisations. There is an interesting study to be written of the ways in which the New Zealand films of the 1970s and 1980s were influenced by the diverse film screenings of the previous decade. In other respects, however, locally made films reflected the continuing dominance of Anglo-American (particularly Hollywood) models. One would not expect a strong art film tradition in New Zealand, though there have been some examples (from sequences of O'Shea's *Runaway*, 1964, to Armagan Ballantyne's *The Strength of Water*, 2009). It is interesting to note that our most specialised maker of art films – Vincent Ward – appears to have owed as much to his German-Jewish family background as to his New Zealand education. There has been an ongoing debate within the New Zealand film industry as to whether we would do better by aligning ourselves with Europe rather than attempting to compete with Hollywood – but such a debate lies outside the scope of the present study, as does the remarkable growth of the industry since the 1970s.

While emphasising the complex range of factors in the growth of film culture, it is still possible to identify some larger trends and regularities. For example, one may see three iconic or representative figures as particularly important; 'the political activist' and 'the educator' shaped much of the local film culture from the 1920s to the early 1960s. These figures continued into the subsequent phase but a new iconic figure emerged, that of 'the Sixties rebel'. We are, of course, deliberately simplifying the cast of characters, in almost cartoon form. Yet this is one way to identify the key movers and shakers in the specific circumstances of New Zealand. The political activist (dominant in the 1930s) saw film as another arena for debate and agit-prop. That figure has been described in some detail in the course of this study.

Equally important was the educator; for in a small country like New Zealand, which placed great importance on education, it was perhaps inevitable that film society organisers would often belong to this profession. This was a remarkably consistent pattern: the first 'film appreciation' courses were offered by the Workers' Educational Association; the executive officers of the 1930 film societies were 'university men'; many post–World War II film societies grew out of WEA classes and were often led by educationalists; 'highbrow' radio programmes were hosted by educators; and the first 'serious' film reviewer in a daily newspaper was an Auckland academic. The list of 'firsts' in which teachers, adult education tutors, and university lecturers figured in the development of New Zealand film culture could be extended considerably. Such people were powerfully motivated by the first of Horace's recommendations concerning the traditional role of theatre, to instruct, and less zealous in advocating the second, to delight. But for all the earnestness of their response to the 'attractions' that enchanted millions, these educators' energies and moral purpose contributed hugely to New Zealand's cultural infrastructure, and film culture in this country would be the poorer if they had not devoted considerable portions of their time to its development.

What shaped the seriousness of their endeavours? Both political activists and educators had grown up experiencing significant material hardship, had felt the dire social and economic conditions of the Depression, had witnessed the rise of totalitarian ideologies that led to bloody war, and were imbued with a valiant sense of 'mission'. Some turned to socialism, some to the churches, and some had an Arnoldian vision of the importance of education.

By the end of the 1960s, it was time for a 'cuppa' and some well-earned recreation; it was also time for a changing of the guard. The late 1960s and early 1970s was a period of cultural transformation and the 'tight society' was loosening its grip. Technological changes (in transportation and media) opened up New Zealand to the world and weakened the many ties that had bound the country to Britain. One of the results of this opening up process for the arts in general, and for minority film culture in particular, was that a more internationalist type of New Zealand intellectual emerged. Coincidence or not, this new type of intellectual (the third of our iconic figures) was perfectly positioned to welcome the arrival of a new wave of filmmaking, sparked by the French *nouvelle vague* and the European art-house cinema of the 1960s. Not all the 'young Turks' of the *nouvelle vague* were welcome in New Zealand. The most frequent visitors were Truffaut, Chabrol, Rohmer, and Resnais (while the cinematically mischievous Godard and underappreciated Rivette were less welcome). There were also innovative films from Italy, Sweden, Germany, and other countries.

The late 1960s and early 1970s represent a watershed of change in New Zealand culture. A younger generation of film society organisers came to the fore and introduced contemporary programming, which placed more emphasis on provocative transgressions of the 'establishment' canon. Lifestyle experimentation, sexual permissiveness, and an inchoate violence figured prominently in the cinematic representations of the baby boomer generation, and to some extent were lived out by many young New Zealanders escaping what they perceived to be the stultifying conformism of the 1950s and early 1960s. Ironically, O'Shea had created his 'rebel without a cause' in *Runaway* (1964) a few years too soon, before this sense of rebellion had taken clear shape.

The new generation had grown up with a love of film and with fewer of the moral or political reservations that previous generations of intellectuals had harboured concerning the rise of popular culture. It saw the battle against censorship as a major priority. Success eventually greeted their campaign for a more liberal approach to film censorship in 1976. With the consolidation of this new era in New Zealand film culture (accompanied by an upsurge in screen production, education, the arrival of new technologies, and the commemoration of an indigenous film 'heritage') this study closes.

References

Adorno, T.W. (1991), *The Culture Industry,* London: Routledge.

Belich, J. (2001), *Paradise Reforged: A History of the New Zealanders from the 1880s to the Year 2000*, Auckland: Allen Lane/The Penguin Press.

Curnow, W. ed. (1973), 'High Culture in a Small Province'. In: *Essays on New Zealand Literature*, Auckland: Heinemann.

Deleuze, G. and Guattari, F. (1980), *Milles plateaux*, Paris: Editions de Minuit.

Easton, B. (2001), *The Nationbuilders*, Auckland: Auckland University Press.

Geertz, C. (1983), *Local Knowledge*, New York: Basic Books.

Horkheimer, M. and Adorno, T.W. (1972), *Dialectics of Enlightenment,* New York: Herder and Herder.

Horrocks, R. (1984), 'No Theory Permitted on These Premises', *And*, (2), February.

Jensen, K. (1996), *Whole Men: The Masculine Tradition in New Zealand Literature*, Auckland: Auckland University Press.

Jesson, B. (1997), 'The Role of the Intellectual is to Defend the Role of the Intellectual', Foreword to *Cultural Politics and the University in Aotearoa/New Zealand*, M. Peters ed. Palmerston North: Dunmore Press.

Phillips, J. (1987), *A Man's Country?: The Image of the Pakeha Male – A History*, Auckland: Penguin Books.

Pound, F. (2002), 'Distance Looks Our Way'. In: L. Bieringa ed. *Distance Looks Our Way: 10 Artists from New Zealand*, Wellington: The Trustees of Distance Looks Our Way.

Renwick, W. (n.d.), 'Beeby, Clarence Edward 1902–1998' [Online]. From the *Dictionary of New Zealand Biography. Te Ara – the Encyclopedia of New Zealand*. Available at: http://www.teara.govt.nz/en/biographies/5b17/1. Updated 31 July 2003. Accessed: 3 September 2010.

Smith, D.I.B. (2003), 'John Reid'. In: N. Tarling, ed. *Auckland Minds and Matters*, Auckland: Auckland University Press, p. 126.

Simpson, P. (1997), 'Bill Pearson's New Zealand Then and Now: Testimony of an Internal Rapporteur', Auckland University Winter Lecture 1996, reprinted in *Landfall*, (194), Spring 1997.

Notes

1 For evidence, see commentaries such as Easton 2001; Horrocks 1984; Jensen 1996; Jesson 1997; Phillips 1987; Simpson 1997.

2 W. Pearson interview, 10 April 2001.

3 *Close Up* published nine translations of Eisenstein's writing between May 1929 and June 1933.

4 See, for example, Allen Curnow's introductions to his two influential anthologies of New Zealand poetry.

5 For a detailed account of the impact his month-long visit had, see Sigley, S. (2013) 'Imperial Relations with Polynesian Romantics: The Grierson Effect in New Zealand'. In: Z. Druick & D. Williams eds. *The Grierson Effect: The International Documentary Movement,* London: BFI/Palgrave.

6 Cf. Jane Campion's account in 'A Memoir of John O'Shea', in *Don't Let It Get You*, pp. 7–9, as one of many.

7 Both Beeby and Harris had been students of the energetic and charismatic James Shelley when he was a professor of education at Canterbury University College.

8 The same functional approach can be seen in the Government's testing of television. A government committee had been studying the new medium since 1949, and experimental broadcasts had been allowed from 1951 – *as long as they included nothing that could be classed as 'entertainment'.* (My italics.) See http://www.tvnz.co.nz/tvnz_detail/0,2406,111544-247-252,00.html.

9 Beeby's religious vocation waned at university as he was introduced to a wider world of ideas but there was an underlying moral purpose to his later work as an educationalist.

10 My emphasis on the Protestant strain of Christianity is not intended to neglect the contribution of Catholics. John Reid was a Catholic of considerable intellect and enormous energy. During his lifetime he worked unstintingly in the service of national cultural development. D.I.B. Smith has referred to this as a form of supererogation – good works done beyond what is morally required that has its source in Christian theology.

11 For example, Georges Charensol (1899–1995), a French journalist and talented critic – art, literature, and, especially, cinema – who began writing about film in 1923 for *Paris-Journal* when Louis Aragon was its editor. Charensol helped establish the Cannes Film Festival (several times a jury member), and was a regular participant of a long-running radio programme on France Inter, *Le Masque et la Plume*, that provided critical commentary and debate about films.

Index